Following the Milky Way

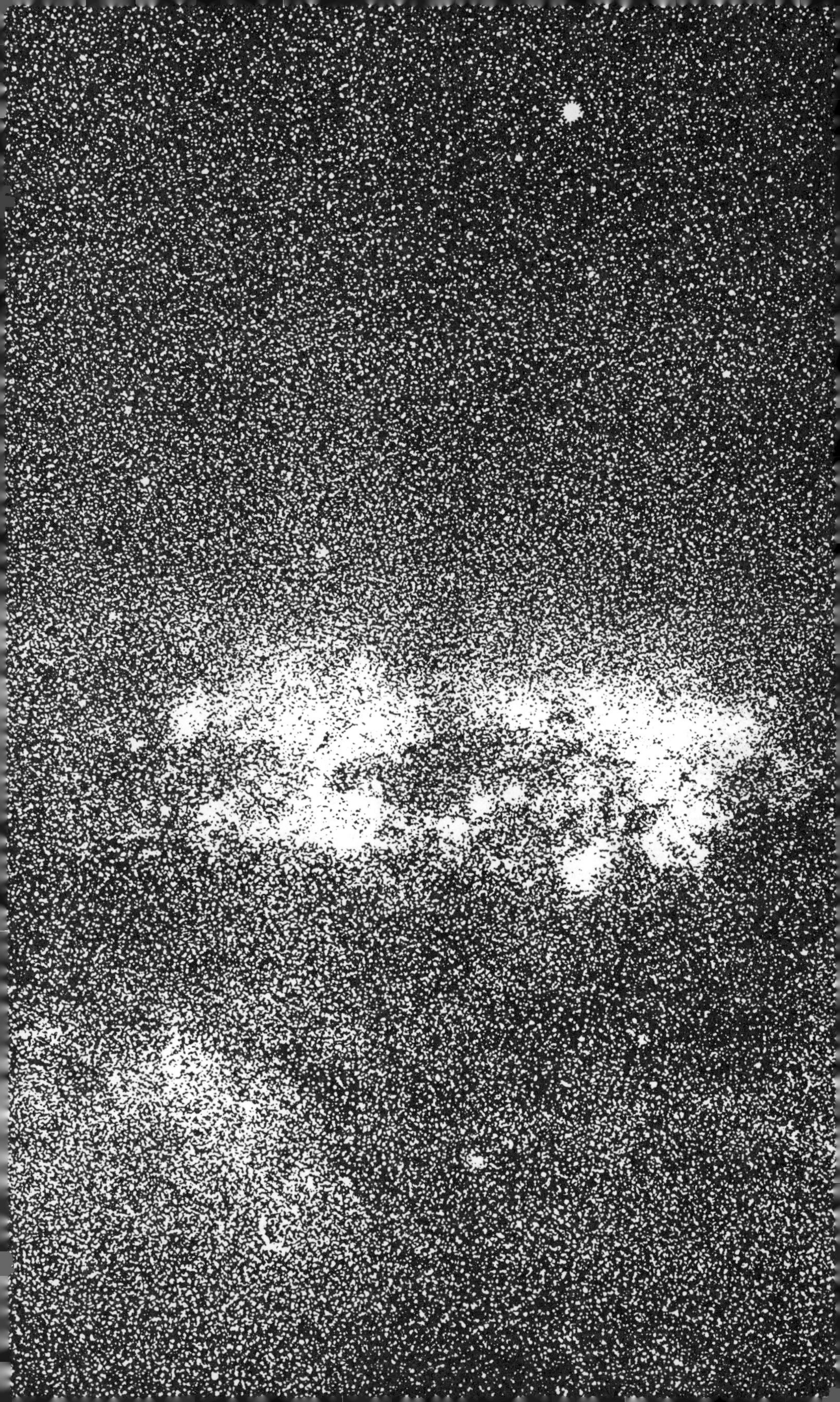

Following the Milky Way

A Pilgrimage across Spain

ELLEN O. FEINBERG

IOWA STATE UNIVERSITY PRESS / AMES

Manufactured in the United States of America

First edition, 1989

Library of Congress Cataloging-in-Publication Data

Feinberg, Ellen Okner.
Following the Milky Way : a pilgrimage across Spain / Ellen O. Feinberg.
p. cm.
Bibliography: p.
Includes index.
ISBN 0-8138-0146-X
1. Christian pilgrims and pilgrimages—Spain—Santiago de Compostela—History—20th century. 2. Spain—Description and travel—1981- 3. Feinberg, Ellen Okner. I. Title.
BX2321.S3F45 1989 914.6′0483—dc19 89-1752

Contents

Grateful Acknowledgments

To my parents, Leonard and Lilian Feinberg, and to my son, Jesse Reynolds, for encouraging me to follow the Milky Way, wherever I found it. To Bill for the lessons I would never have learned without him. To Jim and Renate Fernandez for academic (and personal) support. To Bill Silag, managing editor at Iowa State University Press, for his enthusiasm and suggestions. To the Wenner-Grenn Foundation for Anthropological Research and the Graduate School, Princeton University, for funding my fieldwork. To the American Association of University Women for a dissertation fellowship. To all my friends in Sahagún and to all the pilgrims whose footsteps I have followed. To Santiago for (maybe) starting the whole thing.

Author's Note

The names of some individuals in this book have been changed, as have a few details of their lives. All of the incidents occurred during one or another of my pilgrimages across Spain.

Coquilles St. Jacques and *Madeleines*

Bill and I sat across from each other, separated by the square, linen-covered table, a dark red rose in a clear crystal vase between us. The cafe was dark, lit only by flickering yellow lamps. We were in Paris. Paris in July. I stared out of a nearby window, watching people strolling by. At last a waiter approached our table, balancing two plates on his towel-draped arm. He placed our order in front of us—shells scraped clean of the sea, offering us their bounty: *coquilles St. Jacques,* delectable chewy scallops in creamy sauce, crusty with toasted cheese. Eagerly, we inhaled the sharp odor of ocean, the faint fragrance of white wine. *Coquilles St. Jacques*—the scallop shell of St. James, symbol of the thousand-year-old pilgrimage to St. James's tomb in Santiago de Compostela in Spain.

The waiter placed a wine carafe on the table and left, we poured the straw-colored wine into our glasses and toasted each other: "To Santiago." "To pilgrimage." Then, silently, we began to eat our dinner, savoring the contrasting textures and the crisp white wine.

For dessert—unheard of at that hour, but our whims were being catered to—we ordered *madeleines,* the tiny sugar-dusted sponge cakes that Proust recalled so fondly. *Madeleines:* tea cakes whose sea shell shape echoes the scallop shell, whose delicate flavor commemorates in sweeter, man-made form the pilgrimage to Compostela. The shell of scallop, the cake of Proust, evocative of things past, of things remembered, of things almost forgotten and things imagined.

We finished dinner, dawdling over the thick strong espresso coffee, and left the restaurant, surfeited with food and wine, with recollections, with expectations. The next day we would begin our journey to St. James, our pilgrimage to Santiago de Compostela, but now we strolled leisurely through the Paris night. The sky was clear, full of glittering stars. The

Milky Way, the Via Lactea, spread across the sky. Tradition says it points the way to Santiago, and for over a thousand years pilgrims have followed its star-lit trail.

For over a thousand years pilgrims have come from all over Europe to pray at the tomb of St. James the Greater—Santiago, as he is known in Spain. Son of the fisher Zebedee, brother of the Apostle John; Christ nicknamed James and John the "Boanerges" or "Brothers of Thunder." Sometimes people confused Santiago with Saint James the Less, "brother"—or cousin—of Jesus, a confusion which only added to the fame and the importance of the pilgrimage shrine.

Tradition says that James the Greater came to Spain—Iberia, as it was then called—and spread the words of Christ and founded the church Our Lady of the Pillar in Zaragoza. Then he returned to the Holy Land. Herod Agrippa sliced off his head in A.D. 42 or 44, making him the first martyred Apostle. Miraculously, a boat appeared to bear his body and head and two disciples, Athanasius and Theodore, back to Spain. They landed on the northwest coast of Galicia, at Padrón, called Iria Flavia in Roman times. There, Santiago's body was placed on a stone slab, which miraculously softened like wax to receive it. Other miracles followed in Santiago's wake; the pagan Queen Lupa was converted, and his disciples buried Santiago in a tomb. And there he lay, forgotten, for approximately 800 years.

Sleeping memories were awakened by the sound of angels' voices, by falling stars—falling, perhaps, from the Milky Way. Sometime around A.D. 814 the hermit Pelayo heard angels' singing, or perhaps it was the shepherd Pelayo who saw stars falling on a weed-choked hillside near the River Sar. One of them (the details fall through time as through a sieve) told the bishop Teodomiro, and he dreamt a dream from God. There, in the tiny stone grave, hidden under brush, buried in the hill, lay the bones of St. James and his disciples. Miraculously, they lay now uncovered, rediscovered in Spain's time of need, when Christendom was being challenged by the Moorish conquest of its land and people.

Bishop Teodomiro sent word of his discovery to the Asturian king, Alfonso II, "the Chaste," who came with his nobles and built a church and a monastery at the spot. Soon the site was known as Santiago de Compostela, City of Saint James of the Campus Stellae—the field of stars—or of the Compostum—the cemetery: the meaning has blurred with the centuries.

The faithful prayed for St. James/Santiago to come to their aid, the aid of Spain, in its hour of need. Summoned by their dreams, Santiago appeared, riding out of the sky—galloping down from the Milky Way—mounted on a fierce white charger, sitting tall and fierce, sword hacking at the infidels, slaying 10,000—20,000—50,000 with his mighty blood-stained blade. Santiago Matamoros, Santiago the Moor Slayer, fighting alongside Ramiro I at the Battle of Clavijo in 834 or 845 (if battle there really were), fighting alongside Ramiro II at Simancas in 939, aiding King Ferdinand in the siege against Coimbra in 1064—in which el Cid took part.

Usually alone, once with San Millán, Santiago rode out of the sky to save the Christian forces, forces of Christ, crusading against the infidels in Spain. In one hand he held a fluttering snow-white banner splashed with his blood-red cross, in the other hand a blood-drenched sword. Fisherman, apostle, saint, "Brother of Thunder," slayer of Moors, crusader for the faith, carrying his crusade across Spain to the New World, leading the conquistadores into battle against the Indian heathens. Lending his name to Santiago de Chile, to Santiago de Cuba, to Santiago in the Phillipines.

But that was later.

In gratitude for all his help, they made Santiago patron of Spain. At first, they'd built a humble mud and wattle church over his remains; but soon they built another, more substantial church of stone, and then enlarged that one as well, erecting a massive, lichen-covered, granite cathedral, its tall towers soaring toward the Milky Way. Pilgrims came in droves from everywhere to worship at the tomb. A potent tomb, its sacred power drawing believers like a magnet from Italy, France, England, Germany, Hungary, Scandinavia, the Netherlands, Spain—drawing the pilgrims to pray, to offer up their gifts, to stand close to Santiago's bones, to breathe the sacred air, to be saved, to be healed, to be forgiven, to demonstrate their hope for miracles. Santiago de Compostela and Rome and Jerusalem: three medieval rivals, all with separate claims to fame.

An added attraction soon lured pilgrims to Santiago: the Año Santo Compostelano. First celebrated in 1126 by Pope Calixtus II and then declared in perpetuity in 1179 by Pope Alexander III, the Compostelan Holy Year occurs whenever St. James's feast day, July 25, falls on a Sunday. Pilgrims who perform certain rituals and reach Santiago receive forgiveness of their time in purgatory for all sins committed up to the time they earn their *jubileo.* A plenary indulgence, a jubilee: a benefit worth traveling for, then and now—and worth returning for, again and again, depending on your state of grace or lack thereof. Over the centuries, the tide of pilgrims to Santiago has ebbed and flowed not with the moon but with the Años Santos, rhythmically recurring every eleven, six, five, and six years.

Kings and nobles, monks and merchants encouraged the pilgrimage because of faith, because of politics, because of trade. They made it easy—or easier, since medieval travel was never safe, and pilgrimage requires its sacrifice. Highways were built, monasteries and hospices constructed, cities grew. Pilgrimage routes developed: four routes through France, becoming one in Spain, a network of Roman roads, medieval cobblestones, and forest trails. The Roads to St. James—les Chemins de St. Jacques—The Way to Santiago—El Camino de Santiago—described in detail in the twelfth-century *Codex Calixtinus,* the first tourist guidebook, or so the Spanish claim. The word was spread. The road became so crowded in the twelfth century that the ambassador of Ali ben Yusuf exclaimed, "The multitude traveling to Santiago is so great that they hardly leave room on the road."[1]

They came: pilgrims, priests, merchants, builders, peasants, craftsmen. Together, they built towns and monasteries, palaces and churches, houses and mills, marketplaces and shops. Together, they populated and repopulated the route, developing new architectural styles, inspiring music and song, *chanson* and *geste*: a thriving, exciting medieval hodgepodge, the Age of Pilgrimage, not only to Santiago but to a thousand shrines, most of the rest now long forgotten. But not so Santiago.

Following in each other's footsteps, they marveled at the sights, the thriving cities, the awe-inspiring monuments, paid for by and with the faith of millions. Their pilgrim's way was dotted with exclamation marks of religious fervor, shrines filled with relics and bits of bone, powerful relaying stations of holy power. They prayed beside glorious arcs of silver and gold, housed in jewel-box cathedrals with jewel-like stained glass windows; they admired the ruby, emerald, topaz, sapphire light staining the air, staining the cold marble floors.

Most of the pilgrims who came to Santiago came and went unnoticed, leaving only faint footsteps in the dust—the miniscule, incremental erosion of a stone path, leaving only an anonymous grave, a lost medallion. But some pilgrims left records, or legends, of their pilgrimage. It is said that Charlemagne traveled to Santiago; and Count Fernán González, victor of the Battle of Simancas. And in 997 the Moorish conqueror Almanzor ransacked the town; but, overcome with sentiment (or confusion), he left Santiago's tomb untouched but forced Christian captives to carry the church's bells on their backs to Córdoba. And there they stayed until Córdoba fell in 1236. And el Cid—he went to Santiago to pray for victory. And Matilda, daughter of Henry I of England (1125); St. Francis of Assisi (between 1213 and 1215); St. Louis, Louis IX, King of France (1253); Edward the First of England; Saint Isabel of Portugal (1325); St. Bridgette of Sweden, accompanied by her husband (1340); Chaucer's Wife of Bath (late 1300s); The Flemish painter, Jan Van Eyck (1430); over 3000 English pilgrims by boat (1434); the Catholic Kings, Ferdinand and Isabella (1488); Philip II (1554).

Erasmus's pilgrim Ogygius supposedly made the pilgrimage, later debating its merits with his friend Menedemus. Some 14,000 English soldiers under Sir Francis Drake (1589) threatened to visit Compostela. Richard Ford, the nineteenth-century English traveler came, and saw, and scoffed. The Cardinal Roncalli, who became Pope John XXIII, came in 1954, and Pope John Paul II came in 1982.

And millions more—rich and poor, famous and infamous, innocent and wicked, saints and thieves, faithful believers fulfilling a vow, guilty criminals completing a judicial sentence. All traveled the same road, traveling alone, traveling together, on the way to Santiago. Some died along the way, some made a life of pilgrimage. Some chose to settle on the road. But most returned home wearing the cockle shell, the scallop shell emblem of Saint James, proof and memento of their journey.

Some not only made the pilgrimage—they also wrote about it. The most famous account of all is the *Codex Calixtinus,* compiled around 1130 by Aymery Picaud, a French monk. In an attempt to lend credibility to the work, Picaud falsely attributed it to Pope Calixtus II. The *Codex* consists of five parts, including a list of miracles of St. James, the "Pseudo-Turpin," which describes Charlemagne's fictitious journey to Compostela, and "The Pilgrim's Guide," a twelfth-century traveler's guide which describes four routes through France and thirteen stages of the journey in Spain.

There are other, more personal accounts of the pilgrimage as well, such as those written by William Wey, a Fellow of Eton (1456); the Bohemian Baron Rozmital (1466); Hermann Künig van Vach (late 1400s); the German Arnold von Harff (1499); the English Doctor Andrew Boorde (1532); the Italian cleric Domenic Laffi (1666, 1670, and 1673); and the

English traveler, Richard Ford (1845). Modern guidebooks still use the *Codex*'s thirteen stages and retell the stories told by these literate traveler-pilgrims.

Sacred journey, earthly adventure, spiritual quest, physical hardship. A double image of overlapping experience: spiritual journey from sin to salvation, from penance to peace, from ignorance to knowledge; physical journey from one place to another, eating, sleeping, walking, suffering, avoiding or giving in to temptation. Crossing the landscape of the soul, crossing the mountains and mesetas of Spain. Life is a pilgrimage. Then and now.

Then and now. For the pilgrimage continues today.

Today, most pilgrims go by car, bus, or bicycle instead of by foot, horseback, or litter. Today, people can travel on a modern asphalt highway Camino de Santiago, marked with road signs decorated with the scallop shell. "X" miles to the next town, to the next monument of interest. "X" miles to Santiago. Since how one gets to Santiago is of no importance to the Church, modern pilgrims follow the Camino out of choice, not necessity. Many travelers go on bus excursions organized by travel agencies, combining a sight-seeing holiday with spiritual reward. Some of these travelers are pilgrims, some are tourists, most combine the two—as has been true for centuries.

But not all pilgrim-travelers travel in comfort. An increasing number prefer to walk, starting in France, starting in Belgium, starting in Holland, starting 500 miles from Santiago at the French-Spanish Pyrenees, walking the remains of ancient pilgrim roads, following the traditional Camino de Santiago, following in the dusty footsteps of their ancestors.

The summer before the Parisian dinner of *coquilles St. Jacques* and *madeleines,* I had been in Spain, looking for a research topic for my Ph.D. in cultural anthropology. I stayed in a boarding house run by cloistered, black-robed Benedictine nuns in Sahagún de Campos. Sahagún is a town of 2,500 people, located half-way from the Pyrenees to Santiago on the Camino de Santiago. Sahagún owed its medieval importance to the pilgrimage—an importance long since faded. But the pilgrimage, like Sahagún, continues to exist, and pilgrims once again are taking to the road on foot.

I first encountered some of these "foot" pilgrims when they requested hospitality at the Benedictine boarding house, relying on the millenium-old traditions of hospitality and the pilgrimage. Wearing backpacks and hiking boots, scallop shells sewn on their hats, they were re-creating a "traditional" pilgrimage on the "authentic" Camino de Santiago. They followed pilgrimage guidebooks and yellow arrows painted on the sides of houses, on trees, on walls; they followed the advice of helpful villagers.

Walking on a reconstructed route of ancient Roman roads, medieval cobblestone trails, and asphalt highways, they followed the Camino, that well-worn path, replicating a thousand-year-long journey. Much to my surprise, many of these pilgrims told me that they weren't very religious and St. James, patron of Spain, meant very little to them. They told me it was the journey itself that mattered, not the saint's shrine at the end. For some of these pilgrims, the Camino de Santiago was not even a Christian pilgrimage road—rather, it was a pre-Christian mystical initiation route, marked with esoteric, arcane symbols. Christian or otherwise, these "foot" pilgrims wanted to make a pilgrimage—an authentic pilgrimage, a traditional pilgrimage, figuratively and even literally walking in the footsteps of their ancestors.

I wanted to join these pilgrims of the past and present, these searchers on a quest. Like many of them, I was not religious—in fact, I grew up a Unitarian—but the image of the pilgrimage caught and held me, as it has held so many others: a journey across space, a journey into and through oneself. A time out of place, a sacred time. Not a hike: a pilgrimage. An age-old pilgrimage, a modern-day adventure.

At the end of that summer, I left Spain and continued my graduate studies at Princeton University. I was determined to return to Spain the following summer—an Año Santo Compostelano—and walk the Camino de Santiago. But I didn't want to go alone. I was afraid. A 35-year-old woman walking alone? It seemed too risky. Besides, my idea of exercise was driving to the corner grocery store. I'd had a mild case of polio as a child—no paralysis, but still—and was unsure of my physical endurance. I'd never done much hiking—and never with a backpack. I was eager to test my limits, but not by myself.

Back in Princeton, I wrote grant proposals and avoided reaching a decision about walking the Camino. Clearly, I had to walk it—how else would I know what pilgrimage was like? Obviously, I wouldn't do it alone. Funding was found, companionship was not. Then that spring, Bill, a fellow graduate student I had been going with for a while, said he would walk the pilgrimage road with me. His interest was two-fold: academic (he was a student of history) and personal (he wanted to see what it would do to our relationship—hopefully, it would bring us closer to share this journey).

It sounded great. Bill knew a little Spanish and much more world history; I knew a little history, more Spanish, and much more about the pilgrimage. We'd complement each other, we'd learn together—about the pilgrimage, about ourselves, about each other. Ours would be a multiplex pilgrimage, full of images and intents: a private quest, a shared adventure; a journey across a geographical space, a voyage back in time, walking in the footsteps of the millions of pilgrims who had gone before us.

Following the Milky Way

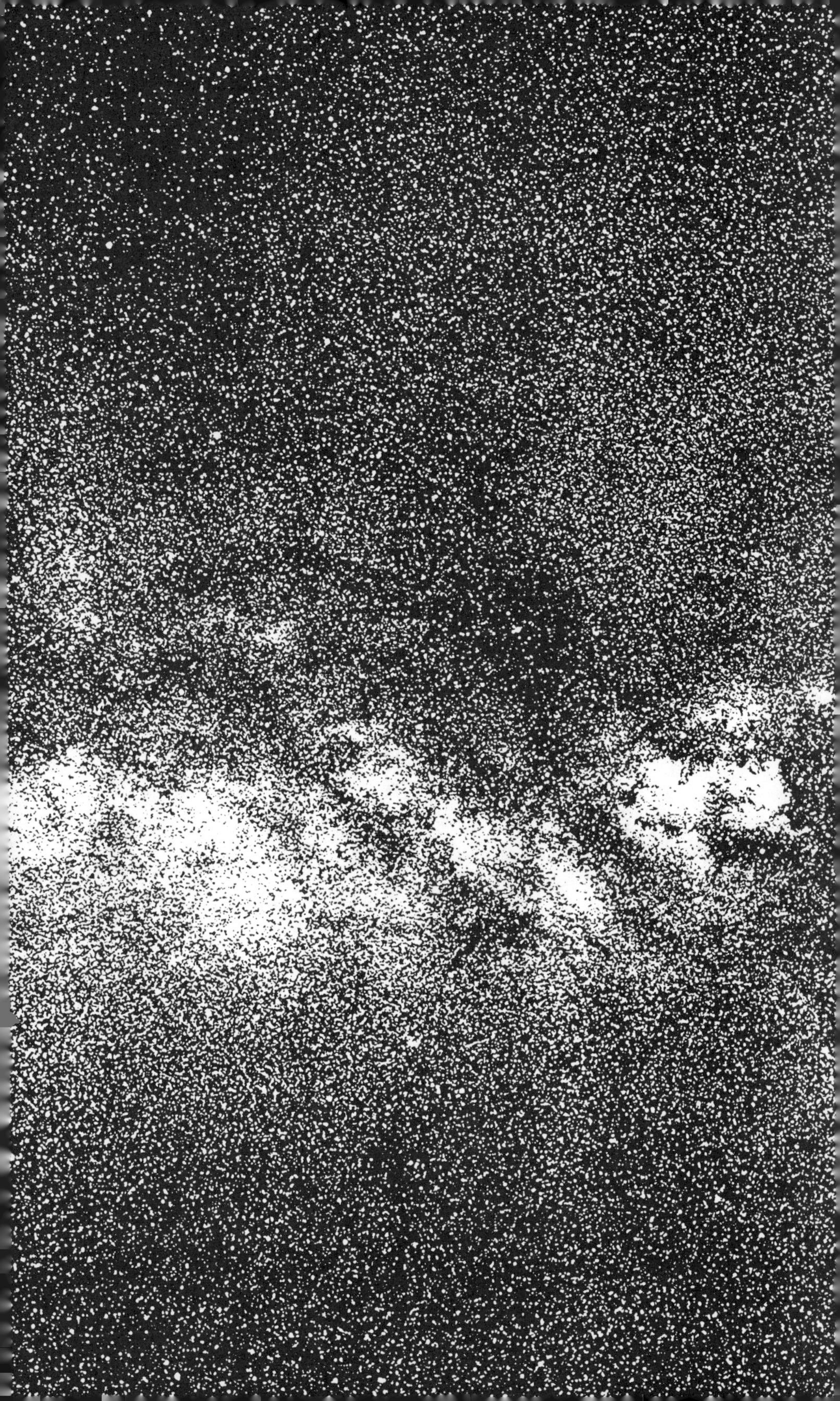

THIRTY KNIGHTS SET OUT FROM Lorraine to Santiago de Compostela, all but one vowing to stand by each other. But when one of them fell ill in the Pyrenees, all abandoned him—except for the knight who had not taken the vow. He stayed behind and nursed his companion, but the sick man died. In despair, the knight called out to Santiago—and Santiago miraculously appeared on horseback. He took up both the dead pilgrim and the living knight and carried them the rest of the way to Compostela—twelve days on horseback—in a single night. At dawn, Santiago left the knight on top of Mount Joy; in the distance, he could see the cathedral spires.

(*Codex Calixtinus,* Miracle 4)

Prelude

In the Middle Ages, a network of roads crisscrossed Europe, carrying merchants to market, soldiers to war, and pilgrims to worship. Four major roads led across France toward Santiago, passing through Paris, Vezelay, Le Puy, and Arles. The road from Arles crossed into Spain at Somport; the other three joined together at Ostabat, ten miles north of St. Jean Pied de Port, on the French side of the Pyrenees, and crossed into Spain at the Pass of Cize, near Roncesvalles. These two routes met outside of Puente la Reina and became one, the Camino de Santiago.

We had between July 7 and August 24 to make the pilgrimage. Then we had to drive to Madrid. Bill's plane to New York left August 27 from Barajas Airport, and my parents were flying into Barajas with my son that same day. Jesse would spend the school year with me in Sahagún. The 800-kilometer trip from the French/Spanish border to Compostela took healthy pilgrims about a month to walk. Given our lack of physical preparation, we would take longer—perhaps a month and a half—so we decided to fly to Paris, rent a car, drive to Bayonne, then take a train to St. Jean Pied de Port to begin our pilgrimage on the French side of the Pyrenees.

Before the trip, we bought Kelty suitcase/backpacks. They looked like luggage and could be carried like suitcases; but, by unzipping a back section and unfolding several straps, we could convert them into finely adjustable, well-padded backpacks. The salesman had shown us how to convert them, but we hadn't had time to try them out. Neither Bill nor I had ever worn a backpack, or done much hiking, but Bill wasn't worried. He assured me he could take care of me no matter what. I found that reassuring.

We arrived in Paris on July 7 and retrieved our suitcases at the baggage claim. Suitcases in hand—after all, we were tourists, still, not pilgrims—we flagged down a taxi and went to our hotel. We checked into the hotel and went to our room—one room with two beds. Weary with jet lag, we stretched out on our respective beds and tried to fall asleep.

Later that day we picked up our Hertz rental car, a tiny Renault Le Car, and drove to the Tour de St. Jacques, located at the corner of the Boulevard de Sebastopol and the Rue de Rivoli—on the north side of the Seine. The tower of St. James is all that remains of the medieval church, a popular meeting place for pilgrims heading south to Santiago. We followed the Rue de la Cité across the Seine, past the Hotel Dieu and over the Petit Pont. From there south, the street retains its original name—the Rue St. Jacques.

I tried to imagine what it was like when medieval pilgrims thronged the road on their way to Santiago. Were they filled with religious exaltation? Were they worried about the dangers—known and unknown—which awaited them on their pilgrimage route? Were they singing hymns as they marched? Were they praying silently as they walked? I could almost see them, dressed in the traditional pilgrimage attire of coarsely woven brown robes, heavy wool or leather capes over their shoulders, water gourds dangling from the top of their tall wooden staffs, sturdy leather sandals on their feet, broad-brimmed hats on their heads, a food and money bag, called a "wallet," fastened to a belt around their waists. Soon we would be following in their footsteps. We drove back to the hotel.

Later that evening, we dined on *coquilles St. Jacques* and *madeleines.* Then we walked back to our hotel room. As I fell asleep, I wondered how people would react to Bill and me traveling together: would they ask if we were married? Would they be bothered that we were not? After all, we were going on a pilgrimage. . . .

July 8: The next day, Bill drove us to Bayonne while I stared out the window or napped, trying to get over jet lag. The distance we covered in one day would have taken a medieval pilgrim weeks to walk. We found a hotel in Bayonne, then drove along the shore at Biarritz, talking a lot about nothing consequential. Suddenly, we weren't very comfortable together; even though we had been going together for months, how well did we really know each other? Yet we were preparing to make a month-long, 500-mile pilgrimage together, planning to walk across Spain together. I began to have second thoughts. I told myself traveling with Bill would take a bit of getting used to, but everything would be all right. After all, I had been afraid to make the pilgrimage alone, and we did want to share this experience.

July 9: I woke up, still slightly shaky from jet lag, walked quietly over to the hotel window, and pulled back a corner of the curtain; the sky was bright blue, the air clear, the sun hot. Bill woke up and we got dressed. Then we checked out of the hotel, put our suitcases—still not converted into backpacks—into the rental car, and drove to a nearby sidewalk cafe. There we drank steaming *café au lait*—coffee with milk—served in huge white mugs, and ate butter-drenched, flaky croissants. Cheerful, well fed, we drove to the Hertz agency and returned the car. Then we took a taxi to the station to catch the train to St. Jean Pied de Port. Our U.S. travel agent had said the train left daily at 11 A.M.; we still had plenty of time.

We reached the train station and went inside, walking to the opposite end of the dingy, deserted waiting room to a partly raised, glazed glass window with a sign over it: "Tickets." Behind the window was a blue-uniformed railroad clerk. In stumbling French Bill asked to buy two one-way tickets to St. Jean Pied de Port. His inquiry was greeted by a rapid outburst: there was no train to St. Jean Pied de Port and never had been—or perhaps there was and we had missed it, or maybe it only ran in June or didn't run in July.

Dismayed, we went outside and sat down on a wooden bench propped up against the station wall. How could we get to St. Jean and start our pilgrimage? Bill walked over to a nearby taxi and asked the driver for advice. The driver said a bus would leave from in front of a church at noon, and he would take us there for five dollars. Five minutes later, he dropped us at the church. We lugged our heavy suitcases to a nearby cafe and waited for the bus. We drank a beer. We drank another. It was hot—the hottest day in years, according to the bartender. I felt queasy with excitement—or was it stomach flu? I had not thought that it would be so hard to start.

I looked at our heavy suitcase/backpacks, leaning against the wall. Mine was stuffed with my new sleeping bag; a pair of bluejeans; a sweater; a jacket; three blouses; a pair of Adidas jogging shoes—my friends had advised me to walk in them, instead of boots, since much of the time we would be walking on roads and I had had no time to break in a pair of leather hiking boots; assorted socks and underwear; a sundress; a nightgown; a plastic rain poncho that could double as a ground cloth; cosmetics; first aid supplies; a novel; a journal; a Spanish dictionary; a guidebook/map of the Camino de Santiago; a compact camera; and a roll of toilet paper. Bill carried only slightly less. We didn't carry foam mattress pads, a tent, or cooking gear—we wanted to travel light.

I looked at our suitcases again. They were quite heavy. Surely, they would be lighter on our backs. But we still had not converted them into backpacks, hesitant to feel their weight, hesitant to convert ourselves into pilgrims.

Medieval pilgrims had elaborate rites of leave-taking that separated them from home, rites in which their staffs, their wallets, their special pilgrim's uniform were blessed. The rites separated them from who and what they had been, transformed them—for the duration of the pilgrimage—into semi-sacred persons with special rights and privileges. Often the whole community participated in the ceremony, celebrating their new—albeit temporary—status, wishing them well, walking with them out of town.

In contrast, we had no special garb, no ritual of separation, no leave-taking ceremony, no community recognition. I'd said goodbye by phone to my parents in Iowa; to my son Jesse, who was spending the summer with his father in Kansas; and to several good friends in Princeton, New Jersey. Bill had also called up friends and family. And that was it. We had no public ceremony to begin our pilgrimage; instead, we had—a name on the map, St. Jean Pied de Port, France, a spot on the pilgrimage road. We were waiting to get there to begin.

I felt nervous. It had seemed so simple, back in Princeton, reading books. It had been a familiar, academic exercise. My preparation for the pilgrimage was intellectual—not spiritual, not physical. The former seemed irrelevant, the latter was too much effort, and besides, I didn't have the time. I'd felt quite confident. I'd told my parents I was going to walk across Spain. They had been shocked—"Walk across Spain? How can you walk across Spain?" And I had blithely replied, "One step at a time." But now I just felt scared. And sick. Something I had eaten—or was it nerves?

The bus came, a great creaking rumbling thing, spewing out exhaust fumes. We heaved our heavy suitcases into the open luggage space in the side of the bus and got on. The bus was half full. The air was grey with the smoke of hand-rolled cigarettes; it reeked of sweat. The men wore black berets called *boinas,* dull black cotton pants, shiny black jackets, scuffed black shoes. The women wore worn black dresses, black sweaters, and low-heeled, black shoes—the black of mourning, once put on so rarely taken off.

The smells, the noise, the jumble of sounds assaulted me. In Paris I'd begun to resurrect my college French—I'd caught the rhythms, disentangled words. But now the sounds I heard made no sense. Were they speaking in tongues? I looked at Bill and saw him leaning forward, straining to understand.

"I think it's Basque," he said.

Basque, a language with no known origins. I'd heard of the Spanish Basque terrorist organization, ETA: *Euzkadi Ta Azkatasuna*—"Freedom for the Basques"—struggling to free País Vasco from Spain. I knew there were Basques in Spain, but I'd forgotten that the French/Spanish boundary was a modern artifact—Basques lived on both sides of the line.

The bus started off, rumbling, shuddering up and down the narrow, curving, hilly roads. It stopped abruptly at an unmarked crossing to let off a passenger. And then another. I felt sick. I held my breath against the stale hot air, the thick smoke, the sharp, sour smell of sweat. We reached a town. St. Jean? No, just a rest stop. We'd have an hour or so to wait. The driver went off down the block, delivering supplies, exchanging boxes.

Bill went off exploring. I sat at the sidewalk cafe, trying not to throw up. How do you ask for a bathroom in French? My mind was blank. I sipped at a tonic water, feeling dizzy in the heat.

I saw Bill walking toward me, wearing faded jeans, a blue work shirt, new hiking boots. Bill, like me, hadn't done any hiking, so he had had to buy new shoes; unlike me, he didn't worry about not having time to break them in before the pilgrimage. He looked healthy, fit, energetic. I felt like throwing up.

We got back on the bus. More hilly curves, more cigarette smoke clogging the air. We were climbing, just a bit, to reach St. Jean Pied de Port—St. Jean, Foot of the Pass. I'd known how to translate Pied de Port, but it was one thing to know, another thing to realize we would have to climb over a mountain pass. At last, we reached St. Jean, and I tottered off the bus and collapsed in a chair at a nearby cafe. I guarded our suitcases while Bill went to find a hotel.

He returned, enthusiastic. He'd found a medieval hotel built into the walls of the old city. We lugged our suitcases the few blocks to the hotel, carrying them by their sturdy leather handles, easing the weight with the shoulder straps. How much simpler it would have been to convert them into backpacks, but we kept putting it off. We had had no ritual of separation, of beginning. We kept putting off their conversion, our transformation.

Surely medieval pilgrims had stayed in this hotel, built into the ancient city walls. Our room had heavy roof beams, tiny windows. It was small but clean, with two swaybacked beds, a wooden wardrobe, a table, two lamps, and an adjoining bathroom. Bill, I noticed, looked a little sick, but he told me his strategy was to ignore illness and it would go away.

After my stomach had quit cramping, we went for a walk, stopping at the tourist office to collect brochures and look at a map on the wall, trying to locate Roncesvalles, our next stop, on the other side of the Pyrenees. St. Jean was in the center of the map, and spreading out from it were zigzag lines. The orange was the road we had traveled from Bayonne. The red was a highway going to Valcarlos—the Valley of Charles, where Charlemagne rested with his troups while Roland met his death—and then to the Puerto de Ibañeta, also called the Pass of Cize, and then to Roncesvalles, our first stop on the Camino de Santiago in Spain. The name Roncesvalles comes either from the Latin *roscida vallis*—deep valley—or from the Basque *rozaballes*, meaning flat or spread out. The narrow yellow line was the route of the Passes of Cize. Part of the old Roman road from Bordeaux to Astorga, it had been the route of the Roman legionnaires, of Charlemagne, of Napoleon. Now it was a trail over the top of the Pyrenees to Roncesvalles.

We wandered around town, walking up a narrow road toward a ruin on the hill, the Citadel. I was winded before we reached the top.

We had dinner at a nearby cafe. Bill praised the food, but I had no appetite. I told myself it must be nerves—but I had a vague suspicion it was something I had either eaten or caught. After a short, tiring walk around town, we went back to the hotel and got ready for bed, politely offering each other the first use of the bathroom. Bill wanted to read for a while, and he hoped the bedside light wouldn't bother me; politely, I assured him that it wouldn't and turned over and pulled the blanket over my head.

Finisterre
Noya
Padrón
SANTIAGO DE COMPOSTELA
Lavacolla
LA CORUÑA
Arzúa
Melide
Disicabo
Palas do Rei
Portomarín
Sarria
Samos
Triacastela
El Cebreiro
Pedrafita
Herrerías
Villafranca del Bierzo
Ponferrada
El Acebo
Foncebadón
Rabanal
Santa Catalina de Somoza
Astorga
Hospital de Orbigo
OVIEDO
LEON
Mansilla de las Mulas
El Burgo Ranero
Calzada del Coto
Sahagún de Campos

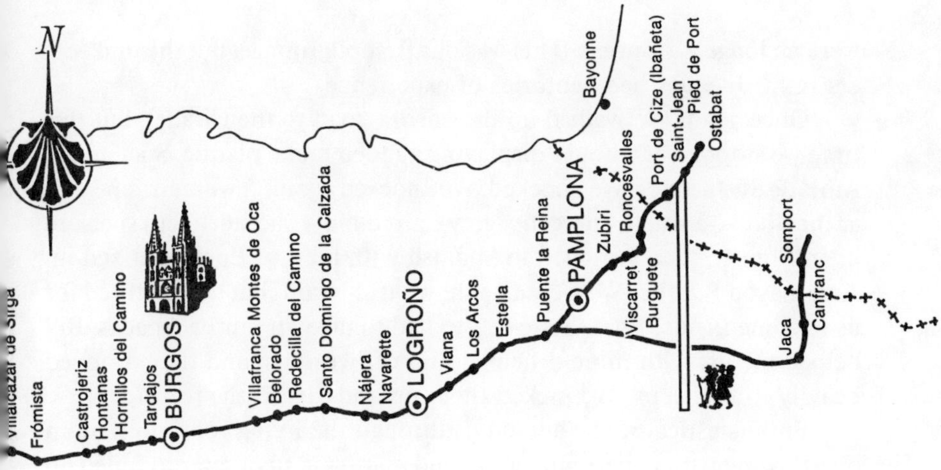

Day 1: July 10 In the morning, we got ready to start our pilgrimage. Bill wore what he had worn the day before; I put on an Indian print, red and black wraparound skirt—my Spanish friends had told me I should wear a skirt, not pants—a white, short-sleeved blouse, cushioned socks, and jogging shoes. Then we converted our suitcases to backpacks and struggled to put them on. Why had I thought they would be lighter when they were backpacks? They might be easier to carry, but they were just as heavy. We adjusted the shoulder straps and the padded hip belts. They were still uncomfortable. Maybe backpacks always felt like that.

"We'll get used to them, right?" Bill said.

I smiled encouragingly. "Sure we will."

We paid the bill and started to leave. The desk clerk called out to us to wait.

"Pelerines?" he asked.

We looked blank.

"Peregrinos a Compostela?" he tried again, in Spanish.

Pilgrims To Santiago. We nodded, yes. He told us, in a mixture of French and Spanish, that we should visit the local representative of the Société des Amis de St. Jacques. She could give us important information. To help us find her house, he drew us a map. I wondered why the innkeeper hadn't mentioned her before, but then I realized that once we had converted our suitcases to backpacks, he knew we were not just—or were no longer—tourists. This was our first pilgrimage, but the innkeepers in St. Jacques had centuries of experience.

Once again, we walked up the narrow road to the Citadel, but this time we stopped at a house displaying a faded metal plaque: Société des Amis de St. Jacques. We knocked. We knocked again. A woman appeared at the door—a small, energetic, grey-haired lady. She started to speak to us in French, then switched to Spanish with a bit of English mixed in. And maybe Basque. We weren't sure what she said, but she gestured for us to come inside. First, however, we had to take off our backpacks. Bill helped me off with mine, I helped him off with his, and they dropped heavily to the steps. We picked them up and lugged them inside.

Enthusiastically, she guided us through the living room to a room overflowing with papers and books and maps and photographs, piled up in corners, stacked on chairs and tables. She was redoing her house, she explained, and everything was in a shambles. She sorted through several stacks, brushing papers off onto the floor. At last she grabbed a few things out of a pile and smiled at us and gestured that we should sit down. We looked around; all the chairs were covered with books and papers.

She had found two Spanish *tarjetas del peregrino*—pilgrimage cards—to give us. Folded in half, they were about wallet size. The front of each tan cardboard card was decorated with a black woodcut print of the sun, fields of grain, and the words, *Peregrino del Camino de Santiago.* Inside, the card was divided into twelve squares, each with a name: St. Jean, Valcarlos, Pamplona, Estella, Logroño, Santo Domingo de la Calzada, Burgos, Frómista, León, Astorga, Ponferrada, Monasterio de Samos. On the back was Santiago de Compostela and more instructions: "Present this card at the Palacio de Rajoy in Santiago in order to obtain the pilgrimage diploma."

She explained that we could get the cards stamped at tourist offices listed in the squares—or at town halls, police stations, or parish offices—to prove that we had made the entire pilgrimage. When we reached Santiago, we were to present the cards and we would be given the *Compostela,* a modern version of a fourteenth-century pilgrimage certificate. And we would also get free meals at the luxury hotel, the Hotel de los Reyes Católicos, located across from the cathedral.

Carefully, she wrote my name, address, and nationality on the back of one card; then she did the same for Bill. Next, she took out a rubber stamp, inked it, and pressed it twice upon a sheet of paper. She cut out the circular designs and pasted one on each card. The size of a silver dollar, it was a picture of castles and medieval pilgrims circled with the Latin words, St. Ioanne Pedis Portus—St. Jean Pied de Port. She gave us the cards and we thanked her.

Telling us to wait, she left the room. Soon she returned with a copy of a hand-drawn map of the "authentic" route over the Pyrenees to Roncesvalles and through the province of Navarra. Canon Navarro, archivist at the collegiate church of Roncesvalles, had drawn the map. He was also in the process of marking the traditional route with yellow arrows painted on tree trunks, stones, walls, and sometimes on the road itself. We paid her for the map and thanked her for her help.

As we lifted up our backpacks and struggled to put them on, she asked us when we planned to start. Right away, we said. She shook her head in warning: the day was very hot, and it was already early afternoon. Better to wait.

I felt queasy, hesitant to start. I thought she was right. "What should we do?" I asked Bill.

"What should we do? You mean, which route do we take? The trail over the mountains, of course!"

Bill glowed with excitement. I cringed. Taking off cross-country over the Pyrenees filled me with misgivings. Besides, I felt sick. Before we had left the hotel, I had taken some Spanish pills I'd used the summer before for "the runs," but I wasn't sure how long I'd last. "I'd really rather not—"

"Come on, Ellen. This is supposed to be an adventure—surely you don't want to walk on the highway when we can walk where Charlemagne and Napoleon walked. There's nothing to worry about. I'll take care of you."

What did he know about hiking and mountain trails? Absolutely nothing. But I gave a mental shrug and fell back on old habits; after all, aren't men supposed to take care of women? Besides, I felt ashamed of being such a coward. But I pointed out that we hadn't eaten and we didn't have any food. It was also late—almost 1 p.m.

Bill replied that the "Société des Amis" lady had said that Canon Navarro walked back and forth in a day, so he thought we should be able to get there by early evening. And he, for one, wasn't hungry.

I wasn't hungry, either, but I felt we should try to eat before leaving. So we went to a nearby cafe and ordered hamburgers. That sounded safe and familiar enough, but they were French hamburgers, not American, and they tasted different. Even the ketchup tasted different. Feeling nauseated, I pushed the plate away. We bought a plastic liter of mineral water and a loaf of bread and started out of town.

We followed the Rue de la Citadele once more, past a church, across a stone bridge over the River Nive. Two-story white stucco houses with wooden, second-floor balconies lined the river's banks. How many pilgrims, how many travelers—how many armies—had passed this way before?

We walked out of town, up the Rue de España, past the Porte d'Espagne, following the Route Napoleon, a narrow, paved, country road. According to the guidebook, this was a sharp ascent. The pavement was uneven, the asphalt soft from heat. After thirty minutes, we paused to rest, helping each other take off our backpacks.

Bill said, "We'll take it nice and slow. We've got lots of time before it gets dark."

I nodded in agreement.

After fifteen minutes, we struggled to our feet and helped each other put on our backpacks. The road wound up the hills, past massive white buildings with big wooden shutters. There was no traffic, so we walked down the middle of the road. At a fork in the road, we stopped and consulted the map, unsure which way to go. There were numbers on the handwritten map, numbers I had thought were meters—or minutes—between landmarks. But they weren't. Maybe they stood for altitude. We stayed on the main road.

Soon we stopped again to rest, taking off our packs, stretching out on a low stone fence by the side of the road. We heard a spring bubbling nearby. I had been told that one could always drink the water in Spain, so we took out our folding plastic cups and scooped up the fresh spring water, drinking some of it, splashing some of it on our faces and our clothes. The cups leaked. Resting in the shade of the rustling trees, shielded from the sun, was delightful. Suddenly, I had an urgent attack of stomach cramps and had to run behind some nearby trees.

We started walking again. Soon the pavement narrowed until it was wide enough for just a narrow strip of pebbly black asphalt winding up into the hills. Always climbing upwards. We walked for half an hour, then rested for half an hour. I took another stomach pill.

Two hikers came briskly up the road. We nodded hello, they nodded back, then they quickly disappeared out of sight. We struggled on. Bill told me not to push—we had lots of time. We rested often and frequently. Frequently, we examined Navarro's map, trying to make sense out of the

Pilgrim's bridge over the River Nive, St. Jean Pied de Port. We crossed over it and left town, following in the footsteps of Charlemagne, Aymery Picaud, Napoleon, and countless pilgrims—or so the guidebooks say. Just outside of town the road begins to climb toward the Pass of Cize.

markings. It was getting late. How much longer to Roncesvalles? We couldn't tell.

We walked, we stopped, we rested, we walked, we stopped, I collapsed, we rested, we walked some more, I collapsed again, we rested. Our lovely summer day had become scorchingly hot. Another hiker came energetically up the road. He was maybe seventeen, dressed like a boy scout in hiking boots, grey knee-high socks, brown shorts and shirt, green backpack.

"Pelerines?" he asked us.

We nodded yes. He pointed to the scallop shell on his pack. In the Middle Ages, wearing the shell showed you had completed the pilgrimage—but he was wearing it for identification on the way. He took off his pack, searched through a pocket on the side, and offered us some fruit. We shook our heads. Food didn't sound good.

Michel told us he was from the north of France and he'd been preparing for the pilgrimage for months, making day-long hikes wearing his pack. Just that afternoon, he'd arrived by bus in St. Jean, and immediately he had begun his pilgrimage to Santiago. For as long as he could remember, he'd dreamed of going to Santiago—his parish priest had gone there a number of times—but his mother hadn't wanted him to walk alone. Now he was almost eighteen, and she had let him go. Or maybe she couldn't stop him any longer. His priest had blessed him before he left.

I asked Michel if he had a pilgrimage card and he laughed. He didn't need one, he said; if he walked to Santiago, it would show on his face. Then I asked him why he was making the pilgrimage. A long discussion followed, which was difficult to follow, but I think he said that for him, walking the Camino and devotion to St. James were the same thing. Maybe something was lost in the translation.

Michel asked us why we were going. We looked at each other. Bill started to say something, then stopped. Curiosity, adventure, suddenly sounded trivial—and insufficient.

Even though we stopped frequently so that I could rest, Michel stayed with us. I rested on the dirt at the side of the road. I rested on the moss-covered roots of a large tree. I rested on a low stone wall. I rested often, but it didn't help very much. My pack felt like an elephant on my back. I leaned over, trying to lighten the load. It was hard to breathe.

Michel seemed puzzled at our leisurely pace, so we explained we were out of condition—it was a lie: we'd never *been* in condition. After an hour at our slow pace, I thought Michel would get impatient—but he seemed to enjoy our company. Or maybe we were part of the adventure.

It was getting late, and I wanted to quit, but Bill thought we should keep walking until we found a spring shown on the map, but our map was no use since we didn't know the distances involved. It started getting dark. I hadn't realized how quickly it got dark in the mountains. Our "Société des Amis" lady had said an afternoon would get us there, but we were still climbing up the French side of the Pyrenees, far from food and shelter.

Suddenly Bill collapsed by the side of the road. He sat down abruptly and shrugged off his pack. "I can't walk any more," he said. Michel and I stopped too, but we couldn't spend the night there. We had to find some level ground off the road to sleep. Michel thought the spring should be close, so he went on ahead to find it. I took off my pack and, lightened by forty pounds, I could walk again. I started up the road.

A hundred meters further on, I found a narrow, rutted dirt path leading away from the road. There would be no danger of being run over by a car. But what about animals? There were lots of tiny rock-like turds—it was an animal trail. Maybe we would be crushed by stampeding cattle. Or sheep. Well, I thought, we would simply have to take that risk.

I went back a few hundred yards and found Bill, still sitting in the same place. Shakily, he tried to stand. Slowly, we picked up our packs and we walked together in the fading light. When we reached the spot I'd found, we dropped our backpacks, took out our rain ponchos to use as ground cloths, and spread out our sleeping bags in the dark. We had no flashlight.

Ten minutes later, a light appeared over the hill; Michel had returned. He had gotten lost, and it had taken some time to get back. He spread out his sleeping bag some five meters away from us, and we could hear him rummaging in his backpack. Then he called out to us to join him. Spread out on a cloth were three loaves of long, narrow French bread, a dozen hard-cooked eggs, and four oranges. His mother, he explained, had wanted to make sure he didn't starve. I had no appetite, but Bill and he ate a late dinner. Then we crawled into our sleeping bags. It was almost midnight.

It was our first night on the Camino, our first night camping out in the fresh mountain air, under the diamond-studded velvet sky. The Milky Way spread out above us, pointing the way to Compostela. But where was the saint who would come and whisk us away on his strong white charger, carrying us effortlessly to Santiago before dawn?

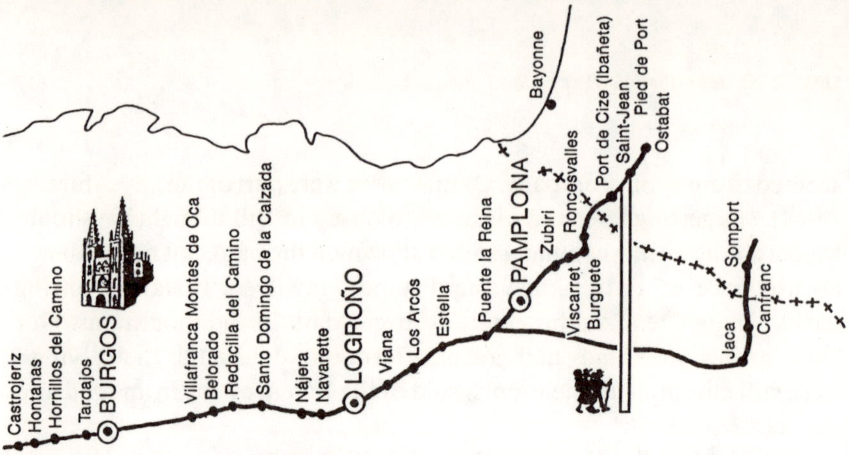

Day 2: July 11 I awoke at 5:30. Fog shrouded the hills below us, like thick whipped cream, flowing into the valleys, filling the ridges. The sun tried to rise through the haze. All was pastel and grey. Michel was awake, standing up, wrapped in his blanket, staring at the dawn. I fell back to sleep and, when I awoke again, Michel was gone. The fog was still creeping up the hills, the air was damp.

We shook out our sleeping bags, then went off in opposite directions. I crouched behind a hillock, in misery. So did Bill. I took more pills and offered some to him. He didn't want them—he thought he was over the worst of it. Then we packed our backpacks and helped each other put them on. They seemed even heavier than before.

I'd had no food since the day before, but I wasn't hungry. Slowly, pausing frequently, we struggled up the road. Three healthy Frenchmen passed us by, out for a morning stroll. One carried a light daypack, probably with sandwiches for lunch. According to Michel, the road we were following was part of the "GR 65"—the "Grande Randonee balises"—a popular hiking route. Red and white numerals, painted on cement, marked the way. Some people hiked this route for pleasure. For me, each step required an effort of will.

Bill thought that if we just rested enough, we'd make it eventually. But the more I rested, the weaker I felt. I could barely struggle 100 meters at a stretch. Exhausted, I wanted to hitch a ride, but Bill objected.

"This is a pilgrimage, after all. We are supposed to do the whole thing on foot, or else it won't count."

Count for what, I wondered. After all, we weren't religious pilgrims, so what difference could it make? But there was a kind of mystique about the pilgrimage road—an urge to struggle on, to push one's limits, not to give in. To walk in the footsteps of one's ancestors—anybody's ancestors—how could we do that if we hitched a ride? But how much further could I go on?

We struggled on. We passed isolated farmhouses, set back in the hills; some had signs in front, advertising honey for sale. According to the map, we were supposed to leave the asphalt road when we passed a painted boulder marked with a yellow arrow. There, we would take off across the meadow to the border. But we couldn't find the boulder with the arrow. Had we missed it? Numbly, I walked up the road; heavy, dull, I concentrating on taking each step, and then another.

A car drove by. In desperation, I tried to flag it down. The driver shook his head no and gestured at the back of the car. He'd already picked up two people. Hikers? Pilgrims with less scruples or more luck? Another car drove by, shifting into low. Even the cars had trouble making it up the pass. We rested, then walked some more. To the right of the road, down the hill, was a small, blackened stone shrine.

Finally, a wizened old man in an old, dirty white *deux chevaux*—a two-horse-powered wreck on wheels—stopped to give us a lift. The car doors were attached with fabric tape. We opened them carefully and climbed in.

"Where to?" he asked.

"The border," Bill said.

The old man concentrated on willing the car up the pass. At last, the road leveled out and the car picked up speed: ten miles an hour. He stopped and gestured toward the right. "The border."

We thanked him and got out. The border? It looked like a picnic spot. Bill walked towards it, then came back. There was no trail, just thick brush and trees, covering a steep hillside. Our ride had driven on. Why had he left us there?

We continued walking on the road. Having missed the turn-off, either in the fog or while we hitched the ride, what else could we do? Turn back? How far? Surely we would reach a village soon. The fog crept up to the level of the road, and the hills behind us disappeared in the fog. We could see the road curving around in front of us and ending in a great white wall.

I collapsed on a rock at the side of the road. I wanted to cry, but I was too tired. We heard a faint noise; another car was coming. Waving the map, Bill ran after them, trying to flag them down, but they disappeared into the white wall of fog. Then we heard a muffled noise; they were backing up. Bill went running after them.

Two men, two women, and two children got out of the cars. Bill told them we were lost, and one man and one woman replied to him in English. They looked at the hand-drawn map and shook their heads. The couple said they knew the route quite well and could take us back to the turn-off we had missed, but they advised against walking in the fog. They knew the mountains and the dangers. They lived in St. Jean Pied de Port and had driven up to the mountains with their children and some friends for a hike and picnic, but they had changed their minds when they saw the fog.

Bill asked them to take us back to the turn-off anyway. He wasn't worried about the fog. They looked at him. They walked towards me, immobile on my rock, and asked me if I felt all right. Paralyzed with fatigue, I could barely shake my head no. They talked a bit in French, then she asked if she could take my pulse. She looked at my eyes and asked if I were hungry. Too weary to talk, I shook my head no.

Bill said that we were lost but that he was sure we would do just fine once we were back on the right road. They suggested we go back with them to St. Jean and start again another day. But Bill wanted to continue on. They asked me if I could make it; but I was beyond response. I felt like a failure. I'd let Bill down.

They said that they would take us back to St. Jean. They were both doctors and it was their medical opinion that I simply could not go on. When Bill began to protest, they said no. I could not continue.

I don't remember much of the trip. I sat in the back seat, wedged between two children. They offered me chocolate, but I wasn't hungry. Maybe I slept.

It took us half an hour to reach St. Jean by car—twenty-four hours after we had left it on foot.

When we got to their house, they stretched me out on the sofa in the living room and fed me glucose pills. Then I fell asleep. Bill and the rest of them ate a late lunch in the dining room. When I awoke, it was late afternoon. Alan, the husband, and Malou, the wife, asked me if I felt better, and Alan took my blood pressure. Then he said they wanted us to stay with them for a few days. My blood pressure was quite low, my heart was beating much too fast. Apparently, I'd used up all my blood sugar. I showed them the Spanish stomach pills I had been taking, and Alan explained that the pills contained belladona, along with other ingredients—a dangerous drug if one plans to exercise.

Later, I asked Alan and Malou what would have happened if they hadn't stopped and if we had tried to continue walking. They said that soon I would have reached a point where I couldn't walk any more. I would have collapsed, and Bill would have had to go for help. Alan was a member of the mountain rescue team that would have come to rescue me, and they would have carried me out on a stretcher and put me in the hospital and fed me intravenously for several days.

If that had happened, I would never have dared to start the pilgrimage again. What a fortuitous escape I had had, being rescued by English-speaking doctors from St. Jean. I told them, "Santiago performed a miracle at the beginning of the Camino, not the end!"

Alan and Malou gave me glucose tablets, French medicine for "the runs," and great encouragement. They were amazed we'd made it as far as we had, given the heat, our poor condition, the stomach flu, my pills. Of course, they also thought we were foolish to have started out so ill-prepared.

I asked them if they often helped out pilgrims and they said no, but they did occasionally take in strangers. We were not the first. Would I take strangers into my house, I wondered?

Malou was French Basque, born in St. Jean but raised in Morocco, where her family had gone to farm. She had been sent back to France for schooling and later earned a medical degree. I'd always thought of boarding schools either as punishment or as something only the wealthy did, but Malou explained it was necessary for her to leave home, since in rural areas there were no secondary schools. Alan was half French Basque, half English, and raised in a nearby town. Like Malou, he'd had to go away to school. But after living for a while in Paris, he had eagerly returned to the land and people that he knew.

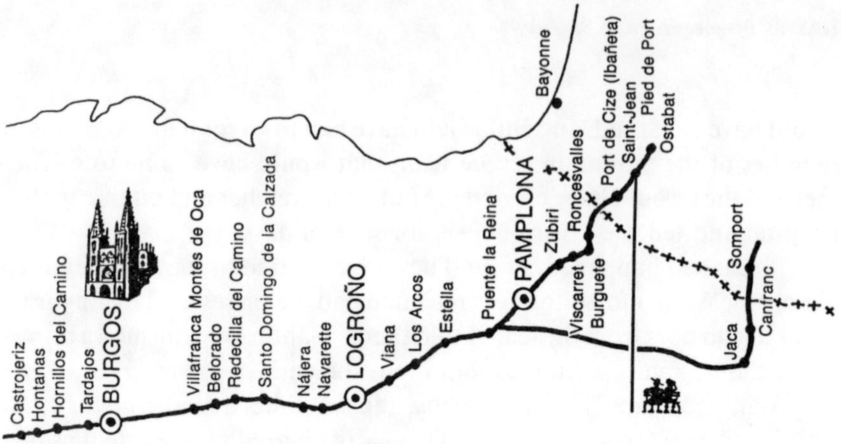

Days 3–4: July 12-13 The next day I had recovered enough to look forward to eating dinner. It was a feast: home-made pâté de fois gras, a *confite* of home-preserved pork ribs, cured in salt. And air-dried ham and specially ripened cheese. Alan said that the sheep's milk cheese made now, in summer in the Pyrenees, was best. He cut a slice for us and held it up. "You see? No holes. That's how it's supposed to be."

Alan and Malou practiced barter, occasionally, instead of charging medical fees. In place of money some of their patients provided them with farm-raised chickens, fresh eggs, pork fed on grain and nuts, home-cured cheese at just the peak of ripeness, fresh-shot game, special home-made sausages.

Alan told us that the ducks had to be force-fed just enough to enlarge their livers enormously—to the maximum size, the peak of flavor—but not too much, or the livers would rupture and decay. He made it sound like a delicate medical treatment. Enforced cirrhosis of the liver, but not to the point of death.

During the next few days, they showed us their herb garden and their cellar full of home-preserved meat and vegetables. In the evening, Alan played us some tapes of New Orleans jazz, his favorite music. As we talked and ate, I was struck by the quality of their lives. St. Jean is a small town, under 2,000 in population, with little in the way of elegant shops or up-to-date entertainment. Bill and Malou's income could not have been very large, but they lived remarkably well.

After we had rested another day, Alan and Malou offered to drive us back to the place where we had gotten lost. We would have a picnic in the mountains and then they'd walk with us a ways—"Just to be sure you find the way this time!"

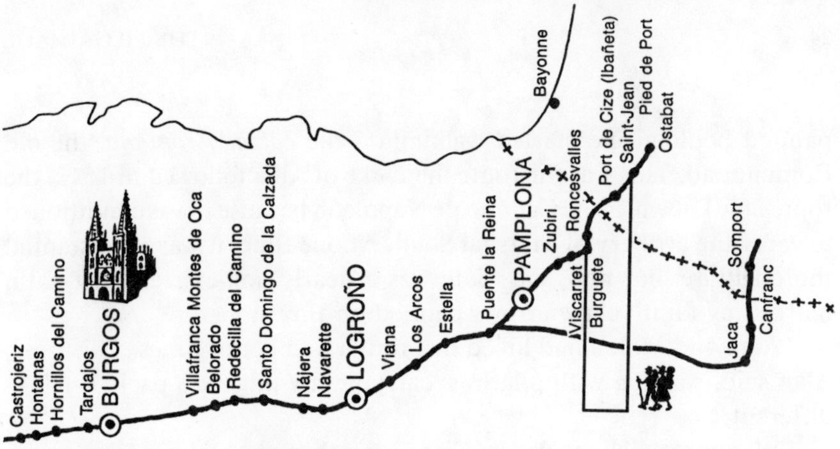

Day 5: July 14 Late in the morning, Bill and I, Alan, Malou, their two children, their large, shaggy sheep dog, and a neighbor piled ourselves, three backpacks, and a large picnic hamper into two cars and quickly, effortlessly drove up the road that Bill and I had so slowly, painfully hiked up four days earlier. We sped by all the places where I had collapsed, flattened with fatigue, and in less than half an hour, we had reached Alan and Malou's favorite picnic spot, a clearing near the yellow marker that we'd missed four days before. We would re-start our pilgrimage from there.

Before leaving, we had a farewell celebration. Boiled eggs and country ham, layered on crusty, chewy bread, spread with sharp, grainy mustard. Ripe tomatoes. Creamy, slightly tangy sheep's milk cheese. Tart, juicy oranges. Between mouthfuls, we talked about the Camino. Alan worried about whether I could make it the few kilometers—all downhill—to Roncesvalles. He wanted me to rest another day at least. I was tempted, but it was clear that Bill wanted to go on, and I decided to risk it. Besides, I was afraid my anxiety would grow in direct proportion to the time spent in anticipation.

Decision made, we put away the food. Alan and Malou admired our backpacks. Their own packs were heavy canvas and unpadded metal, well-worn and battered from years of hiking in the mountains. Our packs were new, lightweight, well-made, with multiple adjustments for different body sizes. They had cushioned shoulder straps that buckled across the chest and a thickly padded belt around the hips, adjustable to ease the load. We had high-tech gear—the best that money could buy. But we needed fitness, not fine equipment.

Alan picked up my pack—"Just to try it out"—and put it on. He was trying to ease my first day on the road again. Then we started out—a raggle-taggle troupe, hiking up a country road. Soon we reached the painted boulder and started walking on the *calzada romana*, the old Roman road. This was the route the Duke of Alba followed in 1512, the route now known as the Camino de Napoleón because it was conditioned to carry the artillery of Marshal Soult. At one time, it was a substantial thoroughfare; but now, the route was a nearly non-existent dirt path, marked by faint yellow arrows painted on tiny stones.

Alan and Malou had hiked this trail a number of times. This time, Alan said, walking with pilgrims, carrying my pilgrim's pack, it felt—different.

We approached the Pass of Cize—or rather, one of them. The Puerto de Ibañeta, on the highway from St. Jean to Roncesvalles, is also called the Pass of Cize. According to legend, it was at the Ibañeta pass that Charlemagne planted a cross—the *Crux Karoli*—and prayed in the direction of Santiago, and it was probably there that his soldiers began digging a road to Santiago. The legend is possibly true, since Alfonso II, "the Chaste," who built the first church over St. James's newly discovered tomb, was in communication with Charlemagne and may have told him of the miraculous find. But since Charlemagne died in 814 and the tomb was not rediscovered until 813 or later, the story is probably false. At any rate, someone planted a cross at Ibañeta, a cross that had disappeared by the sixteenth century. Today, following tradition, many modern pilgrims plant crosses at the Pass at Ibañeta and pray to St. James as they enter Spain.

But we were not at Ibañeta; we were at the other Pass of Cize, where there were no pilgrims' crosses. We were at a slight dip, 1,480 meters high, between green hills. The seven of us—plus the dog, who kept frolicking ahead, chasing butterflies—walked for another fifteen minutes until we reached the ridge where the route of Napoleon and the Roman road diverged. Napoleon's route headed off towards Ibañeta, but we chose to follow the Roman road; it seemed more direct—straight down. In the distance, we could see a wide, flat, green valley. Malou pointed down the hill to a distant clump of buildings, barely visible through the pine trees: Roncesvalles.

Offhandedly, Malou said, "We—the Basques—ambushed Roland near here, you know." So this was where Charlemagne's favorite warrior, Roland, was killed, in 778.

"Will you be all right?" Alan asked again. I nodded, too anxious to speak. We all hugged each other, then posed for a picture on the ridge. Behind us, cloudy sky and blue-green hills stretched as far as the horizon.

Alan took off my backpack and, with his help, I put it on and sagged from the weight. Then Bill and I started down the pilgrimage road, turning frequently to wave. Standing on the ridge, looking down, our friends kept waving back. We walked further down the path and waved again, but they were out of sight. At last, our pilgrim ceremony of leave-taking had taken place.

We continued down the old *calzada romana.* Once, it had been four meters wide, but now it was a narrow leaf-strewn forest trail through the mountains. Pale, dappled sunlight fell through the filtering beech and oak trees; fallen leaves and pine needles softened our footfalls. We walked under a tall canopy of branches crossing overhead. Every so often, we saw yellow arrows painted on tree trunks.

Although there was no way we could get lost—we saw no forks in the trail—I worried anyway. Bill assured me we were on the right path, but now I was wary of his reassurances. Within half an hour, our legs ached. Walking downhill was as difficult as walking uphill, though in a different way. My thighs began to quiver, my knees buckle. But we didn't stop to rest. We kept on going down toward Roncesvalles.

The trees thinned a bit and down below us I could see several large buildings, surrounded by evergreens: the medieval Collegiate church at Roncesvalles, the *hospital,* and the Augustine canons' residence hall. We came down behind one building, then circled around to the front. The multi-storied buildings were made of off-white stone and stucco, with bluish-grey tin roofs and large, brown, wooden shutters.

The Hospital Real—a kind of large-scale hospice—was founded by the Bishop of Pamplona, Sancho Larrosa, and Alfonso I el Batallador between 1127 and 1132. The Collegiate church—so-called because it has no abbot—apparently was founded about 1219 by Sancho VII, he of the Battle of Las Navas de Tolosa, that decisive defeat of the Almohad empire. The Hospital Real and church were staffed—and still are—by canons of San Agustín.

In the Middle Ages, Roncesvalles was extremely well endowed by grateful pilgrims and powerful kings. It was a thriving place, full of canons and visitors. Now it is much poorer, and there are just a handful of canons left, including Canon Navarro, archivist and drafter of our useless map across the Pyrenees. Visitors include more tourists now than pilgrims.

For a thousand years, pilgrims have hiked out of the mountains, walked wearily down from the high mountain passes, in need of shelter, food, and care; for 800 years, they have received it all generously at Roncesvalles. The "Song of the Hospital," recorded in the twelfth-century document, "La Preciosa," describes the welcome travelers received:

> Porta patet omnibus, infirmis et sanis
> Non solum Catholicis verum et paganis
> Judeis, hereticis, otiosis, vanis . . .[2]
>
> (The door is open to all, to sick and healthy,
> Not only to Catholics but also to pagans,
> Jews, heretics, beggars, vagabonds.)

In winter, travelers needed guidance through the snow, and in the sixteenth century a bell rang during the day to guide pilgrims and *caminantes*—travelers, a Spanish word formed from the same root as *camino*—to safety there.

I, like millions of medieval travelers, greeted Roncesvalles with relief. It had taken us four days to travel what we had thought would take an afternoon to walk. Filled with gratitude, I wanted to go to the church and give thanks—a feeling which surprised me. I was not—am not—religious, but offering thanks to someone—or something—seemed appropriate, an acknowledgement of risks overcome, of unexpected aid. But Bill wanted to get a Coke to drink, first, so first we went to a small bar—in Spain, almost every settlement, no matter how small, has a bar that serves food and soft drinks, espresso, and liquor. The Cokes were refreshing, full of sugar and caffein. Then we walked back towards the church.

Near the church was a large grey boulder, veined in pink. The bronze plaque proclaimed: "This is the stone that Roland broke with his sword." It refers to Roland, sung of in "The Song of Roland," the first and best of the *chansons de geste*—the songs of deeds. The *jongleurs* (medieval singers/musicians/jugglers/entertainers) sang or chanted the epic, along with other *chansons de geste,* for aristocratic audiences, for the masses, for pilgrims. They performed in town squares, in monasteries, and outside of sanctuaries along the pilgrimage roads.

"The Song of Roland" is a twelfth-century epic poem based upon actual, historically documented events that led to the death of Roland, warden of the Breton Marches, right hand of Charlemagne. Charlemagne lived from about 742 to 814. A Frank, he was the most powerful leader of the western Christian world in the late eighth century. In 778 Charlemagne entered Spain on the invitation of Sulayman ibn Yaqzan, Arab governor of Zaragoza. Sulayman offered Zaragoza and other cities to Charlemagne in return for Charlemagne's help against the emir.

The expedition was not a success. Sulayman's lieutenant, al-Husain, refused to go along with the plan and surrender Zaragoza. Charlemagne planned to lay siege to Zaragoza, but before he could capture it, he learned that there was trouble back home in Saxony. So he and his Frankish troops started back with Sulayman as hostage, destroying the walls of Christian Pamplona as he went. They retreated through the Pyrenees, through Roncesvalles. Roland was left in charge of the rear guard.

On August 15, 778, Roland and his rear guard were ambushed near Roncesvalles and killed, probably by Basques, in retribution for the destruction of Pamplona—or, possibly, by Gascons, in search of booty. One source says Sulayman's sons Matruh and Aishun ambushed the rear guard and rescued their father, with the help of the Basques.[3] Regardless of who did it, it was a stunning defeat for Charlemagne's troops.

There is a difference between historical events and artistic renditions, and "The Song of Roland," written three centuries after the actual incident, embroiders the facts quite a bit. For example, the Moorish leader is called Suleiman and is governor of Barcelona. And there are new characters, including treacherous Ganelon, who is Roland's stepfather; Roland's wise friend, Oliver; and brave Bishop Turpin, who fights alongside Roland and is the second-last to die; Roland dies last. In the poem, Charlemagne has gone on ahead and is resting at Valcarlos when the rear guard is treacherously attacked by the Saracen army. Roland and Oliver argue about whether Roland should blow his horn, Oliphant, and summon Charlemagne. He refuses to do so until almost all of his troops and the other eleven Paladins—the most famous of Charlemagne's warriors—are dead. At last Roland blows Oliphant and bursts the blood vessels in his brain. Charlemagne hears the horn in the distance and wants to go to his rescue but the traitor Ganelon tries to dissuade him. Soon Charlemagne realizes the treachery and goes, but he arrives too late. Before Roland dies—heroically, of course—he tries to smash his magical sword Durandal against a stone. The stone breaks, not the sword. This was, supposedly, the pink-veined boulder we stood before.

In the poem, the ambushers are all Saracens—not Basques or Gascons. And there is a happy ending for Charlemagne, who victoriously avenges Roland's death and the Christian defeat. In fact, the poem makes the whole military adventure into a crusade—perfectly fitting, since the poem was probably written around 1100—right after the First Crusade—by a man named Turoldus, living in France. It's not certain how much he composed and how much he transcribed from oral versions current at the time. An earlier version probably existed, since it is reported that Taillefer recited it to encourage his Norman troops at the Battle of Hastings in 1066.

It also isn't known if "The Song of Roland" was sung, accompanied on the viol, chanted, read aloud, or mimed. But it is known that it was very popular, and the *jongleurs* of the thirteenth century performed it up and down the pilgrimage roads in France, Spain, and Italy. And artists and sculptors commemorated it by carving or painting scenes from it in churches and monuments along the way.

We left the broken boulder and went over to a nearby chapel, the Capilla de Sancti Spiritus, the oldest building at Roncesvalles, dating from the twelfth century. It is also called the Silo de Carlomagno. A *silo* is an underground storage pit, and, according to legend, the bones of Charlemagne's knights—and perhaps, Roland—were buried there. Excavations have uncovered an ossuary—a depository of bones—there, and some of the bones were reported to be of giants: they were giants in those days, Roland and his fellow Paladins, or else they grew, in memory. Pilgrims were also buried there, pilgrims who didn't recover from the arduous journey over the Pyrenees, pilgrims who died despite the care they received at the hospice.

We walked over to the Real Colegiata, a simple, thirteenth-century stone building. Bill took a quick look inside, then left. I stayed. Walking slowly down the central aisle—the nave—my footsteps echoed through the empty church. At the end of the nave, near the high altar, was a large silver canopy; beneath it was the 600-year-old, silver-clad, jewel-adorned cedar statue of the Madonna of Roncesvalles. Countless pilgrims have prayed in front of her, reciting their pleas, their promises, their creeds. As I approached her silent, sacred form, I suddenly felt out of place; I knew no prayers, nor could I pray to a carved madonna. Yet I wanted to express my gratitude to someone, something. Uncomfortable, frustrated, I sat on a wooden bench and watched the sunlight stream through the stained-glass windows, filling the apse with glowing emerald and sapphire light. Then I left.

We tried to find Canon Navarro, but the clerk at the museum entrance said he was not at Roncesvalles. Off for an afternoon hike to St.

Jean? Perhaps. When we explained we needed someone to stamp our pilgrimage cards, the clerk directed us to an office. We entered and introduced ourselves to a black-robed clergyman sitting behind a desk. We took our pilgrimage cards out of our backpacks and he opened a desk drawer, took out a large, ornate stamp, inked it, and pressed it on our cards. Then he asked us to sign a register.

They had just begun a register of pilgrims, he explained, asking name, nationality, purpose, address, profession, and transport. I glanced at the entries: Germans, Dutch, Flemish, Spanish, French. Two Moroccans. One Japanese had passed through in March, while there was still heavy snow in the mountains. Most gave their occupation as "student," though there were a few teachers and clerics. Most gave their purpose as pilgrimage. Of course. Their transport: foot or bicycle, a few by horse. Many traveled in groups.

It was late afternoon and we needed a place to stay. I had heard that the Augustinian canons still provided shelter and food for pilgrims. In the twelfth century, according to "La Preciosa," at Roncesvalles they washed pilgrims' feet, cut their hair, and repaired their shoes. Someone stood at the door giving bread to all who passed. There were separate hospices for women and men, and those who fell ill were housed separately and nursed by beautiful, virtuous women. There they rested on soft, clean beds and were given baths if they requested them. If they died, they were buried in a special chapel which was, supposedly, visited by legions of angels.[4]

During the centuries since it was founded, Roncesvalles has endured wars and the loss of much of its once-large endowment; even so, in 1660 the canons were still able to distribute over 25,000 rations of food to pilgrims—not counting what was given to the poor and to beggars. In the eighteenth century, according to the Constitution of the House, they were supposed to—and presumably, still able to—give pilgrims a decent bed for three nights, five suppers and dinners, which included a minimum of specified amounts of bread, wine, meat, salad, and cheese.[5]

The canon asked if we wanted to stay at Roncesvalles for the night. I hesitated. What would the accommodations be like? Tired and weak, I needed rest, a comfortable bed, a private bathroom. He said they had a large dormitory set aside for pilgrims, and people slept in their sleeping bags on the floor. I asked him if they separated men and women. Somewhat puzzled by my question, he said they didn't. I thought, either accommodations were better in the Middle Ages or else morality was stricter. The canon added they required their guests to attend mass in the morning.

He told us he and his fellow canons had been disappointed that summer by many of the younger pilgrims. They were noisy, rowdy, played guitar into the early morning hours, and they didn't go to Mass. Shaking his head, he said he wasn't sure if they were really pilgrims. Sometimes he thought most of them weren't; they were just *excursionistas*—excursionists, taking advantage of the pilgrimage traditions of hospitality.

We decided not to stay. The next town, Burguete, was just two kilometers down a flat, straight road. According to my guidebook, there were three hostels—a kind of cheap hotel—in Burguete. Surely, with so much choice, we would be able to find a more comfortable place to sleep.

Just outside of Roncesvalles, we passed a lichen-covered fourteenth-century stone cross on the left side of the road. The guidebook said it was the *Cruz de Peregrinos*—the Pilgrim's Cross. But what did it mean? Did it commemorate a pilgrim's death? Was it a reminder of the sacredness of the journey, like a station of the cross? A boundary marker? Were we to recall the heavy crucifix Jesus carried on his back? We all had our crosses to bear. I took a photograph. We walked on.

Soon we passed a road sign: across the top, the words "Camino de Santiago," embellished with a scallop shell; across the bottom, the words "800 kilometers to Santiago." We walked two of those kilometers to reach Burguete, a small village of large white stucco houses lined up on either side of the road. The houses had large, red wooden shutters; steep, red tile roofs; and wide, grey stone borders around the windows, doors, and base. Substantial houses, they were built to provide shelter from the fierce winter cold. Looking at those shuttered houses, I wondered how much Burguete had changed since Hemingway used it as a fishing base for Jake and Bill in *The Sun Also Rises.*

About half-way through town, we found a place to stay—was it the same inn that Jake and Bill had stayed in?—and, as was customary in Spain, left our passports with the clerk at the desk. Then we went up to our room, collapsed on the soft, yielding beds, and rested our heads on hard, thin, cylindrical bolsters, the Spanish equivalent of American pillows. We flipped a coin to see who would bathe first. I won.

Soon I was soaking my sore muscles—muscles I'd never known I had—in the huge, claw-footed tub. Later, after Bill had bathed, we ate in the hostel's restaurant. The food was marvelous: fresh trout, caught in a nearby mountain stream, stuffed with *jamón serrano*—air-dried country ham—then lightly fried. Trout are a specialty of this region, famous among sportsmen now as in Hemingway's day, for its cold, fish-filled streams.

That evening we strolled through town, looking for a public phone booth. We had promised to call Alan and Malou and tell them we had arrived. They were relieved and pleased and wished us well. I wanted to call my parents in the States, but we couldn't figure out how to use the long-distance system. Although the directions were printed in French, English, and Spanish inside the phone booth, we couldn't figure out how to call collect.

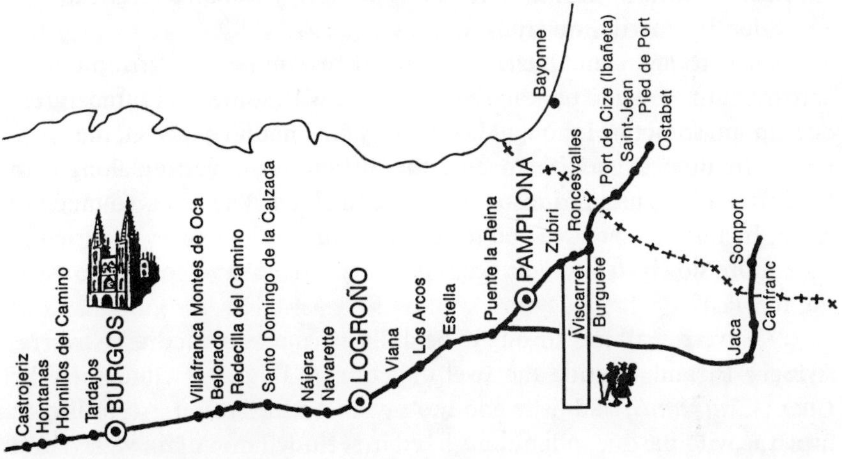

Day 6: July 15

In the morning, we could hardly move: every muscle, every joint ached. But we planned to walk from Burguete to Zubiri, a distance of 17½ kilometers. We repacked our backpacks and filled our plastic mineral water bottle in the hotel sink. Before we left town, I insisted on stopping at a grocery store; this time I wanted to be more prepared against disaster. We bought some oranges, a long, thin loaf of bread—the kind I'd always called "French" bread but which was also Spanish—and foil-wrapped, processed cheese that we could carry without refrigeration. In addition, we had chocolate and glucose tablets that Alan had given me.

Once again we followed Canon Navarro's xeroxed map, trying to stick to the "authentic" route. The Camino de Santiago, the map indicated, went through Espinal, founded in the thirteenth century by Teobaldo II, king of Navarra and count of Champagne. Then—cross-country, uphill. I was walking fast, leading the way, ahead of Bill. Soon I was winded. Out of breath, I paused to rest. Bill caught up with me.

"You're walking too fast."

"I didn't realize it."

"I did."

"Why didn't you warn me?"

"I did, once."

"I didn't realize it—you could have warned me again."

"Why should I? You'll learn."

I blew up. What kind of companion was I stuck with after all? "This isn't a competition, you know. It's a pilgrimage!" I stomped on ahead.

Silently, angrily, we trudged on.

I had thought our pilgrimage would be simple; we'd simply walk across Spain. It would be a shared adventure with someone I cared a great deal about, someone I thought I could rely on. I hadn't expected the physical difficulties; I hadn't expected the difficulties in getting along with Bill; after all, he had promised to take care of me! There was so much to learn. Including how I reacted to stress. Including how to walk. I tried to walk more slowly. It was puzzling: given my fatigue, how could I be walking too fast?

We were walking through the hills of the province of Navarra. Aymery Picaud, writing the twelfth-century "Pilgrim's Guide" in the *Codex Calixtinus*, had little good to say about the region. According to him, the wild Basque inhabitants lived in secluded mountain valleys and spoke a barbarous tongue. They had no food except apples, cider, and milk, and the thieving toll-keepers cheated pilgrims. As to the Navarrese, Picaud wrote little better of them: they wore short dark garments, resembling the kilts of Scots, and rough sandals made from untanned hides. They guzzled their food and their speech was like dogs barking. Picaud thought them savage, dark in face, full of malice, ferocious, perverse, and villainous. However, he also wrote that they were brave and punctilious with regards to paying church tithes.

We reached Viscarret. According to the guidebook, Viscarret was the end of the first of the thirteen stages of the journey given in the *Codex*'s "Pilgrim's Guide." The first stage started at Saint Michel, near Saint Jean Pied de Port. It was supposed to be a day's journey of 22 kilometers. Some of the thirteen stages, which range in length from 21 to 85

Yellow arrows and Canon Navarro's hand-drawn map guided us onto the "authentic" Camino de Santiago: a rough trail gouged into the hillsides. This bit of the route lies somewhere between Burguete and Zubiri.

kilometers, were probably intended for horseback-riding pilgrims, others for pilgrims on foot. Or perhaps the stages were not meant to be taken literally at all.

Or perhaps they stand for something else entirely. Some people believe the Camino was a pre-Christian initiation route; they believe that the thirteen stages were based on an ancient board game, the *Juego de la Oca,* which they believe to be the graphic representation of a secret, arcane initiation. The *Juego de la Oca*—the Game of the Goose—is a popular board game in Spain, said to have been "reinvented" by medieval German merchants, who adapted it from a Greek game, "the Gardens of the Goose," which perhaps had its origins in Crete. The game board is made up of a spiral of 63 numbered squares, which one travels, by throwing two dice, to reach the center. The players travel past bridges, a well, a river, darkness, fire, drink, a labyrinth—and geese. Thirteen of the squares are occupied by geese, an important symbol for teachers of esoteric lore. Thirteen geese, thirteen stages on the Camino de Santiago.

Quickly passing through Viscarret, we began the second stage of the journey. We continued hiking up and down the peaceful mountain trails, resting frequently. Walking side by side through the forests, going up and down the hills on the leaf-softened, tree-lined paths, was tiring but peaceful. We stopped to eat bread and cheese near a large stone, marked—by Navarro—in yellow paint with the cross of Roncesvalles: a cross with the top bent over towards the left, the bottom tip pointed like a sword. Yellow paint spelled out "Pasos de Roldán." What were *pasos*? I didn't know and my guidebook didn't explain.

At the Alto de Erro, our mountain trail crossed the highway. There was a flat, gravel-surfaced rest stop there for cars and buses, and a tour bus had stopped; its passengers had gotten out and were walking around a bit, stretching their legs, and drinking at a nearby fountain. We waiting in line for the bus travelers to finish. They would reach Roncesvalles—or St. Jean or Zubiri—in less than an hour.

After our brief rest stop, we started off again, hiking up and over the mountain ridges. Did medieval pilgrims really walk this "authentic" route? Following the route the highway followed, down in the valley, looked much easier. Bill said Roman legions were so well trained it made no difference if they went uphill or downhill. But surely it mattered to pilgrims.

The distance between Burguete and Zubiri was only 17 kilometers, but it took us all day, walking up, over, and down the mountains on the "authentic" Camino.

Our path came out of the hills and met the highway near Zubiri. At the entry to the town we saw a building and a flag: the barracks of the *Guardia Civil*—the Civil Guard, the national police force, stationed in nearly every town. The *Guardia Civil*: famous for their commitment to law and order—especially Franco's law and Franco's order—infamous for their brutality. As a safeguard, they never station a *guardia* in his own home town and, for protection, the *guardias* always travel in pairs. They are identifiable front or rear by their strange, black, shiny, bi-cornered hats, reminiscent of bull's horns; were they a survival from some ancient cattle cult? After all, bulls are still important in Spain, though now they are fought, instead of worshipped—or is that just another kind of homage?

Somewhat cautiously, we approached a guard sitting in a chair outside the living quarters. I asked, "Is there a hotel in town?"

He shook his head.

"A hostel? A place to stay?"

He shook his head again.

We could ask the parish priest or the mayor to find us lodging—I'd learned that from other pilgrims, the summer before. But Bill didn't want to take advantage of the pilgrimage traditions—it was too much like "taking advantage." After all, we had money, and we weren't religious pilgrims. Besides, I wanted privacy, a comfortable bed, a toilet nearby. I asked the *guardia* again.

"Any other suggestions?"

He thought a bit, then pointed towards a restaurant we had passed at the edge of town, the Restaurante Alamancer. "Maybe the owner will put you up."

We thanked him and walked back. The restaurant was shaped like an L, and the largest part of it was incomplete, either because it was being torn down or being built. Hesitantly, we went inside an open doorway. A short, chubby, smiling man greeted us.

"Hay comida?" we asked, asking if there were food. Although we didn't realize it then, *comida* is also the large, early afternoon dinner.

"No hay."

A restaurant without food? I tried again. "No hay sanwich? Bocadillo?" Aren't there sandwiches? *Sanwiches* are made with white

American-style bread, *bocadillos* with crusty Spanish rolls.

He smiled with pleasure. "Sí, sí. Hay bocadillos. Qué quereis—una tortilla española?" Did we want a sandwich made with the ubiquitous Spanish egg and potato omelet, called a *tortilla española*?

I said yes. "Dos," I added. Two of them. Nodding his head in agreement, he went back to the kitchen. In fifteen minutes he reappeared with two large, crusty rolls, sliced in half, filled with fragrant, steaming, slightly runny potato omelet.

How good it tasted. We had hoped for so much more than an egg sandwich, and yet that *tortilla española* was more satisfying than the three-course meal we had had the night before.

The owner hovered nearby. He wanted to know where we came from and how far we had walked. Next, he wanted to know if we were married. When I said no, he sat next to me and patted me on the knee. I moved away. Pointing at our backpacks, he indicated he wanted to put one on, and he asked Bill to take a picture of him wearing my backpack. Happy to oblige, Bill took a picture of José standing next to me, arm around my shoulder, laughing. Perhaps we were funny: bedraggled, weary, a man and woman in their mid-thirties, traveling all the way from the U.S. to exhaust themselves walking the Camino de Santiago.

We asked José if there were somewhere we could sleep, and he pointed to the second floor of the unfinished wing of the building. Before it got dark, we climbed the stairs up to the second floor and went inside. There were no doors in the door frames, no glass in the window frames. No toilet. The floor was cold cement. It was a roof and walls, a pretense of shelter. Would we be safe? Medieval pilgrims had traveled together for safety and slept in shelters run by priests or brotherhoods. Even so, by the fourteenth century the pilgrimage had gotten a bad reputation because of all the vagabonds and thieves who traveled on the roads. "Ir romero, volver ramera"—"go a pilgrim, return a whore"—was a well-known saying.

I was afraid. In the U.S. there were always news reports of robberies and attacks, of people killed camping out in state parks. I'd never taken such news personally before, but now I did. What a coward I was. How would I ever make it the rest of the way across Spain—even with Bill for protection?

Bill wasn't worried. "Nobody will know we're here. Relax." He was right, of course, except for leering José. As pilgrims we were supposed to be semi-sacred people, untouchable. At least that had been true in the

The innkeeper at Zubiri. He made us supper, then let us sleep in an unfinished building attached to his restaurant/night club. He wanted to wear my backpack for the photo but it was too heavy, so he wore my hat instead.

Middle Ages—in theory, though not always in fact. Pilgrims were given special privileges, excused from paying tolls and debts. And laws were passed which heavily punished crimes committed against pilgrims; not only would the perpetrators be punished on earth but also in heaven. Or hell. But since so many laws were needed, perhaps there was a lot of crime.

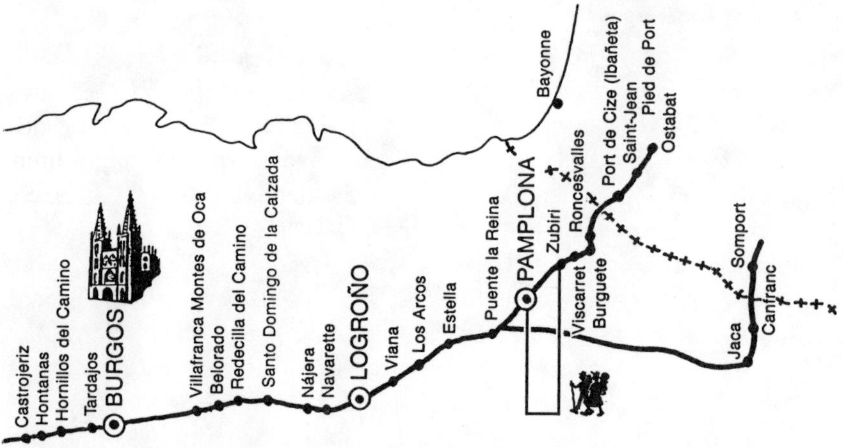

Day 7: July16 We planned to make it to Pamplona, 19 mountain kilometers away. We woke up stiff and sore. With difficulty, we got dressed, picked up our backpacks, and went to wash in the restaurant's bathroom. Our jolly host offered us freshly made espresso. Cheery and well-rested, he was still laughing. We thanked him for his hospitality and left, following the highway through Zubiri. It was an ugly industrial town. There, in the midst of the green mountains, was a magnesium factory, spewing its stench into the air.

We needed to replenish our food supplies. I saw people walking towards a building empty-handed, other people leaving it carrying long, thin loaves of bread. Following them, we entered the building. The heat was stifling. Using large paddles, a man was pulling loaves of bread out of a flaming oven and placing them on a wooden table. As they cooled, a woman wrapped a bit of paper round each loaf. We gave her 25 cents, she gave us a still-hot loaf. Blowing on the bread to cool it, we pulled off fragrant, steaming pieces and ate them as we walked.

My head throbbed. Each step I took pounded into my skull. Soon it started to sprinkle, and we looked for shelter; houses were few, perched on the hillside, scattered one by one along the road. We ran toward the nearest one, a few hundred meters away, and, huddling under a wooden arbor, waited for the rain to stop. I wondered if the owners of the house would mind that we were resting under their arbor. Lulled by the rain and some aspirin, I slept, pillowing my head on my backpack. Soon the rain cleared.

Cutting across farmers' fields, slipping over or sliding under barbed wire, we waded across a stream, soaking our shoes and socks. Why was this the "real" Camino? What made traveling through an unmarked field more authentic than walking on the highway? Somehow, it seemed important to follow the authentic route, as if following it constituted the pilgrimage. Were we engaged in a sort of magical act, trying to follow literally in the footsteps of our ancestors? The guidebooks, Canon Navarro's map, the yellow arrows—all pointed out the "real," "traditional" way, "the" authentic way, "the" Camino de Santiago.

Once upon a time—actually, up to the present day—what mattered on the pilgrimage to Santiago was getting to the goal, not what route one followed to get there. To assist the pilgrimage traffic, and resettlement of the north, and trade, and agriculture, and troop movement, kings, nobles, and clergy had the old Roman roads repaired, new roads built, new bridges constructed. By the twelfth century, specific routes had been developed across France and Spain, the routes described in the *Codex,* routes which still serve as the basis for modern pilgrimage guides and tourist brochures. The routes were lined with famous shrines, with monasteries and hospices often just a day apart. Pilgrims could travel safely on these routes, assured of company, of food and shelter.

The route we were following, the Camino de Santiago, also known as "the French Way" because of the number of French pilgrims who traveled on it and settled along the route, was quite convenient and quite widely used. But there were many roads and many detours, subject to individual preference, to convenience, to popularity. Rather than a single Pilgrim's Way, there were a number of ways, all leading to Santiago. But we modern pilgrims—and the authors of the guidebooks—acted as if there were only one way, one straight and narrow path, one specific road. We seemed to think we were following in our ancestors' footsteps not figuratively but literally. But since medieval pilgrims had actually traveled many different routes, why were people striving so hard to follow this one "authentic" route?

Abruptly, our Camino de Santiago ended in a patch of bushes. There were no yellow arrows and the guidebook was no help. I looked at Navarro's map more closely and saw, in fine print, "impenetrable branch of Camino." We struggled through a weed-choked field until we reached the Río Arga, which we followed until, finally, we found a bridge and crossed the river.

We decided—for the time being—to hell with authenticity. After all, in the Middle Ages, there would have been a road, not a dead end. So which was more authentic, modern highway or trackless wilderness? The highway surface was smooth, newly resurfaced, springy under our feet. A sign said "Peatón, a la izquierda"—"pedestrians on the left." We walked on the side of the road, separated from the sparse highway traffic by a wide white line painted on the asphalt. The road curved up and down and around the hills.

Three pilgrims passed us by, wearing scallop shells on their packs. We called out "Buenos Días." They answered "Buenos Días" and soon were out of sight.

It was 5:00 and we wanted to reach Pamplona before the *Telefónica* closed. We still had six kilometers to go—two or three hours of walking, at our slow pace—so I suggested that we hitchhike. Bill objected.

"I thought we'd agreed. This is a pilgrimage—we should be walking every step."

"But we won't get there in time."

"Then hitchhike by yourself."

I just couldn't. When I was growing up, I was taught that girls should never hitchhike—it was too dangerous. How could I hitchhike by myself in Spain? I tried to explain to Bill, but he thought it was all quite foolish. And simple. Either I hitchhiked alone or I didn't.

Given those alternatives, I decided to walk faster under the bright hot sun. The softened asphalt reflected waves of heat, but I just kept walking, intent upon my immediate goal. Bill was angry; he wanted to go more slowly, but he was determined not to fall behind me.

After an hour, we saw Pamplona in the distance. Pamplona: the end of the second stage of journey in the *Codex Calixtinus.* Another half an hour, we reached the outskirts of the town. Bill suggested we call a taxi so that we could reach the *Telefónica* in time.

I was indignant. "A taxi? After all your objections to hitchhiking?"

"Well, that was 'on the camino.' Now we're in town."

"How can we call a taxi?" I asked him, looking around for a phone booth.

Bill went up to a large, elaborately landscaped house and knocked. An elderly woman came to the door, and Bill asked her to call a taxi for us, which she did.

Soon we were driving past La Magdalena bridge over the Río Arga; at one time, there had been a *hospital* there. In the Middle Ages, a *hospital* was a kind of all-purpose hospice, which might or might not provide medical assistance, depending upon its size and resources. Etymologically, the words hospital, hospice, hostel, hotel, and hospitality are all related; *Hôtel de Ville* means the Town Hall in French, *Hôtel-Dieu* means hospital. According to the German pilgrim Hermann Künig, in the fifteenth century they gave out bread and wine at the *hospital* at the Magdalena bridge. Originally, the *hospital* was dedicated to taking care of lepers, pilgrims, and the poor; pilgrims and the poor often relied on charity, though pilgrims did it out of humility and the poor out of necessity. But by the sixteenth century the *hospital* served only to shelter the poor who arrived after the gates of Pamplona were closed for the night.[6]

The taxi let us off in front of the government-run *Telefónica.* Although the operators were quite helpful, it still took two hours to complete the connections. At last I was able to reassure my parents that all was well. It hadn't been, a week before.

We went to find a hotel. Since we didn't know where to start looking, we asked a passerby for directions. Soon we were walking down a narrow street, full of narrow doorways. Most of the doorways had brass plaques beside them, announcing "H" for hotel or "Hs" for hostel and showing the quality of the place by the number of stars following the "H" or "Hs." The plaque also showed which floor the establishment was on, starting with "1," the first floor above ground floor. Since there were no elevators, the quality of the hostels went down as the floor number went up. Most doorways had several plaques. I waited while Bill went up. No luck. He tried another doorway. No luck again.

Bill thought it was because of his backpack. "Innkeepers don't like pilgrims."

"Why shouldn't they like pilgrims?" I asked him. "It's after 8 p.m., and Pamplona is probably just crowded. After all, the Feast of San Fermín started July 7."

Bill took off the backpack and tried again. This time, he was successful.

After leaving our passports at the desk, we went up to our room. Off-white plaster walls, beige tile floor, two wood-framed beds covered with beige chenille spreads, separated by a small wooden table, a wooden wardrobe—in Spain, apparently, the hostel rooms had wooden wardrobes instead of closets—a private bathroom with a toilet, a sink, and a half-sized bathtub with a ledge on one corner to sit on. The shower head looked like a telephone, attached to a long metal cord, detachable from the wall. There was no shower curtain. Bill and I flipped a coin to see who would wash up first. He won. While he bathed, I slept. Later, we went downstairs and ate dinner at a restaurant on the first floor. I started to fall asleep at the table, but Bill jogged me awake. Then we went upstairs to bed.

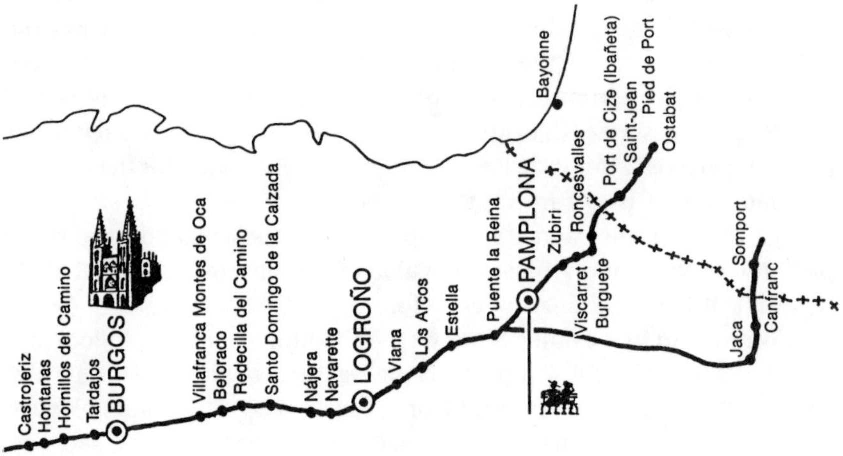

Days 8–9: July 17–18 Bill woke up with a high fever; I woke up exhausted. As the English pilgrim, Doctor Andrew Boorde, observed in 1542, "I had rather go five times to Rome from England, than one time to Compostela: by water it is no pain, but by land it is the greatest [most impressive] journey that one Englishman may undergo." Despite his efforts, all nine of his English and Scottish companions died from eating the fruit and drinking the poisonous water of Navarra. He himself drank only wine or ale.

We spent two days in Pamplona, recovering our strength. Bill was quite sick, so he stayed in bed and I brought him food. Familiar food. When one is sick, one wants familiar comfort. This was not easy to find in Spain, but I located a *panadería*—bread store—around the corner from the hostel. It sold not only bread but sweet rolls and refrigerated dairy products, so I bought a loaf of bread and some *mantecadas*—a not-too-sweet muffin—and some *flan*—an egg custard—and yogurt. Later, I went out to a bar across the street and brought back two *bocadillos,* one filled with *tortilla española*—the potato and egg omelet—and the other filled with the famous Pamplona *chorizo*—dry-cured pork sausage, a bit like salami, redolent with garlic and reddened with *pimentón,* a kind of smoky paprika. I also brought back several cans of Coke. Coke was always easy to find.

Bill didn't want me to help him, but he was too sick to get up. I told him he had to learn to accept help when he needed it; we could help each other, after all.

While Bill slept, I wrote postcards to friends back home and to Alan and Malou. "Wish you were here. Having a great time." It was a lie, but one I wished were true. I caught up with my journal.

"Deciding to walk this 500-mile pilgrimage road wasn't brave—it was naive! I didn't realize there was anything to be afraid of. And now I'm finding out just how much I am afraid of—of getting lost, of sleeping in an empty building, of hitchhiking in Spain. . . .

"I react to the stressfulness by wanting reassurance, wanting to strengthen the bond between Bill and me—we're in this together, I keep saying. We can lean on each other. But Bill reacts to the stressfulness—by trying to be more in control. By getting rigid about the route and not hitchhiking. By trying to act masculine/macho superior. I had thought I was long past getting hooked into those typical male/female stereotypes—but here they are, again. Bill doesn't know any more than I do about hiking—and less than I do about pilgrimage and Spain. But I let him take charge in the mountains—even though the results were almost disastrous. Trying to please. Trying to meet his expectations.

"Pilgrimage. Extremely difficult—but not in the ways one expects. Have I learned anything? Aside from the amount of pain and exhaustion I can endure? I've learned you can't count on when you'll get there—anywhere—not when the experience is new and the terrain unknown. You can't make plans: 'We'll get there by such and such.' Maybe you will, maybe not. The pilgrimage is like a river, flowing through time, flowing across Spain. We have to go with the flow of the pilgrimage.

"The pilgrimage is almost too many new experiences. There is so much to incorporate: pain, fear, pleasure, excitement, achievement, anger, weariness, joy. And the interaction is also intense: with Bill, with the wilderness, with myself. I am saturated with experiences and stimuli and responses."

After a good night's rest we had both recovered, so we went out to explore the 2,000-year-old city of Pamplona. Founded in 75 B.C. by Pompey, it was called Pompaelo, the City of Pompey, by the Romans, Iruña by Castilians, and Iruina ("town") by the Basques. In 466 it was occupied by the Visigoths and, in 542, by the Franks. Still later, it came under the control of Leovigild; the Moors seized it in 738; the Basques and Charlemagne drove out the Moors in 750. But during the Spanish campaign of 778, Charlemagne destroyed the defensive walls around the town—and perhaps in revenge for this, the Basques may have been the ones who annihilated Charlemagne's rear guard and Roland on August 15 of that same year. In 905, Sancho Abarca chose Pamplona for the capital of his newly established kingdom of Navarra, a kingdom which stretched at times from the Pyrenees into León and Castile. Pamplona was to remain the capital of Navarra until the beginning of the sixteenth century, when Ferdinand and Isabella annexed Navarra to Castilla.

Although the people of Navarra were mostly Basque, the medieval town of Pamplona consisted of three *barrios* or districts: one of native Navarrese and two of immigrant Frankish settlers—a word used either for people coming from the areas now known as Germany, France, and Italy, or for privileged, "free" settlers. In 1521, the young captain Inigo López de Recalde, later known as St. Ignacio de Loyola, was seriously wounded during an attempt to recapture the city. The basilica of San Ignacio commemorates the place where the founder of the Society of Jesus—the Jesuits—was wounded. Today, approximately 186,000 people live in Pamplona, including many priests, students, professors, and government officials. The University of Navarra, founded in 1952, the center for the politically powerful and somewhat secretive Catholic layman's organization, Opus Dei, and the provincial government offices are all located in Pamplona.

About 10 o'clock we sat down at a sidewalk cafe, the Irunaberri, under the shade of a green, orange, and blue umbrella, and ordered fresh espresso—25 cents a cup—and croissants, or what passed for that in Spain, a *media-luna* — half-moon shaped, sugar glazed, and dry. I thought of Hemingway's Jake and Bill and Mike and Robert Cohn and Brett, searching Pamplona for excitement, searching each other for answers, each on their own private quest. This had been their cafe, I thought, theirs and Hemingway's. As I nibbled on my *media-luna*, I watched the people walking by. There were lots of Spaniards, of course, but also a large number of young foreigners; we heard English and

French, German, and Italian. Perhaps they had been here for the Feast of San Fermín.

San Fermín was the first bishop of Pamplona and is patron saint of Navarra. Since the 1500s his fiestas, the *Sanfermines,* have taken place in July. Today, the *Sanfermines* run from July 6 to July 15, and the *encierros*—the running of the bulls through the narrow streets—draw tourists from all over the world. Sometimes as many as 100,000 visitors—tens of thousands of them foreigners—watch the running of the bulls each day. Hemingway popularized them and Pamplona in *The Sun Also Rises.*

It has been said that *Sanfermines* made Hemingway famous—and Hemingway made *Sanfermines* famous. Like the festival, Hemingway is still a presence in Pamplona. In fact, the road in front of the bullring is named after him; we saw his books in the stores, and we heard his name spoken at nearby tables. In Pamplona he and his unyielding macho code of risk and bravery live on with each runner dancing before the bulls, each man sprinting 100 to 150 yards alongside the bulls, running in front of death, asserting his consciousness of courage before the dangerous dumb beasts charging after him.

During the *Sanfermines,* each day at dawn the *toros bravos*—fighting bulls, bulls bred for bravery and quick response—are released at one end of the town. A large firecracker explodes in the air, announcing the beginning of the *encierro.* Six *toros bravos,* escorted by *cabestros* (cows or castrated bulls), stampede up the narrow streets to the bullring, where, later in the day, they will be forced to fight in a *corrida* and die. Men (women are not allowed) run just ahead of the charging bulls, trying to keep out of their way. Frequently, people trip as they run and get thrown to the ground, trampled underfoot, tossed up in the air, gored. Although each *encierro* lasts only a few brief early morning minutes, perhaps 40 to 50 men are injured, some seriously, during the festival. On the average, one man dies each year.

But the *Sanfermines* are not only the running of the bulls. They are also drinking, dancing, and parades. After Bill and I finished our espresso, we left the cafe and walked around town, looking in store windows. One window displayed a tableau of Pamplona *en fiestas*: a street scene, full of little dancing figures, dressed in white cloth slippers with rope soles and red laces, white pants and shirts, red sashes wrapped around their waists, red scarves around their necks—the fiesta outfit for San Fermín. Marching behind them down the narrow, cardboard street were *Cabezudos*—Bigheads, people wearing huge, grotesque, papiermache heads; and *Gigantes*—giant figures on stilts, dressed up like kings and queens and Moors; and more white-dressed men, playing a kind of flat drum, called *tamboril* in Basque, a trumpet, and flutes, called *txistu* in Basque.

A well-dressed, middle-aged man stopped by the window and looked at us. He spoke to us in English. "Americans?" We nodded. "Were you here for San Fermín?"

"No," Bill replied. "We arrived yesterday."

"Too bad!"

"Were you here for San Fermín?" I asked him.

With studied deliberation, he took out a Gitano brand cigarette, lit it, and smiled. "This year and every year for the last twenty years. Ever since the summer after my freshman year in college. I spent my first summer in Europe here. And got hooked. No matter where I am, every year I come back here and run with the bulls. There's nothing like it."

Bill said, "Really?"

"Yes, really. It's not just the bulls. All the youth of Europe are here. And my old friends from all the previous years. We meet together here, each year. And everyone drinks and dances in the streets. And drinks some more. And runs with the bulls—for all seven days of the *Sanfermines*."

I asked, "Don't people ever sleep?"

"Oh, sometimes. For a little while."

"Where? Yesterday, we found it hard to find a hotel, and it's already after San Fermín."

"Lots of the natives leave Pamplona during the fiestas, and they rent out their homes to tourists. That's where some people sleep. Some sleep on the sidewalks or in the parks. The police are very lenient." He smiled.

"Maybe we'll see it some other time. We're on our way to Santiago on foot," Bill added.

"Walking to Santiago? Why would anyone do that?"

We looked at each other. I said, "It's hard to explain. Why would anyone run with the bulls?"

He shook his head and walked on down the street.

After asking several people for directions, we found the Pamplona Tourist Office and went in to get our pilgrimage cards stamped. Our "Société des Amis" contact in St. Jean had told us we could get the cards stamped in parish offices, town halls, sanctuaries, and tourist offices. The last choice seemed odd, since the pilgrimage was supposedly religious in orientation, not touristic, but it was obvious that even pilgrims did some sightseeing—and besides, the National Ministry of Tourism had printed the cards. Encouraging pilgrimage? Encouraging tourism? The man at the Tourist Office stamped our cards and gave us tourist brochures describing Pamplona.

We walked over to the cathedral, supposedly built on the site of a Roman capital. The earlier, eleventh-century Romanesque church was added on to in the twelfth and fourteenth centuries, and in 1390 construction was started on the present cathedral, which was completed in 1527. Such building and rebuilding was apparently quite common in the Middle Ages, as fire destroyed earlier buildings, or poorly designed vaults collapsed, or changing fortunes provided revenue for new construction, or renewed city pride called for more impressive buildings. Since it usually took between forty to eighty years to build a new cathedral, I wondered why the cathedral in Pamplona had taken over 130 years to complete. I looked up at the tall, twin towers on either side of the classical facade. The right tower holds the largest bell in Spain, a bell that weighs 12 tons.

According to our guidebook, the fourteenth-century cloister in the cathedral is one of the greatest Gothic works in Spain. Although neither Bill nor I was very interested in seeing the cathedral, we decided to look at the cloister, a covered passageway at the side of an open court. It is quite pretty and delicate; the colonnaded walls are composed of row on row of overlapping, pointed arches and elaborate tracery carved in stone.

We left the cathedral and went next door to the huge Pilgrims' Kitchen. Beginning in the Middle Ages, food was prepared there to give to pilgrims. Pamplona had taken good care of its pilgrims; now it took good care of tourists.

In the eleventh century, the Hospital de San Miguel was located in front of the doors of the cathedral, which gave rise to a famous pilgrims' shelter or *hospital* which was active through the nineteenth century. In the thirteenth century, the *hospital* had fifty beds. Each pilgrim was given a daily ration of bread, wine, a plate of vegetables, meat or beans. By the sixteenth century, the *hospital* was in decline and had only eight beds, reserved for female pilgrims going to or coming from Santiago. This decline was perhaps due to a lessening of devotion to the pilgrimage to Santiago, but in the same century, the Hospital General was built as a stopping place for pilgrims, pilgrims who kept eating at the kitchen of the cathedral.

According to the seventeenth-century Italian pilgrim Dominico

Laffi, while mass was sung, twelve pilgrims were fed at a table near the church door. Pilgrims went to the exit of the kitchen and were given a bowl of soup, and then they walked in single file to the cathedral and sat at the table. There they were served bread, boiled meat, a slice of pork, and a glass of wine. In the eighteenth century, according to the traveler Guillermo Manier, pilgrims (including himself) were given soup, cod, bread, and two glasses of wine.[7]

By the twelfth century there were a number of private hospices in Pamplona, and the *Codex Calixtinus* warns travelers to be wary: it was not unheard of for dishonest landlords to take unfair advantage of unsuspecting pilgrims. There were also other *hospitales* and hospices for pilgrims, run not by the Church but by lay brotherhoods. The Cofradía de Santa Catalina supported two different hospices, one for Spanish pilgrims, the other for foreign pilgrims. From 1534 to 1680 this latter hospice took in a number of Belgian, French, and German pilgrims, some of whom died there. The *hospitalero* who ran it was required to give the pilgrims a bed, light, fire, and dinner for three nights.

Today the *hospitales* and the cathedral kitchen are closed. In their place are a number of hotels and hostels of variable quality, and a number of restaurants, bars, and cafes. But none of them provides charity.

Outside of the cathedral we saw an older, white-haired pilgrim. He was wearing jeans, a cotton shirt, and hiking boots. We knew he was a pilgrim because he wore a carved wooden scallop shell around his neck. I asked him in English, "Are you a pilgrim?" He looked blank. I tried again. "Peregrino?"

Smiling, he nodded yes. A Frenchman, he was traveling alone, fulfilling a vow he had made during the "War in the Pacific." He had begun in Paris, about a month earlier. Usually he traveled 40 or 50 kilometers a day, mostly on foot, sometimes by hitchhiking or bus. Eager for conversation, he asked us about ourselves, and we explained we were from the U.S. He was surprised that we had come from so far away to walk the pilgrimage road.

"You must have a lot of faith!" he said.

We shook our heads no, and said goodbye.

I thought: now there goes a real pilgrim, a pilgrim motivated by faith. Not like us, motivated by—curiosity? Sixty or seventy years old, he was traveling alone, averaging 40 or 50 kilometers a day. We could barely manage 20! Of course, he did hitchhike some, he had said. I was puzzled; he was fulfilling a religious vow made during World War II, yet he found nothing wrong with taking a bus occasionally or hitching a ride, while we, having little or no faith, had scruples about not walking every foot of the way! Was it because we were substituting external ritual for interior belief? Was I a pilgrim? I surely was suffering enough, but did suffering make a pilgrim?

We started slowly walking back to the hotel. Sightseeing was amusing, but we were worn out. On the way, we passed through a small plaza in which several young boys (called *maletillas*) were practicing bullfighting. The bull—a scaled-down model of the front half of a fighting bull—had wheels in place of rear legs, and one boy was wheeling it around while the other boys dodged. The girls stood on the sidelines, watching. They started early, in Pamplona, learning the ways of bulls and boys.

Back at the hotel, we ate *la comida,* the big meal of the day, served after 2 p.m. The waiter gave us a printed sheet of paper, showing both *el menú* and *la carta. El menú* listed the fixed price meal of the day—or rather, the several fixed price meals. By law, Spanish restaurants are required to have a fixed price tourist menu available. *La carta* was the a la carte list.

After examining *la carta,* Bill ordered a Pamplona specialty—*chuleta de buey*—a huge steak, made from ox meat—*toro* meat, according to the waiter—served almost raw. I ordered *entremeses variados*—mixed appetizers—and *ensalada mixta*—a mixed salad. Soon the waiter brought our orders. Sitting in a pool of congealing blood—or was it juice?—Bill's enormous steak was, indeed, barely cooked. Bill looked at it a bit skeptically, but cut off a piece and chewed it slowly. He swallowed, then looked at me.

"Now I know what *toro* tastes like. Strong."

Tame by comparison, my appetizers consisted of a plate of cold cuts, including *jamón serrano*—the dry-cured country ham, regular ham, *chorizo,* several kinds of salami, and a serving of mayonnaised potato salad. My mixed salad was a huge platter of lettuce, tuna, white asparagus, green Spanish olives, slices of onion and pimento. I took a bite of Bill's steak; it was essence of beef intensified—appropriate in Pamplona, with its cult of bulls.

After lunch, we went up to the hotel room and took a nap, trying to recover from the excursions of the day. About 5 o'clock, we went back to the plaza, drank more espresso at a sidewalk cafe, watched more people walking by, and wrote more postcards. Then we returned to the hotel and ate a small dinner—*la cena,* at 9 p.m. By ten p.m. we were in bed.

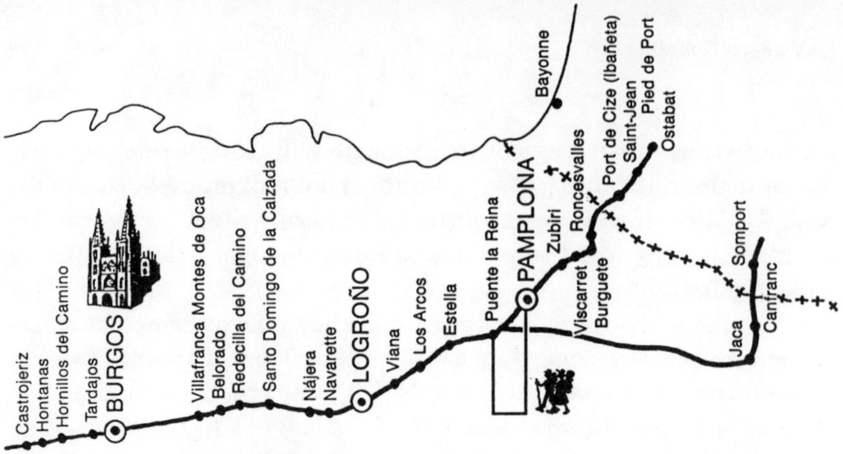

Day 10: July 19 The third stage of the *Codex* journey is from Pamplona to Estella—43 kilometers. Perhaps medieval pilgrims could travel that distance in a day, but we knew we couldn't. Since Pamplona lies in a treeless basin between the Pyrenees and the sierra zone, to reach Estella we would have to climb up—and presumably down—hills. We planned to walk as far as we could and then stop in the nearest town.

About 9 a.m. we left the hotel and started walking. Half an hour later, we were still in Pamplona, so we stopped at a cafe for our morning coffee. During the time we stood at the bar drinking espresso, half a dozen men came in, ordered a *copa*—a shot of cognac—or *vino*—a glass of wine, drank, and left. We hoisted up our backpacks and left. Soon the street forked and we asked two passersby which road to take. They started arguing about which was the "real" Camino de Santiago. After five minutes of unresolved discussion, we thanked them and continued on.

As we passed by a large cement apartment building complex, I heard a faint, eerie sound—it sounded like scales being played on a flute. The music reminded me of Greek myths and Shakespeare's *A Midsummer Night's Dream.* Looking around, I saw a tiny, blue-overall-clad man sitting on a bicycle-like contraption: a knife grinder. While I watched, he brought a musical instrument to his mouth and again I heard the haunting music; he was playing the panpipes to announce that he had come to sharpen knives.

It took a long time to get out of Pamplona. Since we had arrived by taxi, not on foot, we had had no concept of its size. Unlike the villages we'd walked through, which ended abruptly, Pamplona kept on going for several kilometers until it finally petered out.

We decided to follow Navarro's map again; the day was fresh and cool and we felt energetic enough to strive for authenticity. So we followed a country road through fields of grain that stretched into the dark grey distant hills. We walked silently, concentrating on the weight of our backpacks, the measurement of meters. On the highway, we could read the numbered kilometer posts, but on the "authentic" Camino our only judge of distance was our increasing weariness and the gradual approach of distant landmarks.

Above us, the sky clouded up and suddenly it was as if we were in a gilded, grain-filled bowl, covered by a pewter lid streaked with black. In the distance, lightning streaked across the clouds and thunder echoed off the hills. Although the sky was dark, the fields seemed brighter than before; the patches of metallic grey sky intensified the golden fields. We watched the storm moving closer and closer, watched the rain blotting out one distant hill, passing over it, and blotting out another. It was beautiful—and violent.

"Bill, do you know what you're supposed to do in a lightning storm?"

"No, do you?"

All I could remember from high school science courses and growing up in Iowa was that you're not supposed to be the highest object—or near one.

We looked around. There were no trees around us, only fields of grain.

I suggested we get down in a ditch, but Bill thought we should head for the hills. Following a path at an angle to the storm, we hurried towards the nearest hill and found shelter along the side of a ridge, next to a tree. We took our rain ponchos out of our packs, covered ourselves and our packs with plastic, and leaned back against the hillside.

I wondered if the tree would draw lighting, but Bill thought not. We stayed where we were.

It poured. It thundered. Lightning flashed—but not too near. Our resting place was sheltered from the wind, but the rain ran down the hillside behind us. Soon our backs were soaked. But the storm passed over us rapidly, leaving behind the smell of damp earth.

The green hillside sparkled. The black road surface glistened. Our orange plastic ponchos gleamed. The trees rustled in the wind, sprinkling us with another shower. The air was warm and steamy. Scattering raindrops, we headed up the road to Cizur Menor, located on top of a hill.

According to the map, there is a Cizur Menor and a Cizur Mayor. According to the guidebook, in the twelfth century there had been a hospice for pilgrims in Cizur Menor, and in 1508 there was a house called the *Hospitalecoa,* with six beds for poor pilgrims. Nothing now remained except some ruins.

Before reaching Cizur Menor, we collapsed in a dense grove of pine trees on the side of the hill, overlooking the highway and a gas station, five kilometers from Pamplona. We spread our ponchos out to dry, ate some oranges, some bread and *chorizo* we'd bought in Pamplona, and then Bill went to sleep. While he slept, I put moleskin on a blister on my left heel. My jogging shoes were comfortable, but the left one rubbed the left side of my heel. To fill the gap, I experimented with wearing two pairs of socks, but then the shoes were too tight.

After an hour's rest, we started walking again, following Navarro's map to Guendulain. The route was hard to find, the ancient Camino obliterated. We had to clamber down and up a steep, mud-filled arroyo, made slippery by the storm, but at last we reached Guendulain, a semi-abandoned, shaggy village, huddling at the base of a hill. Our narrow trail skirted the houses and kept going up; after a sharp ascent, it leveled off. In front of us was a grove of trees and a meadow and, visible through the trees, a beautiful medieval palace—the palace of the Counts of Guendulain. It looked like a Disneyland commercial, with stone walls, narrow, high-placed windows, and decorative stone edging around the roof. I expected to see knights in armor, bowmen peering out of the corner watch-towers. But the palace was abandoned—or semi-abandoned, since we could not open the massive wooden doors.

We heard bells: sheep. We saw their tiny black turds, we heard their bells, then we saw a flock of them, accompanied by a black sheep dog. Unfortunately, there was no sign of the shepherd; we would have liked to ask him about the palace. Walking around the palace, we came to an open door in a small, attached building. We went inside. After our eyes adjusted to the dimness, we saw that we were in the abandoned chapel of the deserted palace, empty, now, except for a painted coffin, broken bottles, and a tattered rusty black curtain. Was someone using it for a theatre—or for forbidden midnight rites?

Hoping to make better time on a paved, well-marked road, we took a shortcut back to the main highway. We'd only traveled eight kilometers since morning and already it was getting late and we were exhausted, once again. Following Navarro's trail had been a mistake—once again. Perhaps it *was* authentic—but it was unreliable and full of surprises. Some of them were pleasant, like the abandoned palace; others were unpleasant, like the disappearing Camino. Surely the highway would be easier.

Since our rest stop at Cizur Menor, I had developed a large blister on top of another blister on my left heel. The first 200 meters on the highway it felt as if a knife blade were sticking into my flesh. Each step was another twist of the knife. Sharp pieces of glass were being driven into my heel with a jackhammer. My attention narrowed to my left heel; my body felt as if it were all excruciatingly painful foot; the pain expanded until it surrounded me and it was all I was aware of. And then, slowly, the pain contracted into a dull, localized ache. It was continuous, but dulled. It was bearable. There was more of me than my foot, more to me—and to the moment—than layers and layers of pain.

We took another half-hour break. When I put no weight on my foot, it did not hurt. But then we started walking again and the pain was excruciating. Tears came to my eyes, my throat constricted each time I forced myself to lift my foot and put it down. I gasped with the effort to override my nerves and place my left foot on the ground and put my weight on my left foot and lift it up again for a momentary cessation from pain and then again repeat the same excruciating procedure. And then, just as before, the shattering pain turned gradually into a dull ache, like the pounding of distant music which one feels but cannot hear.

I asked Bill if he knew why the pain diminished: did the nerves short-circuit?

"Maybe so. Maybe the nerves can only stand so much—and then they go dead for a while. I've noticed that when one part of me hurts a lot—like my foot—I don't notice the pain in my back or my shoulders. It's as if only one pain can be felt at a time."

I hadn't known there were so many kinds of pain. The numb disassociated pain of exhaustion. The sharp splintering pain in my foot when I started to walk, the dull throbbing pain in my foot after I'd walked awhile. "Funny, isn't it? We're on a pilgrimage—supposedly a spiritual experience. And all we can think about is pain!"

"If we were religious, would it hurt less? Or be more edifying?"

"Maybe, Bill, the idea is that it hurts so much you are willing—eager—to give up this vale of tears and sorrow. Maybe it enforces the idea that the body is just a source of sin and agony and that the spirit is what you had better think about."

"Maybe so."

"If part of pilgrimage is penance, pain is a suitable kind of sacrifice to make. If the pilgrimage were too easy, it wouldn't mean as much. It wouldn't be a pilgrimage, right?"

"Right."

After fifteen minutes, we passed a roadsign: "Camino de Santiago. Zariquiegui, fourteenth-century Romanesque church. Santiago: 736 kilometers." The highway Camino was well labeled, even though our "authentic" Camino was not. Zariquiegui was somewhere to the left of the highway, so we would have had to take a detour to see it. Medieval pilgrims made detours all the time, going from one shrine to another, visiting their old favorite saints or virgins or a new one that had just gained in popularity by performing an impressive miracle. But we were too tired for detours. All we could manage to do was follow the road, when we could find it.

We walked on, silently, concentrating on not concentrating on the pain of walking. The road kept going upwards. After half an hour, we reached Astrain, a small town spread out to the right, sloping down the hillside. It was late afternoon and we decided to stop, just as we had planned that morning: to walk until we are tired, then stop in the nearest town and spend the night. So we left the highway, crossed an unpaved street, and sat down on a narrow stone bench in front of a building. Wearily, we took off our packs. We rested awhile.

A woman dressed in black, wearing flat black felt slippers called *alpargatas*—a woman dressed like most of the older women we had seen in Spain—walked over to us.

"Peregrinos?"

We nodded yes and asked her, "Is there a hostel in town?"

Shaking her head, she said no.

"A restaurant?"

Another negative.

It hadn't occurred to us that the town we chose to stop at wouldn't have a place for us to stay.

The woman was joined by a well-dressed younger woman in high heels—dressed like most of the younger women we had seen in Spain—pushing an elegantly dressed little girl—again, like most of the little children we had seen in Spain—in a dark blue, ruffled, parasol-shaded carriage. The daughter nodded hello, then they all said goodbye and left. A family stroll.

We could ask the priest or the mayor to find us lodging, but we still didn't want to. The traditions of the pilgrimage—was it fair for us to use them? Besides, we thought we would get better accommodations if we paid for them. But how far was it to the next town with a hostel? As we talked over our alternatives the old woman returned, carrying two cans of luke-warm orange and strawberry Kas—Spanish Fanta—and offered them to us. The traditions of the pilgrimage included charity. Grateful, we thanked her.

While we drank the soda pop, she talked with us, standing beside us on the unpaved street. "I went on a pilgrimage to Santiago once, by train. It was beautiful! The old medieval city was so lovely, with its narrow streets and its beautiful cathedral. I embraced the Apostle, too."

"Dar un abrazo al Apóstol" meant to give the larger-than-life-sized statue of the Apostle an embrace. The jewel-encrusted image sits under a golden baldachin—an ornamental canopy—in the cathedral, and there are steps behind it so that worshippers can climb up behind the figure and hug it around the neck. Since the Middle Ages, embracing the Apostle has been considered to be meritorious. But a Basque friend of mine described it with revulsion—he didn't think one should get so familiar with the saints, not even with their statues.

The old woman asked where we were from and we told her. Smiling, she said, "Santiago is a very powerful saint, to bring you from so far away!"

I asked her, "How far to the nearest hostel or restaurant?"

"Not far at all—there's a town, just the other side of the Alto del Perdón."

"How far to the pass?"

"Three kilometers."

We thanked her and hoisted up our backpacks. As we started to leave, she gave me some coins and asked me to "light a candle for her in the cathedral." I wasn't sure what that meant, but I agreed.

The altitude of Pamplona is 449 meters, of the Alto del Perdón, 734. Although the road had been going up gradually, for the next three kilometers the incline was quite steep. The road surface was old and pebbly, hard on our feet, and the road had no shoulder where we could walk. Luckily, there was no traffic. As soon as we started walking, my left heel started to hurt again; this time, the sharp splintering pain took at least 150 meters to diminish.

At the top of the pass there was a three-story abandoned stone building, its corners and rows of large empty windows edged in darker stone. On one side, facing us as we came up the hill, was a large sign, sponsored by the Caja de Ahorros de Pamplona—a savings bank. The sign, labeled "El Camino de Santiago, Navarra," showed a map of the highway going from the Alto de Perdón, through Puente la Reina, Estella, Los Arcos, Torres del Río, and Viana. The map showed the road going up, from lower left to upper right. I hoped not. I wanted to go down. Bill took off his pack and sat down next to the building to rest. I took off my pack, took out the dwindling roll of toilet paper, and went behind the building. The jarring of the backpack was affecting my kidneys.

Somewhat recovered, we started the descent. In the distance we could see forests and hills; on either side of our road were pine trees. The air was filled with the fresh green scent of evergreens. Despite the pain, despite the exhaustion, I was glad to be walking. Inside a car, I would have missed the wild flowers, the pine-rich air, the accomplishment, the lessons of pain.

The old woman in Astrain had said there would be a town close by, but close for her was not close for us. It was at least two kilometers further and almost 9 p.m. before we saw a few houses by the side of the road and a sign advertising a restaurant/bar/*fonda.* We stumbled towards the door.

Pushing aside the multicolored bead curtain that let in air and kept out flies, we entered a smoke-filled, noisy room. Half a dozen men in dark, dirty clothes, *boinas* on their heads, were standing at a bar, drinking, smoking, watching and listening to a blaring color television attached high up on the wall. A bartender was standing behind the bar, looking at the T.V. There was litter on the floor. There was usually litter on the floor of a cafe/bar in Spain, since so many of the *tapas*—appetizers served at bars—come served on tiny papers or stuck through with toothpicks, and the sugar cubes are also individually wrapped. There are no wastebaskets, and people drop the paper on the floor. The trash accumulates on the floor until someone sweeps it up. This bar, however, was dirtier than most.

Sitting down at a table in the corner, we ordered two *tortilla española* sandwiches and Cokes. The omelets would be safe for my stomach, which was still upset. Besides, nothing else was available. Bill asked him if there were a place to stay—beds? a room? The sign outside said this was a *fonda,* but the bartender shook his head no.

I knew I couldn't walk any further; neither could Bill. I decided to ask the local priest for a place to stay, so I went up to the bartender. "Please, is there a *padre* around?"

He looked at me, puzzled. "A *padre*? You mean, a *cura*?"

I nodded yes. He left, came back with a woman, perhaps his wife.

"You need a priest? What for? There isn't one here. You have a problem?" She didn't sound sympathetic, and, due to my weariness and frustration, my Spanish deserted me. I couldn't explain myself.

"No, no, excuse me. I'm sorry."

I had known you could ask for the help of the priest, but now I realized I didn't know how, and that not all towns had priests in them.

The woman was still standing there. I tried again. "We need a place to stay."

"Puente la Reina—there are hotels there."

That was six kilometers away—and it was almost dark. We'd never make it.

During this exchange, the men at the bar had been silent. Now they starting talking again. One called out to us. "I'll give you a ride—but there's only room for one of you!" Everybody laughed. The men stood at the bar, elbowing each other. It was clear which one of us they meant.

And I had thought that pilgrims were looked on as sacred persons! If I had ever had doubts about hitchhiking alone, they had just been reinforced. The men kept looking at us, talking, and laughing. As quickly as we could, we finished eating, paid the bill, and left.

We looked at the highway stretching in front of us. It was still light out, but it would be dark in another half an hour. Six kilometers more. We'd never make it. Then I heard a car coming and stepped forward, sticking out my thumb. *Autostop,* or *a dedo*—by finger—it's called in Spanish.

The car, a small Seat—the Spanish Fiat—stopped. Inside were two young, clean-cut kids. "Where do you want to go?" they asked.

"Puente la Reina."

"Hop in."

Bill protested: he hadn't agreed to hitchhike. I looked at him. "Do you have a better suggestion?" He shook his head.

So we squeezed into the back seat and drove off. The driver turned his head to look at us and asked, "Peregrinos?" We nodded yes. "Americanos?" Again, we nodded yes. They smiled and introduced themselves. Jaime was the driver; his companion, Ramón. Ramón said he had gone to Santiago once, by train and by hitchhiking. It was a nice city.

I asked him, "When did you make your pilgrimage to Santiago?"

He replied, "Oh, it wasn't a pilgrimage. It was an excursion. A couple of years ago."

I wondered what the difference was, but before I could ask, we had reached Puente la Reina. Six kilometers by car doesn't take very long. They drove up to the wide, tree-lined alameda and we got out. Grateful, we thanked them.

"It was nothing. Goodbye!"

While Bill looked for a place to stay, I waited with the backpacks. He returned quickly and said he'd found a room in a new hostel.

It was indeed new—so new, it was not yet open officially. But the owner was very friendly and showed us the second-floor—in Spain, first-floor—rooms. We chose one with a balcony overlooking the alameda.

Downstairs there was a bar, so we bought a small bottle of Spanish champagne to celebrate our safe arrival and then we went upstairs to bathe. How I looked forward to soaking my aching muscles, steaming my stiff neck. But the owner had forgotten to mention there was no hot water. So I skipped the bath and went to sit out on the balcony, watching the young couples, the old couples, the children, the groups of teenagers strolling up and down the alameda for pleasure.

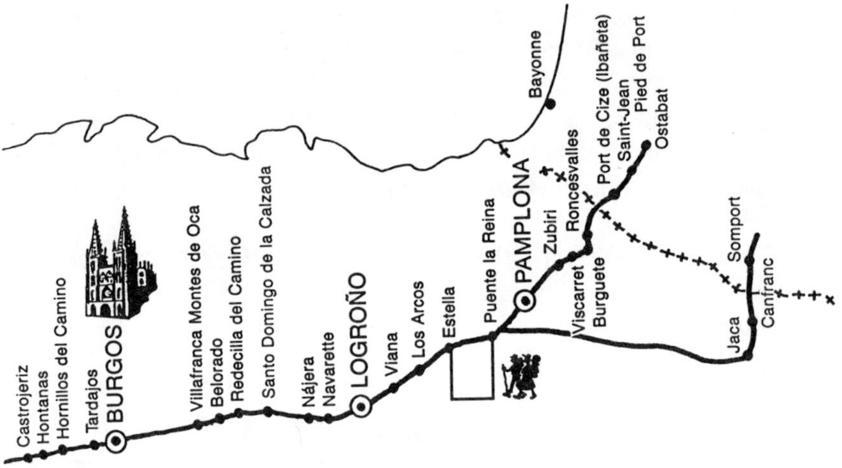

Day 11: July 20 Puente la Reina is a town of 2,000 people, a few kilometers from Obanos, where the two traditional Caminos de Santiago from France—the one entering at Somport, the other at Roncesvalles—unite. According to the "Pseudo-Turpin Chronicle," one of the five books compiled by Picaud to form the *Codex,* after Charlemagne destroyed Pamplona, he stopped in Puente la Reina.

In the eleventh century, Puente la Reina was known as Ponte de Arga or Ponte Reginae. It was named in honor of Doña Mayor, wife of Sancho el Mayor of Navarra, who had had a stone bridge built over the River Arga in the eleventh century—a bridge which is still intact. By 1090, Puente la Reina was a town populated by Franks, people from the area we now know as France, Germany, and Italy.

In the Middle Ages there were several *hospitales* for pilgrims run by clergy or lay brotherhoods. The Hospital del Crucifijo, founded in the mid-fifteenth century, gave out bread, wine, firewood, and fire, and took care of the ill. In 1585 it had five beds; in 1629, seven. And there were other *hospitales* as well. The seventeenth-century Italian pilgrim, the cleric Domenic Laffi, mentions he had hoped to stay in one but it was full. Nothing remains of any of them. Instead, today there are privately run hostels.

We visited the Church of the Crucifix, begun in the late twelfth or early thirteenth century. We admired the fourteenth-century crucifix, probably from the Rhineland, that has its arms nailed up on a cross in the form of the letter Y; the sculptor took advantage of the natural shape of the wood. On our way out of town on the Rúa de los Romeus—the Road of the Romeros, or Pilgrims—we stopped at the twelfth-century Church of Santiago and examined its Romanesque doorway: five concentric layers of stone columns and carvings frame the heavy wooden door decorated with metal studs. The archivolt—the intricate carvings over the rounded arch of the door—were worn and weathered but still impressive.

Inside, we saw the fourteenth-century painted wooden statue of Santiago Peregrino, its original gay polychrome faded to shades of brown and beige. The statue was nicknamed *el Beltza*—which means Negro in Basque—because it was recently found, all darkened, in a loft in the church. There was a picture of this statue on the cover of our guidebook: a swarthy Santiago dressed in a long, gracefully draped robe; on his head, a tri-cornered hat decorated with his scallop shells. In his left hand he holds a Bible, in his right, a staff. He has an elaborate, curly beard and long curling hair, falling in ringlets over his shoulders. He is calm, gentle, solemn—a trustworthy guide on the Camino de Santiago, on the camino of life.

We followed the Rúa de los Romeus towards the eleventh-century stone Pilgrims' Bridge. Passing through a large stone doorway in what remains of the city walls, we stepped onto the bridge. The center of the pavement is made of cobblestones; on either side and in the middle,

Looking through the archway at the eleventh-century bridge over the Arga River at Puente la Reina. Although the photograph doesn't show it, the bridge is shaped like a wide, inverted V.

heavy square paving stones stabilize the cobblestone surface. As we walked across, the bridge seemed steep, almost an inverted V; but after we had crossed it and looked back, the angle didn't look so exaggerated. Apparently, it was an illusion caused by the incline and length. The six arches of the bridge stretch across the Río Arga, each supporting pillar open in the middle to form another arch, framing the distant hills.

According to a legend about the bridge, occasionally a bird of an unknown species would appear and dip its wings in the river. Then it would fly to the statue of the Virgin that stood on the stone parapet, and it would clean the statue with its wings. This was supposed to be a good omen for the community, which gathered round en masse to watch the bird at work.

Perhaps it was the heat, or perhaps the champagne from the night before had weakened our muscles—or our resolve. At any rate, it took a great deal of effort to keep walking. We decided to follow Navarro's map again, still striving for "authenticity." While the highway curved gently through the green valleys, we walked across the sides of fire-scorched, barren hills. There were no trees, no shade. It was terribly hot—perhaps it was in the 90s—and we spent the day walking over mirage-like hills on a disappearing trail. My blister-layered heel had improved overnight, but now the pain began again. And Bill was having trouble, too; he had blisters on both little toes and was losing his left big toenail.

By 2 p.m., we were looking for somewhere cool to stop and eat lunch. Our "authentic" route rejoined the highway near Cirauqui, near a large building with "bar/restaurant" painted on one side. Gay, lilting, Celtic-sounding music poured out of the open windows. We went inside.

Five young people were sitting at a table, just beginning to eat *la comida.* We went up to the bar at the other end of the room. Periodically, one of the young men got up from the table, went into the kitchen, and came out with more food. But no one asked us if we wanted anything. Finally, we walked over to the table and asked.

"Hay comida?"

They looked at us. "No hay."

We were in a restaurant, they were eating, and they told us there was no food. We tried again, the old standbys.

"Un bocadillo? Tortilla española?"

"No hay."

One of the women looked up and said, "Hay Coca Cola."

There was Coke. Grudgingly, one of the women got us two bottles—no glasses—and went back to the table. Bill thought: they don't like pilgrims. I thought: maybe it's a family reunion, or they live here but are on vacation. We took some stale bread and warm, processed cheese out of our packs and made ourselves some unappetizing sandwiches.

An hour later they had finished eating and cleared away the dishes. I asked for another two Cokes and started a conversation about the music with one of the young women. She explained it was a tape of a group called Gwendal, from Brittany, in northwestern France. Gwendal was very popular around there, and the group was going to give a concert in Estella in a week. I thanked her for the information and asked her where the nearest hostel was. She said there was one in the next town down the road. Shouldering our packs, we left.

Navarro's map indicated we were to leave the highway and walk through Cirauqui: a yellow arrow marked the spot. Why is it "authentic," I wondered, to leave one asphalt road for another? We walked up into the town, built on a hillside, presumably for security reasons during the Reconquest. It was 3 p.m. and the streets were empty; everyone was staying indoors to avoid the heat. The narrow, cobblestone streets wound past large stone houses, three or four stories tall. We followed the cobblestone streets through and out of the silent town onto a pebble-strewn path. Soon we were walking on actual *calzada romana*—made with real Roman paving stones, over 2,000 years old. Older than the pilgrimage, older than Christianity.

Rome had established provinces in Iberia by 197 B.C., and by 19 B.C. Augustus had fully incorporated the Iberian Peninsula into the Roman Empire. Seneca, Lucan, and Martial, the Emperors Trajan, Hadrian, and Theodosius—all came from Spain. The Romans built roads to last—and they had, nearly 1,500 years longer than the Empire.

Roman stone pavements, medieval cobblestones. Built to last. The modern asphalt and concrete highways were already crumbling at the edges, split at the seams, pock-marked in the middle.

We crossed a medieval stone bridge over the Río Salado. Aymery Picaud, in the "Pilgrim's Guide" in the *Codex,* advised twelfth-century travelers neither to drink the water of the Río Salado nor let their horses drink it, for the river is poisonous. He also warned that the Navarrese waited with sharpened knives to skin the dead beasts of the pilgrims. I tasted the water; it was salty, but not deadly.

Still following Navarro's map, we walked on more Roman pavement. But then we lost the route. At last we made our way back to the highway, near the one-street-wide town of Lorca. Many towns on the Camino are only one street—the Camino—wide, the settlement developing around the pilgrimage road. A group of women dressed in black called out to us: "Peregrinos?" We nodded yes. They smiled and said, "Vale la pena!" "It's worthwhile."

Tired and thirsty, we stopped at the town fountain and filled our water bottle with the fresh, clear water. Then we rested on the stone steps. I wondered why the older women were friendly, the younger people were not. Anti-religiousness? Anti-Franco feelings?

Franco had been a supporter of Santiago—and vice versa, apparently, since in 1937 Franco called on Santiago to come to his aid at the battle of Brunete—a crucial battle in the Civil War—and Franco and his forces won. After coming to power, Franco reinstated the national offering to the cathedral in Santiago, a national levy that had begun in the twelfth century and had been terminated in 1812. Franco's Minister of Tourism, Manuel Fraga, was also a supporter of Santiago, and it was during his ministry that the Camino de Santiago highway was completed and labeled across Spain and a major promotional campaign was launched to encourage travel on the Camino.

It was early evening and we were tired. We saw another bar/restaurant. A bit hesitantly, after our last two experiences, we went inside. This bar was clean, well lit. Encouraged, we asked for *la comida.* Again, no *comida,* but they did have Cokes and we ordered two apiece. After a few minutes, I asked the woman at the bar if there were a place to stay.

She was eager to help. "You could sleep in the parking lot around behind the bar, but it's safer to go to Estella. I've seen some strange people hanging around here recently—they looked like gypsies. Go to Estella—that's only eight kilometers from here."

Eight kilometers. By car, a few minutes. For us, a few hours. We could go no further.

A nicely dressed man standing at the bar walked over to us. "Do you need a ride to Estella? I would be glad to give you one."

We hesitated, and he repeated his offer. He lived in Lorca but would be pleased to give us a lift to Estella. "I just want to help, that's all." While he talked, the woman behind the bar nodded at us in reassurance.

Bill explained, "We are walking to Santiago."

The woman behind the bar said, "Santiago will forgive you eight kilometers!"

We rode to the edge of Estella, end of the *Codex*'s third stage of travel.

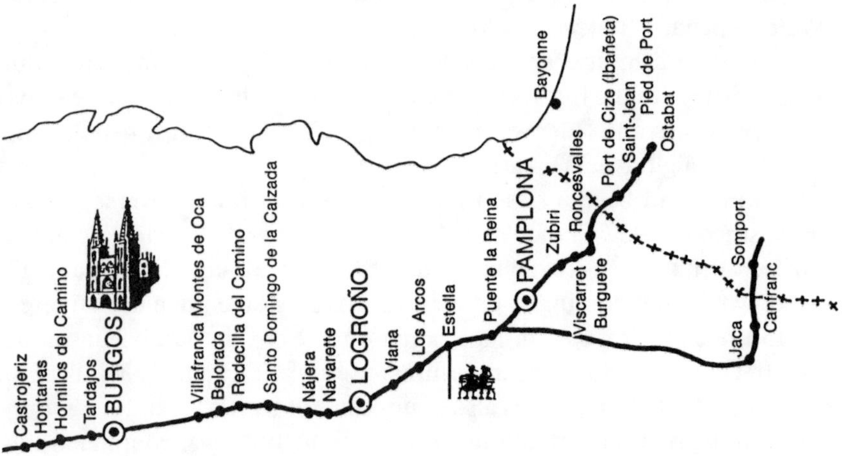

Day 12: July 21 We stayed in Estella, recovering from the day before. We seemed to be unable to walk for more than two days at a time. Hopefully, our stamina would improve with time—it had to, since we wanted to reach Santiago by August 22 or so, to spend a few days there before going on to Madrid. We had to be in Madrid no later than August 26, and it would take two days to get there from Santiago.

In the morning we washed our laundry in the bathroom sink, hanging it up to dry on a braided elastic line I'd brought. Then we went out for breakfast. First, we went to a *pastelería*—a pastry shop—and bought assorted butter cookies and sweet rolls, including a local specialty, a custard-filled puff pastry horn, sprinkled with cinnamon and powdered sugar. Then we stopped at a nearby sidewalk cafe, ordered *café con leche*—coffee with milk—and ate our breakfast, the powdered sugar falling like dust from our fingers.

In 1090, Sancho Ramírez had Estella repopulated by Franks as part of the Reconquest and development of the Camino de Santiago. As late as the fourteenth century, Provençal, the language of southeastern France, was the common language of its inhabitants. During the Middle Ages, Estella was the residence of the kings of Navarra. It was well situated, located at the foot of a rock where there had been a castle and on the banks of the Río Ega; surrounded by mountains, yet in a green and fertile valley. Originally called Lizarra, by the twelfth century the town was known as Estella and by the fifteenth as Estella la Bella. Today, some 10,000 Navarrese live in the midst of new buildings and medieval monuments, many dating from the twelfth century: San Pedro de la Rúa, Nuestra Señora de Rocamador—formerly a pilgrims' hospice—Santa María Jus del Castillo, Santo Sepulcro, San Juan Bautista, the Basílica de la Virgen del Puy.

After crossing a reconstructed medieval bridge over the Río Ega, we visited the twelfth-century palace of the kings of Navarra, one of the best preserved Romanesque civic buildings in Spain. The struggle between Ferragut, the giant, and Roland, the hero, described in the "Pseudo-Turpin Chronicle," is carved on one of the sand-colored capitals of the building. There they are, mounted on horseback, struggling against each other still.

The "Pseudo-Turpin Chronicle," one of the five books in the *Codex,* is called "pseudo" because, despite its claim, it was not written by Bishop Turpin. The pseudonymous author tries to tie Charlemagne and Roland to the pilgrimage to Santiago. According to the "Chronicle," Charlemagne had conquered a great deal of territory and reached a point where he had to decide between more war or a much-needed rest. Looking up into the sky, searching for an answer, he saw the Milky Way stretching from the North Sea all the way to Galicia. What could it possibly mean? Santiago suddenly appeared to tell him: he was to lead an army to Spain and save it from the infidels. Santiago also pleaded with Charlemagne to deliver his remains, buried in Galicia, from Saracen domination. The "Pseudo-Turpin" is filled with stories and legends which helped publicize and promote the pilgrimage and the Camino de Santiago. Along the Pilgrim's Way, artists and sculptors carved and painted scenes from these stories, providing a vivid visualization of heroic and fantastic deeds.

We continued walking through the Barrio de la Rúa, where Franks and Jews lived in the late Middle Ages. In 1492, when the Catholic Rulers Ferdinand and Isabella expelled the Jews from Spain, the King of Navarra, Juan Labrit, and his wife wrote to the authorities in Estella and urged them to settle as many Jews as possible in the town, for "Jews are gentle people and submit easily to reason."[8]

As we strolled around town, we nodded hello to a number of pilgrims. Sometimes we would stop a few minutes and talk, but we were spending the day sightseeing in Estella, while they were on their way out of town, backpacks heavy on their backs. I remembered the weight of our own packs. Surely, we could lighten them. After all, there was no reason to carry excess baggage: we weren't performing a penitential pilgrimage.

After much discussion, Bill agreed, so we went back to the hostel and sorted through our belongings. All I needed, besides my walking outfit of skirt, blouse, and Adidas, was an extra blouse, two pairs of socks and underwear, a light jacket, a cotton shift to sleep in or use as a sundress, my sandals, my first aid kit, my journal, my camera, and the guidebooks. I didn't need blue jeans, a sweater, a Spanish textbook, a novel, four additional pairs of socks and underwear, two more shirts, a cotton robe, and a bag of cosmetics. Why had I thought I needed all this stuff? Maybe pilgrimage was learning how much baggage one could do without.

But sorting through our possessions was just the beginning. Next, we had to get rid of them. We decided to mail them to my friends in Sahagún, a town half-way along the pilgrimage road, in the province of León, where I'd stayed the summer before. So we bought tape and string at a nearby bookstore, borrowed a cardboard box from our landlady, and prepared our package. Then we went to find the post office.

Following directions in Spain was not easy. First, there was the problem of language. Second, there was the problem of directions. In a medieval town like Estella, streets don't run at right angles, they don't make tidy corners. They run up and down, at odd angles, in circles. People tried to help us by telling us what monuments the post office was near, but since we didn't know any of the landmarks, that didn't help.

At last we found the post office, but they wouldn't take the package. It was too heavy by a mere eight ounces. We argued with the postal clerk: couldn't we mail it anyway? Definitely not. There were rules. We were angry and frustrated. I thought I had been learning patience on the pilgrimage—but my tolerance for petty bureaucracy had diminished markedly.

The postal clerk suggested we try to send the package by bus. So we went, with many missed turns, to the bus depot. Unfortunately, the buses were all local or regional: none went to Sahagún. The bus driver was quite pleasant and suggested we try a trucking firm. When he tried to explain where it was, I threw up my hands in frustration.

Bill was ready to forget the whole thing, but I wasn't. After lugging the package all over town, I knew how heavy it was and refused to carry even half of that extra weight on my back again. Besides, I had decided that "pilgrimage is learning how much you can do without." Now I was learning that it isn't always easy to get rid of excess baggage! I refused to give up.

The bus driver waited while Bill and I argued. At last, ignoring Bill, I turned to the driver and explained how hard it was for us to follow directions in Spanish; he understood and motioned to a young clerk to join us. After talking it over, the young man offered to show us the way. Bill didn't want to go, so Jesús and I went off to find the trucking company.

Jesús asked, "You're from the U.S.?"

"Yes."

He looked at me cautiously. "Many people don't like Americans."

"I'm not surprised."

"They don't like your politics. What you are doing to our economy."

"I understand. I don't like some of those things either."

"No?"

"Of course not. There are lots of Americans who don't like the very things you don't like about Americans. We are not all alike, after all."

Jesús pointed out interesting landmarks as we walked. Then he said, "You're a pilgrim to Santiago?"

"Yes. Have you ever been there?"

"No, and I'm not interested in going. I'm told it's a pretty city, but one old city is just like another, as far as I'm concerned." He pointed out another monument.

"But Santiago is patron of Spain. Doesn't that make a difference?"

"Not to me."

At last we reached the trucking firm. Unfortunately, they didn't go to Sahagún either. I looked at Jesús.

"What else can we do?"

"Make two packages and mail them. I'll get you another box," Jesús suggested.

So he did, and we did, and we went back to the post office. If we had done that to begin with, we would have saved two hours and several kilometers of walking in circles. But all wasn't wasted; I'd stood up for what I wanted and, in addition, I'd had a guided tour of Estella.

We had wanted to get our pilgrimage cards stamped in Estella and now I knew where the town hall was, so Bill and I walked over to it and went upstairs. Behind the information desk was a congenial-looking woman. After stamping our cards, she asked how our pilgrimage was going. We muttered commonplaces about how beautiful Spain was.

Pleased, she smiled warmly. As an afterthought, I asked her for the address of Los Amigos del Camino de Santiago, the group, located in Estella, that published our guidebook.

"They don't exist any more. Sorry."

Disappointed, we thanked her and left. While we were standing on the steps outside of the town hall, wondering what to do next, a young Spanish pilgrim came up to us.

"Peregrinos?"

We nodded yes.

"Have you visited Los Amigos del Camino?"

I said, "We were just told they no longer exist."

"Of course they do! I just visited with the president, and he gave me this pilgrimage card."

He showed us a large card, the front of which was decorated with a cartoon-like drawing of Santiago, an illustration taken from the *Codex*. Inside, the traditional stages to Santiago were listed, and there was space for getting stamps along the way. When I told him I'd like to meet the man, he gave me his phone number.

"He's very friendly. Give him a call."

We said goodbye, walked over to a phone booth, and called the president. Sounding pleased to hear from us, the man invited us up to his apartment. We followed his directions and, after a few wrong turns, located his building. At the entrance, we had to ring his apartment number and wait for him to buzz open the door so that we could enter. We took the elevator up to the fourth floor.

A distinguished looking gentleman, the president of Los Amigos was a lawyer and ex-city council member. He had been active in community affairs for many years but now—apparently since the change of government into more liberal hands—he was less involved. I asked him about Los Amigos.

"We're a loosely knit group of community-minded Estellan citizens, interested in promoting the history and folklore of Navarra. For a dozen years or so we organized an annual Medieval Week conference of music and lectures in Estella. It was famous all over Europe."

He went on, speaking lovingly of the Camino de Santiago and of his efforts to promote travel on the "authentic" road. He wanted to set up a series of shelters, each a day apart, and have cement markers constructed to mark the traditional Camino. Before we left, he showed us correspondence he had received from all over Europe, correspondence addressed to Los Amigos in Estella. He also showed us articles he had written on the history of the region. Then he gave us each the pilgrimage identification card, which he said Los Amigos had printed to distribute at the Hermitage of Rocamador, across the river. The most famous shrine of the Virgin of Rocamador is in France, on one of the French Caminos de Santiago; apparently, her devotees spread her worship into Navarra.

Bill asked how many members there were in Los Amigos, and he said he thought there were a dozen or so dues paying ones. Many more were unofficial. Had they all made the pilgrimage on foot? No—none. They were just concerned citizens, helping to preserve traditions. I told him I would like to join Los Amigos, and he looked a bit surprised. There was no application form, but there was a membership fee, which I offered to pay. He told me to send him a postal money order made out to him, and he would take care of it.

Since the Middle Ages, there have been brotherhoods of Compostelan pilgrims. Usually the members were people who had made the pilgrimage to Santiago at some time in their lives. Members would march together in processions and financially aid others who wanted to make the pilgrimage. This organization, Los Amigos del Camino de Santiago, and the Société de Les Amis de St. Jacques were in some ways modeled on the medieval brotherhoods.

Bill asked why the woman in the town hall said Los Amigos no longer existed.

The president replied angrily. "They're not very helpful these days. In the old days, we got financial support and assistance from the local—and regional and national—government. Now, nothing. It's all politics."

I knew that up until a few years ago there had been a medieval pageant at nearby Obanos, a pageant connected with the pilgrimage to Santiago; recently, however, government support for that had been discontinued. Nationally, there used to be well coordinated promotional campaigns for the Años Santos, orchestrated out of Madrid. But now those funds and other more subtle forms of support appeared to be less forthcoming.

We thanked him for his help and left. It was after 2:30—time for *la comida.* According to the *Codex,* twelfth-century Estella was rich in good bread, fine wine, meat, and fish, and full of all sorts of happiness. And that is still true.

We ate *la comida* in a fine restaurant located in the arcade of the main plaza. Our meal began with mixed appetizers: a half-dozen little plates, each filled with something different—pickled mussels, pâté of rabbit, smoked salmon, white asparagus with a delicate vinagrette sauce, deviled eggs, and *chorizo.* For a second course, we ordered the local specialties, *gorrín asado*—baked suckling pig—stuffed green peppers, and *pollo al chilindrón*—chicken baked in olive oil, garlic, onion, ham, and roasted red peppers. Since we were not walking the Camino, I could drink alcohol; so we selected a fine red wine produced by the Señorío de Sarriá, a winery located just outside of Puente la Reina. For dessert, we shared a *tarta helada*—a slice of ice cream, frozen in the shape of a pie, covered with whipped cream and laced with rum and chocolate. Then Bill ordered a cognac and I ordered *manzanilla*—camomile tea. The waiter brought Bill a box of cigars and offered him one.

To walk off this enormous meal, we decided to visit the sanctuary of the Virgen del Puy, located on top of a hill. Sanctuaries are usually located on a hill or in a cave: closer to heaven, closer to earth. The Virgin was reported to have appeared at that site on May 25, 1085; shepherds, guided by falling stars, found her statue there. The same legend is told about the discovery of the tomb of Santiago. Did those stars showering on Estella also fall from the Milky Way, the route which guided Charlemagne to Compostela, the route which we were following with such determined authenticity?

Leaving the restaurant, we walked through the oldest section of Estella, past decrepit, sand-colored, medieval houses leaning against each other, leaning towards each other, separated by narrow cobblestone streets. For part of the way, the incline of the street was so steep that the pavement had been divided into steps. We clambered up the broad stone steps and reached the asphalt road that wound around the hillside to the shrine at the top.

The sanctuary was an impressive, contemporary building, bright with light pouring in through the modern, abstract, stained-glass windows. In the center of the large, circular sanctuary was the figure of the Virgen del Puy, flanked by two large urns filled with waxy calla lilies. Entirely covered in silver, except for their faces and hands, the Virgin and her child are perched on a silver crescent moon.

The Christian church has always practiced syncretism. The Mexican Virgin of Guadalupe was first an Indian cult figure, and numerous churches have been built directly over pagan shrines. The crescent moon of the Virgen del Puy presumably went back to some Roman cult, or even perhaps to an ancient Celtic Mother Goddess. Similarly, the shell of

Santiago may be linked to some Roman cult, perhaps of Venus. Some people think that the Camino de Santiago was a pre-Christian initiation route, taken over and disguised by the Benedictine Cluny Order, which came from Burgundy to organize the pilgrimage route.

Throughout history, there have been certain recurrent images: the shell, the crescent moon, the sun, the journey—images which carry with them faint imprints of older, other meanings, faint fragrances of other, ancient rituals. They do not stand—or signify—alone. Whether we hear the echoes, and how clearly, is another matter.

I wondered what stories lay behind those blank glass eyes. Venerated virgin, earth mother, mother goddess—why was it that for Christians only virgin martyrs and virgin mothers were venerated, and the earth mother, the mother goddess, who so abundantly celebrated her fertility, who so joyfully enjoyed her fecundity, was hidden away, disguised? Beneath the robes of the Virgin of Guadalupe, the goddess still remained, and the Indians prayed to her, hiding behind the Christian sacraments. What difference did it make, after all, if they added another manifestation to the many that had come before? I looked again at the silver, crescent-perched virgin mother and child. The room was filled with the sweet, musky scent of incense and the oily odor of burning wax.

Slowly, we walked down the curving asphalt road and back through town. I saw an open music store—since it was after 5 p.m., the shops were open again—and went in and asked for music by Gwendal. They showed me three different tapes and I bought all three. They wouldn't weigh much, after all. And I knew the next time I heard the lilting Celtic music I would remember not only Cirauqui and the unfriendly restaurateurs but also the pagan antecedents, the mystical undercurrents of the Camino.

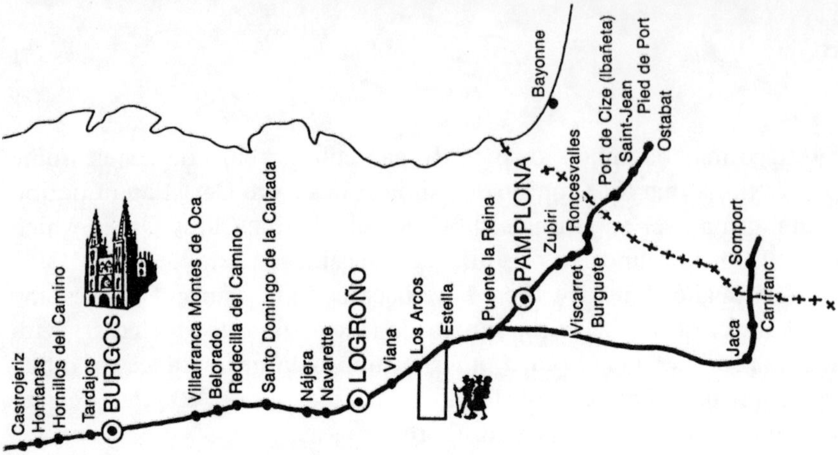

Day 13: July 22 We planned to reach Los Arcos, 17 kilometers away. The guidebook indicated we would follow a relatively flat highway most of the way, so it looked like an easy day. Just outside of town, we met a tan, healthy looking Spanish pilgrim with short-cropped hair, wearing hiking shorts and boots and carrying a large pack, from which dangled a pilgrim's water gourd. He looked about 28 years old. Hanging from his neck was a scallop shell painted with the blood red, pointed cross of Santiago. But he was going the wrong way: he was walking into, not out of, Estella.

He asked, "Going to Santiago?"

"Yes, and you?"

"Yes, but I was sick for four days with stomach trouble. I stayed at the Monastery at Irache—two kilometers further down the road. They took care of me for free."

The next day he was supposed to join up with some friends at Santo Domingo de la Calzada. They planned to make the rest of the pilgrimage together. But he was behind schedule now, so he was going to take the bus to Santo Domingo. Next time, he said, he'd go by bicycle.

I asked him where he got his shell.

"At Santiago, when I went there before, for the last Año Santo."

Since the thirteenth century, an Año Santo Compostelano—Compostelan Holy Year—occurs whenever the feast day of Santiago, July 25, falls on a Sunday. During an Año Santo, people who perform certain prescribed rituals and go to Santiago will earn a plenary indulgence for their sins. This means they will be forgiven their time in purgatory for the sins they have committed up to the time of the indulgence.

Many people repeat the pilgrimage to Santiago every Año Santo. During a Holy Year, numerous bus excursions are organized by parish offices and travel agencies. They frequently combine a brief stay in

Santiago with a holiday excursion to the north coast of Spain, the Portuguese markets, or off-shore islands. Condescendingly, some Spaniards call this kind of pilgrimage *turismo aprovechado*—"taking-advantage tourism"—but the people I knew who went on these excursions seemed to take their religion—and their indulgences—seriously.

We, too, combined pilgrimage and sightseeing. But our excursion was much slower and much more painful. Did that make it more authentic? After all, what was a pilgrimage without some kind of sacrifice? Or was I merely trying to justify the pain and exhaustion?

We wished the Spaniard well and started off down the highway. He called to us to stop.

"That's not the Camino de Santiago."

We didn't care. "That's all right—we'll just follow the highway for a while—"

"No, no, don't do that!" He pointed at a stone wall in the distance. "There's a yellow arrow on it. Follow the path to the right."

We thanked him and started towards the wall.

"Bill, what difference does it make which road we take?"

"Well, if we want to do this right, we should walk the 'real' Camino."

"Says who?"

"The guidebooks. Tradition. That pilgrim. It's expected of us, obviously."

"But that 'real' pilgrim is taking a bus to Santo Domingo de la Calzada."

"Well, he can't help it. He's late to meet his friends. But we can try to be 'authentic,' anyway."

"And he says that next time he'd ride a bike!"

Bill made no reply.

We followed the yellow arrows and got lost.

An hour later we stopped in a bar for a Coke: sugar, caffein, cool refreshment, an excuse to sit in a chair and rest. The woman behind the bar told us there had been lots of pilgrims this year—she didn't know why, but there was definitely an increase from previous years.

Slowly, the terrain was changing. We were still walking through foothills, but now the hills were covered with low scrubby olive trees, and there were wheat fields interspersed with fields of grape vines. Wine country. Soon two young French pilgrims, walking our direction but traveling much faster, passed us. They were in their early twenties, from Paris. Like us, they'd been sick with *la gripe*—stomach flu. We compared distances traveled—they averaged 35 to 40 kilometers a day—and reception received—they said they found the Spanish unfriendly. In Lorca, however, where we had had that unpleasant offer of a ride "for only one," they had found a storekeeper who let them sleep in an empty house.

Friendly and unfriendly receptions. Was it because of language differences? Personalities? Politics? There has been a connection between the pilgrimage and politics since the very beginning, when Alfonso II, the Chaste, honored the discovery of the Apostle's tomb by building a church over it. Alfonso III of Asturias (866-910) considered St. James his patron, and Sancho III of Navarra, Alfonso V of Castilla-León, Sancho Ramírez of Aragón and Navarra, and Alfonso VI of Galicia/Asturias and León-Castilla all contributed to the development of the pilgrimage and the Camino, actively enlisting the aid of the Burgundian Cluny order to develop hospices and support systems along the way. "Santiago y cierra España"—Santiago and close Spain [Spanish fighting ranks]—was a rallying cry for the Reconquest.

The royal patronage continued actively throughout the centuries. The Catholic Monarchs Ferdinand and Isabella visited Santiago, as did later monarchs. Kings, merchants, and clergy promoted the pilgrimage for their own ends for 1,000 years. And Generalísimo Franco continued the tradition. Perhaps the association of repressive dictatorship, military conquest, and conservative religious observance was so strong that the liberal, and the younger, Spaniards disliked the whole idea of pilgrimage to Santiago. For us—and many other pilgrims on the road—politics and religion had little personal significance. We just wanted to make a pilgrimage.

Our guidebook said the road flattened out after Estella. Instead, it looked like a roller coaster. Although our packs were lighter, we were exhausted and our feet hurt. But we were getting used to the pain. Or had the pain diminished?

Late in the afternoon we reached Los Arcos and decided to quit for the day. We walked through town, looking at the old men dressed in faded black sitting on benches in front of the cafe/bar, their canes leaning against the wall behind them. Women dressed in faded black strolled down the streets. Soon we came to a hotel and asked for a room.

Smiling, the woman behind the reception desk asked, "You're walking to Santiago, aren't you?"

We nodded yes.

"I saw you an hour ago, on the highway. I had to drive to Estella for something, and there you were!"

She gave us a "pilgrim's discount" on the room and took us upstairs. Unfortunately, again, there was no hot water. But at least there was water, a toilet—my stomach was still not right—and beds. We rested, ate in the hotel dining room, and went to bed early. We were exhausted.

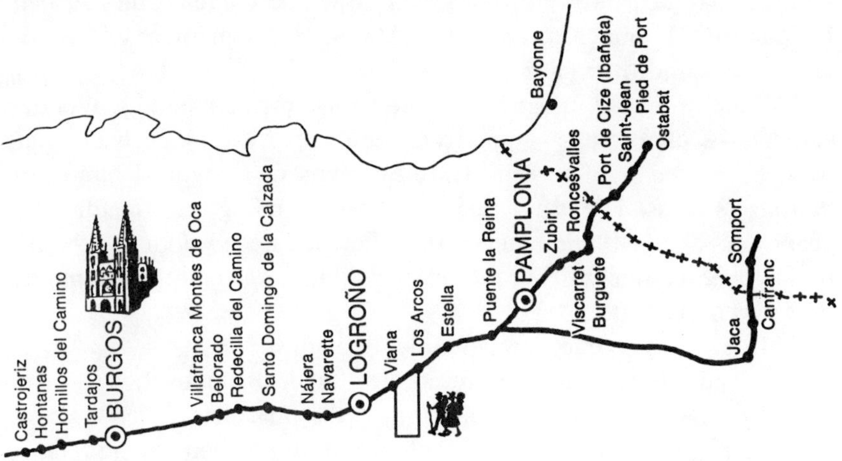

Day 14: July 23 Before leaving Los Arcos we visited the local church, built in the fifteenth century. It looked quite imposing from the outside, as if it were larger than it actually was; parts of it no longer fit. The tall, beige stone church tower was typical of the region: cylindrical, with short, turret-like structures around the top. Inside, the church walls and columns were painted with colorful designs, as if they were covered with embroidered brocades and oriental carpets. All the other churches I'd seen had bare grey stone or white-washed plaster walls.

Many buildings in antiquity were multi-colored inside. The Romans often used mosaics; later artists preferred frescoes. The insides of early churches were covered with paintings—scenes from the gospels, lives of the saints, done in bright colors. Even the stone statues were colored. The Gothic artists painted not only with pigment but also with stained glass, an effect even more dazzling and impressive. But through the centuries, as tastes changed and painting deteriorated, frequently the multi-colored walls were masked with whitewash or plaster and churches looked much more austere. The vivid pictures, visual instructions for the illiterate, hid behind blank white surfaces. The ornate *retablos*—gilded altar screens composed of darkened oil paintings framed with gold or carved statues placed in gilded niches—that I had seen in other, white-walled churches, looked out of place. Here, against the multi-colored walls, the ornateness fit.

On to Viana. For the most part, we followed the highway, but every so often we found a yellow arrow painted on the pavement, directing us off the road onto a narrow dirt or gravel path. Was that really the "authentic" Camino? I wondered, as we walked briefly through furrowed fields of grape vines and then back to the highway.

While we rested under a tree, three pilgrims marched by. Wooden conchas—scallop shells—hung from their necks; their t-shirts and hats were decorated with screen-printed designs of a stylized hand and Santiago's cross. They said they had been planning the trip for three years. Averaging 40 kilometers a day, they had been walking without a break for three weeks, from the tip of Brittany. At night they slept outdoors or in haylofts.

"In France, people were friendly. But not here."

I asked, "Is Santiago an important saint in Britanny?"

"No, not at all. What's important is the pilgrimage!"

After giving me a copy of their carefully planned itinerary, they started briskly down the road. I looked at the paper. How could they have planned, day by day, where they would spend the night? For us, each day was a challenge, and we had only tentative hopes of reaching an inhabitated town by evening.

We walked on, up and down, up and down. Not rugged mountains, but still hills. In the distance we saw Viana, climbing up the side of yet another hill. Just before we reached Viana we passed the Hermitage of the Virgen de Poyo, an ancient shelter for pilgrims; we stopped and rested on the stone steps. It was already 5 p.m., and we had walked seventeen kilometers.

Viana was ugly—heavy industry, stacks of unadorned, multi-story cement apartment buildings. Several grubby little children came running up to us. It was a startling contrast to the well-kept villages, the well-dressed children we had seen along the Camino.

"Peregrinos?"

We nodded.

"Where do you come from?"

"Los Arcos."

"No—no! Where do you come from?"

"Oh—the U.S."

"Americanos!"

We nodded.

"How many kilometers do you walk per day?"

"15 or 20."

They laughed at that and told us there was one pilgrim—an old man—who walked 60 kilometers a day. Was it true, or was it a new legend of the Camino?

We walked on into town. The old city, on the hill, was actually quite attractive—and full of noise and people. Viana was *en fiestas,* celebrating its patron saint. The plaza was full. All sidewalk cafe tables were full. The bars were full. The streets were full. When we asked a man for directions to a hotel, he shook his head.

"Everything is full."

In the plaza, we saw a bar with a sign on the window, "Habitaciones"—rooms. Shouting at the bartender over the din, we asked for a room. He shook his head no; everything was full. Everyone had come home for the celebration. He suggested we could try a hostel down the street. At last we located it and went in. A middle-aged man was sitting in a chair near the door and we asked him if there was a room. Looking us up and down, he said, "Perhaps." He'd have to check with his wife, who was out shopping and would not be back for another hour.

Rather than wait there, we went to a nearby bar, one that was not too crowded, and ate some *tapas.* We pointed to several different ones, displayed behind a covered glass shelf, and the barman served them to us. *Boquerones*—a kind of *ceviche*, made of tiny anchovies marinated in oil, vinegar, and garlic, flecked with parsley. Wedges of Spanish omelet—but this time the omelet was made with *chorizo* as well as potato and onion. *Pulpo*—spicy boiled octopus, radiating garlic and smoky Spanish paprika. And *calamares fritos*—squid rings dipped in batter and fried until crisp, served with lemon. With the *tapas,* we drank cheap red wine.

Refreshed, we walked back to the hostel and interrupted the man and his wife having an intense conversation. The man turned towards us, apologetic. "Sorry, no room."

Bill turned to me. "It's because we are pilgrims. Just like Pamplona."

"Come on, Bill. It's because they are crowded. Why are you so paranoid?" I looked at the man. "Is there anywhere else we can go?"

After talking with his wife a moment, he offered to take us to a *pensión*—he knew a woman who rented out rooms in her home. We went there and the woman explained that normally she had an empty room for rent, but during fiestas her sister and her family were staying with her. However, she had another place—an old apartment on the other side of town. We could stay there, if we wanted to, for $5.00. We thanked her and waited for her to finish feeding her family.

As we walked across town, she told us she had made the pilgrimage to Santiago—by bus, of course. She thought it was a lovely town. She'd also been to Rome and Jerusalem. By far, she preferred Jerusalem—after all, that was *tierra sacra.* After showing us the apartment, she gave us the key and left.

Staying in someone else's house instead of in a hotel was like staying in a furnished apartment, I told myself, but it still seemed strange. Were Spaniards more trusting? I doubted it, since all the houses we had seen had metal grillwork in front of the windows and bars across the doors.

Bill and I took a brief stroll around town. People were playing trumpets and drums, people arguing, people shouting. We looked at the once impressive, now decaying Renaissance buildings. Most of them had the sign, "En Obras"—In Works—on the door; they were closed for restoration. A bystander told us they had been *en obras* for years. We came across a large bronze monument to César Borgia, who was buried in the nearby church of Santa María. Born in 1476, son of the future Pope Alexander VI, he was the most violent member of the Spanish-Italian Borgia family and is considered the prototype of Machiavelli's ruthless, opportunistic, Prince. He was killed in Viana in 1507, while serving as captain of the Navarrese Army.

Hungry again, we stopped at a restaurant called Bodega Ramón. According to my dictionary, a *bodega* was a wineshop, but apparently it could also be a restaurant. A waiter came up to the table and recited the menu by courses. We ordered a mixed salad. It came, made with succulent black ripe olives, not green ones. And onions. Usually, oil and vinegar are provided in cruets on the side, but this time the salad already had a delicate herbal dressing. For the second course, Bill ordered grilled *salmonetes*—red mullets—and they came garnished with parsley, lemon, and anchovy butter, a delightful combination of tart and salty, crisp and smooth. I ordered baby lamb, and it was juicy, tender, rubbed with garlic. At the table next to ours, people were eating an intriguing dessert that looked like a textured white custard, served in a small ceramic cup. The waiter called it *cuajada* and explained it was similar to yogurt. Actually, it was fresh rennet pudding, similar to curds, flavored with cinnamon and drenched with local honey. I ordered it for dessert.

"Bill, do you think 'real' pilgrims eat like this?"

"We're 'real' pilgrims, aren't we?"

"Well, we're certainly not practicing abstinence—or mortification of the flesh."

"It seems to me we suffer enough walking the Camino."

"We seem to find different parts of the tradition important. Following every foot of the 'authentic' Camino is important to you—but dietary abstinence is not."

"Right. And how about you?"

I thought awhile. "I guess the process of making the pilgrimage seems most important—the experience of endurance, of overcoming my limits, of achieving something I never thought I could do. What I eat, or where I sleep, doesn't seem important. That doesn't 'make' the pilgrimage."

"I agree. It is the Camino that matters. That's why I want to make sure we follow the 'authentic' route on foot."

We left the restaurant, went back to the apartment, and tried to sleep. It was 11:30. Getting to sleep was difficult: Viana was exuberantly *en fiestas* all night long.

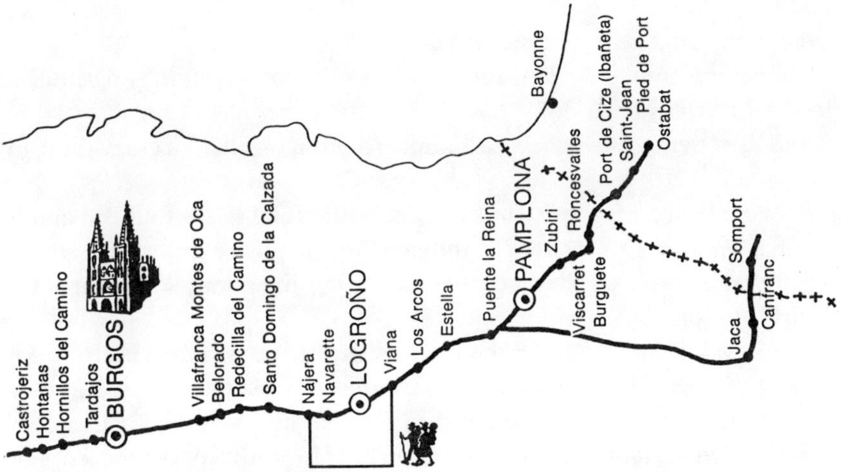

Day 15: July 24 Eve of St. James' Day. We planned to walk just part of the day, from Viana to Logroño. 10 kilometers. A piece of cake. As we passed through the now-deserted plaza on our way out of town, a young Spaniard came stumbling towards us.

"Hello! Hello!"

We stopped and waited for him to catch up with us.

"You speak English?"

"Yes—"

"I want to practice English. Let me buy you a drink."

Very cheerful and very drunk, he smelled of stale cigarette smoke and sour wine. He guided us into a nearby bar and ordered wine; we thanked him but requested coffee, instead. While Bill talked with him, I talked with the bartender.

"Americana?"

"Yes."

He shook his head. "I don't like Americans. Look at how they are ruining our country! The missiles, the strong dollar! I don't like your country. Me, I'm a communist!"

I said something neutral and then tried to change the topic, thinking this would be a good test of my theory about liberal politics and distaste for the pilgrimage. "Have you ever been to Santiago?"

"No."

"We're going on pilgrimage to Santiago. Walking."

"Parece bonito," he said—that is, "that seems like a nice thing to do."

"You think so?" I asked, surprised.

"Yes. Of course, Jesus is the son of a true whore—but the pilgrimage, that's a nice thing to do!"

Bill's friend overheard. "Walking to Santiago? That's a crazy thing to do!"

We talked a bit more, finished our coffee, and left. I told Bill about the bartender's comment. He thought he was just being polite, but I wasn't sure. After all, he hadn't been very polite about Americans. Or Jesus' origins.

A few kilometers down the road we met a Spanish pilgrim from La Coruña, north of Santiago, riding a motorcycle. He looked about 25 years old. He had traveled up the coast to France, across to Cologne, down through Switzerland, and was now returning to Santiago. On the front of his motorcycle were a scallop shell and a number of travel stickers. Tourist or pilgrim? He proudly displayed the scallop shell and a map of the Camino. Living close to Santiago, he had traveled a long distance away in order to make his pilgrimage.

The road evened out at last, and in the distance we could see

Logroño. We had left the province of Navarra and entered La Rioja, the heart of Spanish wine country. La Rioja takes its name from a tributary of the Ebro, the Río Oja, and is a region where the northern Atlantic climate (cold and wet) meets the southern Mediterranean climate (hot and arid). These are supposedly ideal conditions for growing grapes. Wine production in the region has a long history and is mentioned as early as 1102. By the sixteenth century, Rioja wines were exported to France, Flanders, and Italy; by 1560 growers had formed a control board to regulate its production. One of the world's first trademarks was that of the Rioja wine producers.[9]

La Rioja is divided into three parts: the more mountainous and better watered region, Rioja Alta—Upper Rioja—extending south of the Ebro and west of Logroño to Haro; Rioja Alavesa—northern Rioja—comprising part of the province of Alava north of the Ebro; and Rioja Baja—Lower Rioja—stretching east from Logroño to Alfaro. Riojas Alta and Alavesa are the northernmost, more influenced by the Atlantic climate, better for producing fine wines.

The red Rioja wines are noted for their taste of vanilla, which develops from being aged in oak, usually for at least a year, sometimes for as long as eight to ten years. Originally, the reason for the oak aging was to stabilize the wine; now it is a matter of custom and style.

There are over fifty different *bodegas* in the region, each making wines from its own secret blend of four kinds of red and three white grapes. Three are native red grapes: the *tempranillo,* which gives the wine a fruity spicy flavor and deep ruby color; the *graciano,* which gives the wine a perfumed bouquet and freshness; and the *mazuelo,* which is high in tannin and contributes to the wine's acidity and color. The fourth red grape, the *granacha,* also called *grenache* and found elsewhere in Europe, gives the wine a high degree of alcohol. Approximately 90% of the Rioja wines are red, but there are white wines produced as well from mixtures of *viura* or *macabeo*, *malavasía,* and *granacha blanca.*

Just over the provincial border, four or five kilometers from Logroño, we took a path to the left of the highway and ended up walking along a ridge between vineyards, olive trees, and fields. Soon we passed by an important archeological site: a prehistoric, Roman, and high medieval city, apparently destroyed by the Goth king Leovigildo in 574. In front of us was a clear view of the Ebro valley and Logroño, with its famous towers.

Walking over a long—198 meters—stone bridge over the Río Ebro, we entered Logroño. Today, Logroño has a population of 96,000 inhabitants; but in the tenth century, it was nothing more than an agricultural granary on the banks of the Ebro. The Camino de Santiago was the impetus for its growth, beginning in the eleventh and twelfth centuries. A linear city, going from east to west, it follows the orientation of the Camino.

As we walked into town, we passed the fifteenth-century church of Santiago el Real. Over the doorway was an enormous, seventeenth-century, beige stone carving of Santiago Matamoros—Santiago the Moorslayer—riding on a muscular charger, wielding his sharp-edged sword, decapitating heathens. This Santiago was a far cry from the thoughtful, gentle Santiago Peregrino we had seen in Puente la Reina.

As one of Christ's Apostles and as a Christian, he was automatically a pilgrim; after all, the New Testament says "we are all strangers and pilgrims on this earth," and the Church teaches that life is a pilgrimage, from sin to salvation, from this world to the next. According to a most unreliable tradition, Santiago wandered through Iberia as a missionary, thus combining religious wandering with proselytizing—two additional kinds of pilgrimage. Later—again, according to unreliable tradition—his body was miraculously transported from Palestine and buried in Galicia; even death didn't stop his pilgrimage. And even after his body was buried far from his homeland, even then his pilgrimage was not completed, for Santiago Peregrino still travels the Camino. In churches all along the pilgrimage road, images of Santiago abound, carved in wood and stone, glazed in stained glass, painted in oil. In different guises, in different forms, Santiago is always there—traveling alongside, traveling ahead of the weary pilgrim on the Camino. He is always there. Both as pilgrimage companion and pilgrim's saint, he shows the way.

But there is another, less gentle side to Santiago. He is represented not only as the peaceful evangelist but also as the armed crusader, practicing another, more forceful, way to spread the faith. As warrior saint, slayer of infidels, Santiago aided Spain and Christendom in its battle against the Moorish invaders; later, he crossed the ocean with the conquistadores, not as gentle pilgrim but as sword-wielding crusader, slaughtering the heathen natives. Cervantes describes this Santiago Matamoros in glowing terms in *Don Quixote*: "Yes, this is indeed a knight of Christ's squadrons; St. James the moorslayer, one of the most valiant saints and knights the world ever had, and that now the heavens have. . . . this great knight with the vermillion cross has been given by God to Spain for its patron and protection."

It was as warrior saint that Santiago appeared above the portal of the church in Logroño. And it was as warrior saint that he appeared in the dreams of kings and warriors—of Charlemagne, of Ramiro I, of Franco. In fact, it was at the fictitious Battle of Clavijo in 844 that Santiago Matamoros was first reported to appear, riding on a white charger, wielding a bloody sword in one hand and holding a banner with a blood-red cross emblazoned on it in the other. According to the legend, the battle was fought because Ramiro I refused to pay Abderrahman II, the Emir of Córdoba, a tribute of 1,000 virgins. Santiago helped Ramiro I defeat the Moors and himself supposedly slaughtered 60,000 of them. Spain—and the Reconquest—had found its patron saint. Clavijo is located just 17 kilometers from Logroño, so it was not surprising that the church commemmorated the battle scene.

Although the Battle of Clavijo is legend, there was an actual battle at Simancas, in 939, in which Ramiro II was victorious over Abderrahman III—with, according to legend, the help of Santiago—and this time, St. Millán as well. It was at this battle that Ramiro II supposedly pledged Spain to pay the *Voto de Santiago*—the nationwide annual offering to the cathedral in Santiago. Actually, the pledge was not documented until the twelfth century and its authenticity has been called into question for centuries. It was frequently the subject of bitter legal dispute. But in 1634 Philip IV officially established—or validated—the National Offering to Santiago, consisting of 1,000 escudos of gold per year; in 1646 another offering of 500 ducados of silver was added. The veracity of the documentation of Ramiro I's offering became irrelevant. The *Voto* was finally abolished by the Cortes of Cádiz in 1812, but it was reinstituted by Franco in 1948 as the *Ofrenda Nacional.*

Leaving the bellicose saint, we went to the Tourist Office to get our pilgrimage card stamped, but it was closed. So we went to the parish office in the cathedral, but the priest we asked said that no one was there and he was too busy to help us. We weren't sure if we had to get the card stamped in Logroño or not, but the empty square on the pilgrimage card said "Logroño." Maybe that meant province. The priest shook his head and hurried away. A man standing nearby called out, "They're never any help!"

While trying to decide what to do, we wandered around an arcaded plaza in the old part of town. A man tapped on the back of my pack. I turned around, and he made gestures of eating. I nodded encouragingly, and he pointed to a nearby restaurant, Escalerias. Did he help us because we looked lost? Because we were pilgrims? The restaurant was crowded, but we found two places at one of the long wooden trestle tables. There was only one item on the menu: baked suckling lamb. It was delicious.

Afterwards, we walked around the city, looking in store windows. Travel agencies were advertising pilgrimages to the Holy Land and to Santiago: $60 for a weekend in Santiago de Compostela and the scenic Rías Bajas. What kind of a pilgrimage was that?

It felt unpleasant to be in a city. Logroño, a city of nearly 100,000 people, was definitely urban. Heavy traffic. Noise. Fancy shops. A prison. Noise. Traffic. I wanted to get back to the Camino and Bill agreed. Although we had already walked ten kilometers, we were not tired, and it was a pleasant, cool, breezy day, a good day for walking. We decided to continue on to Navarette, ten kilometers away. In 1367, Peter the Cruel, aided by the Black Prince, vanquished his brother Henry II Trastamara at Navarette. According to our guidebook, there was a hostel there, so we would be able to spend the night.

Instead of agony, walking was almost a pleasure. My blisters had healed and I was used to the weight of my pack. I felt good. So did Bill.

Energetically, we marched down the road to Navarette. About half-way there, the sun started to burn up the road. The road had been flat but suddenly it got hilly. It was hot. Bill twisted his ankle. It was terribly hot. My feet started to hurt, with blisters forming on the soles from walking on the hot pavement. At last we saw Navarette in the distance, curving up the side of a hill.

Bill wanted to rest, but I hated to stop and rest when we were so close to the end. It took me more effort to start again that it did to just keep going. Bill was the reverse, preferring to stop a quarter-mile away from our destination and enter it refreshed. We argued, and then we stopped at the ruins of the Hospital of the Order of Saint John of Acre, founded in 1185 as a shelter and aid for pilgrims. We rested in the shade for half an hour, then got up and trudged towards the town.

We saw a young couple, out for a late afternoon stroll. Spaniards often take late afternoon or early evening strolls, either around town or just outside of town. I envied them, remembering how just a few short hours before I had been eager to walk, basking in a sense of fitness and well-being. God—or Santiago?—was watching and letting me know, just in case I had forgotten, that this was a pilgrimage. Footsore and weary, we hobbled towards the couple.

"Is there a hostel in town?"

"No."

"Oh. Our guidebook said there would be a place to stay."

"There was, but it closed down."

"Nowhere to stay?"

"No, sorry."

Bill and I discussed what to do.

"We could try to ask for the priest or the mayor."

"You know I don't feel right about that, Ellen. We could sleep outdoors, too, and not bother anyone."

"You know I need a toilet close by. I've still got 'the runs.'"

"So what do you suggest? The next large town—Nájera—is 16 kilometers from here. We won't make it tonight, walking."

Just then a car drove up beside us and stopped at a stopsign. I ran up to it and stuck my thumb out. The woman in the passenger's seat rolled down the window.

"Peregrino?"

I nodded yes. "Could you give us a ride to the next town? There is nowhere to sleep in Navarette."

She talked with her husband, who clearly did not approve, but she was adamant.

We slid our packs into the back seat and climbed in after them. The car was air-conditioned, the seats covered with plush upholstery. Cool air, comfortable seats—what a contrast to five minutes before.

The woman was Spanish, in her mid thirties. She talked enthusiastically. "I'm from Santo Domingo de la Calzada—that's on the pilgrimage road, you know. We've had lots of pilgrims this year. They're following the Camino, the real Camino de Santiago, not the highway. It's a lovely thing to do."

I asked her, "Have you been to Santiago?"

"By car, several times. A lovely city."

"Have you ever walked there?"

"Oh, no! Spaniards don't walk! It's mostly foreigners who do!"

I wondered why. After all, I had seen lots of Spaniards walking, in villages, along the alamedas—and even a few Spanish pilgrims on the Camino, though not many.

She pointed out attractions by the side of the road: "Look—there's the Alto de San Antón and the ruins of the convent of San Antón and another of the Templars, so they say. In the Middle Ages—and, actually, more recently—this area was covered with woods, and it was very dangerous for pilgrims. There were bandits in the region, some of whom dressed up like monks. So they built a refuge for pilgrims here. And see that little white house on top of the ruins? The inhabitants still offer hospitality to pilgrims."

If we'd known that, we could have stopped there and asked for help. As it was, we had asked for a ride.

Bill asked, "What kind of trees are those?"

"Almond trees. And there, on the left—the Poyo de Roldán—the Stone Seat of Roland. The story is that Ferragut, a Syrian giant descended from Goliath, lived in the castle in Nájera. And he fought against and conquered the warriors of Charlemagne. But one day Roland came to fight him. He climbed up to the top of the ridge there and saw the giant sitting in the doorway of the castle. Roland took up a huge round stone and—like David—he measured the distance, gritted his teeth, and let fly with the stone. It went like a speeding ray and smashed into Farragut's forehead. He was knocked out immediately and all of the imprisoned knights were freed. That's why they call the place where Roland stood the Poyo de Roldán."

That wasn't the same battle carved on the stone capitol in Estella, but it was more exciting. I told the woman, "You really know the history of the area!"

She smiled, pleased. "I like the stories of the Camino."

Stories of the Camino. We were walking in the footsteps of our ancestors—both real and imaginary. Other pilgrims had walked this way, seeking shelter in hospices which were now in ruins. We had sought shelter and found none; we had asked for help and it had been given.

At the edge of Nájera was a roadsign: "San Millán de la Cogolla, 20 kilometers." She said, "You really have to go there. The two monasteries are very famous. Besides, San Millán is the patron and protector of Castilla."

We nodded in agreement, but I thought: walk twenty kilometers out of the way? No way! I knew that the two monasteries at San Millán, the monasteries of Suso and Yuso, were worth a visit, and I knew we wouldn't go. The Monastery of Suso, built in the mountains and partly into a mountainside, is the older of the two; it is part Visigothic and tenth-century Mozarabic. Gonzalo de Berceo, the earliest known poet to write in Castilian, spent his life among the Benedictine monks at Suso, where he was buried, perhaps in 1246. He wrote about the lives of Santo Domingo de Silos and San Millán de la Cogolla; he wrote of pilgrims and of the Virgin. Rustic and charming, Berceo's poems are full of local color. The Spanish poet Antonio Machado says of him, in "CL: Mis Poetas":

> Gonzalo de Berceo, poeta y peregrino,
> que yendo en romería acaeció en un prado,
> . . .
> Su verso es dulce y grave; monótonas hileras
> de chopos invernales en donde nada brilla;
> renglones como surcos en pardas sementeras,
> y lejos, las montañas azules de Castilla.[10]
>
> (Gonzalo de Berceo, poet and pilgrim,
> That going on a *romería,* happened upon a
> meadow,
> . . .
> His verse is sweet and dignified; monotonous
> rows
> of wintry poplars where nothing shines,
> lined up like furrows in brown sown
> fields,
> and, in the distance, the blue mountains of
> Castilla.)

The Monastery of Yuso, built in the valley and called, for its magnificence, the Escorial of the Rioja, was begun in 1053, but the present monastery is Renaissance in style. Yuso guards the remains of the centenarian, San Millán de la Cogolla—St. Emilian of the Hood, who lived from 473-574. Although a gentle hermit shepherd, San Millán, like Santiago, was transformed after death into a slayer of Moors. According to legend he appeared, mounted on a huge white charger, to fight beside Santiago at the Battle of Simancas. He is represented as San Millán Matamoros on the doorway of the Monastery of Yuso, where his relics are kept in an eleventh-century Byzantine casket, adorned with plaques of ivory which depict miracles he performed. Additional miracles are attributed to the relics.

But we would not see them—not the monasteries, not the relics. To walk twenty kilometers out of our way was unthinkable.

We crossed the Río Najerilla and entered Nájera, end of the fourth stage of journey in the *Codex.* The bridge we rode over was originally built by San Juan de Ortega, a twelfth-century hermit who achieved sainthood by helping pilgrims on the Camino. Once, to the left of the bridge, there had been the Hospital de Santiago, also built by San Juan de Ortega. Nothing remained. I knew that somewhere ahead of us, past Villafranca de Montes de Oca but before Burgos, was a national monument to San Juan, located on the "real" Camino de Santiago. Would we see it?

We stopped in front of a two-star hotel—the only hotel in town. The hotel had a room for us and it even had hot water. A month before, I never would have been grateful if a hotel had hot water. But I was learning not to take anything for granted.

Nájera. The name is Arabic or, perhaps, pre-Roman. In 923, Nájera was taken from the Moors by Ordoño II of León and Sancho Garcés of Navarra. The first Christian money of the Reconquest was coined here by Sancho el Mayor; he also redirected the pilgrimage route, which previously had gone through País Vasco, through Nájera. During the tenth and eleventh centuries, the town was the capital of the Kingdom of Nájera, and it became an important stop on the Camino.

In 1052 Don García of Nájera, King of Navarra, decided to build a large church and monastery on the site where he had discovered a statue of Santa María, la Virgen de la Terraza. According to the legend, he was hunting and a dove crossed his path; he released his hawk, and the two birds disappeared into a cave by the river. Don García followed them and saw a brilliant light shining from a lamp, next to a statue of the Virgin. In front of the statue was a *terrraza* (a pot) of lilies and a bell.[11] The monastery was originally under the rule of San Isidoro, but in 1079 Alfonso VI gave the church and monastery to Cluny, in order to help develop the pilgrimage to Santiago. This didn't please the bishop of Nájera, who moved the see—the seat of the bishop—to Calahorra. Since 1895 the monastery of Santa María la Real has been under the Franciscan order.

We went to see the Santa María la Real Monastery, subject of so much politicking, and admired the elaborate choirstalls, carved in 1495. Then we went below the gallery to visit the royal pantheon—the burial chamber—of the eleventh- and twelfth-century princes of Navarra, León, and Castilla, as well as the seventeenth-century dukes of Nájera. The air smelled faintly musty.

The intricately carved, twelfth-century sarcophagus of Doña Blanca of Navarra, great-granddaughter of el Cid, was beautiful. Placing my hands on the elaborate marble sepulchre, I traced the rounded figures carved in high relief. How many centuries death had rested beneath these ornate tombs. Warm flesh turning cold, soft flesh melting off the bones, bones coming clean and slowly crumbling, the weight of the body gradually lessening as blood and flesh and bone desiccated into dust. Their power and fame forgotten, their love and treachery beyond remembrance, voices and caresses stilled, the disintegrated remains of warriors and kings, mothers and queens lay encased in cold, chiseled stone.

At the center of the pantheon, between two carved, kneeling figures of the founders, was the entrance to the cave where the figure of the Virgin was found. Unlike the Virgen del Puy in Estella, who was found on a hilltop, this Virgin was found in a cave. Perhaps it is not so surprising that in Spain holy images were hidden away from Moorish invaders, hidden and forgotten, and then miraculously rediscovered. But stories of similar discoveries are told throughout the world—stories of earth mothers, sky fathers, made visible.

We left the pantheon and walked around the Cloister of the Caballeros, a delicately carved, lace-like stone gallery, dating from the sixteenth century. In the patio inside the cloister was a stage. Our guide explained that in the summer townspeople performed a colorful pageant called the "Crónica Najerense" that included scenes of medieval pilgrims and knights in colorful costumes. Unfortunately, they were not performing it that night.

On the way back to the hotel we passed a restaurant and went in. We ordered the standard mixed salad, which we split, and then we requested the specialty of the house. The waiter said there were two: *chipirones en su tinta* and something else, a word I couldn't catch. We ordered both. The *chipirones* were tender little squid, an inch or so long, braised in a dark sauce made with their own ink, garlic, and a bit of cinnamon. They were quite unusual, combining sea and spice. The other dish came. On closer examination we realized it was a fried fish head, brains and all.

I looked at the waiter. "A fish head?"

"Delicious. Our specialty."

I looked at it. I couldn't eat it.

"Bill, can you—"

"Not a chance."

At the table next to us, an elegantly dressed woman was eagerly attacking the fried fish head, drawing out the brains, sucking on the eyes. I looked away.

"I'm sorry, but this was a mistake."

"A mistake?"

"Yes. Could you take it back? Could I please have a *tortilla espanola* instead?"

Although puzzled, he was pleasant and helpful. We saw him shaking his head as he walked off, wondering at the strange dietary preferences of Americans.

Back at the hotel, I asked the clerk what festivities were planned for the Día de Santiago. She looked surprised. "None," she said. I was surprised. "But tomorrow is a national holiday, and Santiago is patron of Spain." She shrugged and replied, "So what?" and turned away.

Last year on the Eve of Santiago, I had been in Santiago de Compostela with some friends. We had watched a folkloric dance contest in the Plaza de las Platerías near the cathedral, one of an ongoing series of events commemorating the Día de Galicia, not the Día de Santiago. Gallego separatists took advantage of the celebration to honor their own separate heritage and to call for political separation from Spain. Bright red, white, and black Gallegan costumes; lilting Gallegan music, similar to the music by Gwendal that we had heard in Navarra. Wafting out of the noisy bars was more Celtic-sounding music, and we saw a band of costumed *gaita* players parading through the streets with their brightly colored bagpipes slung across their shoulders.

Later that evening, we had crammed ourselves into the Plaza del Obradoiro, along with thousands of other people, to see the fireworks. The front of the cathedral was covered with a complicated arrangement of fireworks, designed to look like a Moorish palace. Rockets went off and the fireworks ignited, seeming to set the front of the damp, lichen-spotted cathedral on fire. Supposedly, this was a recreation of Almanzor's sacking of the city in 997. We were wedged into the crowd, unable to move, unable to avoid the bits of fireworks that came showering down on us from the sky. At last the crowd broke up, and we stayed behind to look at the now-darkened cathedral in the near-empty plaza. Now, a year later, I was a pilgrim on the road, part way to Santiago.

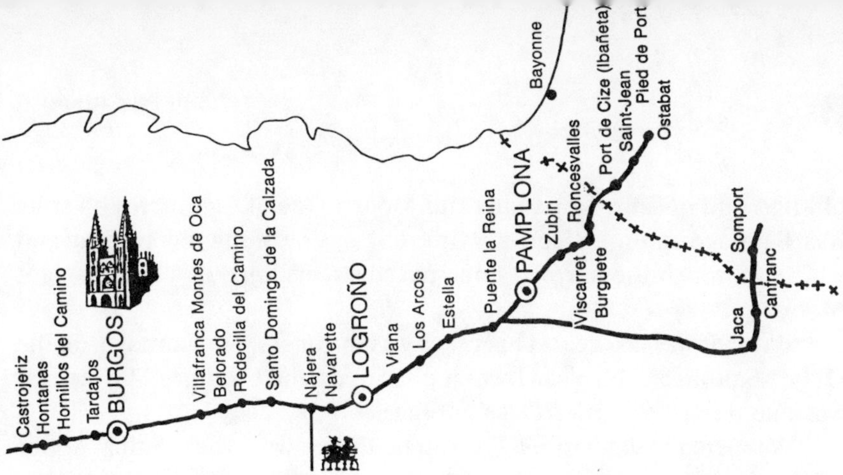

Day 16: July 25

The Día de Santiago. In the morning in the cathedral the king of Spain would present the National Offering—that twelfth-century *Voto de Santiago* which had been reinstated, after a lapse of more than a century, by Franco. During a non-Año Santo, some other high official would do it, but this was an Año Santo, and the king would make the offering himself. And that meant there would be violent demonstrations in the streets. The previous year, I had seen riot police of all sorts standing, rifles ready, guarding the cathedral and its dignitaries from crowds of brick-throwing demonstrators who used the day as an opportunity to express their desire for a Galicia separate from the rest of Spain. Somehow, my friends and I had managed to get around the crowd and the police and went to the cathedral for the special mass. But try as we might, we could not enter the cathedral; it was crammed with people. So we had gone down a side street and into a bar, and we had watched the proceedings on the television set while we drank espresso. We watched the elaborate rituals, and listened to the lengthy speeches. We saw the colorfully dressed men swing a five-foot-high incense burner—the *botafumeiro*—from a rope hanging from the cathedral ceiling—it swung higher and higher, faster and faster, perfuming the air with purifying scent.

Once the mass was over, there were religious processions, and several reliquaries and a statue of Santiago mounted on his horse, slaying Moors, were carried through the streets. The procession consisted of cathedral hierarchy; we saw a heavy-set, red-faced priest, town officials, devout female worshippers carrying long, unlit yellow candles, and young boys dressed in long black robes, sprinkling incense. The small procession wound its way through the streets.

Off and on during the day, there had been another sort of parade: Giants and Bigheads—the figures we had seen in the store window display in Pamplona—danced through the streets, re-enacting imagined dramas of kings and queens, Christians and Moors. One of the figures on stilts was Santiago, mounted on a white horse; gracefully, he twirled and whirled through the narrow, stone-paved streets, pursuing fleeing giant Moors.

But that was last year. This year I was in Nájera, not Santiago, on the Día de Santiago. This year I was a pilgrim on the Camino. The festival was one thing—the pilgrimage another.

We spent the day resting. We watched TV news in the evening. About three minutes was devoted to the procession—the mass, the demonstrations. That was it. I was glad to be resting, far away from Santiago. The festival, after all, had nothing to do with pilgrimage.

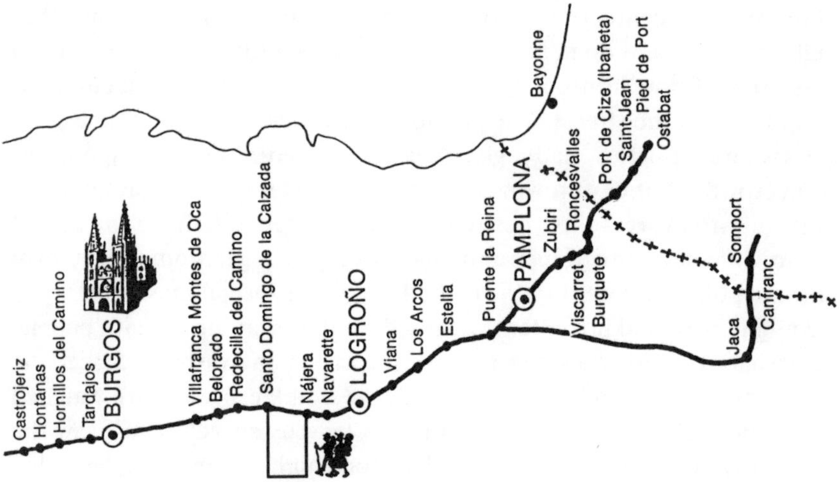

Day 17: July 26 We left the hotel around 9 a.m., hoping to reach Santo Domingo de la Calzada, 19 kilometers away, by late afternoon. Just outside the hotel we saw a young Spaniard sitting on a bench, scallop shell fastened to the backpack on the ground beside him.

"Walking to Santiago?" I asked.

He looked at us ruefully and pointed to his feet. He explained that he and three friends had begun walking the Camino at Roncesvalles a week ago. But his friends had gone on without him when they reached Nájera: he couldn't walk any further. His feet were covered with blisters.

"I've played soccer for years—but this pilgrimage is something else! Walking, day after day! And sleeping on the ground—I'm not used to it. My back hurts, my feet are a mess, and I'm tired all the time."

I asked him where they slept at night, and he said they had no money, so they usually slept outdoors, or in shelters, or wherever people would let them stay for free. Last night he had stayed at the Franciscan monastery.

In the eleventh century, Don García and Doña Estefania founded a special hospice just for pilgrims at the same time that they founded the monastery of Santa María. There were other hospices in Nájera. In the fifteenth century, the pilgrim Künig praised Nájera's accommodations, saying they gave willingly for the love of God, and pilgrims had all they wanted. Except in the Hospital of Santiago, everyone bantered a lot. The women of the hospital made a lot of commotion, according to Künig, but the rations are very good.[12] Apparently, the Franciscans were continuing the Jacobean traditions.

The Spaniard told us he was going to catch a bus that afternoon at 5:30 and meet his friends in Santo Domingo de la Calzada at 6 p.m. We hoped, by starting at 9 a.m. and walking all day, to reach Santo Domingo by evening. He asked us if we had heard about the 40-year-old Frenchman who walked the whole 800-kilometer Camino de Santiago in eight days? Had he heard about the three Brittany pilgrims walking 40 kilometers a day? Yes, he'd met them, several days before. Wishing him good luck, we started jauntily down the road.

Nájera backed up against a large, abrupt hill, which shed reddish-purple pebbles onto the road. Our route curved around the side, then between two small hills, then through pine trees, vineyards, and open countryside shimmering in the heat. We counted guideposts: each kilometer of highway was marked with a cement post and a number, and occasionally a road sign gave the kilometers to the next town. We counted our progress kilometer by kilometer.

The day passed quickly. We fell into a steady rhythm of walking, stopping, and walking again. There were no steep hills, no vast uncharted plateaus, no disappearing yellow arrows. Keeping on the recently resurfaced highway, we did not get lost, and the highway was easy to walk on, its smooth, yielding surface cushioned our feet. Seventeen kilometers from Nájera we came to a medieval *rollo*—a Cross of the Pilgrims—indicating, according to the guidebook, that we were walking on the *verdadera ruta jacobea*—the real Camino de Santiago—even if it was asphalt.

As we approached Santo Domingo de la Calzada, a rattling, open-bed truck drove slowly by.

"Did you see that?" Bill asked me.

I looked up from my plodding feet. "See what?"

"The driver looked at us and turned away and spat."

"So?"

"What do you mean, so? That was intended for us!"

"Oh, Bill, don't be paranoid."

"I'm not paranoid—I know a look of disgust when I see one! And it's not the first. There've been several hostile stares."

"They don't even know us!"

"They don't like pilgrims. I've told you before—there are people who don't like pilgrims."

"Maybe so." I wondered, as I had wondered before, how much of our reception—of any pilgrim's reception—depended on personality—ours and theirs. On the one hand, I thought bad interactions were generated by distrustful and suspicious personalities. After all, I never thought we were refused a room because we were pilgrims—but Bill always thought so. On the other hand, those people driving by didn't even know us. Did Bill just imagine hostility? Or were they really hostile? If so,it had nothing to do with anything we had done—except to be pilgrims.

Just outside of town we saw a building with a sign painted on it:

Santo Domingo de la Calzada
Donde canto la gallina
Despues de asada

(Santo Domingo de la Calzada,
Where the chicken sang
After being roasted)

According to a legend recounted by the sixteenth-century English pilgrim Dr. Andrew Boorde, a white cock and hen were kept in the church of Santo Domingo to commemorate the following event. A young pilgrim to Santiago rejected the advances of a serving girl, so she hid a piece of silver in his wallet, then treacherously reported him as a thief. He was condemned, hanged, and left on the gallows as a reminder to all. His parents continued the pilgrimage, and when they returned from Santiago they went to the gallows and prayed for his soul. At which time the young man spoke up: "I am not dead; God and Saint James have preserved me. Go to the judge and tell him to cut me down." They did so, but the judge had just sat down to a dinner of a baked hen and cock, and he refused to believe them. He scoffed: "Your tale is as true as that these two chickens will stand up and crow!" And lo and behold, they stood up and crowed. Whereupon the judge went with a procession of others to fetch the young man from the gallows.[13]

This legend of the unjustly hanged pilgrim was first told by Aymery Picaud as one of the miracles of St. James in the *Codex*. That version, however, referred to a German father and son, arrested on the false charge of a dishonest innkeeper in Toulouse. One of them was condemned to be hanged, and the son sacrificed himself for his father. He was resuscitated by St. James. By the sixteenth century, the story had been elaborated on and included the crowing white cock and hen, and now it was reported to have occurred in Santo Domingo, not Toulouse—and the miracle was credited to Santo Domingo, not Santiago.

To honor the miracle, a cage with two white chickens in it is kept inside the twelfth-century cathedral. Traditionally, pilgrims would pick up white feathers from the birds and put them in their hats. As late as the early twentieth century, French pilgrims would push crumbs of bread into the cage, believing that if the birds ate the crumbs, the pilgrims would have a safe journey; if not, they would die on the Camino.

Santo Domingo is famous for more than miraculous birds, however. Santo Domingo de la Calzada—St. Dominic of the Causeway—was a famous protector of pilgrims, a builder of pilgrimage roads and bridges during the eleventh century. According to one story, he tried to join the Benedictines but was rejected and retired as a hermit. According to another, he was an Italian who sold all his possessions and came to Spain as a pilgrim. He settled on the banks of the Río Oja, where the forests were thick and filled with robbers and wild animals. He cleared the forest and laid a causeway between Nájera and Redecilla, thus shifting the Camino de Santiago to the south of the Roman road which had been used. He built a bridge over the Río Oja, settled the lands, and constructed a church and *hospital,* which is now a first-class hotel, in Santo Domingo. Before he came, there was neither bridge nor settlement; by the time he died, there was a town which catered to pilgrims. Because of his labors he is called the "engineering saint of the pilgrimage." San Juan de Ortega, who had built the bridge in Nájera, was a colleague of his.

We decided to stay in the hotel. Founded in the eleventh century by the saint, the building was reconstructed in the fourteenth century and, until the eighteenth century, served as a hospice for pilgrims. In this century, the government has turned it into a first class hotel—for paying tourists, not charity-seeking pilgrims. There are a number of these government-run *paradors* along the Camino, encouraging tourism.

Inside, the building resembled a medieval palace, tastefully modernized. The walls were bare stone, with arches criss-crossing over the lobby; the floor was covered with dark burnished tiles. A contemporary skylight of brilliant blue and green stained glass had been cut into the ceiling, and yellow bulbs glowed warmly in the wrought iron chandeliers, and the lounging areas were furnished with dark wood and red leather sofas and chairs. On one wall there was an impressionistic map of the Camino de Santiago, a copy of which I had seen at the Spanish Tourist Office.

Soon we were relaxing in a luxurious room with a balcony facing the cathedral. The beds had firm mattresses, soft pillows, and there was even a small refrigerator, stocked with cold drinks and a small bottle of champagne. The bathroom had hot water and, on the spacious countertop, there were packets of black Spanish Magno soap and shampoo. Hanging on rods were huge, soft, white terrycloth bath sheets. I raved about the accommodations. Bill was more restrained.

"It's nice."

"Bill—it's gorgeous!"

"You just think that because you're comparing it to the other hotel rooms we've been in recently."

"So?"

"So it's nice, but it's not fantastic."

I walked into the bathroom and locked the door. It didn't matter on an absolute scale how luxurious the room was. What mattered was that the pilgrimage was teaching me to appreciate things I used to take for granted, like hot water, a firm mattress, feet that didn't hurt all the time, a toilet when I needed it.

I finished soaking in the steaming bath, rubbed myself pink with a huge, absorbent towel, and got dressed. Stepping out onto the wrought-iron balcony, I saw a group of pilgrims kneeling in front of the cathedral. Most were wearing shorts and holding straw hats in their hands, but one was dressed in a long dark robe and carried a cross. Standing behind them were three priests in long cassocks. In unison, they prayed out loud, then entered the cathedral. We went downstairs to find out more about them. The receptionist thought they were from a religious high school in Barcelona.

We went out to talk with them, but by that time they were gone, so we went to find the parish priest to stamp our pilgrimage cards. Neither communicative nor informative, he complained about being bothered at all times of the day to stamp these cards. He added that there were a lot of pilgrims that year—more than ever before. A real nuisance. We left and went to the El Peregrino—The Pilgrim—restaurant for dinner.

Restaurateurs, as well as the Church and the State, get a lot of tourist mileage out of the pilgrimage to Santiago. But pilgrimage has always been an industry, in the Middle Ages as well as now. Most of the towns we'd walked through developed because of the pilgrimage road. No matter where the mind is traveling—no matter what journey the spirit is engaged in—the body still needs food and shelter.

Lured to the restaurant by its evocative name, we soon found we had been misled; the food was awful. We finished quickly and went back to the hotel. On the way back, I saw a sign advertising a pilgrimage to Santiago, complete with a few days for shopping and sightseeing in Vigo, Bayonne, and León. A holiday vacation, with a bit of religion thrown in?

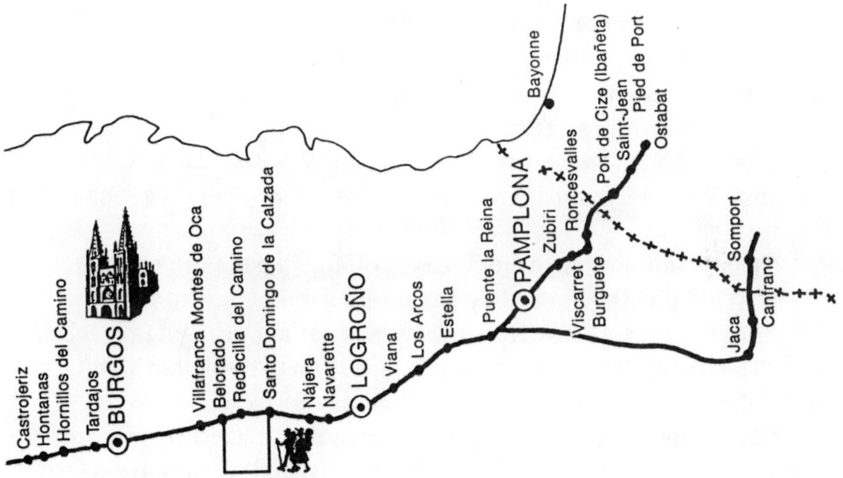

Day 18: July 27 Twenty-one kilometers to Belorado. Crossing over the Río Oja on a 24-arch stone bridge built by the saint, we left Santo Domingo. The road was getting hilly again. Our path cut through an extensive valley, protected on both sides by black poplars. The walking was easier now than in the Pyrenees, but it was still tiring. And it was still hot. We saw the group of twenty pilgrims again, all male and about 15–17 years old, except for the three older priests. A van drove ahead of

them, carrying their baggage and supplies. As they marched in unison, we heard them recite the rosary. Every so often, one of the priests would see someone working in a field and would hike up his cassock to walk quickly and go over to talk with him.

What would it be like to travel in a group of twenty other pilgrims, reciting prayers along the way? More spiritual? Bill thought not. He thought most of the kids were just along for the ride—or the excursion. Besides, they weren't even carrying packs. What kind of pilgrimage was that?

The highway crossed the border between the province of La Rioja and Burgos. We trudged up the hill to Redecilla del Camino and went into town to see the church, which has a famous twelfth-century stone baptism font. There were four bicycles in front of the church; appliqued on each bicycle pack was the cross of Santiago. Inside, a priest was giving a tour of the church's art treasures to four Spanish pilgrims, each wearing the red cross of Santiago embroidered on his shirt. They ranged in age from 17 to 30. They told us they were from Madrid and Pamplona and had started their pilgrimage in Roncesvalles.

"Why are you going to Santiago?" I asked.

They looked at each other. "Sports." "Exercise." "Religious motives." "To be with my friends."

They told us about the group of thirty young men walking the Camino. We told them that a van accompanied them, carrying their luggage.

"That's not a pilgrimage!" they scoffed. "That's too easy!"

We said goodbye and they got on their bikes and rode away.

"Bill, if it's 'too easy' to use a van, what about riding bicycles?"

"That seems 'too easy,' too—but they seem to think they're pilgrims, maybe because two of them have religious motives."

Was it the motive or the performance that makes the pilgrim? We lacked religious motives, but we were walking, and we were trying to follow the "authentic" route in an "authentic" fashion. Even if the "authentic" route was a modern fiction.

People used to make the pilgrimage on foot or horseback, or in a litter, and walking wasn't the only "authentic" way, although walking was supposed to be more humble and fit the pilgrimage ideal of penance and humility.

Bill continued, "We're pilgrims because we're walking."

"No—the point is, we might be walking because we're pilgrims—it's

This pilgrim follows the modern highway between Redecilla del Camino and Belorado. The original Camino lies buried beneath layers of asphalt. The rolling hills are typical of this part of the route.

not the other way around."

We walked up and down the hills, following behind the twenty—or thirty—straw-hatted pilgrims. The bicyclists were long gone. Soon we took a rest stop in the shade of a small building in a field, and a middle-aged farmer came up to talk with us; we were resting in the shade of his storage shed. He was curious, not hostile; but it was clear that he felt our pilgrimage was a sort of luxury, an indulgence. He explained he couldn't walk to Santiago—he had to work. He added, he'd probably walked to Santiago and back half a dozen times, behind his plow horse. We laughed.

People seemed friendly. Truck drivers honked and moved aside to give us more room on the road. When we stopped for lunch in a cafe outside of Villamayor del Río, a man in his 70s started talking with Bill about the pilgrimage.

"Vale la pena—it's worthwhile," he said, approvingly. "The walk is hard and your packs are heavy, but the pilgrimage has more value that way. It is a sacrifice and worth more. Qué sacrificio! And more for her"—he pointed at me—"a woman, than for a man, because women are not as strong." He recited the route at length, beginning with Valcarlos. He repeated the route several times, as if he enjoyed the sound of the words. "My niece went, by car. But that's not the same as walking."

Bill asked him, "Have you gone to Santiago?"

"Yes, six or seven years ago. It's beautiful. Of course, I drove there."

We walked on. My arms blistered from the sun.

Each day was different. At first I had thought: once I get used to walking and my blisters heal, it will be easy. But it was never easy. It was just different things that were difficult. Bill thought the pain was a necessary part of the pilgrimage, and maybe he was right. If so, how could pilgrims go by bus?

But what, after all, was edifying about pain and exhaustion? Chronic pain and weariness were just boring. Pleasure, enthusiasm, excitement—coherent thought—all became impossible when I was in pain or exhausted. I had to have some energy left over in order to experience positive emotions. Too much suffering left nothing. I had no sense of spiritual renewal or transcendence. Maybe I hadn't suffered enough. Or long enough.

It was 7:00 in the evening and we were still walking. We met two more travelers to Santiago, a French woman and a Flemish man, riding bikes. They rode 60–80 kilometers a day. They had begun their pilgrimage in Biarritz, rode to St. Jean Pied de Port, over the Pyrenees to Valcarlos. They had left Santo Domingo just one hour earlier. We had left it ten hours before and had been walking ever since. Eager to reach Belorado, they rode on.

Trucks tried to push us off the narrow highway, rather than giving us more room. But there was no shoulder, and bushes and weeds grew up to the edge of the pavement. Eventually, the winding road cut through a ravine and, after a final curve, at the bottom we reached Belorado. We turned a corner and in front of us was a park. Hot and weary, we collapsed on a bench. Leaving my pack with Bill, I walked over to a group of people sitting together on a nearby bench. They watched me warily, then looked away. I spoke to their averted faces.

"Excuse me, could you tell me where there is a hostel?"

They turned and looked at me again. What had they thought, that I would ask them for money? They said there were two and pointed towards the nearest one. Bill and I walked over to it and got a room for the night: two swaybacked beds, a rickety table, a water pitcher and a washbasin. No sink. The bathroom was down the hall. No hot water. No plug for the tub. Just the day before, luxury. Now, the bare necessities.

After an early supper we went out for a walk and ran into the French-Flemish couple. We went to have a drink at a sidewalk cafe in the plaza. They told us they were following the Camino for its art history—he was interested in Romanesque churches. About ten years before, when he was a teenager, he had read Mullins's book, *The Pilgrimage to Santiago,* and he had decided to make the pilgrimage. A few years later he had traveled part of the Camino in France. It was easier there, he said, since you could ride on the back roads on bicycle, unlike in Spain, where the "real" Camino was usually gravel or footpaths.

Disappointed, he complained: "It's all so modern in Spain! It takes a lot of imagination to see the medieval pilgrimage way. And the older places are off the highway, so we can't reach them by bike."

I was surprised. "Modern? It doesn't seem that way to me."

"Maybe it looks different on foot."

His wife said, "It must be very hard to travel the Camino on foot, carrying backpacks. And so slow!"

I thought: "Vale la pena."

We asked where they had stayed in Santo Domingo, and they told us they had asked a policeman where to get the pilgrimage stamp for the pilgrimage card they had been given at the Pamplona Tourist Office. He took them to a shopkeeper, who took them to a place called the Casa del Santo, where pilgrims could stay for free. There was a book there signed by a number of pilgrims, mostly Spanish.

The couple showed us their Flemish guidebook, which described the route in detail. According to them, although it showed the "real" Camino, it was intended for people in cars who wanted to take an occasional excursion on foot. Traveling by bicycle, they could rarely follow the medieval route—they had to stay on a smooth surface. We told them we didn't always follow the "authentic" Camino because the Camino was often poorly marked and much harder to walk on—the surface was uneven, the path nonexistent. They were surprised.

Although it was already late, we strolled around town, admiring the beige stucco buildings and the arcaded plaza. Belorado is now an insignificant hamlet, but once it was a more important city. It had been the ancient episcopal see for the region until 1076, when the see was transferred to Burgos. In 1116 it was repopulated by Alfonso el Batalladoro, and in the Middle Ages it had had a *hospital* for pilgrims.

We said goodbye to our fellow travelers—not fellow pilgrims, it seemed, since their only interest was art history. Would we meet again? Not likely. They planned to be in Santiago in ten or twelve easy days, then take the train back home.

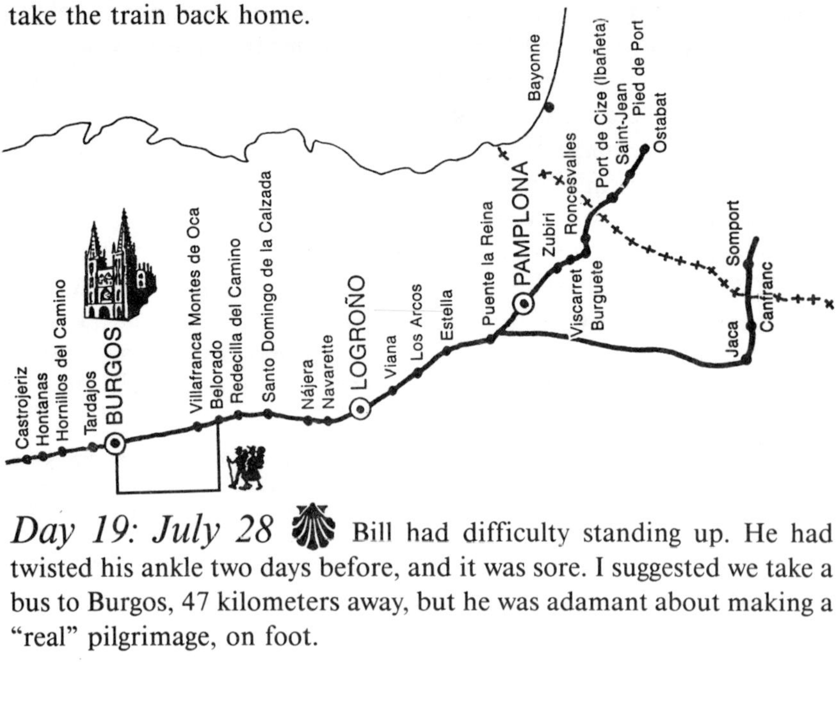

Day 19: July 28 Bill had difficulty standing up. He had twisted his ankle two days before, and it was sore. I suggested we take a bus to Burgos, 47 kilometers away, but he was adamant about making a "real" pilgrimage, on foot.

So we walked out of town and down the road. Or rather, up the road, past Tosantos, past Villambistia. The day had begun cool and overcast, but it soon cleared and got hot. We had been walking past patchwork fields of green and gold. Now we were walking up into tree-covered hills.

While taking a Coke break in a bar at Espinosa del Camino, we talked with the bar owner. He said he'd seen a group of thirty or forty young pilgrims, one of whom carried a cross. We said we'd seen them too—but their numbers must have grown. Bemused by such activity, he shook his head, then asked why we were going to Santiago. We tried to explain about being curious about the history, the experience, about wanting to make a pilgrimage. He didn't seem to understand.

"Isn't it expensive to make the pilgrimage? How can you afford to take a month off of work?"

Bill said, "If we were home, we would have to buy food, pay rent. Walking is free. And we have sleeping bags."

I added, "And we have the summers off, anyway. Besides, in Europe, lots of people get a month's vacation, don't they?"

"Only if they work for a big business or the State. If you work for yourself, you work all the time."

Curious, I asked him, "Have you ever gone on pilgrimage to Santiago?"

"No. Nobody around here has. Santiago isn't important here—San Juan de Ortega is. Nobody cares about Santiago, here. Our local saint is San Juan."

San Juan, who lived from 1080 to 1163, was a collaborator of Santo Domingo. Like him, he built roads and bridges to help pilgrims on the way to Santiago. In the Montes de Oca there was a dangerous stretch of road, where robbers frequently attacked and robbed pilgrims. Knowing the difficulty and danger of the route through the mountains, he built a church and hospital there to provide help and assistance.

Although San Juan de Ortega was important, I was surprised that the bartender had no interest in Santiago. "But Santiago is patron of Spain!"

"So what! He's just not important here." Changing the topic, he commented, "It must be hard to walk the road."

We agreed.

His wife came into the bar and looked at our backpacks. "Pilgrims to Santiago?"

We nodded. Her husband came over and lifted up my backpack,

then went back behind the bar. "That pack of yours is very heavy!"

His wife said, "It's supposed to be. It is *un sacrificio*—a sacrifice—to make the pilgrimage."

Her husband added, "We make the *romería* to the sanctuary of San Juan de Ortega every year—that's 10 kilometers, up in the mountains. But we don't carry packs. By the way—don't take that route. Stick to the highway."

Bill protested, "But the highway's not authentic."

"So what? The road through the Montes de Oca is terrible. It is much longer, and it is very hard to walk on."

We thanked him for his advice and left. Wearily, we walked towards the Montes de Oca, the ancient eastern border of Castilla. According to the *Codex,* a miracle had occurred in these mountains. A French couple and their son were making the pilgrimage to Santiago. The son died in the Montes de Oca, but when they started to bury him, the Apostle interceded and their son was brought back to life. Together, they completed the pilgrimage.

At last we reached Villafranca de Montes de Oca. It had taken us four painful hours to walk the ten kilometers from Belorado. Villafranca de Montes de Oca was known in Roman times as Auca; later, it was called Villa de los Francos de Montes de Oca—Town of the Franks in the Mountains of the Goose. Because of the word *oca* in its name, it is one of the important places on the pre-Christian initiation route, that mystical route purported to be a path of spiritual death and rebirth, a route continuing past Santiago to Noya, where Noah's ark supposedly landed. Perhaps the *oca* is related to the death-conquering phoenix, or to the crowing, death-denying birds in Santo Domingo. Remnants of ancient rites, repeated by word of mouth; shards of ancient symbols, engraved in stones along the way. Only the initiates knew, and they can no longer speak; only coded messages remain to mark the way.

There was a restaurant/truck stop on the outskirts of Villafranca and we stopped there and asked about the bus schedule. Rudely, the waiter said he didn't know and told us to ask at the breadstore across the street. Bill went to the breadstore, but they said they didn't know either.

Frustrated, he told me, "I know that they know—they just aren't telling!"

"Bill—why wouldn't they?"

"I don't know. Because we're pilgrims. Because we're strangers."

Bill saw the owner or manager of the restaurant standing behind the cash register, so he asked him about buses. He said there were several buses in the morning, but none after 12:30 p.m. Since it was after 2:00, we had missed the last bus for the day. We decided to eat lunch at the restaurant and then hitchhike.

The late-fifteenth-century German pilgrim Hermann Künig wrote that they provided good food in Villafranca at the Hospital de la Reina. And the seventeenth-century pilgrim Domenic Laffi agreed, saying that they gave fine charity and good food to pilgrims, and in particular at the Hospital. The Hospital was established in 1380; in the eighteenth century it still had 36 beds for pilgrims. Now, however, it was empty and provided nothing. So far, the hospitality in Villafranca had been most noticeable in its absence.

But *la comida* was excellent. That day, the specialty of the restaurant was *conejo a la cazadora*—rabbit, hunter's style, baked with wine, tomatoes and herbs. Aromatic and succulent, it was delicious.

By 3 p.m. we had finished our meal and were back on the road. Bill had agreed to hitchhike, but no one stopped. We kept walking up the steep highway that led through and out of town, and soon we were walking into hills covered with oak trees and thick vegetation. Laffi got lost in these mountains and had to eat wild mushrooms to survive.

At last a car stopped for us. The driver, in his mid-thirties, was going to Valencia. He said he would be glad to give us a ride to Burgos. As we rode through the evergreen-covered Montes de Oca, he told us at length about the "real" Camino. According to him, the crosses by the side of the road mark where pilgrims had died.

"They built special pilgrimage churches on the outskirts of town, so pilgrims wouldn't infect people. Pilgrims carried diseases and parasites, and townspeople wanted to keep them separate. The *botafumeiro* in Santiago—the huge incense burner that they swing up and down the aisles—was used to disinfect the pilgrims."

I wondered if he was correct about the separate churches for pilgrims. Maybe so. After all, many pilgrims were sick—that's why they were making the pilgrimage. And many others got sick from the stress of walking the Camino. San Roque, patron saint against the plague, is the patron saint of many villages along the Camino. I had seen his statue many times; dressed as a pilgrim to Santiago, with the scallop shell on his cloak and hat, he points to an open sore—a plague pustule—on his leg. A dog stands near him, with a piece of bread or a stone in his mouth. According to the legend, either it is a piece of bread to feed the saint or it is a curative stone.

It had taken us half the day to walk 11 kilometers; it took us half an hour to be driven 32. Since morning, we had traveled into the Montes de Oca, across a 900-meter-high, tree-covered plateau, and down into a shallow, grain-filled river valley.

According to Aymery Picaud, once we left the Montes de Oca we were in Castilla: "Land full of treasures, abounding in gold and silver, cloths and strong horses. It is rich in bread, wine, meat, fish, milk and honey." Actually, we were in the modern province of Burgos, which until recently was part of the region called Castilla Vieja and is now part of the autonomous region known as Castilla-León; political boundaries keep changing. Soon we arrived in Burgos, home of el Cid, end of the fifth stage of journey in the *Codex.*

Our friendly driver dropped us off in front of a two-star hotel, the Fernán González, named after the great Count of Burgos who fought at the Battle of Simancas and later established the virtually independent County of Castilla. He died in 970. A popular thirteenth-century epic poem, written in Castilian, celebrates his feats. We went inside the hotel and took a room for two nights: we had had enough of pilgrimaging. The room cost $28 for the two of us—twice what our room in Belorado had cost. Leaning against the back wall of the elevator—this was a two-star hotel, so there was an elevator—we rode effortlessly to our third floor room. L-shaped, with two beds, a private bath, and a door which opened onto a patio on the roof—the room was spacious. When we stepped out onto the rooftop patio, we could see the Río Arlanzón, which winds through the city, and, across the river, the city gates and the towers of the cathedral, described in our guidebook as "floating lace pointing towards infinity."

It was only 4:00, but we were exhausted. Once again. As always. Not being tired was something I could only vaguely remember.

While Bill slept, I took a bath and washed clothes. The bath water was steaming hot, the tub was huge, the towels were large and fluffy—not quite as large as in Santo Domingo, but large enough. A change from the stiff, face-cloth-sized towels in Belorado. Unsuccessfully, I tried to soak the weariness from my body; unsuccessfully, I tried to generate energy with a shower massage. Afterwards, I carried a chair out to the rooftop terrace and sat, staring at the river and the rooftops.

I felt off-balance. Somehow, arriving in Burgos by car had left me unprepared to arrive. I had gotten used to getting places on foot, at a slow pace, savoring the expectation of arrival, the satisfying sense of achievement, the cessation of effort. This time, I felt like a tourist. It had been too easy—I hadn't suffered enough. At Santo Domingo I had revelled in the luxurious hotel, but here I felt self-indulgent—and unappreciative.

It wasn't just because we had hitchhiked—we had hitchhiked before: four kilometers to Puente la Reina, eight to Estella, sixteen to Nájera. But always before, we had hitchiked when we were near our goal or had needed to find a place to sleep. This time was different. We had driven in half an hour what would have—should have—taken two days to walk. I had missed 32 kilometers of the Camino. I would never know what they looked like, what they felt like.

I tried to write in my journal but I couldn't. Every moment on the Camino was filled with experience, intense awareness of my feet, my shoulders, the ground, the sun, hunger, pain, thirst, friendship, accomplishment, exhaustion. Now, I wanted to escape. I fell asleep.

Later that evening we went downstairs to the hotel restaurant. The dining room was filled with members of a French pilgrimage tour, organized by a French travel service called SIP that specialized in guided bus trips to major pilgrimage shrines throughout the world. Gaily, the tourist/pilgrims chatted away, probably exchanging impressions of sights they had seen through the bus windows as they drove rapidly down the highway. But just what could they have seen? Only those things large enough, or unusual enough, and big enough to be visible at 60 kilometers an hour. It was what they—and I—hadn't seen that mattered: people's faces, wild berries by the side of the road, a scallop shell carved on an abandoned building, pilgrims' crosses, the changing texture of the highway.

Hoping my gloom would be dispelled by a good dinner, I suggested we order the house specialties. Bill didn't want to and reminded me of the fried fish head in Nájera, but I was determined to have an adventure. After all, Bill didn't have to agree with me: I could order what I wanted, even if we were splitting expenses.

The waiter came, we ordered. Bill played safe, ordering the standard *entremeses variados* as a first course. I ordered *morcilla burgalesa,* recommended by the waiter. It came: steamy, moist slices of shiny black sausage.

Looking at the glistening slices, smelling the strong, pungent odor, Bill wondered what it was.

I looked it up in my pocket dictionary. "Blood sausage." I tried it, and it was delicious: spicy, peppery, almost chocolately rich.

Next, I ordered *cochinillo asado*—baked suckling pig—and Bill ordered *lechazo a la parrilla*—grilled baby lamb. The *cochinillo* came, a haunch of baby pig, golden, crisp skin stretched over tender, juicy white flesh. I had a momentary qualm at the sight of the tiny leg and thigh. For dessert we had fresh local cheese and flan. The flan was excellent: rich in egg yolks, creamy smooth, the brittle caramel coating just slightly bitter. A cognac followed, to settle my stomach—the *cochinillo* had been greasy—and Bill had a cigar and an espresso. After we were done, I asked Bill if he wanted to go for a walk.

"No, my ankle hurts." He looked at me. "That's a real admission, coming from me."

It was. Did it hurt more, or was he learning to acknowledge pain?

Although I could have gone for a walk alone, I didn't feel comfortable walking alone at night—not in the U.S., not in Burgos. So we both went into the lobby to sit for a while. On a table was a newspaper—*El País*, the liberal Spanish daily. It was the first newspaper we'd seen in over two weeks.

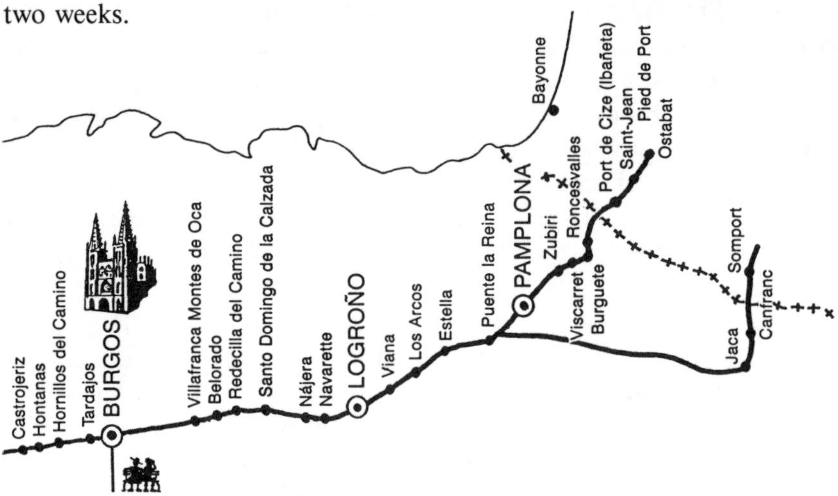

Day 20: July 29 A day of rest. We crossed the river to the thirteenth-century Gothic cathedral to get our pilgrimage cards stamped. Although it is constructed out of white limestone, somehow the builders managed to make the chiseled stone look like fragile lace; the delicate-

appearing, 276-foot-high twin towers are covered with statues, arabesques, and topped with elegant, open-work spires. Begun in 1221 as a replacement for an earlier, Romanesque cathedral, the impressive building was designed by Master Enrique, the same architect who built the Gothic cathedral at León.

The priest, like the priests in Logroño and Santo Domingo, was busy and officious. He asked no questions, made no conversation. Maybe the priest preferred pilgrims who go by bus. After all, they are more predictable, more routine. More controllable. Maybe the priests are more supportive of people whose motives they are sure of—and less supportive of those who were "doing their own thing" by walking the road. The canon in Roncesvalles had thought a lot of the young people on the road were just excursionists. And were we pilgrims? Was I a pilgrim? People were treating us like pilgrims.

When I began the pilgrimage, sometimes I felt like a voyeur—standing back, observing. But that had changed. The pilgrimage got more meaningful, more important, the longer I did it, the more I suffered. Montaigne wrote, "I know well what I am fleeing from but not what I am in search of." I didn't think I was fleeing from anything—but I was on a quest for self-knowledge, for understanding. Bill said his attitude had also changed, from feeling he shouldn't take advantage of pilgrimage traditions to feeling that of course he should—after all, he was a pilgrim.

The psychological explanation would be—at least in part—that it is like an initiation ritual: the more you suffer to join something, the more valuable it is to be a member of the group. But which group? I had nothing in common with those French bus tourists from the night before, or the group with the cross, or the bicyclists. Fellow *caminantes*? Perhaps.

Bill and I sat silently for a while, then Bill spoke. "It's not only my attitude towards the pilgrimage that's changed—so is my attitude to other things. I'm not pushing myself so much, anymore. And I'm more cooperative."

There had been changes in both of us. Bill was less controlling; I was more confident, more assertive.

We stopped talking, each thinking about the weeks we'd been traveling the road, becoming pilgrims. Then we got up and went into the cathedral.

In the Capilla del Santísimo Cristo, we saw the famous Cristo de Burgos, a thirteenth-century crucifix of Christ covered with buffalo skin and wearing a skirt for modesty. It is a highly realistic, full-size figure, its skin covered with bleeding wounds. Popular devotion says that it sweats blood and its beard grows. I found it overwhelmingly realistic and thoroughly dreadful.

Tetzal, who traveled to Spain with Leo of Rozmital between 1465-1467, described the figure with these words:

> No one knows whence it came. It is made neither of wood nor stone, and the body is composed like that of a dead man. Its hair and nails grow, and when one touches its limbs they move. When one grasps the skin it feels like a man's. It has a dreadful and solemn countenance.[14]

Richard Ford, the nineteenth-century English authority on travel in Spain, described it with a bit less awe.

> As a work of art it is admirable. . . . nor will the lace petticoat displease our fair readers.[15]

We found images of Santiago throughout the cathedral. In the Chapel of Santiago, we saw his image on the retablo and on the iron railings. In the choir, one of the carved walnut seats shows the appearance of the Virgen del Pilar to St. James. In the museum, there is a woodcarving of the saint. And in the Condestable Chapel, there is a figure of Santiago dressed in a carefully draped robe, holding a staff; on his head is a round-brimmed hat with the scallop shell.

On a column in the cloisters is carved a pilgrim's head: shaggy beard, vacant eyes, hair spread out around his craggy face, worn hat turned up at the brim. How many pilgrims had looked at that stony head and seen themselves? I remembered a verse from Shakespeare's *Hamlet*:

> How should I your true love know
> From another one?
> By his cockle hat and staff
> And his sandal shoon.

Not only Shakespeare was familiar with the standard pilgrimage attire and the scallop shell. The Elizabethan poet Sir Walter Raleigh described the costume in one of the stanzas of his poem, "The Passionate Man's Pilgrimage." But, typical of the times, he gives each part of the pilgrim's outfit spiritual significance:

> Give me my scallop shell of quiet;
>   My staff of faith to walk upon;
> My scrip of joy, immortal diet;
>   My bottle of salvation;
> My gown of glory (hope's true gage)
>   And then I'll take my pilgrimage.

Our pilgrimage attire was lacking in symbolic significance. We had chosen our clothes for comfort and, in my case, modesty. We didn't even wear the scallop shell as identification. I wished we had.

Not only Santiago and pilgrims are present in the cathedral; so is el Cid. Burgos was the home base of Rodrigo Díaz de Vivar, more commonly known as el Cid Campeador: el Cid, from the Arabic title *sidi* or lord; and Campeador, meaning surpassing in valor. In 1921 the remains of el Cid and his wife Jimena were buried under the 177-foot high, rosette-covered, star-ribbed dome of the cathedral. Their funerary stones are inlaid in the crossing pavement. In the Capilla del Corpus Christi, in the cloister, is a wooden chest el Cid left as security for a loan. According to the "Cantar del Mío Cid"—the "Song of My Cid"—el Cid needed to borrow money in a hurry in 1081 when he was exiled by Alfonso VI. Craftily, he filled an iron-bound chest with sand and used it as surety on a loan of 600 marks, pledging to the Jewish money lenders that it was full of gold. In St. Catherine's Chapel in the cloisters, one can see the marriage contract of el Cid and Jimena.

El Cid lived from about 1026 to 1099. Born in Vivar, 10 kilometers north of Burgos, he was of noble stock on his mother's side—his great-uncle, Nuño Alvarez, was an important figure in the court of Ferdinand I—and lesser, though noble and famous, stock on his father's side. As a child, he saw numerous battles; by the time he was twelve he had participated, with his father, in a successful campaign in Navarra. Raised with Ferdinand's eldest son, Sancho, Rodrigo received a liberal education; he learned to read and write, though his spelling was awful, to ride a horse, and to use arms. He also became knowledgeable in law and was called upon to settle disputes. Most important of all, he became a courageous and powerful warrior, Ensign—supreme commander of the army—of his boyhood companion Sancho, now King Sancho II of Castilla.[16]

Unfortunately for el Cid, Sancho II was treacherously killed—probably through the machinations of his sister, Doña Urraca—and succeeded on the Castilian throne by his brother, Alfonso VI of León. In 1079 el Cid was sent as ambassador by Alfonso VI to collect tribute from Motamid, ruler of Seville; he returned in glory. But his glory soon displeased Alfonso VI and his envious nobles, and by 1081 el Cid had fallen into the king's bad graces and was exiled. He became a mercenary leader, frequently serving such Muslim rulers as the king of Zaragoza. At the head of an army of 7,000 men, mostly Moors, he captured Valencia and ruled it independently from 1094-1099. In 1099 he was defeated at Cuenca by the Moors, and he died soon afterwards.

El Cid died just after the First Crusade, begun in 1096, a year after Pope Urban II made his rousing speech at Clermont; he died just before the *Codex* and the "Song of Roland" were written. His victories made him a national hero in Spain, and a major epic poem, the "Cantar del Mío Cid," written around 1180 to 1207, popularized his exploits.

According to some, el Cid was an unscrupulous mercenary leader. But according to others, the story of el Cid represents the drama between the upwardly mobile warrior-noble and the entrenched nobility.[17] El Cid, an *infanzón*—hidalgo—of Vivar, was noble by birth but not an aristocrat. A chivalrous, brave, daring leader of men, he was able to gain power and wealth through conquest and booty. And he was resented by the more "noble" nobles, of greater lineage—such as the Infantes of Carrión de los Condes, the Beni Gómez brothers Diego and Fernando González—who married el Cid's daughters and then mistreated them viciously. In the "Cantar del Mío Cid," el Cid is described as superior to the established aristocrats—an attractive role model for upwardly mobile warriors.

Although Santiago has been dead for almost 2,000 years, and el Cid for almost 900 years, they both were present in Burgos. A statue of el Cid presides over one of the bridges over the Río Arlanzón. At the west end of the Calle Fernán González—named, like our hotel, for the medieval hero—are the ruins of the ancient castle on the hill where el Cid and Jimena were married. Beneath the ruins, a stele and two obelisks mark the site of the Solar del Cid, supposedly his ancestral home.

Nor is Santiago confined to the cathedral. At the nearby Monasterio de las Huelgas Reales, there is a thirteenth-century figure of Santiago, with articulated arms. Called Santiago del Espaldarazo—of the Accolade—the figure was used to knight Ferdinand III, John I, and other kings of Castilla and León—so that they would not have to receive the accolade of knighthood from an inferior.

Leaving the cathedral, we strolled around town. There were a lot of monuments and statues to see in this town of 120,000 people, with its long and impressive history, headquarters for Franco's *Movimiento Nacional* from 1936 to 39. Alfonso III of León reconquered Burgos from the Arabs in 882; soon afterwards, the Castilian Count Diego Rodríguez Porcelos built a castle there—the ruined castle on the hill—and, using troops as settlers, repopulated Burgos. By 920 Burgos was already a city. With the help of Fernando I and Alfonso VI, it continued to develop.

Burgos was a major stop on the pilgrimage to Santiago, the meeting place of the Camino de Santiago from Puente la Reina and a road from the Basque country and Bayonne. In the Middle Ages there were over 32 hospices and *hospitales* in Burgos catering to pilgrims, and numerous churches and palaces and a castle. In addition there were a number of important monasteries and convents on the outskirts of Burgos, including the illustrious Monasterio de las Huelgas Reales and the Hospital del Rey, founded by Alfonso VIII, and la Cartuja de Miraflores.

We strolled around the old part of the city, looking in store windows. Centrally displayed in the window of one hat store was a black, broad-brimmed pilgrim's hat, complete with scallop shells, one of which was painted with the cross of Santiago. Bill was disgusted by the commercialism. I wondered who would buy it—a "real" pilgrim?

We ate lunch in a cafe advertising two local specialties: *olla podrida*—rotten pot—and *lentejas medievales*—medieval lentils. The *lentejas medievales* is a lentil soup, full of lentils, pork, vegetables, and sausage. The *olla podrida* is an ancestor of the Spanish *cocido,* a kind of all-purpose boiled meat stew composed of cabbage, beans, onions, garlic, ham, beef, *chorizo,* blood sausage, and so on. It is the subject of a scene in Cervantes' *Don Quixote.*

Sancho Panza, Don Quixote's squire, is appointed governor of an island. He sits down to eat and is presented with sumptuous plates of food, but all are taken away from him when his physician says they are dangerous to his health for one reason or another. At last Sancho suggests an *olla podrida* would be acceptable, since "it is a hodge-podge of many meats, surely I'm bound to light upon somewhat that'll be wholesome and toothsome." The doctor replies, "Olla podrida indeed! There is no dish in the world more injurious. Leave olla podrida to canons, college rectors, or lusty gluttons at country weddings: but never let them be seen on the tables of governors, where delicacy and daintiness should be the order of the day."[18]

After eating, we ambled slowly back to the hotel. It was hot. There are two common descriptions of the weather in Burgos: "Nine months of winter, three months of hell"; or, "Summer begins on St. James Day, July 25, and ends on Santa Ana's Day, July 26." Perhaps it would cool down later that night. Taking two chairs out to the patio, we sat outside for an hour, watching the sun set. Slowly, the lacy cathedral spires faded into grey shadows, then disappeared entirely in the night.

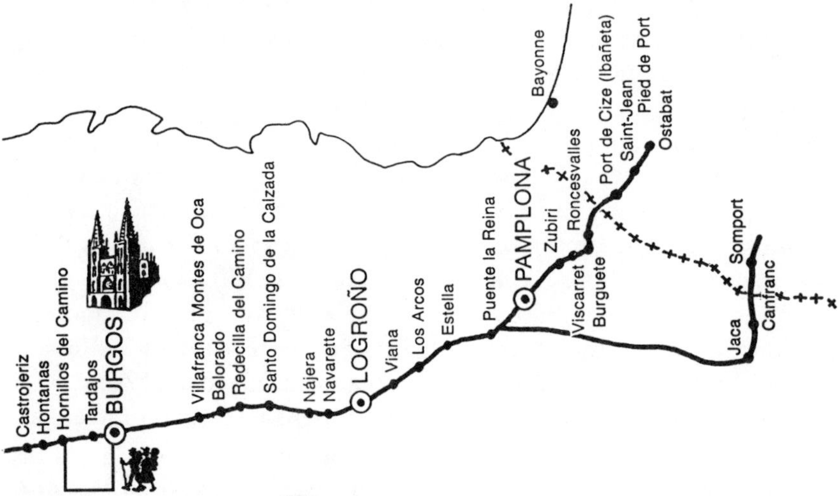

Day 21: July 30 The sixth stage of journey in the *Codex* is from Burgos to Frómista, a distance of 59 kilometers. Picaud's medieval pilgrims might have reached Frómista in a day, but we figured it would take us three.

We started walking out of Burgos on the highway—or, rather, on the highway shoulder. Athough a wide white line separated where we walked from where trucks and cars drove, it was not wide enough and it was only a line; traffic was heavy, forcing us off the road. Everyone was heading out of town on the only road there was, the highway Camino de Santiago. The early morning air was filled with exhaust fumes and dust, the oily smell of engines, the screech of brakes, the squeal of tires, the blare of radios. How I longed for the pine-scented mountain trails of the Pyrenees, the deserted highways of Navarra.

We noticed a number of French cars speeding by. There is a great deal of French tourism to Spain—just as in the Middle Ages. Then, it was pilgrims on foot; now, it is tourists in cars. Some still go to Santiago, but most cut across central Spain to Portugal, or, perhaps, to the southern beaches of the Costa del Sol. Frequently, the French tourists travel in caravans of four or five cars.

We made a game out of recognizing the different countries of origin of the cars whizzing by. Most of them had an oval sticker on the trunk which identified them: "E" for España, "F" for France, "GB" for Great Britain, "I" for Italy, "D" for Germany.

Although we had been walking for over half an hour, we were still in Burgos. On the left side of the road we saw a sign, "Monasterio de Las Huelgas Reales," and I suggested to Bill that we do some sightseeing: it would get us off the highway. He protested, but I pointed out that taking the detour would get us out of the heavy traffic. So we headed down the side street, following signs to the Monastery of Las Huelgas Reales.

Las Huelgas was a Cistercian nunnery founded by Alfonso VIII at the request of his wife Eleanor, daughter of Henry II of England. It was built between 1180 and 1230 on the site of a country residence of the Castilian kings; its name comes from the Spanish word *huelga*—rest or leisure. Las Huelgas was quite an exclusive convent, only ladies of the highest rank were admitted as nuns, and they were addressed not as "sisters" but as *señoras doñas.* The abbess had the title of princess, second only to the queen, and possessed power of life and death over between fifty-one and sixty-four manors. Cardinal Aldobrandini reportedly said, "If the Pope were to take a wife, he could not find a fitter one than the Abbess of Las Huelgas."

Schaseck, a traveling companion of Leo of Rozmital, described their visit to the nunnery in the mid-fifteenth century:

> In that nunnery are the most beautiful nuns which with their Superior are none of inferior birth, but of the highest rank, namely belonging to the families of the dukes, counts and knights of noble birth. They received my lord and his attendants most kindly, entertaining us with various delightful games such as dances and the like, and conducted us into the most delightful gardens planted with many trees and plants.[19]

Hamlet's suggestion to Ophelia, "Get thee to a nunnery!" takes on a different sense, given the luxurious life at Las Huelgas.

Las Huelgas was important to Castilian royalty in the Middle Ages: kings were knighted there by the articulated arm of the statue of Santiago; kings and queens were buried there. And it has continued to be politically important. It was in the monastery chapterhouse—the building where the monastic chapter convened—that General Franco assembled his government for the first time and the Falange swore loyalty to him.

In the impressive pantheon of kings, we saw numerous royal sarcofagi, some carved, some polychromed, including the tombs of Alfonso VIII and his wife Eleanor of England. Then we visited the chapterhouse to see the *pendón*—banner—of the Moorish king Miramamolin, taken at the Battle of Las Navas de Tolosa in 1212, the decisive battle at which Christian forces defeated the Moors. The pennant is actually the tent-flap of the Moorish king. Next, we toured the Romanesque cloister, which houses a museum displaying the jewelry, fabrics, court dress and regalia found in the tombs.

Leaving Las Huelgas, we walked over to the nearby Hospital del Rey, founded by Alfonso VIII to provide hospitality to poor pilgrims. We passed through the Gate of Romeros; carved on the walnut doors of the Hospital del Rey is a powerful relief: pilgrims marching to Compostela, guided by Santiago himself. San Miguel is using his lance to hold open the jaws of a dragon; a friar is imploring protection for the pilgrims; a family of pilgrims walk behind: the mother, nursing an infant, the father, helping another son, wearied from the pilgrimage. Hats, shells, calabashes, walking staffs—all of the accoutrements of pilgrims to Santiago are carved on the doors. In the sixteenth century, the Hospital del Rey had confessors who spoke all languages, in order to serve the many pilgrims going to Santiago. Until the nineteenth century, it continued to provide aid to pilgrims. Now it is partially in ruins.

After we left the Hospital del Rey, we rejoined the highway and again dodged traffic and breathed exhaust fumes. When we saw a rough gravel path ten meters to the side of the road, we walked on that instead. Soon that disappeared and we were walking on the side of dirt and gravel mounds made out of road fill.

Six kilometers from Burgos we reached Tardajos, a town that had existed in Roman times. We stopped at a pharmacy to replenish the stomach pills Alan had given me in France; unfortunately, there was nothing like them in Spain. The pharmacist suggested another pill. I was surprised I didn't need a prescription, but apparently many drugs are available in Spain without one. While the pharmacist located a box of the pills, Bill and I chatted with his wife.

Noting our backpacks, she started to tell us about other pilgrims she had seen: a group of 125 French pilgrims that had walked by a few days ago, accompanied by a physician; the group of thirty or more from Barcelona; and, just that morning, four pilgrims dressed in long brown capes, carrying pilgrim's staffs. Some pilgrims not only walked the "authentic" Camino but dressed "authentically" as well. The woman told us that it was here, in Tardajos, that the authentic Camino de Santiago separated from the highway, and she urged us to be sure to take the left fork outside of town.

Just outside of town, a shepherd pointed out the way to the Camino de Santiago, telling us to watch for yellow arrows painted on the side of the road. Suddenly, the day turned grey and overcast. We walked on a stony road through hilly fields dotted with small, solitary, twisted trees. After half an hour, we met another shepherd, standing near his flock of sheep.

He had on a black beret, a leather cape polished with wear, faded and patched pants, and scuffed black shoes. His skin was as leathery as his cape, red and wrinkled from the years spent out under the sun, spider-veined from drinking too much wine. He offered us a drink from the leather winebag, called a *bota,* he had slung over his shoulder. He tilted the kidney-shaped leather bag up and aimed the spout at his mouth, squeezed, and swallowed. Bill tried to mimic him and succeeded; I tried but forgot to swallow—I choked, and wine spilled down my chin. We all laughed. Then Bill offered him a cigarette, which he took and lit. Watching clouds darken overhead, we stood there by the side of the road.

The shepherd asked, "Where do you come from?"

"Burgos."

"No—where do you come from?"

"The U.S."

"Ah—Americanos!" He took another puff on his cigarette. "How much does this pilgrimage cost you? It must be expensive!"

Bill explained, "We have to eat at home, anyway, and walking is free."

The shepherd nodded, then looked away. "This is a difficult road. Be sure and follow the yellow arrows."

Bill asked, "How far do you think we can get today?"

"Probably to Hornillos del Camino. Stop in Hornillos and ask the monks or the priest for a place to stay." He nodded and walked off.

Soon it started to rain, a grey, steady downpour. But this time we didn't run for shelter—we just put on our rain ponchos and kept walking through the drizzle.

Outside Tardajos, a pilgrim encounters a flock of sheep. Soon it started to rain, and the Camino turned into a mucky trail of mud. We carried much of it with us as we slogged over the hills to Rabé de las Calzadas.

The road got bad, rapidly. Soon there was only a newly bulldozed gash in the hills. Of course, the rain didn't help, since it turned the earthen trail into mud. Dirty water filled the ruts in the mud, turning it into glue. Slogging along, we stopped frequently to scrape the accumulated muck off our shoes. This must have been what infantry soldiers had to endure. I wondered which was better—or worse: soaking wet jogging shoes or soaking wet leather boots.

It was only 1.5 kilometers from Tardajos to Rabé de las Calzadas but it took us two hours to get there. The "Calzadas" in Rabé de las Calzadas meant it was a town on the traditional *calzada* or road. But we were not following any *calzada*, we were walking in a muddy slash up the side of the hill.

There is a popular saying: "From Rabé to Tardajos you will not lack work; from Tardajos to Rabé, free us, Lord." But it got even worse after Rabé. We had to climb a path up to the top of a *meseta*—a plateau—and the rain had made the clay soil slippery and clingy at the same time. We kept on slogging. Finally the rain stopped, and we reached the top of the *meseta* and looked down. There below us in a wide golden valley was Hornillos del Camino. We slipped and slid down the rain-slicked path towards the bottom of the hill and the road to Hornillos. It was about 7:30 at night.

A single unpaved road wound through the village. "Authentic" camino? Tired, muddy, thirsty, we stumbled through the town. Groups of black-dressed women seated in chairs on the sidewalks were knitting and making lace. At their backs were grey houses, made of rough stone blocks, with deeply set-in windows and doors. Each house was joined to the ones next to it at the side walls, forming an unbroken line on either side of the street. On some of the houses, the second floor hung over the first a few feet, perhaps to provide some shade; dark timbers showed under the overhang. I could imagine that in the Middle Ages pilgrims walked through Hornillos on the same dirt path, seeing just what we were seeing. As we walked by, people came out of their houses to look at us—but avoided looking at us directly.

Bill said, "I think they're hostile."

"Bill, there you go again! I think they're just curious—and shy."

We stopped at the church but it was closed. Nobody spoke to us, so we kept walking down the only street, the Camino de Santiago, until we were near the edge of town. I saw a sign, "Club," on the right, but no sign of a bar. Then I saw a group of older people dressed, as usual, in black, standing nearby.

Going up to them, I said, "Excuse me, is there a bar or cafe in town?"

They conveyed the idea, "No, go somewhere else," and turned away.

We walked on, trying to figure out what they had said. On a hunch, I turned back to look at them. They were watching us, and one man made the gesture of drinking from a *bota* and pointed at Bill and I nodded and he pointed to the club and I nodded again and he talked with another man and they gestured to us to go with them.

Bill said, "What was that all about?"

"A bit of 'male solidarity,' I think—they realized you, a fellow male, need a drink!"

The two men took us to the club and unlocked it. It was a large room with half a dozen wooden tables and a number of chairs; apparently, it was the town social club. Going up to a well-stocked bar, one of the men asked what we wanted to drink. We both ordered Cokes, which clearly surprised them: they had thought Bill wanted wine. But, with a puzzled smile, one of them took two warm bottles of Coke out of a crate, opened them, and gave them to us. We drank them quickly and asked for two more.

While we drank our Cokes, they told us they had seen other pilgrims—the group of thirty, the four in costume. They commented on our backpacks, which we had dropped heavily to the floor beside the barstools. Playfully, one of them tried to lift mine and, surprised by the weight, dropped it on the floor. We all laughed. They told us about people getting lost and about yellow arrows someone had been painting to mark the route.

Out of curiosity, I asked, "Who do you think is marking the road?"

Looking at Bill, one of them replied, "Maybe someone from the Ministry of Tourism and Information."

Bill asked them, "How far is it to the nearest fonda?"

"Eleven kilometers, to Hontanas. It's over the mountains."

Over the mountains. Dismally, Bill and I looked at each other. We'd already walked 20 kilometers through the mud. To reach Hontanas would take us three hours or more.

After they had talked with Bill awhile, one of them asked, "Where do you plan to spend the night?"

Bill asked, "Is there somewhere we could stay in Hornillos?"

They talked to each other, then one of them said, "Ask the mayor if you can stay in the *sala.* Go look for Maríalupe."

We thanked them, finished our Cokes, and went to find the mayor. At last, traditional hospitality—but a female mayor?

We walked back down the street, past the same group of older people. We asked them for Maríalupe and they pointed down the road. Soon we came to a group of young women, gaily dressed in flounced red or yellow or white skirts, t-shirts, and black high heels. Even in the villages, the girls dressed up. I asked for Maríalupe.

"I am she," replied a dark-haired girl dressed in a full red skirt and white blouse.

"You're the mayor?"

She laughed. "Of course not! I'm the mayor's daughter!"

After we explained that we needed a place to stay, she said we could stay in the *sala,* a small cement building next to the church. She went to find the key and returned.

"Just lock it in the morning and bring me back the key."

The one-room building was unpainted but clean. There was one bare electric light dangling from a cord. Old maps of the province were taped to the walls; there were several shelves of dusty old books and town records and two long wooden tables and eight wooden chairs, scattered around the room.

Soon after we had spread our sleeping bags on the cement floor we heard blaring music, and a truck drove up in front of the church. We went outside to see what was happening. Summoned by the loud music, women carrying mesh bags were coming from all over the village. The open back of the truck was filled with crates of fruits and vegetables: this was how the villagers shopped during the week. I waited patiently in line, which was a mistake. There was no line. There was only the loudest, most insistent voice. At last, someone helped me and I pointed at the oranges and plums I wanted.

That night, we sat on the steps outside our cement hotel room, eating fresh plums, looking at the clear night sky, tracing the path of the Milky Way. This was the first time we had taken advantage of the traditions of the Camino. It had been relatively easy—once people had decided to be helpful. I wondered why the mayor was in charge of helping pilgrims. Perhaps it was because small towns no longer have priests. I wondered if we had asked for the mayor in Lorca or Ciraqui, would we have been given a place to stay? Somehow, I doubted it. In Navarra, people didn't seem as helpful.

Maybe in Hornillos the traditions of the Camino were stronger—perhaps because of isolation, perhaps because no one but pilgrims would walk down that road. But even so, we had almost left town before anyone offered to help. According to Bill, people were hostile when we first walked into town. Perhaps they were cautious, not hostile.

We finished eating our fruit, washed our hands in the round cement fountain in front of the *sala,* and went inside our room and locked the door.

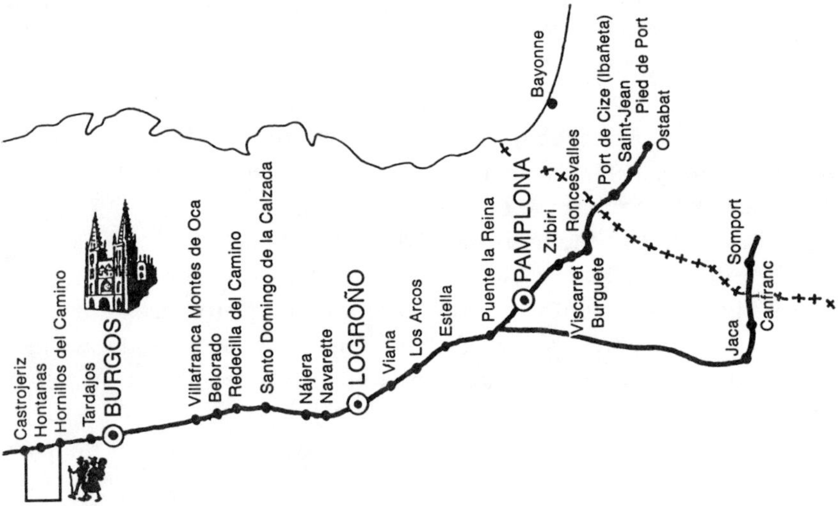

Day 22: July 31 We woke up terribly stiff and sore from sleeping on the cold cement floor. It would have been more comfortable to sleep on the ground.

We repacked our backpacks, washed at the fountain, and started off, hoping to reach Castrojeriz, 18 kilometers away, by evening. We walked out of town and up a narrow gravel cart track and then down an arroyo and up to the top of a huge *meseta.* The countryside was dry and deserted, filled with abandoned buildings and collapsed stone corrals. We tried to follow the yellow arrows, but found none. In the distance, we could hear combines.

Soon we were lost, surrounded by rolling hills covered with grain. Following a narrow path over the plateau, we passed slumping piles of stone, the remains of someone's home, of a village. We saw an endless vista of blue sky, golden fields, grey stone ruins. We heard machine noises, wheat blowing in the breeze, birds chirping, but no voices. For an hour, we wandered aimlessly from one ruin to another, looking for a way off the plateau.

In the distance, we saw a large building with a TV antenna sticking up from the top. We walked over to it and found it was on the edge of the plateau: below us, far below, there was a small village with a number of large churches. Carefully, we climbed down the steep, stepped path to the town below. Once in town, we walked over to some young girls jumping rope in a plaza.

"Where are we?"

"Iglesias."

We were in a town called Churches. According to the map, we had wandered three kilometers out of our way.

I asked the girls, "Is there a cafe?"

One girl, blonde, about eight years old, nodded yes, and they all took us over to a bar. Telling us to wait, she went next door and came back with a young woman—about fifteen—who opened up the bar and made coffee for us.

Refreshed, we started out of town. A tiny, wrinkled old woman, dressed in black—black scarf on her head, black felt slippers on her feet—offered to show us the way. Under one arm, she carried an enormous round loaf of bread. She chatted with us as we walked up the steep path. Soon we were winded, but she wasn't even breathing hard.

"Vale la pena. It's worthwhile to make a pilgrimage—but it costs women more, doesn't it? But it has more value that way!"

At the edge of town, near the cemetery, she stopped and gave us directions for a shortcut: we were to turn right at an abandoned hermitage on top of the *meseta.*

Soon we were lost again. So much for the straight and narrow path. One abandoned building looked like another to us. I had thought it difficult to follow directions in Estella, with its twisting medieval streets; how much more difficult it was in the country. Obviously, the old woman knew which ruined building she meant—but we did not.

We walked on and on under the hot sun, through burnished fields. In the distance we could hear the sound of combines, but we saw no one. We wandered from one clump of ruins to another. It felt as if we would spend the rest of our lives wandering through yellow fields, past crumbling ruins—and someday pilgrims would stumble on our bones and raise a cross to commemorate our deaths. I tried to console myself: dying while on a pilgrimage is supposed to mean immediate access to heaven—but, unfortunately, I was not a believer.

At last, far away, we saw some people and started to walk towards them. We heard a voice calling us from a distant hill. We stopped. In the distance, we saw tiny black shapes and a red combine; two of the figures started running down the hillside and up to our hillside. Very quickly, they got closer—a young man in blue jeans accompanied by a shaggy brown dog.

Not even breathing hard, the man asked, "Are you going to Santiago?" We nodded yes. "Don't go that way—people have been getting lost that way! It happened yesterday, too. Someone in Iglesias must be giving them bad directions." He would show us the way.

While we walked, he asked us questions. Where were we from? Where had we stayed the night before? We told him, in the *sala* of the town hall in Hornillos.

He nodded: "They keep the custom of providing hospitality there—they are 'of the Camino.'" He went on to say that many places used to, but that times had changed and many villages no longer followed the old customs.

"Have you seen many pilgrims?"

He'd seen a number, including the thirty or so with the cross, and a group of four on horseback, and a number of French women. In his opinion, as many women walked as men. We were surprised since we had seen very few women: maybe he just noticed the women more.

At the edge of the plateau, near an abandoned building, he stopped. We were back on *the* Camino, though it looked like any other path to us. Since he had to get back to work, we said goodbye. Before he left, I asked him his name.

"Santiago."

After he left, we continued down the path to Hontanos. Our path went downhill through a desolate, stony countryside. We rested in the shade of some large boulders, then followed the trail. Just before Hontanos, it turned into a narrow path flanked by high stone walls, then buildings. Exhausted, we asked a woman standing in a doorway if there were a place to buy a Coke. Her little daughter took us to a nearby house, and the woman there sent her daughter to open up the club for us. While we drank warm Cokes, we asked the girl if there were a bus to Castrojeriz, but she said there was none. So we rested a bit longer, then we picked up our packs and started off again.

As we walked through town, several people directed us to the "real" Camino; we thanked them for their advice but planned to ignore it. Half a kilometer from Hontanos we sat down in the shade of a large tree and ate some cheese and bread. We had eight kilometers to go to Castrojeriz.

We followed a tree-lined country road through a narrow valley. Although the highway surface was old and pebbly, hard on our feet, at least we knew where it was leading us. Still, we were tired—from the heat, the sun, the exertion, the extra kilometers, the anxiety of getting lost. We still had five kilometers to walk when a pickup truck came by and Bill stuck out his thumb.

"Bill—you want to hitch a ride?"

"Well, Ellen, I'm learning to be flexible. Besides, if you count all the extra miles we've walked today—we've covered more than our quota of 'real' camino!"

The truck driver was a tiny man, wearing faded blue work clothes and a black beret. A hand-rolled cigarette stuck to the edge of his lips. As he drove, he pointed out the "real" Camino for us, differentiating it from the highway. He told us lots of people had gotten lost that year in the hills—the road was badly marked. Then he told us stories of the Camino, stories he had learned from a lost pilgrim from Burgos, stories he had read. Although he had never been to Santiago, he loved to talk about it. Someday he would go, when he had time and money.

There was a cluster of ruins in front of us, and the road passed through the middle of a beige stone Gothic arch. Jorge stopped the truck so that we could see the ruins of the once-great Convent of San Antón. Most of the buildings are from the fourteenth century, but it was founded by Alfonso VII in 1146 under the rule of the Order of the Antonians, an order which was suppressed in 1791. The priests of San Antón were supposed to have the power to cure the "sacred fire" or "San Antón's fire," an illness that appeared in the tenth century in Europe. Now all that remained were scattered stones, pieces of walls, walls without ceilings, doorways without doors, an archway through which a highway passed.

In the distance, winding up the side of a hill, was Castrojeriz. On top of the barren, earth-colored hill were the crumbling earth-colored ruins of an eighth-century castle. Castrojeriz itself was a mixture of white and adobe buildings, with red tile roofs. Just outside of town, our truck driver drove off of the highway onto a narrow road leading towards a church.

"This is the 'real' Camino de Santiago," our truck driver said. "You should enter town on the 'real' Camino, not the highway!"

He was more concerned about authenticity than we were, at this point, but we thanked him anyway. He dropped us off at Our Lady of Manzano, a national monument. Santa María del Manzano originated in the ninth century, though much of it was built in the thirteen century. Alfonso X, el Sabio, in his famous *Cantigas,* ascribed many miracles to the statue of the Virgin in this church. But we didn't want to see it, however famous it was; we just wanted to find a place to stay for the night. We followed the Calle de los Romeros—the Street of the Pilgrims—through town, looking for a lodging sign. People were helpful and told us to ask in a nearby bar.

We went in and asked the teenaged barkeeper for a room; he said we had to ask his mother and he went to get her. A heavy-set woman in a print dress, she came into the bar and looked at us. Was this a screening

The modern Camino passes under the arches of the fourteenth-century convent of San Antón. A loquacious truck driver (truck in background) gave us a lift and regaled us with pilgrimage stories; on the way, he insisted on stopping at the ruined convent. Note the elaborate doorway on the left.

process? If so, we passed it. She took us to an unmarked fonda across the street and gave us two keys, one for the front door and one for our room. Was it a fonda or a private house? It didn't matter: we were grateful just to be able to rest and to wash in a bathroom with running water. We dumped our packs on the floor and collapsed. After a few minutes I went to take a bath, hoping there would be hot water. There was no hot water. There was no water at all. Except in the toilet, which flushed. I went over to the bar and asked the owner about the lack of water. According to her, there was a drought in the area. Maybe later there would be water. I told myself: last night, I didn't even have a toilet—or a bathroom—or a bed.

I ordered an espresso and sat down to write in my journal.

"Today and yesterday felt truly 'pilgrimy.' Getting lost in the hills, drinking wine with the shepherds, sleeping on the floor of the cement *sala.* And walking, walking, walking, asking directions, getting lost, having help come when we needed it—the old woman guiding us out of Iglesias, Santiago—himself?—appearing out of nowhere and running over the hills to put us on the right road, the truck driver with his scenic tour.

"I had forgotten the pain for a few days, but today I remembered. After sleeping on a hard floor, walking all day up and down and up and down stony paths and rocky trails—I ache all over. It's not a hike, it's a pilgrimage—so there must be some purpose to this pain.

"I'm still driven by curiosity and by a desire to test my limits. But testing limits is a static idea, as if limits stayed in one place, like geographical boundaries. I've expanded my limits, strengthened myself, become more courageous, more sure of myself, less reliant on Bill. And he's changed, too.

"I still don't have a religious motive, though I have seen repeatedly what faith can do—the churches, the monasteries, the hospices built for pilgrims. Mine is an inward pilgrimage, a private quest—not fulfilling a vow to some deity, not requesting a boon from some God.

"I am learning about the importance of the 'real' Camino to people who help along the way. They tell us we have to walk the real, authentic road. They say it's shorter but it's not. They send us on our way—our authentic way—and we get lost. A metaphor for life? The difficulties in finding one's way? Life is full of detours, wrong turns, dead ends, but you keep on going, anyway. What would help is a good map—or a trustworthy guide.

"I am reminded of other images of 'the road': Frost's poem about

'The road less taken.' Tom Paxton's song, 'I Can't Help But Wonder Where I'm Bound.' Kerouac's *On the Road.* Steinbeck's *Travels with Charlie. Pilgrim's Progress.* Lagerkvist's *Pilgrim at Sea. Perceval.* The *Book of Jonah.* Gypsies, hippies, vagabonds, migrant laborers, Mexican wetbacks, homeless heroes, drifters, wandering saints, skeptical graduate students—pilgrims, pilgrims all."

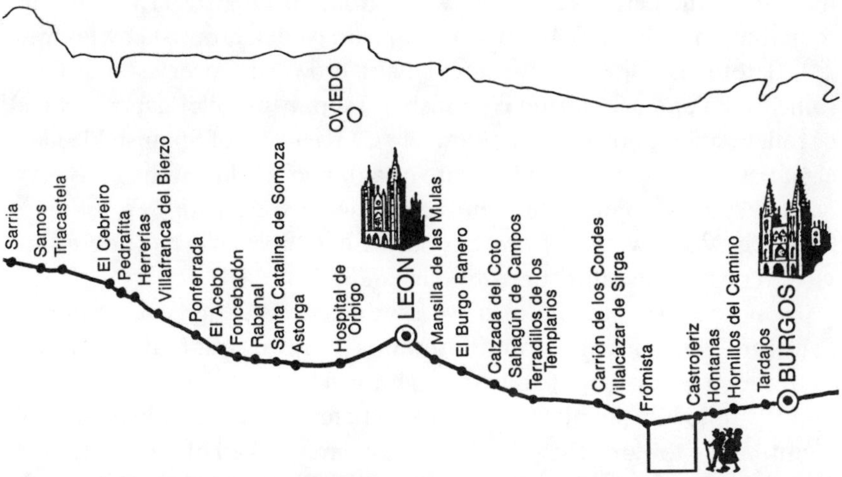

Day 23: August 1 We slept well—the mattresses were new, still firm—got up, and tried again to bathe. Still no water. Bill thought either the water was not even connected or else the owner was saving money by turning it off.

We ate breakfast in the bar. A middle-aged woman sitting next to us looked at our packs and shook her head. "What a sacrifice!"

Her companion, another middle-aged woman, asked us, "Are you Catholic?"

Bill said yes, I said no.

Looking at me, she said, "It has more merit if you're Catholic—maybe you should convert!"

I replied, "Well, who knows!"

She continued, "I, for one, am a free thinker!"

Her companion said, "It costs women more."

The owner had been listening and she added, "There's a doctor in his 50s who's already walked the Camino twice this year!"

Another legend of the Camino? Or someone doing a lot of penance?

We finished our breakfast of coffee with milk and bread with jam and paid the bill. As we left, the landlady called after us: "Going to Frómista?"

We nodded. Hopefully, we would reach Frómista, twenty kilometers away, by early evening.

"Don't take the highway. Take the Camino de Santiago—it's shorter and easier. Besides, it's authentic. Just follow the path over the hill over there, past the hermitage. There was a group of pilgrims last week who went that way. They left here at 6 a.m. and arrived in Frómista by 1 p.m."

Before leaving town, we stopped at a crowded grocery store to buy some bread and cheese and replenish my supply of toilet paper. Instead of toilet paper, I bought several travel-size packages of Spanish kleenex: each tissue was the size and texture of a dinner napkin. When they saw our backpacks, some of the other customers asked if we were going to Santiago, where we were from, how far we had traveled. They offered advice, repeating the directions of our landlady.

On the way out of town we saw a highway sign, "Camino de Santiago," with an arrow pointing towards the town. Was that the authentic route, a block-long detour through town?

We followed the highway for a kilometer or so, then took a narrow country lane towards the Cuesta de Mostelares—the Hill of Mostelares. According to the guidebook, this was both the traditional Camino de Santiago and a shortcut to Frómista. The countryside was flat, the only shade an occasional clump of black poplars. After crossing the Río Odrilla, we started to climb up the *meseta* which separates the valley of the Río Odrilla from that of the Río Pisuerga. It was a prolonged ascent of several kilometers on a rocky path. At one point, our route wound around to the top of the *cuesta*; the path was badly eroded, and we slipped on the loose, chalk-grey stones and gravel. At the top we stopped, exhausted.

Bill said, "Whoever figures this is the easy way must never have walked it!"

"Not only that, but the distances in the guidebook have nothing to do with topography—they don't take into account going up this hill and back down!"

"I read somewhere that Roman soldiers paid no attention to hills—they were so well trained."

"We're not Roman soldiers."

We had stopped near a wooden cross at the top of the hill and, after recovering from the exertion of the climb, we went over to look at it. There was a scallop shell on the crossbar. Did it mark the authentic Camino—or a dead pilgrim?

Shouldering our backpacks again, we walked over to the other side of the hill, passing two more crosses. An immense panorama spread out before us: a deep, broad valley, the Río Pisuerga lined with trees, patches of gold and brown fields, clumps of dark green trees, a few hills, distant, flat-topped *mesetas*—the vista stretched on and on. Frómista was not in sight.

Trying not to slide, we picked our way down the side of the hill. At the bottom, the path petered out, but at last we found a trail and followed it through the fields until we reached the Fuente de Piojo, a cement trough filled with water and marked with the yellow cross of Roncesvalles.

Left or right? There were no markings. Why did our yellow arrows fail us when we needed them most? There we were, trying to follow the straight and narrow path, the "real" Camino, the right road—and we didn't know which way to turn. We arbitrarily started off to the left and walked for a kilometer, looking for the ruins of a hermitage. Nothing. We kept walking. The tree-lined Río Pisuerga, the same river we had seen from the *cuesta*, was to the right of us, and Bill suggested we just try to cut across it. I refused; I didn't think that would get us anywhere.

Finally I saw a man working in a field and, dropping my backpack on the road, I cut across the thistle and weed filled field to ask for directions.

"Excuse me, but where is the Camino de Santiago?"

Looking up from his work, he looked at me, then looked back at his work. I tried again.

"We're lost. Can you tell us the way to Frómista?"

He looked up, gestured back the way we had come, looked down again.

I walked back across the field, legs covered with welts from the thistles. Bill looked at me, questioningly, and I pointed back where we had come from.

Annoyed at getting lost, annoyed at wasted kilometers, we retraced our steps. Yesterday when we had gotten lost, we had been anxious; today, it was just an annoyance: uncomfortable, but neither dangerous nor disastrous.

At last we picked up the road again, twenty meters from where we had turned left instead of right, and followed it to the river, passing close to Itero del Castillo, with its ruined medieval tower. The tower had been built by 934 to guard the frontier between the Moors and the kingdom of León. We crossed over the Río Pisuerga on a stone bridge raised by Alfonso VI. The bridge is the Pons Fiteria mentioned in the *Codex;* 800 years later, pilgrims can still walk over its eleven arches to cross from the province of Burgos to the province of Palencia. In the Middle Ages, there was a hospice and a monastery next to the bridge to shelter pilgrims. Today there was not even a roadsign.

We were entering the "Campos góticos," flat expanses of golden fields, rich in grain, poor in water. Walking slowly down the road, we passed quickly through Itero de la Vega, a town of some 400 inhabitants, and on to Boadilla del Camino, an even smaller town of some 300 inhabitants. Outside of Boadilla we passed some dug-out caves in the side of a small ridge. There were doors in front of them and ventilating pipes on top of them; villagers make—or store—wine in these *bodegas.* One was open, and we could see narrow stairs leading down into darkness. Dug down into the hillside, the *bodegas* are cool in summer and warm in winter. Some of them, I knew, had large, well-furnished rooms, and the owners—a family, a group of friends—hold parties in them.

The guidebook mentioned an important fifteenth-century *rollo gôtico* in Boadilla and we found it: a large, elaborately carved stone pillar ornamented with scallop shells. According to the guidebook, it had been associated with some judicial process. The wind began to blow and it started to pour, so we ran for shelter to a nearby bar, fleeing past whitewashed adobe houses, each attached to the one next to it.

The bar was long, narrow, smoky, full of people taking shelter from the rain. We found an empty table, sat down, dropped our packs on the floor. Everyone was talking, playing cards, eating, drinking. Nobody talked to us. Bill got us two ice cream cones and two Cokes, and we ate and drank, listening to the rain beating against the windows.

That morning, when we left Castrojeriz, I had hoped to reach Frómista for the night and stay at the Hostería de los Palmeros. The inn was a sixteenth-century—or earlier—pilgrimage hospice, converted to a modern hotel. I had looked forward to sleeping in the same room as pilgrims had slept in for centuries. But now it was pouring, and we had five more kilometers to go. Bill and I discussed what to do. Since Boadilla did not seem very welcoming, we decided, rain or no rain, to walk on. Although we had walked approximately twenty kilometers already, it was still early and we felt as if we could walk five more to Frómista. We put on our rain ponchos, hoisted up our packs, and walked out into the rain.

A man came running out of the bar after us.

"Peregrinos a Santiago?"

Gesturing with one hand, he pointed out the "real" Camino de Santiago and gave us specific instructions: follow the yellow arrows, turn left at the Canal de Castilla, an irrigation canal, and follow it to Frómista. After waving goodbye, we walked in the direction he had pointed out. As usual, the yellow arrows failed at a crucial juncture, but this time it didn't matter; we followed our guide's directions and turned left.

It poured. The wind lashed the rain to a 45-degree angle; it whipped our ponchos around our legs, making it hard to walk. My shoes squished with every step, Bill's boots squeaked. But the rain was warm, so it was like walking in a shower with a massage head at full power. Our visibility was quite limited, however, so it helped that the large cement irrigation canal was easy to see, despite the heavy rain.

At last, after 8 p.m., we arrived in Frómista, end of the sixth stage of journey in the *Codex*. We had walked further than ever before: twenty-five kilometers. Ready to collapse and enjoy a well-deserved rest, we followed signs to the pilgrims' inn. We walked up to the Hostería de los Palmeros, a white stucco building in the arcaded plaza. It was named after the pilgrims to Jerusalem, called *palmeros* after the palm fronds associated with the city. Eagerly, we went into the open door under the columned porch and asked the first clerk we saw for a room.

"No room."

"No room?"

"No. Go to the Casa de Peregrinos."

I said, "But we have money!"

He looked at me, brushed by. "No room."

Bill and I went outside.

"Ellen, I'm sure it's because of the way we look. They don't want us ruining the tone of the place!"

I was tired, disappointed. "I can't believe it—it says it is an inn for pilgrims—well, we're pilgrims!"

"Maybe they want pilgrims to stay somewhere else and let tourists stay here."

Drenched and forlorn, we sat on a wooden bench under the arcade. Passersby looked at us out of the corner of their eyes. No one spoke to us, no one offered to help. I was beginning to share Bill's opinion—we weren't wanted. What was that bumper sticker: "You're not paranoid: they really are out to get you!"

Once it stopped raining, Bill crossed the puddle-filled plaza and went to find a place for us to stay. An hour later he returned, frustrated.

"I've tried five different hostels. No luck in any of them! Everyone I ask tells me to go somewhere else. This place must really have it in for pilgrims!"

"The clerk in the inn suggested we go to the Casa de Peregrinos. We'd better find out about that."

"I can't believe it! I've seen posters all over this town advertising the Camino de Santiago—and here we are, pilgrims on the Camino—and we can't find a place to stay!"

An elderly man walked by, and I asked him if he knew of a place to stay. He said we should ask the priest or the mayor. So we went to the parish office and looked for the priest, but no one was there. A neighbor heard us knocking and came out; she told us the priest had gone out for the day. So we went back to the plaza and asked a passerby if he knew where the mayor was, and he said he was out of town. Then a woman who had overheard stopped and told us the mayor was standing with the group of men on the corner across the street. So we went up to them and asked for the mayor.

"I'm the mayor." He was an attractive middle-aged man, dressed in sharply pressed grey pants and a white shirt, wearing well-shined shoes, despite the mud.

Almost in tears, I said, "We need a place to stay for the night."

He smiled, reassuringly. "Do you have sleeping bags?" We nodded. "Good. You can stay in the Casa de Peregrinos."

Bill asked, "What's that?"

"It's a school teacher's apartment that we have kept vacant this year for pilgrims. It's a nice place—there is no furniture, but there is a bathroom and a kitchen."

It sounded good.

"I have to get the key for you. The priest has a key, but he is out of town. Wait here and I'll come back soon."

So we took off our packs and sat down on another bench against a wall in the plaza. Soon we were surrounded by half a dozen young kids who wanted to practice English with us. Just a short while before we had been avoided, but now we were the center of attention. After a half an hour, the mayor returned with a teenaged girl who had the key and would take us to the apartment.

Before we left, I asked the mayor, "Is it true that the hostels are all full?"

He looked surprised. "Of course it is. Why?"

"Well, we were beginning to think it was because we were pilgrims."

He shook his head. "No, no. It's not like that. In the summer, many people return home for the holidays to visit their families. And this is a popular spot for car tourists on the Camino de Santiago. So, frequently, all the hostels are full. That's all."

Bill still looked doubtful.

The Casa de Peregrinos had no furniture, no electricity, and the sink in the kitchen was broken. But the toilet worked. I wanted to take a shower but there was no hot water. Oh, for hot water and a bath. I was exhausted, freezing, wet. And hungry. So we dried off, changed clothes, and went back to the Hostería de los Palmeros to eat dinner. It was 10 p.m. At least they couldn't claim there's no room in the restaurant.

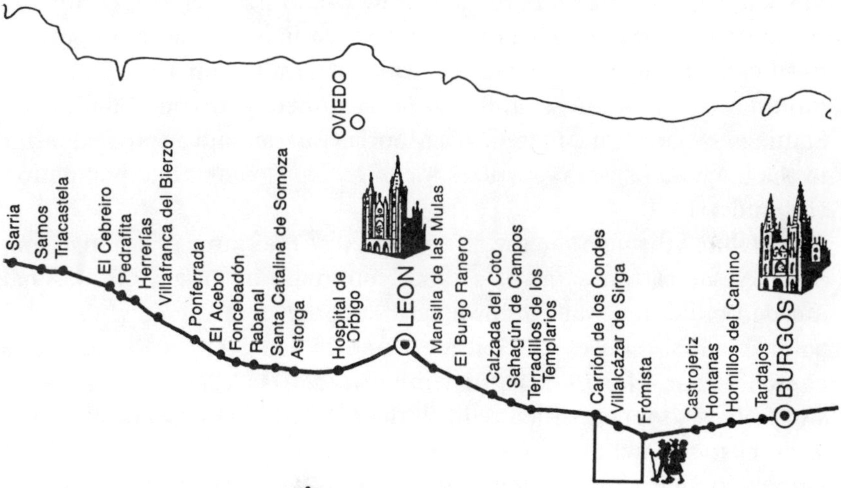

Day 24: August 2

Although we had planned to spend a day in Frómista resting, the reception we had received was not very friendly. We wanted to leave, but we were too tired to walk. So we tried to find out about a bus. There was no bus. In Spain buses don't work on the same system as in the U.S., where a single busline travels across the continent. Here, it seemed, there was a patchwork of local or regional bus service, geared to commuting to work. Nor was Frómista on the train line.

Bill suggested we rent a taxi. Near the plaza there was a taxi stand, and there was a car with a taxi insignia parked in front. Bill asked for the driver in a nearby bar, and they directed him to a nearby adobe house. A woman answered our knock and said she would take us on a "guided tour" to Carrión de los Condes, a distance of 20 kilometers, for $8.00. Relieved at the relatively low cost and her availability, we agreed to meet her at noon in front of the taxi.

We went to the tourist office to get our cards stamped, but it was closed, so we went to the Town Hall—several rooms on the second floor of a building in the plaza. The mayor was there and we thanked him for his help. He stamped our cards and told us to be sure and visit the church of San Martín. We thanked him again and went to get some breakfast.

After drinking coffee in a bar and chatting with a family of French car-pilgrims, we went to find the church.

The name of the town, Frómista, comes from the Latin Frumenta; the Romans named it for its abundance of grain—even though to us the town looked dessicated. Frómista was colonized by the Romans, repopulated in the tenth century by the Castilians. It was an important town in the Middle Ages, a place at which the route from the Cantabrian mountains via Reinosa and Cervatos joined with the Camino de Santiago. At one time, there was a Moorish quarter and a Jewish quarter in the town and several hospices for pilgrims. Now its total population was under 1500.

Walking through the town, we paused at the statue of a native son, San Telmo, patron saint of sailors, continued on past white-washed arcaded buildings, walked down earth-colored streets lined with earth-colored adobe houses. At last we came to the famous Romanesque church of San Martín, constructed between 1035-1066. Built of beige stone blocks, topped with a reddish tile roof, its oblong shape contrasts with the two matching round towers on either side of the main door and with the round-arched windows and doors, each of which has several layers of arches, providing a contrast of light and shadow. Staring at the roof, I saw its fanciful decorations: 315 carved spouts, carved into bizarre beasts and grotesque faces, adorn the edge of the roof. The inside of the church is serene: simple in plan, all sand-colored stone, but, like the outside, deceptive in its simplicity. The neatly lined-up pillars all have intricately carved capitals. San Martín was quiet, cool, dark: a thoughtful church, worth spending time in. Unfortunately, a tour bus arrived and

The entry to the thirteenth-century church of Santa María la Blanca, Villalcázar de Sirga. Alfonso X, el Sabio, expressed his devotion to La Virgen Blanca (and other Virgens) in his Cantigas, *a marvelous, illustrated, medieval collection of verses set to music. (Recordings of these hymns of praise, some of which were sung by pilgrims to Santiago, are available.)*

disgorged some thirty noisy French tourists, so we left.

Outside we saw a dark-haired pilgrim, about our age, looking disappointedly at the crowd entering the church. We went up to him and started talking. Stefan was Dutch and had walked alone from Saint Jean Pied de Port. In his hometown he was an assistant burgomaster and active in his political party. They had just held elections, and he had promised his colleagues that if they lost, he would walk to Santiago. And if they won, he would also walk! Although this sounded like a religious *promesa,* and maybe it was, Stefan added that he was a student of Arabic and medieval history, and he had always wanted to see Spain. Besides, when he was eighteen he had had tuberculosis and had been bed-ridden for a year. Ever afterwards, he had thought of himself as physically weak. Preparing for the pilgrimage had given him an opportunity—and a motive—to get himself into shape, to test his limits. Stefan carried a small daypack with just a change of clothes; he asked for and always found shelter, with a bed, for the night.

It was time for our taxi ride to Carrión de los Condes, so we shook hands, wished each other well, and left. Our driver was waiting for us, and we talked about the pilgrimage as we sped out of town and down dusty roads. She said there were a surprising number of pilgrims that year—many more than in previous years. Perhaps it was a reawakening of true religious feeling, she suggested. As she drove, she told us stories of the Camino. Did we know that there were tunnels under Frómista, probably for hiding from the Moors? And that the Gothic *rollo* in Boadilla had been the site of beheadings?

When we reached Villalcázar de Sirga, our driver insisted on stopping. Although the town was now poor and faded, at one time it had been rich and famous. It had been under the control of the Order of the Templars, and there had been a pilgrimage *hospital* here, as well, under control of the Order of the Knights of Santiago. Most famous of all was the church of Santa María la Blanca, a Virgin whose fame was widespread in the thirteenth century and who was commemorated in the *Cantigas* of Alfonso X, el Sabio.

Alfonso X, the Learned King, was born in 1221 and died in 1284, alienated from his family and deserted by his followers. Although called wise, he was neither politically nor militarily astute; but he did make tremendous contributions to Castilian learning. He made a beginning at legal reforms in the *Siete Partidas*—the *Seven Divisions of Law;* and he had a famous Arabic collection of tales and philosophical tracts, *El Libro de Calila e Dimna,* translated into Spanish. This made him the first to sponsor a translation from Arabic into a western vernacular.

Sometime in the middle of the thirteenth century, Alfonso X began work on the *Cantigas de Santa María*—the *Canticles of Holy Mary,* a series of over 400 verses praising miracles of the Virgin. It is probable that he was the author and composer of most, if not all, of the canticles. The collection of canticles is not only poetry but also contains marvellous colored miniatures and musical notations; the *Cantigas* are one of our richest resources for visualizing what life was like in the thirteenth century.[20] Written in Galician-Portuguese, approximately two-thirds of the canticles describe miracles of the Virgin; the rest are songs of praise, lauding her virtues. Many of the canticles are based on miracle stories current at the time; others appear to be based on miraculous encounters with the Virgin by the royal family and friends. In Villalcázar, although we could not see the *Cantigas* themselves, we could see the statue of a Virgin commemorated in them.

We entered the sand-colored stone church through an impressive Romanesque-Gothic carved doorway. Once inside we found the thirteenth-century statue of the Virgen de la Cantigas leaning against a pillar. Formal, austere, the carved stone image is seated on a throne, holding a headless infant in her arms. In the Capilla de Santiago we admired the elaborately carved sarcofogi of an unnamed knight of the Order of Santiago, of Don Felipe, son of Alfonso X, and of his second wife, Leonor de Castro. Faded paint still colors Leonor's tomb, which rests on the backs of large stone animals. Her costumed effigy is carved on top of the tomb in minute detail, so finely done that I expected the lace-like veil over her mouth to move in the breeze. I asked our guide why Leonor wore the veil; she wasn't sure but thought it was because she had died of a contagious disease.

When we left the church, our guide pointed out a nearby building with the sign, "Mesón del Peregrino." The innkeeper fed pilgrims for free. He served excellent food, and the restaurant was widely used for wedding receptions. One of the attractions was a medieval feast, complete with costumed serving wenches. Unfortunately, we didn't have time to eat at the restaurant: our guide was in a hurry to reach Carrión de los Condes. She rapidly drove the six kilometers to Carrión and let us out in front of a hostel. We paid her and she drove off. By car, it had taken just an hour to travel twenty kilometers—including a half-hour stop in Villalcázar. By foot, it would have taken us a day.

I was getting used to arriving places either slowly or quickly. When we had hitchhiked to Burgos, I had felt shaken by the speed of our arrival. This time, it didn't matter. I was just glad to be out of Frómista. But when we went into the hostel and asked for a room, we had an unpleasant surprise: it was full. But the second place we tried was eager for our business. It was a new hostel, just opened, above a thriving restaurant and a bowling alley. We didn't know about the bowling alley when we took the room, but we couldn't help but find out. The place vibrated. But the hostel had plenty of hot water—the first hot water we had enjoyed since Burgos—and the landlord assured us the restaurant, which he also ran, was excellent. When we asked him about the bowling alley, he explained that he had worked in Germany and bowling was popular there; so after he returned to Carrión, he had decided to start a new trend.

We took hot baths and washed our clothes. Then we ate in the restaurant downstairs. The food was excellent, beginning with a *sopa de ajo*—garlic soup, made with hot water, garlic, smoky *pimentón*, bits of bread and ham—and a *menestra*—mixed vegetables, including green beans, peas, artichoke hearts, and potatoes, sauteed in oil, flavored with chopped ham, garlic, and onions. By the time we had finished with our first course I was already full, but we had ordered another course: stewed partridge, a restaurant specialty. Then coffee and a long walk.

Carrión is built on a hill above the east bank of the Río Carrión. In the Middle Ages, it was a very important city, seat of royal councils and courts. The *Codex* describes Carrión as "a rich and very good villa, industrious in bread, wine, meat, and all kinds of products."

In the Middle Ages, Carrión was the capital of an earldom presided over by the family Beni Gómez, rivals of el Cid in the eleventh century. The treacherous Infantes de Carrión, Diego and Fernando, married el Cid's daughters, Doña Elvira and Doña Sol. Ridiculed for their cowardice when a lion escaped its cage, they planned a vicious revenge. Loaded with booty, the Infantes and their wives departed from Alfonso VI's court to return to Carrión. Then, in a deserted woods, the Infantes stripped their wives of their clothes and beat them, leaving them for dead. They boasted to each other that now they were avenged for the ridicule they had suffered—and, besides, their wives had been much too low for them to have married anyway.

Unfortunately for them, Felix Múnoz, nephew of el Cid, had followed close behind and discovered the vicious deed. He found the women, helped them recover from their wounds, and took them to safety.

When el Cid heard what had happened, he sent a trusted vassal to find the king and tell him of this shameful act. He found Alfonso VI in Sahagún—35 kilometers further west on the Camino de Santiago—and, after lengthy discussions, a court was called in Toledo and the Infantes were forced to make financial restitution. Later they were forced to do battle with the followers of el Cid. They were, of course, vanquished, and the honor of el Cid and his daughters was restored. The daughters went on to marry the princes of Navarra and of Aragón. Although the story might sound apocryphal, the noted Spanish scholar Ramón Menéndez Pidal believes the account is based on truth.

Carrión is the town where the Infantes had lived in the eleventh century and where the rabbi Sem Tob lived in the fourteenth century. Author of the "Proverbios Morales," dedicated to Pedro I—Peter the Cruel—of Castilla, Sem Tob was one of the great, early Castilian poets. Carrión is also the town where Iñigo López de Mendoza, Marqués de Santillana, was born in 1398. Born into a wealthy and distinguished literary family, influenced by Dante, Petrarch, and Boccaccio, he became the chief Spanish literary figure of his century. His "Refranes"—proverbs—were translated into English in 1579 and his philosophical poetry is still read. In those days, Carrión de los Condes was an important city; now, it is a small town of 2,600. How fleeting, glory.

There were a number of important medieval churches and convents to visit, including the thirteenth-century Convent of Santa Clara, the twelfth-century Church of Santa María del Camino or de la Victoria, the twelfth-century Church of Santiago, and the Monastery of San Zoilo, with its famous Renaissance cloister and the tombs of the Infantes of Carrión. We didn't really feel like visiting any of them—we'd seen enough churches—but we walked by one by accident: the Church of Santiago, with its splendid twelfth-century Romanesque doorway. In a carved stone frieze above the doorway sits a one-armed Christ, flanked by the twelve apostles. Around the arch of the doorway—the archivolt—are twenty-four other figures, including a musician, a warrior, a cobbler, a barber, a potter—typical artisans and people of the Middle Ages. Unfortunately, the delicate sand-colored carvings are being eaten away by the exhaust fumes of the cars driving by on the narrow street.

That evening in the restaurant we met a family of six French bicycle pilgrims, riding from northern France to Santiago.

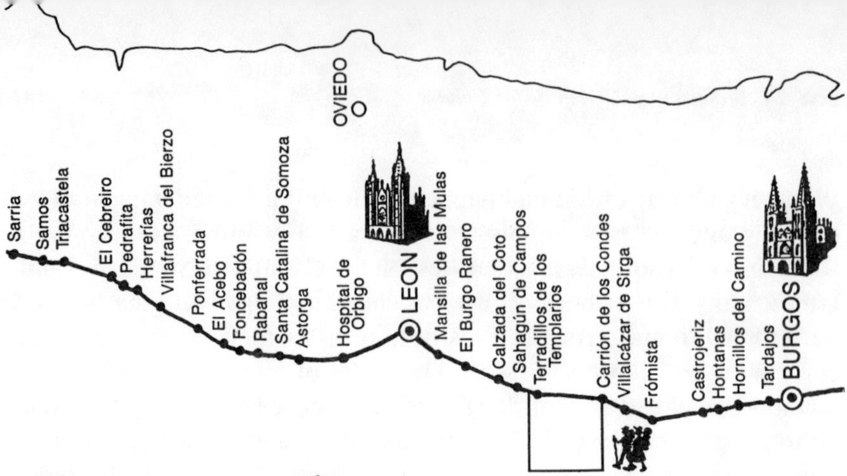

Day 25: August 3 On the way out of Carrión we stopped at a *pastelería* and bought some local specialties: *almendrados* from Villalcázar de Sirga—a delicious sweet made from puff pastry and almonds, and *mantecadas* from Carrión—the not-too-sweet muffin/cupcakes. The Spaniards don't divide cakes, muffins, and breads into the same categories we do.

Licking our fingers, we walked down the street. Near the outskirts of town, we stopped at a bar for some coffee. An old man, already cheery from an early morning shot or two of cognac or a glass of wine, greeted us.

"Going to Santiago?"

We nodded yes.

"Let me buy you a drink!"

We accepted. But while we drank the espresso, he left the bar. Soon he returned with a large tourist brochure, "El Camino en Palencia," which he autographed with a flourish: Pedro, the mason. We thanked him, but he brushed aside our thanks. However, when we left the bar, he leaned out of the doorway and called after us, "Give an embrace to the Apostle for me!" We assured him that we would.

We crossed the Río Carrión and passed by San Zoilo without stopping. The Camino was buried under the flat, straight highway; there was almost no traffic. It was a pleasant morning for walking and the road was shaded by poplars. Soon we left the pavement and walked down a gravel path; according to our guidebook this was the real, authentic Camino de Santiago.

To the right, hidden in a verdant field, were the ruins of the Abbey of Benevívere—the Abbey of Good Life. Our gravel road continued, winding between groves of black poplars. It got hot. We got tired. To the right we saw a small cement-roofed spring marked in yellow: Fuente de Peregrinos. In the Middle Ages this stopping place was known as "la parva de los peregrinos"—the light breakfast of the pilgrims—referring to the fact that pilgrims would stop there and eat something to regain their strength. We stopped and sprinkled cool water on our hot faces; then we took off our shoes and sprinkled cool water on our hot feet.

A man and a boy rode by on bicycles and stopped to talk with us. They said the fountain had been labeled by someone in the nearby village. They also told us they had seen forty young men walking with the cross. There were lots of pilgrims this year, the father added.

We put our shoes and packs back on and continued walking down the flat, unshaded road. The road was made up of a multi-colored collection of pebbles: authentic medieval Camino cobblestones?

After walking a kilometer or so, we came up to a man sitting at a table beside his car, which was parked just off the road in a field. He was either supervising some work or else enjoying sitting on his land.

He offered us grapes, saying apologetically, "I'm sorry, but all I have to offer you is grapes!"

We thanked him and discussed the "real" Camino. Yes, he said, from Benevívere to Calzadilla de la Cueza, twelve kilometers, the cobblestone path was the authentic Camino, and it was still called the "Calzada de los Peregrinos." That meant we were literally, not figuratively, walking in the footsteps of our ancestors. And the fountain we had stopped at—there had been a *hospital* there long ago.

We said it was hot and he said it had been worse—and then one really couldn't walk. After eating the grapes, we thanked him again and continued walking down the real, authentic, Camino de Santiago. Actually, it didn't look much different from a gravel path—except for the color and the smoothness of the stones, worn by the footsteps of pilgrims through the centuries.

"Bill, have you noticed that people are offering us food?"

"That's right—the man in the bar, that guy in the field. It must be a custom of the region."

The old lady in Navarra, near the pass, had given us soda pop, and the old man had bought us coffee. It's a tradition of the Camino to give to pilgrims. It is also a Christian act of compassion. One of the miracles of Santiago tells of his coming in disguise and asking for bread—and being told there was none. And then the bread, which was there all the time, was turned into stone.

We kept on walking. It got hotter. Cobblestones might be authentic, but they were also hard to walk on, especially in jogging shoes; since the soles of the shoes were so flexible, the soles of my feet were constantly accommodating the changing surface of the Camino. We climbed up a small hill; as we started down the other side, we entered Calzadilla de la Cueza. Walking down the narrow dirt street, past tall adobe houses melting together in the hot afternoon sun, we looked for a bar. There was no bar. The village seemed deserted.

On the outskirts of town there were some trees, and we sat down in the shade and rested for a while. Then we got up and started walking again, this time on the highway. So far, we had walked seventeen kilometers, but it felt like more. The next town was six kilometers down the road—or rather up the road, since the highway had started climbing gradually. There was a sign by the side of the road: "Camino de Santiago," pointing towards a stretch of cobblestones, preserved alongside the asphalt pavement. We walked on it for a few hundred meters till it ended, buried beneath the fields.

According to our guidebook, the route we took should have been shorter than the highway—but, according to the signpost, it was longer. Maybe the guidebook didn't take topography into account. Compared to medieval guidebooks, our guidebook gave a lot of information: a map, mileage, festivals, lodging. The medieval *Codex* was, for the most part, a list of place names, with a few descriptive sentences about terrain and kilometers between major stages. On the other hand, although there was no detailed map, it did provide vocabulary lists and colorful descriptions of the dangers to avoid.

As we stumbled wearily along, we passed the ruins of Santa María de Las Tiendas on our left. Tiendas once belonged to the Order of Santiago and there was a *hospital* maintained there for pilgrims until the last century. Now there were only ruins and a still-standing piece of wall. We walked through a small valley, full of poplars and evergreen oaks. We were too tired to appreciate it.

A car drove up beside us, and the driver honked and offered us a ride. We hadn't been trying to hitchhike—but a ride was being offered to us, so how could we refuse? Although the driver offered to take us to Sahagún, 15 kilometers away, we asked him to drop us off at Ledigos, four kilometers away. In five minutes, he had driven us up and over and down the hill to Ledigos and let us out next to a bar.

We walked in, took off our packs, and went up to the counter. The owner was a cheerful, plump woman, dressed not in black but in a faded print dress. We asked if she had any food and she offered to make us egg sandwiches.

"Bill—this is what I had expected to have happen in Navarra, but it never did!"

"Perhaps the people are different here."

The owner took me behind the bar into an enclosed yard lined with sheds. In one of them she stored canned goods, wine, fruit, meats, and produce. Apparently, she not only ran the only bar in town but also the local supply store. She selected some fresh eggs and then we went to a room behind the bar, where she cooked the omelets. Then, back in the bar, she took down a haunch of ham hanging from a ceiling hook through a cord attached to the hoof, and, after laying it down on the counter, sliced off a few paper-thin pieces of *jamón serrano.*

As we chewed the dry ham slices and ate the steaming, tender egg omelet sandwiches, she told us about her brother who had gone to Germany to work and about her sons who had gone to León to work. A man came in for a drink and joined in the conversation, telling us about his experiences working in France. A couple came in and talked about Germany, where they had lived for ten or fifteen years; they had only returned a year ago to their old home in Ledigos. There had been a lot of migration in the region. After a while, I mentioned that we might stop walking for the day, and the owner offered to let us stay in the school house. We considered this friendly offer but decided to go on a little further. Politely, regretfully, we declined her offer.

We talked some more, this time about the pilgrimage. The woman had seen the forty with the cross—the number, or their numbers, kept growing—and a number of other pilgrims—many more than usual. She thought it was a rebirth of spiritual feeling. Looking at my pack, she shook her head and said, "Qué sacrificio!"

Relaxed, rested, well fed, we continued on our way. A short old woman dressed in black stopped us just outside of the bar. She pointed out the "real" Camino to follow. I was puzzled, since our guidebook said all vestiges of the traditional Camino de Santiago were gone, plowed under the fields of grain. But rather than continue on the highway we followed her lead and scrambled up an arroyo and over a hill into Terradillos de los Templarios.

Terradillos is an undistinguished, brown adobe village, once under the jurisdiction of the Templars. We walked past the outskirts of the village; there were two women working in a clearing, separating wheat from chaff. They had on wide-brimmed straw hats and were bent over large mesh frames, which they shook by hand. Amazed that such work was still done by hand, we walked by silently, looking at their bent forms, thinking of the literal meaning of back-breaking labor. This was indeed poor country. And yet, it was supposed to be rich in grain.

The sun was setting, suffusing the fields with soft, pastel light. We found a place to camp in a grove of poplars just off of the trail. No longer worried about sleeping outdoors, I actually looked forward to it—a welcome change from stuffy rooms. We spread out our sleeping bags and sat down on them, watching the peach-colored sun set into the gold hills, watching the star-filled Milky Way come out in the night sky. The air smelled like fresh-cut grass. As we drank some cognac Bill had bought in Carrión, we listened to the buzzing cicadas, the breeze ruffling the trees, and the distant clanging sound of church bells. We were almost half-way to Santiago.

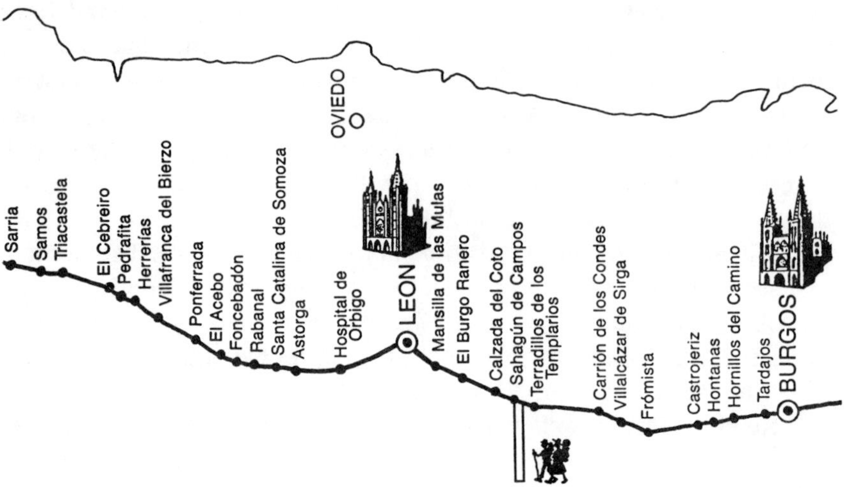

Day 26: August 4 We woke up with the sunrise. Although the ground was hard, it was softer than sleeping on a cement floor. And it was so much pleasanter to sleep under the *belle etoile*—the lovely star—than under a roof. Just three weeks before, I had been afraid of sleeping in an unfinished building in Zubiri!

We followed the highway past the Arroyo de los Templarios. Once, there had been a house of the Templars there; now, nothing remained to mark the spot. We walked past the adobe village of San Nicolás del Real Camino. In the twelfth century there had been a *hospital* for lepers there, under the regular canons of San Agustín. The *hospital* also provided services to needy travelers. Clearly, this part of the Camino had been well supplied with hospices for pilgrims—better supplied in the past than now.

After we crossed the Río Sequillo, we passed the boundary marker between the province of Palencia and the province of León. At that point we left the highway and took off across a stony, scrubby field on a faint path, supposedly the "authentic" Camino. We reached the edge of the desolate hilltop and looked down and out; four kilometers away, in an enormous valley, was the town of Sahagún, end of the seventh stage of journey in the *Codex.*

Beyond Sahagún stretched a great expanse of flat land, broken by occasional clumps of green: the Tierra del Campos, an immense, nearly treeless plain, stretching as far as we could see. We would have to cross it—cross all of it—and then, further away than we could see, climb up into the lush, green hills of the Bierzo, and then up into another mountain chain to the pass of Cebreiro, and then through more mountains and eucalyptus forests until, finally, 400 kilometers away from the flat dry plains of León, we would reach our goal: Santiago de Compostela. We were half-way there.

Scrambling down the dry, hard, eroded edges of the hillside, stumbling over tufts of weeds, tripping over fissures in the rock-hard ground, we reached the bank of the Valderaduey. Across the dried-out riverbed was the Hermitage of the Virgen del Puente. This simple, reddish-gold brick building was constructed in the twelfth century and reconstructed ten years ago. Once there had been a *hospedería* there for pilgrims, and until the end of the nineteenth century there was a farmstead nearby where pilgrims were given food and shelter. Now, the hospice and the farmstead are gone, as is the ancient bridge which used to cross the river. We reached the hermitage and rested in the shade of the trees beside it, grateful for the cool shelter, grateful for the hospitality so near. This must have been how medieval pilgrims felt, coming down from the dry hilltop, approaching the first large city they had seen in many kilometers.

Heading for town, we followed a cobblestone path through the stony fields. A mule cart rattled by and the driver offered us a ride. What a way to enter Sahagún—on the back of a creaking cart! The ride was bumpy and slow but faster than walking. And, after all, it was authentic. Soon we

Just outside Sahagún de Campos is the twelfth-century Hermitage of the Virgen del Puente; for centuries, barren women have prayed to her for children. In the early 1900s, the hermitage began to fall into ruin. It was recently rebuilt, however, and people once more celebrate the novenas of the Virgen at the hermitage each September.

reached Sahagún, and the cart driver dropped us off at the gas station.

Sahagún is shaped like a triangle: its apex, near the train station, is at the top of a fairly steep incline; its base spreads out below, stopping at the Río Cea. As we walked into town from the gas station, we passed the crumbling, golden-brown brick church, la Trinidad, and the gleaming white plastered church of San Juan de Sahagún, native-born patron of this town and of Salamanca. On top of the church tower of San Juan was a large nest of twigs and branches, the nest of the *cigueña*—the white stork—so often found on church towers in León and Castilla. As we watched, one of the graceful birds floated to its resting place: bright blue sky, white feathered form, rough brown nest, rounded-edged white church tower. We continued downhill, walking past new brick apartment buildings and old adobe houses, pressing side to side.

In front of us was the Church of San Lorenzo and a small plaza planted with plane trees, their feathery green leaves spreading out like shaggy mopheads from the narrow brown trunks. We rested for a few minutes on the grey stone benches in the plaza, enjoying the shade, admiring the thirteenth-century San Lorenzo, one of several such brick churches in Sahagún. Sahagún was one of the first northern cities to employ *mudéjares,* Moorish workmen from the south, authorized to remain and work for Christians, as builders. They brought with them building skills and a particular kind of architectural style, noted for horseshoe-shaped arches and "blind"—purely decorative—arcades attached to walls.

Since there was a shortage of building stone in Sahagún, in the Middle Ages they built out of mud. Although adobe houses made of mud and straw were most common, builders also used the mud to make thin, sun-dried, earth-colored bricks. Built from brick out of necessity, the churches represent an important architectural style: Romanesque brick Mudejar churches.

The front of San Lorenzo is creamy colored, the individual bricks covered long ago with plaster and paint. But the three apses—the semicircular, projecting extensions at the east end of the church—and the tower are bare, stripped of their concealing coating. Perched above the central apse is the square brick tower, made of four levels, each decorated with ornamental brickwork and arched windows of varying size. There is no glass in the openings, only light. The apses are decorated with purely decorative horseshoe arches with square borders, typical Mudejar style. Some of the bricks form elaborate designs: the builders laid most of the bricks horizontally, but some of them they recessed more than others, and some they placed vertically, or end to side, forming chevrons, diamonds, or the horseshoe-shaped arches. Earth-colored bricks, cream-colored mortar, light and dark, shadow and shade, the patterns change as the sun moves across the sky. The church is still in use: a bent old woman dressed in black came out of the entry and greeted us briefly as she hurried by.

Shouldering our backpacks, we started walking again down the cement street which flowed between buildings and sloped gently towards the main plaza. Once, all the streets were made of earth or cobblestone. It looked as if one day, not long ago, someone had simply poured out an enormous quantity of concrete at the train station at the top of town, and the concrete had flowed downhill to the river, swirling around buildings, thickening in corners. The narrow, winding streets, the hodge-podge of brown adobe, earth-colored brick, and white-washed buildings with red tile roofs—Sahagún is not an example of careful urban planning. Sahagún is, instead, an example of a 1,000-year-old town, surviving long after its former greatness. For great it was.

According to Walter Muir Whitehill, an expert on Spain,

> One cannot read a page of Castilian medieval history without finding its name, yet today only a few unintelligible ruins remain. I know of no sadder nor more desolate spot in Spain: destruction has brought a curse with it, and one flees from the dust and the savagery of dissolution.[21]

Another expert voices similar feelings. Georgiana Goddard King, whose books on the Camino de Santiago are classics, states:

> I had been—not sitting, indeed, in the ruins, for not a stone lay anywhere to sit upon, but prowling like the hyena or the jackal, striving to realize where once were aisles and courts, apses and galleries and Gothic cloisters: and coming home along the sordid alleys and across the sorry squares.
> . . . the slow corruption of Sahagún has corrupted nearly all the race, and the children are ready to spit upon or to stone a stranger as they would a strayed dog. . . .[22]

I, personally, did not share their sour views. In fact, I was tired of guidebooks which described Sahagún as a decayed, faded, disappointing town. I happened to be very fond of the place—I'd lived there, the summer before; I'd made friends, met pilgrims, and learned about life in Spain. To me, and to the Sahagunese, there was more to Sahagún than monuments and ruins, although these were an inseparable part of the town.

The word Sahagún is a contraction of Santus Facundus, the name of a Roman martyr under Diocletian, whose body was purportedly tossed into the Río Cea, along with that of his brother, San Primitivus, in 303. Originally called Domnos Sanctos, after Alfonso III founded a monastery there in 905 the name was changed to Sant Facund, which, over time, became Safagún, and, finally, Sahagún.

A small martyrs' shrine was built and, in 874, Alfonso the Great built a new church for the martyrs in Sahagún. The church and monastery were destroyed by Abohalid, governor of the King of Córdoba, in 883. They were rebuilt and destroyed again, this time by Almanzor, in either 988 or 996. But they, and the surrounding town, continued to prosper, and again they were rebuilt. The humble pilgrimage shrine of the two martyrs, joined later by San Mancio, was to become the nucleus of an extremely important community.

In the eleventh century, Alfonso VI took refuge—"religious prison"—in the monastery in Sahagún after having been defeated by his brother Sancho II—and el Cid—at Golpejera. After his brother's death, he regained power and became King of León and Castilla. Because his fondness of and gratitude to the clergy of Sahagún was enormous, he gave the monastery to the powerful Burgundian-based Cluny Order. With his aid, the monastery in Sahagún became extremely wealthy, the most powerful Cluny monastery in Spain, with feudal dominion over 90 other monasteries. Its monks spread throughout Spain, controlling politically powerful religious posts, further spreading the influence of Sahagún. Alfonso VI continued to return to Sahagún, off and on, and held court there—el Cid sought him there, after the treacherous beating of his daughters—and he lies buried there, along with several of his wives, Doña Constanza, Doña Berta, and the Moor Zaida.

Alfonso VI gave the monastery valuable privileges in 1079, and the *Fuero de Sahagún* of 1085 further established the Cluny monastery's feudal rights and privileges over the inhabitants of the town—a source of frequent altercations and even warfare between the growing bourgeoisie population of the town and its Benedictine overlords. For with the growth in power and wealth of the monastery came the growth of the town; by the end of the eleventh century, the population of Sahagún included merchants, ironworkers, carpenters, tailors, furriers, sculptors, and other craftsmen from many countries, including Gascons, Bretons, Germans, English, Burgundians, Provençals, Lombards, Jews and Moors.

In 1087, 1110, 1227, and 1245, there were repeated uprisings of the townspeople against the clergy, only suppressed by the intervention of kings. The abbey not only retained its feudal power, it even expanded; in the fourteenth century, there was a university in Sahagún, run by the abbey; it existed until 1494. Eventually, however, changes in the religious power structure and the battles between the independent villagers and their autocratic Cluny masters ended the importance of the monastery and of the town.

Now, the gigantic abbey of San Benito lies in ruins, its power and wealth destroyed by the *desamortización* (state-ordered loss of property) of the early 1800s and by fire in 1810 and 1835. All that is left is the huge southern doorway, built in 1662, part of an apse of the chapel of San Mancio, a portion of the wall of the nave, and a clock tower, whose discordant chimes ring out the time, more or less accurately, every fifteen minutes, day and night.

The summer before, a friend of mine, a middle-aged native of the town, had pointed at the ruined walls and proudly said, "We burned the monastery." She meant, of course, her ancestors had—but she obviously felt that she participated in that act, striking out against oppression and the autocratic feudal Church, so foreign to Spanish individualism. Just as at San Antón, outside of Castrojeriz, a road now passes underneath the still-standing doorway.

Sahagún is mentioned by Picaud in "The Pilgrim's Guide" in the *Codex.* He says that it possessed every blessing of nature and claims, erroneously, that Charlemagne erected the chapel of the martyrs Facundo and Primitivo. Charlemagne and Sahagún also appear together in the "Pseudo-Turpin." According to that chronicle, there was a great battle just outside of Sahagún between Charlemagne and the Moors. The night before the battle, Charlemagne and his troops camped beside the Río Cea and stuck their lances upright in the ground. By the next morning, the lances of the Christian warriors who were to die in battle had sprouted bark and leaves—divine indication that they would enter Heaven as martyrs. Today, villagers point to the rows of black poplars beside the Cea and tell the traveler, "Those are the lances of Charlemagne's warriors."

But Sahagún was not only the site of ancient and imagined battles; it was also the starting point of Sir John Moore's retreat to La Coruña in 1809. And Sahagún was one of the first towns in Spain to declare its support for the Second Republic, although during the Civil War the district was on the Nationalist side. Sahagún was also the birthplace in about 1500 of Fray Bernadino de Sahagún, "Father of Anthropology in the New World," author of the important firsthand account of the collision of European and Aztec cultures, *General History of the Things of New Spain,* written both in Spanish and Nahuatl. There is a statue commemorating him in front of the Caja de Ahorros Saving Bank, one of ten banks in the town, and next to the Bar Zamora, one of thirty cafe/bars in Sahagún, and near the Hotel Codorniz, one of half a dozen inns.

Although Sahagún obviously is full of ruins and faded glory, it is also full of life. It is a thriving community of 2,500 people, a popular place on tourist itineraries and for summer visitors who come to Sahagún to enjoy the clean, dry air. None of the four *hospitales* of the fifteenth century exists—including the one of the monastery, with seventy beds for pilgrims, and the one next to the Virgen del Puente—but half a dozen hostels cater to tourists and pilgrims.

Since Sahagún is the municipal center for the surrounding township, it has the regional schools, the public health clinic, several courts, the barracks of the *guardia civil,* the fire station, a movie theatre, a library—and a number of restaurants, bars, discoteques, pubs, grocery stores, fish markets, bread stores, sweet shops, hardware stores, television and electrical appliance stores, pharmacies, variety stores, fabric stores, beauty and barber shops, music stores, and clothing stores. Dull and disappointing? Hardly!

We passed by the town hall, walking in the shade of the arcaded plaza of wood columns supporting the overhanging second story of the buildings lining the square; then we turned right and walked past the Retirement Home to the Monasterio de la Santa Cruz. Although the all-powerful Benedictine monastery San Benito was destroyed, the unobtrusive monastery of the Benedictine nuns was not; it remains active today, although the number of resident nuns has dropped in recent years to fourteen, most of whom are old. In order to support themselves—for cloistered nuns are not permitted to leave the monastery walls—they have a garden, sew ski clothes, bake tea cookies and cakes, specializing in the macaroon-like *amarguillos,* and run a boarding house attached to the monastery.

Without leaving the monastery walls, the nuns take turns in supervising the hospice. The thirty places are usually filled with retired couples from the humid, northern mining province of Asturias who come to Sahagún to ease their bronchial problems and arthritis. Often, they stay a month or more, eating and sleeping in the hospice, taking long walks in the countryside, drinking coffee and cider in the bars, and going for sightseeing or shopping excursions in nearby towns.

The summer before, I had spent a month and a half in the Benedictine boarding house. The rates were reasonable, the food was good, the companionship was excellent. It was there that I had first seen pilgrims, identity cards in hand, requesting hospitality for the night. Last summer I had come to the monastery as a tourist; this summer I returned, as a pilgrim.

We rang the doorbell—the door is always locked—and waited. Sor Angela opened up the door. A tiny, wizened nun, she was dressed in a floor-length grey habit, grey and white coif around her reddish face. Her eyes gleamed when she recognized me, and she opened wide the door and ushered us inside. Bending down, I kissed her on both cheeks, and she kissed me. Then I introduced Bill and she greeted him warmly.

"We got your postcard so we knew you were coming!"

"Do you have room for us?"

"For you? Of course we do! Some of your friends from last summer—María and Lupe and Isabel, and their husbands—are here again and they are eager to see you, too!" She looked at us, looked at our backpacks. "Qué sacrificio!"

We nodded in agreement. She ushered us into the waiting room and asked us to wait while she fetched the abbess. We took off our packs and sat down. On the wall was a sign commemorating pilgrimage and charity:

"We are all Pilgrims and Strangers. Giving hospitality is a rule of the Benedictine Order and a truly Christian act."

There was also a map, showing the Benedictine monasteries across Spain. Travelers, with the proper introduction, could stay in them. There was even one in Santiago de Compostela, directly behind the cathedral.

Sor Angela reappeared with the abbess, who greeted us and kissed me on both cheeks. Holding my hands, she told me how pleased she was to see me once again—and this time as a pilgrim. Had we heard about the sixty-year-old French pilgrim traveling with his dog? He had stayed there, several days before. According to the abbess, the man had had open heart surgery several months before; at that time, he made a vow to

Santiago to walk the Camino if he recovered; he recovered and set out on the pilgrimage with an enormous dog to carry his pack. Although his doctors had said he could walk, he could not carry any weight. The dog slept beside him when he was cold and protected him from robbers on the road. We were impressed.

The phone rang, Sor Angela answered it; it was for the abbess. We took our leave, and Sor Angela led us upstairs to our rooms. My room had white stucco walls, dark tile floors, a wooden bedstead, a small table and lamp, a wooden wardrobe, and a sink with a mirror. Clean and bare, the only decorations were a crucifix and a plaster wall cast of the Virgin and child, with the title, "O Virgin, do not abandon me." A bathroom with a shower was down the hall; a bathroom with a tub was downstairs. There was hot water.

At 2:30 we went to the dining room for *la comida.* Everyone had assigned places, including us. We sat at a table in a corner. As Bill and I walked in, I saw familiar faces and went over to several tables to greet my friends from the previous summer. They returned the greeting, asking how I was, looking curiously at Bill. I introduced him as my companion on the pilgrimage road. The women nodded, approvingly, and one of them, Isabel, commented that it was much safer to travel with a male companion. Were we really walking all that distance? I pointed at my jogging-shoe-encased feet and nodded. More murmurs of approval, including "Qué bonito" and "Vale la pena."

Sor Angela and Consuela, the nuns' assistant, a young girl from the town, started bringing in the food on large serving platters, so we went to our table and sat down. First a huge mixed salad, made with lettuce, tomatoes, and onions grown in the monastery garden. Then the second course: *fabadas asturianas*—a thick soup of large white beans and bits of sausage, the regional dish of Asturias. And then the main course, pan-fried, thinly sliced beef steaks and french fried potatoes. For dessert—fruit, coffee, or camomile tea.

I had forgotten there was so much food—and the guests ate it all. Since we were pilgrims, they wouldn't ask us to pay anything, but they would accept a donation. I knew that not all the nuns were pleased at giving charity to pilgrims—some of them complained that they have to work so hard to make ends meet, there isn't anything extra to give—even though giving charity and hospitality are an important teaching of Saint Benedict.

After the enormous meal, we went upstairs to our separate rooms. I took a nap. Around 4:30, Bill knocked on my door, and we went out to visit my other friends from the summer before. We walked back to the central plaza and, across from the Caja de Ahorros, we entered the Librería Luna bookstore/curio shop/printing shop. There, behind the counter, was one of my dearest friends, Julia Tovar, known as Paca, the dark-haired, energetic, middle-aged wife of Segismundo Luna, owner of the store. Dressed as usual in a faded print dress, shoulders covered with a black sweater, Paca was delighted to see me and scurried around the counter to kiss me on both cheeks. I introduced Bill and she kissed him, too. Then she stood back, looking at me.

"Elenita! How are you? When did you get here?"

"Just before lunch—we went straight to the Benedictines—"

"How could you! You should have stopped here first! We knew you were coming—Antonio told us!"

"Antonio?"

"Antonio—the man with the mule cart! He told us you had arrived. And Jorge, he saw you, too. We were wondering where you were!"

"We wanted to drop off our backpacks and bathe. And then it was time for lunch."

Paca looked me up and down. "You look thinner than last summer."

"It's the walking."

Segis came in and kissed me, shook hands with Bill. He had been setting type by hand in the back room. Grey haired, solid, he was a self-educated, self-made man. When he was twelve, he had had to quit school in order to help support his family. He had taken the cattle out to the fields and worked hard at a number of different jobs, studying, on his own, at night. Somehow, he had managed to open up a print shop/book store. With Paca's help, the shop had expanded and now they sold curios, souvenirs, porcelain, toys, and regional ceramics, as well as books and school supplies.

Paca's mother had been widowed at an early age, her husband a victim of the Civil War. Working day and night, the mother had raised her six children on her own. Paca, like Segis, had had to quit school at an early age and work to support the family.

During the years, the couple had become well respected in the community; Segis had served on the City Council, at one time. Their daughter Piedad, in her mid-twenties, had an advanced degree in philology and worked at the University of León; their son Pedro, just over thirty, was a bank teller in the Caja de Ahorros across the street. He's married to

Tinina, from Grajal, five kilometers south of Sahagún, and they have a little girl, María.

I had gotten to know the family through Piedad. Told that there was an *americana* in town, Piedad had introduced herself to me. She practiced her English, I my Spanish, during our long walks around town. It was she who had first taught me about the history of Sahagún and it was her family who had shown me what living in an extended family—grandparents, parents, grandchildren, in-laws, aunts, nieces, nephews—was like.

Paca asked, "How long are you here for?"

"Maybe just tonight, maybe tomorrow too. We need to rest a while."

"I can imagine! But stay tomorrow at least—we are going on a picnic in the country."

A picnic in the country. I remembered one with them the summer before: it had begun at noon and lasted till 9 p.m. There had been wonderful food and card games and music and napping in the hot afternoon sun and dancing and eating and drinking. . . .

I looked at Bill. "We'll try to stay."

Some customers came into the shop, and Segis went back to his typesetting and Paca waited on clients. We waited till the shop was temporarily empty.

"Where's Piedad? And Pedro?"

"Piedad's in León—but she'll be back for the picnic. And Pedro's in Grajal, at Tinina's parents. They'll be back late tonight."

"Tell them we're here."

"Of course!"

We left the store and walked back the way we had come, but we cut off towards the right before the monastery. There, in front of us, were the ruins of San Benito, the clock tower, and the twelfth-century church, San Tirso.

San Tirso is very similar to San Lorenzo, except that the lower third of the central apse is made of stone—apparently there was only that much available, so the builders had to switch to brick. There was a sign, "En Obras," by the door, but a man I knew was sitting at the doorway, resting in the shade, and he smiled at me and said that we could go in. He followed us and explained: they were almost done removing the stucco covering on the walls and repairing the wooden ceiling. The interior was now shades of beige and reddish-brown: the walls were reddish-brown brick, set in beige mortar; the floor was beige cobblestones and brown paving stones; the roof was exposed wooden beams and crossbeams.

Stripped of plaster, the clean simplicity of the church was beautiful: the bricks outline the arches that form the entrances to the apses, contrasting with the horizontal pattern on the walls; and, where the walls joined the ceiling, one row of bricks had been laid vertically, the next row in a chevron pattern. There was no elaborate carving, no sculptured niches, no baroque ornaments or colorful paint, no distractions from the geometry of the place.

I noticed a Star of David in the floor in front of the central apse and asked our guide about it. There had been a Jewish neighborhood in town, and a Moorish one as well—one street is still called Calle de la Morería. But our guide assured me I was mistaken. I knew that the church had been built by *mudéjares* from the south; I wondered if perhaps they had had their private joke.

When we left, we gave the guide some money for his time and bought some postcards from him. Under the overhang, he showed us several stone sarcofagi. They had just been found during archeological excavations around the church; they were probably from a Roman burial. There had been several Roman villas near Sahagún, one near the Virgen del Puente; perhaps there had been more.

To see what was left of the chapel of San Mancio, we had to ask permission from the *guardia civil*, whose barracks are built alongside the remains. The crumbling, roofless chapel smelled of hay and manure; the *guardia civil* had used it as a stable. Leaving quickly, we walked over to what remained of the monastery entryway. Free-standing, it resembled a left-over movie set facade: a massive doorway, decorated with elaborate statuary, plaques, and a royal seal, attached to nothing. The road that circled Sahagún passed under the archway. We walked around the arch and towards a small hill on the southern edge of town.

On top of the hill is the semi-ruined convent of the Franciscans, the Sanctuary of La Virgen Peregrina. Founded in 1259, the convent has been abandoned and most of it is in ruins, but the central sanctuary is still standing. We circled the large brick structure, looking at the Mudéjar blind arches, the horseshoe windows. To the west, below us, was the Río Cea and fields of grain; to the south, the town of Grajal, with its fifteenth-century castle, and more fields. As we walked around La Peregrina, I exchanged greetings with various people; the sanctuary is a popular picnic spot for townspeople and Asturian summer visitors. Even on hot summer days, the hilltop is cool; usually there is a slight breeze blowing, and the building itself provides shade from the scorching sun.

The large wooden doors to the sanctuary were open, so we entered the large, two-story room, white-wash slightly stained, stucco crumbling, but still in use. On the altar was the statue of La Peregrina, a work attributed to the seventeenth-century Andalucian sculptor, Luisa Roldán. La Peregrina's festival had been held on July 2; the statue was still in the sanctuary and the altar was full of flowers. La Peregrina is dressed like an elegant pilgrim to Santiago: her rich brown-velvet and gold-embroidered outfit is decorated with scallop shells, and scallop shells adorn her short shoulder cape—called a *pelerín,* from the French word for pilgrim, *pèlerin.* In her right hand, she holds a pilgrim staff and gourd. In her left, she holds the infant Jesus. Her face is delicate, her hair is real.

The same man who had been at San Tirso appeared and showed us a back room, recently stripped of its stucco covering. There, beginning eight feet up on the high walls, was a plaster frieze of elaborate arabesque designs, reminiscent of the Moorish work in Toledo. The colors were still faintly visible. It was possible that this room had been a private chapel, decorated with Mudéjar work that had been concealed for centuries with thick white plaster. Or, the guide suggested, it might have been a synagogue for the Jews. Once there had, indeed, been Jews in Spain—they formed an important population, contributing to trade, to literature, to philosophy, until all those who refused baptism were finally expelled in 1492, the same year as the final conquest of the Moors by Ferdinand and Isabella—the Reconquest of Granada, the same year as the discovery of the New World.

After climbing down the cobblestone path from the sanctuary, we stopped at the nearest bar, El Peregrino, for an aperitif. I drank *jerez*—sherry, named after the town of Jerez in southern Spain—and Bill drank Campari. Then we walked back to the nuns for dinner.

We were not the only extra guests. At a table next to us was a group of seven French boy scouts who had ridden their bikes from Paris, requesting hospitality along the way. They said it was a custom in Paris for boy scout groups to make a bicycle pilgrimage on the Camino de Santiago. Had we gone to Mass, they asked? We shook our heads. They told us to be sure to visit the chapel of the Benedictine nuns—the *retablo* was incredibly ornate, a baroque masterpiece of gilt columns encircled with twining vines, gilt cherubs, gilt virgins and saints, hanging from the ceiling, overflowing the tiny room.

Dinner came. Smaller and lighter than lunch, it was still impressive:

salad, fried river eel, french fried potatoes, flan for dessert. We ate and then went out to find Segis and Paca, to tell them we would go with them the next day. Then we sat at a table outside the Bar Zamora, drinking cognac, watching the people strolling up and down the plaza.

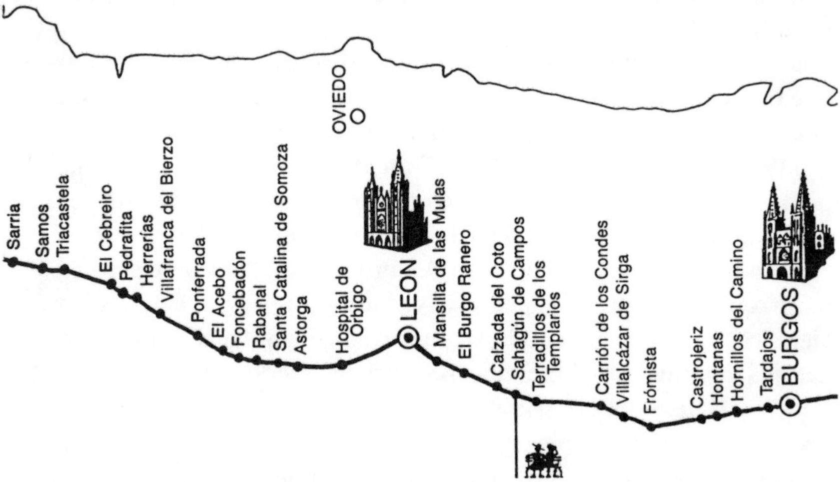

Day 27: August 5 We got up around 9 a.m. and went out for *churros. Churros* are made from a batter of oil, water, and flour, extruded through a narrow fluted tube into a large frying pan of bubbling oil. As soon as the coiled spirals of *churros* turn golden brown, they are removed, snipped into finger-long lengths, and served. When *churros* are steaming hot, freshly fried, they are light and absolutely delicious; if allowed to sit, they solidify and taste like congealed grease. Spaniards sprinkle *churros* with sugar or dip them in thick hot chocolate; I preferred to eat them plain. (In different areas of Spain, these are called *porras.*)

Although ten or fifteen years ago there were several *churrerías*—*churros* shops—in Sahagún, today there is just one, located in a *confitería* in the Plaza Mayor. We got there just in time; the line quickly formed behind us. Out of a dark, smoky room, a sweat-drenched man appeared, carrying a pan of *churros.* His assistant quickly snipped the snake-like spiral into shorter lengths, then counted out the number we requested and put them in a cone made out of newspaper. We walked down the street munching them.

One of the bars advertised "Hay chocolate," and we went in. Bill ordered hot chocolate. If properly done, the drink is made of melted chocolate bars, milk, and lots of sugar, slowly simmered and steadily stirred together. It is thick and sweet and coats the *churros* like a frosting. I found it much too rich, but Bill enjoyed it. I was surprised at how popular chocolate was in Spain. I knew it had been brought back from the New World by the Spanish conquerers, but the 400-year fascination seemed a bit much. In the grocery stores, there are shelves and shelves of chocolate bars, and kids are given chocolate and bread sandwiches for snacks. And chocolate in chicken dishes, too. Perhaps it had something to do with the shortage of chocolate—and sugar—during the war years.

We finished our *churros* and our drinks and started over to Paca and Segis's. Outside of the Bar Caracas we saw a tan, healthy looking blond man, perhaps in his late 20s. Beside him was a guitar.

We walked up to him and asked, "Peregrino?"

He smiled and nodded, gestured for us to sit down beside him. His name was Jean, and he explained that he was a guard at a youth prison in Belgium. For the last two years, he and another guard had been taking hard-core juvenile offenders on the pilgrimage to Santiago. They walk for three months, following the Camino de Santiago through France and across Spain. When they get to Santiago, the prisoners' sentences are commuted and they are free.

In the Middle Ages pilgrimage was often used as a punishment; for certain crimes, civil and ecclesiastical courts would impose the sentence of going on a particular pilgrimage. There were different pilgrimages for different crimes, depending on the severity and the distance to be covered. Pilgrimage-as-punishment was most popular in the twelfth and thirteenth centuries. It was even possible to pay a set fee instead of making a particular pilgrimage, and different pilgrimages had different values. The practice lost popularity by the mid-fourteenth century, in part because so many criminals and thieves were making pilgrimages that it became dangerous for others; in part because of serious doubts about the spiritual value of enforced pilgrimage; in part because of changing penal codes. I asked Jean if this Belgian practice was a holdover from the Middle Ages.

He shook his head, no. "Three years ago, my partner and I saw a film on the American Outward Bound project. It seemed to us that kind of experience would be a fine way to rehabilitate young offenders."

"And does it work?"

"So far, it seems to. The prisoners volunteer and sign a contract, agreeing on certain rules. We've had to send one prisoner back to Belgium this year, for unacceptable, violent behavior. But the ones who went last year are all doing fine—they've got jobs and are living on their own."

Bill asked, "Why the Camino de Santiago?"

"Because it is well known, well marked. Next year, maybe we'll go to Greece instead."

I asked, "Did you know that in the Middle Ages pilgrimage was used for criminal sentences?"

"Yes, but we're not religious, and we're not making a religious pilgrimage. The idea is to have these kids learn to work with others, to change their image of themselves through overcoming hardship."

A group of young men, escorted by a middle-aged man, walked up to him and he stood up. "I've got to go."

We walked the few blocks to Paca and Segis's to help them with preparations for the picnic. Paca put me to work peeling the skin off of tiny squids; then we cooked the squid and some chicken. Paca was busy boiling eggs and frying thin beef steaks. She had sent Piedad out to buy bread and garden-fresh lettuce and tomatoes at the market. The kitchen was hot: the wood and coal burning stove radiated a lot of heat—useful in winter (their sole source of heat in the apartment) but stifling in summer.

Bill went downstairs to keep Segis company while he set type for a funeral announcement. An elderly woman had died the night before, and the relatives had asked him to print the standard announcement: the names of the deceased and of the surviving relatives, topped with a cross, edged with a black border. They would post copies of it on telephone posts and walls all over town.

Piedad came in and Pedro, and we warmly embraced each other and exchanged pleasantries about the strong U.S. dollar destroying the Spanish economy, about the Camino destroying our feet, about the current Socialist government in Spain, about work, health, relatives, and the weather. Then we packed the cars. It took two cars to transport us and the food, and there were more cars and people coming later.

We headed thirty kilometers north, over the flat brown plains of Tierra de Campos, towards the not-so-distant, blue-hazed mountains of the Cordillera Cantábrica. At the village of Villazanzo de Valderaduey the pavement ended, but we continued driving on a gravel path towards a grove of trees to the northwest of town. On a hill towards the northeast was a small hermitage of San Roque, patron protector against the plague, patron of many villages along the Camino. Perhaps pilgrims had come down through the mountains here, as well—or, just as likely, illness traveled every road.

We reached the picnic site, famous for its clear spring water. We numbered two dozen people or more—I lost count, since families came and went during the day. There were Segis and Paca and their children Piedad and Pedro. There were Paca's sister and brother-in-law from León and another sister and brother-in-law and their daughter from Oviedo. And some friends of theirs. There was Segis's brother, a priest, visiting from Brazil. There were Piedad's boyfriend and his parents and his sister and her husband and their daughter, and an uncle of the boyfriend. There were Pedro's wife, Tinina, and daughter, María, and Tinina's parents and Tinina's sister and her husband. There were several friends of Pedro and of Paca and Segis. And us. Each family had brought food to share, and Pedro and a friend had brought guitars. Someone had a radio.

The main dish was *paella,* that varied and variable rice *pilau* of Spain. Purists say the only true *paella* is made in Valencia, but even purists disagree about what goes into—or stays out of—*paella.* In fact, there are numerous *paellas,* the content determined by taste and availability; all are good, most are delicious, as long as the rice is not over-cooked. Our *paella* was made with rice, oil, and saffron, with mussels, squid, shrimp, clams and chicken, with peas and artichokes, and garnished with hard-cooked eggs and red pimientos. Although some of the meat had been precooked, all of it was cooked together in stages in an enormous *paella* pan—perhaps a yard across—over an open fire. The bottom of the *paellera* had tiny raised bumps, designed to help the rice cook.

While waiting for Piedad's boyfriend to cook the *paella*—outdoor cooking is the domain of men in Spain—we women set up the tables and got out the rest of the food: wine, bread, salad, spicy stewed rabbit, thin, fried beef steaks. The women worried: would there be enough? And then there was dessert—an ice-cream cake that Bill and I had brought. Afterwards, the women washed dishes, the men relaxed. Then they got out cards, and a table was cleared for the game. During the afternoon, the players alternated. Bets were made, tempers lost, apologies given.

Bill, Segis, and I went for a walk across the fields and up to the hermitage of San Roque. It was locked, so we could only peer in through cracks in the thick wood door. Segis asked us why we were going to Santiago.

Bill answered first. "I guess, out of curiosity. About Spain, about myself."

I added, "That's true for me, too—I wanted to make a pilgrimage. You know, Segis, I'm not religious—I'm not even Catholic! But when I was here last summer, I met pilgrims walking the Camino and I was fascinated by it—by the history, by the continuity of experience, by the fact that people were still making the pilgrimage today."

Segis listened to us and nodded. "You know—and I only tell you this, because we are *de confianza*—a lot of people make the pilgrimage just so that they can brag about what they've done! They do it out of pride, not curiosity."

I looked at Segis. I knew he was a deeply religious man: he went to Mass at least every Sunday, if not more often. "Would you make the pilgrimage to Santiago?"

He laughed. "Not me! If I had the chance, I would rest for a few days. I wouldn't walk across Spain."

Bill asked, "Have you ever been to Santiago?"

"No, but my chidren have. They went on a bus excursion, during high school. They say it's a lovely city, but I have no desire to visit it."

"But Santiago is patron of Spain."

"So?"

I added, "And Sahagún is on the Camino—I've heard the mayor tell people that if it weren't for the pilgrimage, Sahagún would never have become so important."

"That's true, and the pilgrimage is part of my life—I grew up with it, growing up in Sahagún. But that doesn't mean I want to walk to Santiago or make a pilgrimage."

I asked, "Do you know anyone from Sahagún who's gone on pilgrimage to Santiago?"

Segis thought a moment. "Well, there are two women who went. One of them is a very Christian woman—a fine woman, there should be more like her! She even takes in pilgrims and lets them sleep in her home. She went once, with a friend, during an Año Santo. I think they walked from Samos—about 100 kilometers." He thought some more. "She's the only one I can think of."

We walked back to the party. The card game was over, and people were sitting around, reading newspapers, or napping on blankets. Some people had already left. I went over to Paca, who was knitting under the shade of a tree. She was almost always knitting, like many Spanish women, knitting sweaters, or vests, or socks, for children or grandchildren or husbands—rarely for themselves.

"Paca, what do you think of the pilgrimage to Santiago?"

"I think it is *muy bonito*! I would like to go myself."

"By car?"

"Not by car—on foot."

"Why?"

"Just because it is such a beautiful thing to do, to walk through the countryside, to sleep under the stars. Once, a pilgrim came to our door, asking for water. She was a fat woman, from Chicago! We invited her in and gave her yogurt. She spent the night at the nuns, but the next morning she came back to say goodbye. She sent us a postcard from Santiago."

Jorge, a middle-aged friend of someone in the family, overheard our conversation and he joined in.

"You know, of course, that most of those pilgrims are not really pilgrims."

I looked at him. "No?"

"No. They are excursionists, taking advantage of the traditions of hospitality of the Camino."

"But they are walking."

"They may be walking, but so what. If they don't have the right attitude, then they are not pilgrims."

I thought about myself. What would he think of us? I knew I was a pilgrim.

He continued. "Not that I believe in any of it. The priests—the Church—they're just out to take your money! Besides, you realize, of course, that there is nothing there in Santiago."

"What do you mean?"

"The tomb is a fraud. The whole thing was concocted by greedy priests. There is no proof, no proof at all that the bones are those of St. James—or of any other saint."

I knew that argument. In fact, Dr. Andrew Boorde, the sixteenth-century English pilgrim, claimed that he was told as much by a cleric at Compostela. According to the cleric, all there was at Compostela was Santiago's staff, his prison chains, and the sickle used to cut off his head. All the bones, according to the cleric, had been transported to Toulouse by Charlemagne. The sixteenth-century Spanish historian Juan de Mariana raised similar doubts, but he did so very cautiously, not wanting to cause trouble. More recently, other historians have also been skeptical—but, as one of them points out, regardless of "the truth," millions of pilgrims have traveled the Camino for centuries, and their belief is real and has accomplished miracles.

Bill started arguing with Jorge. "But millions of pilgrims have been going there for 1,000 years—and in 1884, Pope Leo XIII validated the bones when they were rediscovered, after having beeen misplaced for several centuries."

"They're all mistaken," Jorge said, and he got up and walked away.

What difference does it make, I thought. I just want to make a pilgrimage.

Paca shook her head, disapprovingly. "My great-grandmother walked to Santiago. And my grandmother used to live in a farm next to the Hermitage of the Virgen del Puente. She and her husband gave shelter to pilgrims in need. Later, when she was widowed, she left the farm and moved into town and ran a *fonda.* Even there, she gave food to pilgrims who needed it."

Bill told her, "We stopped at the Virgen del Puente on our way to Sahagún."

"You should have seen it a few years ago. It had started to fall down. But our family got together and we rebuilt it—Pedro and a friend of his did the brickwork, and my aunt made new clothing for the Virgen—we used some of Piedad's hair to make a new wig for the Virgen—and now, once again, they hold the Virgen's novenas there, in September. People come from all around—there is a lot of devotion to the Virgen del Puente; she's helped a number of women have children. Including the parents of San Juan de Sahagún, 400 years ago. Every year, we get donations from people, in gratitude."

Suddenly, the sound of guitar music drowned out the radio. Pedro and his friend were playing their guitars and singing. Soon they were playing a *jota,* a regional folkdance, and people started dancing in the clearing, arms raised above their heads, fingers snapping. They circled around the clearing. Paca came over and pulled me up to join them, teaching me the simple step-hop-step.

It was time to eat again. Angel had brought raw sardines, six or eight inches long, and he placed them, ungutted, on a rack over the still-glowing coals. He watched them carefully, making sure they grilled evenly, the skin blackened but not burned. He gave one to each of us and showed us how to eat them, stripping the meat from the bones.

Someone had brought home-made *chorizo,* and that was added to the rack as well. And someone else had brought *tortilla espanola.* Paca put slices of each on pieces of bread and handed them to us.

We protested: "We're stuffed!"

"Eat some more—you're much too thin!" Paca said.

It was getting late, so we all packed up the food, put out the fire, folded up the tables and chairs, and repacked the cars. We drove back to Sahagún, just as the sun was setting. The sky was a rich, deep blue, intensifying the colors, sharpening the outlines of the brown adobe walls, the white-washed buildings, the red tile roofs of the town. It was after 9 p.m., but our companions planned to continue the party at someone else's home. We thanks them, declined their invitation to join them, and waddled back to the nuns.

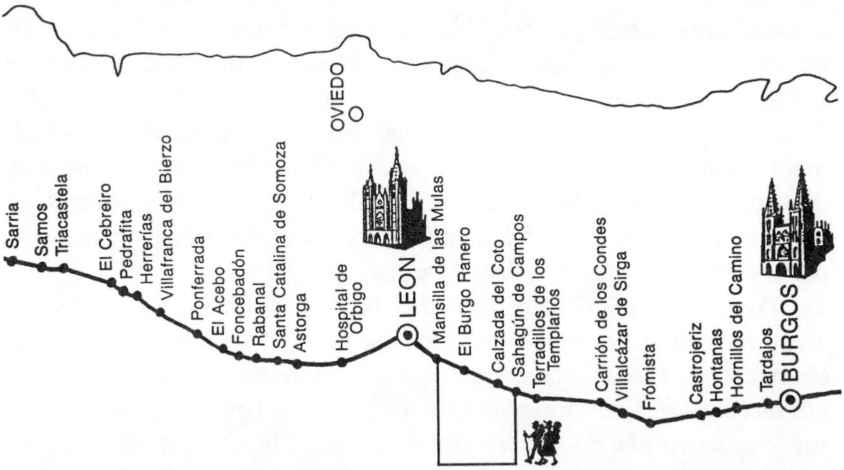

Day 28: August 6

Half-way there, half-way to go. We'd had our time off, our celebration, our intense day of socializing with my old friends. Now, once again, we would be pilgrims, strangers and pilgrims, walking down the road.

In the Middle Ages Sahagún had a reputation as a "den of iniquity." It had gambling houses and whorehouses, serving the needs not only of the kings and courts but also of pilgrims falling from grace. I could believe it; after weeks on the road, it was tempting to have some fun, to forget about serious things, about pain and weariness. Besides, one's sins would be forgiven in Santiago! No wonder major pilgrimage shrines were associated with festivals and fairs.

Bill and I gave the nuns a donation, said goodbye, and walked over to the *librería.* Paca had a surprise for us, a foil-wrapped *tortilla peregrina*—a pilgrimage omelet, her own invention. It was a *tortilla española* encased in a large, circular loaf of bread. Paca had cut the loaf open and hollowed out the center, then placed the potato, *chorizo,* and egg omelet in the center, and covered it. That way, it would be easy to transport. She also gave us a small bottle of *puchiri,* a homemade coffee liqueur. We thanked her, kissed everyone goodbye, and walked out of town.

We crossed the Río Cea on the Puente Canto. Once a Roman bridge spanned the river, but it had been destroyed; in the seventeenth century, its stones were used to construct the present bridge. It was very narrow. When a truck came towards us, we had to step off the pavement into a small triangular extension from the central arch. After crossing the river, we passed a grove of black poplars, the distant descendants of Charlemagne's army's lances. Until we reached Calzada del Coto, five kilometers away, we would be walking on the highway that covered both the ancient Roman road and the medieval Camino.

Near the municipal sports complex—a pool, tennis courts, a soccer field, a restaurant—we saw a road sign with a scallop shell emblem on one side: "Camino de Santiago. Santiago de Compostela: 473 kilometers. León: 65 kilometers." Sahagún to León was the eighth stage of journey in the *Codex,* a distance of 52 kilometers.

We'd made it half-way there. My blisters had healed, my stomach was calm; Bill's toenails were growing back, his shoulders had quit cramping up. It had been good to relax with friends, to be with friends, not just strangers met by chance on the Camino. The pilgrimage took all stability away, since we were always passing through, always leaving. Everything was impermanent except the pilgrimage—and that was a permanent state of transit and quest. No wonder pilgrimage was a Christian metaphor for life—but what was it a journey towards?

As we walked along the edge of the road, I pointed out some circular adobe buildings, called *palomares.* Villagers keep doves or pigeons in them. A truck came roaring around the curve, and we stepped off the side of the road onto the hard-baked, reddish soil. After an hour, we reached Calzada del Coto, the ancient Villa Zacarías, once the property of the monastery of Sahagún. We had to make a choice: take the Calzada de los Peregrinos, which passes through Calzada del Coto and Calzadilla de los Hermanillos, to Mansilla de las Mulas, 34 kilometers away; or, take the Real Camino Francés, which passes through Bercianos, El Burgo Ranero and Reliegos, to Mansilla. According to the guidebook, the first route was the same as the Roman road, the Vía Trajana, and was isolated and unpaved. The second route, a bit more to the south, was paved and easier to travel. We chose the latter.

The church in Calzada del Coto. In front of it is the main plaza. During the village fiestas, this plaza is blocked off with carts and barricades, and small, horned cattle are driven into the enclosure. The men of the community practice bullfighting in this improvised ring, while the rest of the community watches and cheers.

On the outskirts of Calzada we passed the Hermitage of San Roque on the right and a wrought-iron statue of a man and a cart on the left. The statue commemorates Eufrasio of Sahagún, who, in 1981, turned the merchants of *aceite de colza* away from Calzada. He told them everyone was in church and there would be little business for them that day; not wishing to waste time, they left. The *aceite de colza* was machine oil which had been reprocessed and was falsely labeled and illegally sold as cheap olive oil; unfortunately, the oil was poisonous and ingesting it could, and did, cause death or chronic illness. Although Calzada del Coto was spared, most of the surrounding villages were not. Olive oil, staple of Spanish cooking, is expensive in León, and the people are poor.

Calzada is a small agricultural village of 350 people who earn their hard living by raising sheep, growing grain and soybeans, selling cow's milk, and, at one time, cultivating grapes. Now only a few people make wine and sell it; it is hard work to tend the vines and the quality was never very high.

The pavement ended, and we walked down a dirt street. Everything in the village looked brown and dry—unbroken blocks of adobe walls, brown streets. No green lawns, no landscaped yards. Sometimes, the adobe was the front of a house; sometimes it was a blank wall. We looked in through one cracked wooden door and saw not the interior of a house but a lushly blooming garden, shut off from casual, public view. We heard bells: cattle were being taken out to pasture.

On one corner we saw a bar and went inside. The two teenage girls behind the counter barely stopped talking long enough to serve us. The fact that we were pilgrims to Santiago, the fact that we were strangers, the fact that we were foreigners, did not interest them at all. We drank our Cokes, left, and crossed over to the Camino Real Francés.

The summer before, the successful wine-maker/farmer/mayor of the town had proudly shown me some of the Camino, buried beneath a field. But a friend of his told me that nobody had cared about the "real" Camino until the early 1970s, when the State Ministry of Tourism started promoting its existence. The mayor had also introduced me to his 82-year-old mother, a wrinkled, nearly toothless woman dressed in black. Around her neck were several medallions, including a gold cross; proudly, she had taken it up and kissed it: it came from Santiago and had been touched to the back of the Apostle's cape.

Outside of town we saw farmers with mule-pulled carts, working in the fields, and there was a clearing where some people were winnowing the grain. A man sat on a *trilla*—a wooden platform, lined underneath with teeth—and a horse walked around in a circle. The man's weight, and the teeth, broke up the grain.

Bill shook his head. "I had no idea farming was still so primitive here!"

I remembered how shocked I had been, the summer before, to see such primitive agriculture. One family I knew had a small vegetable garden outside of Sahagún, and I used to see the son riding the horse to the field; I would think how poverty-stricken they must be, using a horse instead of a tractor. But the mother told me the horse was very convenient: their plot was small, and the horse could be used not only to till the soil but to carry produce back from the fields. The horse's upkeep cost very little. Unfortunately, the horse died, and then her son had to ride his bicycle—they had no car—to the fields and back. She didn't know how they would plow the garden the next year.

The countryside was flat and barren, but at last we came to a few low scrub trees, *encina*—evergreen oak—and a small building on the left, the Hermitage of la Virgen de Perales. Legend says that once there was a *hospital* for pilgrims beside it. We decided to take a break and eat our *tortilla peregrina* in the shade. We took our shoes off while we rested. My feet were sore and swollen, although they had been in good shape when we started, just a few hours earlier. While we sat and ate, two young pilgrims dressed in walking shorts, t-shirts, and hiking boots came by; they saw us and walked over. Blonde, pretty Dutch girls, they had started walking the Camino in Vezelay in France. We offered them some of our *tortilla peregrina* and they offered us some fruit.

I asked them, "How is it going?"

Between bites, the shorter one replied, "Fine. The first few days were rough, but now we're used to walking."

Bill asked, "Do you walk every day?"

"Every day. Some days are tougher, some days are easier. But we're in a hurry and we don't have time to stop."

Bill asked, "How many kilometers a day?"

"Oh, between 30 and 35."

The taller one added, "Of course, sometimes we hitchhike. We hate walking on the highway and dodging trucks."

Bill and I looked at each other: we'd managed 25 kilometers to Frómista and had collapsed.

I asked, "Why are you going?"

They looked at each other, and the shorter one said, "Well, we had the summer off, and we wanted to take a long walk together, and we knew about the pilgrimage—not much, just that the Camino still existed—so we went to Vezelay and started."

The other added, "It was hard to find out about the Camino in France—the road's not marked. But we have a copy of Picaud's 'The Pilgrim's Guide' and we followed that."

"Have you had any trouble along the way—being women, traveling alone?"

The tall one nodded. "Only once. We were sleeping in the porch of a church, and the village guys kept pestering us. It was annoying—"

Her friend interrupted: "Not dangerous, just annoying. And only once."

Bill asked, "Where do you sleep?"

The tall one said, "We always ask the mayor or the priest for shelter. We're art students, so we don't have much money—we really can't afford to pay. In fact, Sahagún was the first place we had to pay for shelter."

I said, "Didn't you know the nuns would let you stay for free?"

"We tried them, but they were full. And we couldn't find the mayor."

As we ate, we exchanged stories of the Camino. Had they heard about the forty with the cross? Yes. Had we heard about the woman from Barcelona who was traveling alone—for the fourth time? Or about the two French women, one of whom was going to get married in Santiago? She was going to meet her fiancé there, at the end of the pilgrimage.

We finished eating and brushed the crumbs off our clothes. The Dutch girls stood up.

The shorter one suggested, "We can walk together for a while, if you like."

Bill said, "I think we need to rest a little longer."

Although I was surprised at Bill's response, I didn't argue. "Maybe we'll see you later."

They left, and I asked Bill why he didn't want to walk with them. He explained he was exhausted. So was I, and I had a new set of blisters as well from tying my shoes too tight.

We stretched out in the shade and took a nap. Later, we walked the remaining kilometer to Bercianos del Real Camino Francés. Bercianos is a small adobe village, quite similar to Calzada, though a bit smaller and more poverty-stricken in appearance; none of the streets was paved.

There hadn't been a telephone in Bercianos until 1970, or running water in the houses until 1975.

We walked through town and saw a sign, "Bar Café El Camino." Since it was already time to take another break, we went in, ordered two Cokes and started talking with the barkeeper. She told us that just the day before, four French pilgrims on horseback had passed through. They had spent the night in the Casa de Peregrinos, an eighteenth-century *posada* which had, until recently, been used as the parish priest's house. Now there was no parish priest, so the mayor had decided the house should be used to shelter pilgrims. And a few days before, there had been a group of 40 or so with a cross, and a German traveling alone, and a Dutchman, also alone. And a Belgian, who spoke neither French nor Spanish but some language all his own. She shook her head: he'd seemed a little odd. And there were four Spaniards, wearing traditional pilgrimage garb. Had we seen them? No, we hadn't. There were a lot of pilgrims, she added, more than usual.

"I remember when I was a little girl, there were pilgrims then, too—but not as many. And we took turns—*la vez del pobre*—helping poor people or pilgrims who needed shelter. They would go to the mayor and get a *palo*—a stick—that gave them permission to ask for shelter. All the families took turns."

"Did they sleep inside the house?"

"Oh, no—they slept outdoors, in the hayloft, or in the barn. But we fed them. And I remember sitting on the floor after dinner, listening to their stories. In those days—thirty, forty years ago—none of us had traveled very much. But the pilgrims had, and they would tell us stories about far off countries, and places they had seen. Once, two of them stole the blankets we lent them—but I think they were just pretending to be pilgrims. And once my mother let someone stay in the house who was absolutely crazy! But I don't remember if he was a pilgrim or not."

Her teenage daughter had been listening, and she spoke up.

"I'd like to go on pilgrimage to Santiago, but my mother won't let me."

I looked at her mother. "Why not?"

Rubbing her thumb and forefinger together in a standard Spanish gesture, she said, "No money."

I asked the girl, "Why do you want to go?"

Her mother answered for her: "She likes *cosas raras*—unusual things!"

We all laughed, including the girl. Then the barkeeper turned to a rack of cellophane snack food on the wall behind her and pulled off a package of kernels of some sort, in liquid. She handed it to us. “It's *chochos.* Take it—it's a gift.”

We opened the cellophane package and ate the kernels, spitting out the skins, and then we ordered another two Cokes. She wouldn't let us pay. “Vale la pena,” she said, and smiled. “Un abrazo al Apóstol.”

We thanked the woman, put on our backpacks, and started to leave.

Her husband came in and, seeing our packs, asked if we were pilgrims. Then he told us about pilgrims he had seen over the years—a young couple and a baby, traveling in a mule-driven cart; a group of four Frenchmen on horseback. Then he asked if we knew where the Camino de Santiago was. We said we thought so, but he told us anyway.

“Go to the church and follow the yellow arrows out of town.”

Everyone seemed to know where the “real” Camino was. I remembered what someone had told me the summer before—that interest in the Camino was fairly recent. In the 1960s Franco and his Minister of Tourism, Manuel Fraga, had made a concerted effort to promote and publicize the pilgrimage to Santiago. Was that when villagers—some villagers, at least—actually became aware of, or interested in, the “real” Camino? Maybe he was wrong and some of them had always cared about the tradition.

Although we found the church, we didn't see any yellow arrows. So we followed a dirt path out of town, down a small hillside honeycombed with *bodegas.* We saw no arrows, but how could we be lost? The countryside was almost completely flat, bare, without shade. The earth was dry, the sun was bright, the air was shimmering with heat. Gradually, the road began to rise and fall a tiny bit. When we saw a small arroyo and some trees on the left, we headed towards the shade, took off our backpacks and our shoes, and fell asleep. We were awakened by the sound of sheep and bells; a shepherd and his flock were passing by. He walked over to us.

“Pilgrims?”

We nodded yes.

“I see you're lost.”

Bill and I looked at each other.

Pointing with his shepherd's crook, he said, “Cross over that ridge and you'll come to a road. Turn left and follow the road to El Burgo Ranero.”

We thanked him, put on our shoes again, put on our backpacks

A typical settlement in the Bierzo region: one-house deep on both sides of the Camino. The houses are massive, with large windows and doors and thick walls. The settlement, like the Camino, winds around the hill. Pilgrims must dodge traffic as they walk on the unyielding, pebbly pavement.

again, and started over the ridge. The day was hot, our packs were heavy. Soon we reached the road and followed it towards El Burgo Ranero. In 1681, Laffi and his companions encountered the dead body of a pilgrim being eaten by wolves a league from El Burgo Ranero. When they reached the town they looked for the priest in order to give the body a proper burial. Then, as now, the countryside was deserted. Laffi reported that the village was incredibly poor, nothing more than humble shepherds' huts, thatched with hay. He and his companions had had to sleep on the floor.

During the last three centuries, El Burgo Ranero has improved. Now, red brick buildings are interspersed with adobe houses; the town is on the railroad line and is next to a major highway, and there is industry. We saw a granary and a large sign on a warehouse, "El Burgo Ranero Chorizo." At a bar advertising rooms, we stopped and went in. But the room was not too appealing, so we left and went to another bar and drank a Coke.

Looking at our backpacks, a young man drinking wine at the bar said,

"Qué trabajo!"

We smiled.

"Peregrinos?"

We nodded and he told us he had gone three times to Santiago—but always by car.

I asked, "On pilgrimage?"

He shook his head: "No, never. On excursion."

Despite our protestations, the young man paid for our drinks. Then he left.

The next town with a hostel was probably Mansilla de las Mulas, eighteen kilometers away.

Bill said, "I don't want to walk those eighteen kilometers. Not today, not tomorrow. Frankly, I'm tired."

"I'm tired, too, Bill—but we've been tired before. We don't just quit because we're tired."

"Who's talking about quitting? I'm talking about taking a taxi."

"But Bill—"

"You didn't mind, before, when you were tired or needed to get somewhere. So why do you mind now?"

I thought about it, struggling to find the words. "It just seems like we're 'copping out.' We've only walked eighteen kilometers. We're not exhausted or desperate—we're just tired and bored. Besides, we could stay here and rest."

"You may not be exhausted, but I am. And I don't want to stay here. You've accused me of being rigid—what about you?"

"Okay, Bill. Sometimes I need to quit walking, sometimes you do. But let's take a bus, not a taxi."

We asked the barkeeper about a bus, but there was none that late in the day. How about the train? The train didn't go to Mansilla. So Bill asked about a taxi, and we were directed to a house down the block. It was an imposing edifice: a two-story adobe building, with tiny, boarded-up windows on the second story. We knocked at the heavy wooden doors. No answer. We knocked again. Still no answer. At last, Bill pushed on the door and it opened. We looked inside and saw that instead of knocking on the front door, we had been knocking on a gate. Inside, cats and chickens scurried across a courtyard, a cow mooed from a nearby stall. Leather harnesses hung on one wall and rusty equipment was scattered about. The yard was inside walls, hidden from view. We walked over to a small building with windows and knocked at the door. A man, dressed in blue overalls, answered. After Bill explained that we wanted a ride to Mansilla, he agreed to take us there for $10.00.

Soon we were in his car, effortlessly traveling across the flat, boring, hot Tierra de Campos. Dust followed behind us. In ten minutes we had arrived in the partly walled town of Mansilla de las Mulas, and our driver dropped us off at the Hotel La Estrella. We went in, got a room with a private bath and hot water.

Mansilla, called Manxilla by Picaud, was founded sometime before 1188. It was surrounded by medieval stone walls and towers, parts of which still remain. Originally there were four gates into the city; now only one, la Concepción, remains. Once Mansilla had had a convent, a monastery, seven churches, and three *hospitales* and several inns. One of these was the site of a famous seventeenth-century picaresque novel, *La Pícara Justina.* The picaresque novel, originating in sixteenth-century Spain, had as its hero a rogue or *pícaro* who undergoes a number of intriguing adventures. *La Pícara Justina* is a witty, first-person account of an adventurous innkeeper in Mansilla de las Mulas named Justina.

Today, Mansilla's walls and churches are in ruins, and instead of *hospitales* there are several fondas and a "hospitality complex" which includes the Hotel La Estrella, a spectacular discoteque with fake Greek statuary, revolving strobe lights, and a gambling hall. We went inside but soon left, driven out by the noise, and walked over to a restaurant we had noticed as we drove into town. Called "El Horreo," it was a square building on stilts, designed to look like the Asturian grain storage bin. It was early—only 9 p.m—so there was no crowd. I ordered grilled lamb chops, Bill ordered the specialty of the house, *mollejas.*

"Bill, what are *mollejas*?"

"A kind of shellfish—a mussel, I think."

They came. They were not mussels; they were something else, something grey, soft, and spongy, covered with a wine, tomato, and mushroom sauce.

I checked the dictionary. "Mussels are *mellijones.* What you've got are *mollejas*—sweetbreads."

"What are those?"

"I'm not sure."

We asked the waiter, who pointed towards his throat and explained that *mollejas* were thymus glands, taken, in this case, from the throats of young calves.

Bill looked back at his plate. "Well, I'll try it. It's not quite as bad as your fish head in Nájera, at least." He took a sample. "Actually, it's quite good. Want a taste?"

I tried it. It was good.

Spanish cuisine seemed to include most parts of the animal. Paca used chicken feet and odds and ends of bones and greens for stews. And people ate *callos*—tripe—and fish heads. When I was young, Mother served beef heart for dinner sometimes, and liver—but tripe, head cheese, sweetbreads—these were not standard American fare.

After dinner we walked on painful feet back to the hotel. But rather than go to bed, we sat downstairs in the bar, drinking sherry and talking to the hotel owner, a heavy-set, well-dressed gentleman. We told him we had friends in Sahagún and he proceeded to extoll the virtues of Mansilla, a town full of history: Juana la Loca and Queen Urraca had lived there. He wondered what we were doing in Mansilla, and we told him we were pilgrims, traveling to Santiago. He told us that 100 Swiss pilgrims on bicycles had slept in the Town Hall the night before. And a few days ago, he had seen thirty with a cross—both boys and girls, he told us. I wondered whether this was a new group, or whether the same old group was changing its membership.

I asked him the difference between *peregrinación*—pilgrimage—and *romería.*

"A *romería* is a fiesta, a pilgrimage is a sacrifice. You might have to travel for a *romería,* say, to a hermitage outside of town, but it doesn't matter how you get there. And once there, even if there is a Mass or some religious celebration, there is also—first and foremost—a festival, with a picnic, and music, and dancing. The religion is just an excuse for having a party. But a pilgrimage is different. A pilgrimage means making a sacrifice. Everyone does it their own way—by bicycle, on foot, by car—but it has to be a sacrifice, any way you do it."

Bill said, "I've seen streets called 'Calle de los Romeros.' What does that mean?"

"*Romeros* are pilgrims going to Rome. *Peregrinos* are pilgrims going to Santiago."

Alfonso X, el Sabio, wrote in the thirteenth century that:

> Men become *romeros* and *peregrinos* to serve God and honor the saints. And because that is what they want to do, they separate from their families and places and wives and houses and all that they have and they go through foreign lands, lacerating their bodies and leaving their belongings, looking for shrines. . . .[23]

According to him, a *romero* was one who went to Rome; a *peregrino* was one who went to Jerusalem or Santiago or some other shrine—however, again according to Alfonso the Wise, people used the terms indiscriminately. Writing at the end of the same century, Dante made a different distinction. In *Vita Nuovo* he wrote that *romeros* were those who went to Rome, *palmeros* were those who went to Jerusalem, and *peregrinos* were those who went to Santiago. Since this definition gave primacy to Santiago, Spaniards tend to prefer it.

In subsequent centuries, the word *peregrino* came to mean vagabond, thief, and gypsy, as many disreputable types took to the pilgrimage roads and either disguised themselves as pilgrims or simply outnumbered the honest ones.

The word *peregrino* comes from the Latin *peregrinus,* one traveling in strange lands. Titus Livy, writing in the first century A.D., mentioned a Roman official called the Praetor Peregrinus, responsible for all foreigners in Rome. The familiar Biblical phrase, "we are all strangers and pilgrims," is, technically, redundant, but it didn't feel redundant; it felt emphatic.

It was late, we were tired, so we said goodnight to the hotel owner and went to bed.

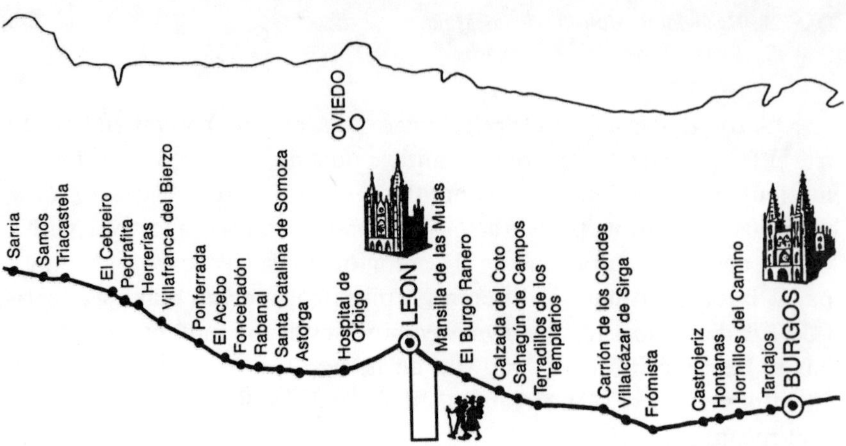

Day 29: August 7 I woke up crying. I had dreamt that I was back in the U.S., that we had quit the pilgrimage at Mansilla. In my dream I was asking, "How did this happen? How could we quit, just because we had sore feet and were tired?" I was sobbing with disappointment. In my dream, I knew I had to return to Spain and finish the pilgrimage.

Preoccupied, I got up and looked out the window. In the plaza, in front of the public fountain, a middle-aged pilgrim was washing. He had taken off his shirt and was washing himself under the arms. As I watched, he dried himself, attached the damp towel to the top of his pack, put on his shirt again, lifted up his pack—there was a scallop shell on the back—and started down the road.

My blisters had popped and were bloody; my feet ached—the arches felt as if they were ready to collapse. Bill was exhausted, too. Why were we so tired? We were more used to our packs than before, but our backs continued to hurt. And our feet. Maybe I should have worn boots; they would have given my ankles and arches more support—walking on uneven cobblestones and slippery gravel was very hard on the feet. But Bill wore boots and his feet were in terrible shape. He had lost some toenails, he had blisters, and, he informed me, he had just developed a case of tendonitis.

The morning before we had been rested and even cheerful—but the enormity of what still lay before us had suddenly hit both of us. Somehow, once we had accomplished the short-term goal of reaching Sahagún as honestly as possible—on foot—we were ready to quit. We were tired. Tired of being strangers passing through. Tired of the pain, tired of being tired.

Bill looked at me as he laced up his boots, then looked at his backpack. "I've lost my momentum."

I nodded. “Me, too. But we’ve got to go on. We’re running out of time.”

“Maybe if our packs were lighter—”

I looked at our packs, sitting there on the floor. “Maybe if we had balloons? Or trained birds?”

“Come on, Ellen, I’m serious. Maybe we could lighten our packs again, like we did in Estella.”

“That sounds wonderful—I’d love to walk with nothing on my back to weigh me down! But what do you suggest we leave? We need the sleeping bags and the rain ponchos—”

“Why?”

I felt anxious and depressed. No sleeping bags—a risk. No rain ponchos—another risk. I remembered the disastrous beginning in the Pyrenees. It frightened me to feel so exposed, so unprotected, so unprepared. Besides, I felt as if I were always leaving bits and pieces of myself behind. In Estella I had laughed about getting rid of “extra baggage” and thought there was a profound lesson to be learned. Now, I found there was some baggage I didn’t want to give up. I missed my friends in Sahagún. I missed my family in the States. I missed my nice clothes, my comfort. I was tired of sacrifice, tired of shedding protective layers.

I was unwilling, but Bill convinced me we should at least try an alternative. So we went to a store and bought two nylon duffle bags—about two feet long, one foot wide—with shoulder straps. We packed them with just the necessities: no sleeping bags, no rain ponchos, one change of clothes. And we took a trial walk for one kilometer down the road. Almost immediately, the carrying strap began cutting into my shoulder. After twenty minutes, we turned around and walked back to the hotel.

Frustrated, Bill said, “Well, there must be something we can do. Maybe if we walk earlier in the day, or take a longer rest. Let’s not walk today, either. Let’s take a taxi to León. Maybe that’ll help.”

“All right. At any rate, since we don’t have time to walk all the way to Santiago, maybe we should make plans for when, and where, we take a bus or taxi.”

“I don’t want to plan it. Let’s just play it by ear.”

“But look, Bill, I think it would be better to know we’ll skip a certain stretch and walk the rest, rather than just taking a ride whenever we feel tired. That’s an ‘easy out’ that weakens my resolve, makes it harder to keep going.”

“I don’t want to make plans. We’ve walked over 500 kilometers and that's more than half-way. We just need to make a big, final push. We've got time—two weeks."

I looked at him. There was no point in arguing. We were both so—changeable. Yesterday, just yesterday, we had felt energetic, rested, enthusiastic—and by mid-afternoon, we had collapsed and Bill had wanted to quit walking and find a ride. And I had objected. But today I agreed, without arguing, to take a taxi to León at the same time that Bill was talking about a "big, final push." We seemed so—mercurial. Maybe it was because every day was so full, so over-filled with challenges and decisions, that what felt right at one time, at one place, felt absolutely wrong just an hour, a kilometer later.

A big, final push. Sacrifice, sacrifice. We'd gotten lazy. But for what was the sacrifice? What was the lesson now? We'd been walking for almost a month: enough of a lesson. Now, it was just exhaustion, tedium, repetition. Was that the lesson, to keep on going on and on, just to get there? You can't quit on the pilgrimage of life?

We took a taxi the fourteen kilometers to León, end of the eighth stage of journey in the *Codex.*

We drove down from the flat, brown Tierra de Campos into a broad green and brown valley formed by the rivers Torío and Bernesga. In front of us was León, capital of the province of León. As we drove across the stone bridge over the Río Torío, our driver wanted to know where to drop us off. León was a large city, with over 120,000 inhabitants and a number of hotels. I suggested we give ourselves a treat and stay at the five-star hotel, San Marcos, run by Entursa.

San Marcos was begun in the sixteenth century as a monastery for the Knights of Santiago. According to the guidebook, the poet Francisco de Quevedo was imprisoned there from 1640 to 1643 by Philip IV for his lampoons against Olivares. More recently, it was used as a barracks and, rumor has it, as a headquarters for Franco's inquisitions. In 1964 work was begun to convert it into a luxury hotel. Though our driver found it odd that pilgrims wanted to go to a luxury hotel, he drove us there.

It was impressive. San Marcos was begun in 1513, when King Ferdinand was head of the Order of the Knights of Santiago, founded in 1170 as the Brothers of Cáceres and a year later officially called the Order of Santiago. The Knights of Santiago were one of several military-religious orders established in the twelfth and thirteenth centuries to help fight the Moors, protect pilgrims, and ransom prisoners in Palestine. Like Santiago Matamoros, they combined priestly devotion with soldierly blood-thirstiness. Their motto was *Rubet ensis sanguine Arabum*—"My sword is red with the blood of the Arabs"—and their symbol was a sword-like cross with the scallop shell on the crosspiece.

Several of these Orders—the Knights Templar, the Knights Hospitalier, and the Knights of Santiago—became extremely powerful, so much so that they threatened or were perceived as threats by the monarchs of Spain and France. King Ferdinand had a novel solution: he had himself made leader of the Order of Santiago, thus gaining for himself the power and wealth of the Knights of Santiago. Soon the Order no longer posed a threat.

After he took over the Order, the King had a new convent built on the banks of the Río Bernesga, next to the hospice for Christian paupers founded by Doña Sancha in 1152. Perhaps he had the convent built to assuage the Knights' suspicions about being taken over by the Crown. Construction took place in stages; much was done between 1513 and 1549, but some of the work was not completed until the eighteenth century. Recently remodeled on the inside, outside the modern hotel retains the original, impressive 100-meter-long Plateresque facade, with its carved frieze of mythological and historic busts, including kings and queens, priests and warriors. The ornate two-story facade is a balanced composition of windows and niches, columns and pilasters. Over the elaborate main door is a horseback-riding figure of Santiago, and the legends of his life and death are graphically shown.

To the right of the convent is the church of the Order, consecrated in 1541; the front of the church is decorated with *vieiras*—the scallop shell of Santiago. Row after row of evenly spaced shells form patterns of light and shadow as the sun moves across the sky. The scallop shell, the cockle shell, the *vieira*: sea shell in the shape of the foot of the *oca* or goose, in the shape of the rising sun, in the shape of a cupped hand; used in ancient cults, found in ancient tombs, emblazoned on the side of the church of the Knights of Santiago.

To the right of the church is an unprepossessing building, the pilgrim's *hospital,* a several-centuries-old replacement for a pilgrim's shelter that had existed in the Middle Ages. In 1528 this hospice was quite imposing, two stories tall, with a painted portal. A registry was kept of all pilgrims, and weary travelers were treated with care. There were separate dormitories for men and women, and sheets were hung between the beds for privacy. The Pícara Justina from Mansilla mentions the *hospital*, saying that "there they kept ill Frenchmen and other gents, but didn't want *gallofos* [vagabonds]." Laffi, writing in the seventeenth century, called it a "very fine hospital." Today, the thriving pilgrim's *hospital* is gone, replaced by a shabby, abandoned-looking building.

After admiring the outside of the hotel, we went in and asked for a room. The desk clerk looked skeptically at us and our packs. Although we had changed into our more presentable "sightseeing" clothes in Mansilla, we still had our backpacks. Bill looked at me, expecting the worst. Quickly, I smiled at the clerk and started telling him in Spanish how much we were enjoying our trip, and about our friends in Sahagún, and about how much we were looking forward to staying in this famous hotel. While I talked, I took my money out of my wallet. I had cashed travelers' checks in Sahagún, so I had plenty of money with me. After looking at us again, the clerk gave us a room; apparently he had decided we were eccentric—but not poor.

We walked through the stone-walled lobby, up the stone steps, past the huge, gilt-framed oil paintings of aristocrats dressed in elaborate velvet and lace outfits, then down a long stone hallway, past sofas of deep red velvet and tables of deep, rich wood. Finally, we reached our room. It was posh: finely carved wooden bedsteads, velvet bedspreads, upholstered chairs, oriental-looking rugs—the warm colors and rich textures contrasted pleasantly with the rough, sand-colored stone walls.

I went into the bathroom. There were huge white bath sheets, an enormous tub, a tray full of soaps and creams, special cloths for shining shoes. I turned on the tap; there was, of course, hot water.

The rest of the afternoon we relaxed. Rather than walk around town, we decided to explore the hotel. We went into the *Bar Americano* (a *barra americana* is a house of ill repute) and ordered Cinzano—a bitter alcoholic drink, like Campari. While we relaxed, we admired the impressive reddish-pink brocaded canopy over the bar, the glittering chandeliers, the dark brown leather covered chairs, the plush red carpeting.

By going through a glass doorway in the lobby we entered the Provincial Archeological Museum; when the convent was remodeled, the chapterhouse, the sacristy, and part of the cloisters were set aside for the museum. On the pavement and walls of the Gothic cloisters are randomly placed chunks of inscribed and decorated Roman stones. The rest of the museum is filled with Roman, Celtic, Visigothic, medieval, and Renaissance treasures, remnants of the various conquerors and acquisitive nobles who temporarily resided in León.

León takes its name from the Seventh Roman Legion, the *Legio*

Séptima Gemina, encamped there by Augustus to defend the plains against the wild Asturians. In 586, León fell to Leovigild; then it fell to the Moors in the first onslaught of the Moorish conquest, but it was recaptured by Ordoño I in 850. Ordoño II made it his capital, and in the tenth century the Asturian kings built new walls around their new capital, adding to the third-century Roman fortifications. Despite the walls, Almanzor burned the city in 988; it was rebuilt, destroyed again, and rebuilt again. Fernando I was crowned King of León and Castilla in León in 1037, and later his son Alfonso VI, with the help of his vassal el Cid, made Castilla subject to the crown of León. By the eleventh and twelfth centuries, León had been resettled with Christian refugees from the south, called Mozarabs, and had become the center of Mozarabic Spain. In 1324 Alfonso XI built more walls around the city. However, later in that century, Pedro the Cruel moved the royal court to Sevilla and León lost its political significance.

When we entered the Provincial Archeological Museum, we saw an array of inscribed Roman stones, including an altar to Diana; Celtic artifacts; Byzantine, Arab, and Jewish textiles; Flemish paintings; and assorted statuary and crucifixes from various centuries.

The most impressive piece was a small ivory crucifix, El Cristo de Carrizo, carved in the eleventh century. Palms nailed to a wooden cross, large black eyes staring unblinkingly at the floor, the figure looks solemn and slightly puzzled. The delicately carved body is out of proportion: the hands and feet are long and large, the arms and legs are short; the head, with its tight rows of curly hair and its curly beard, is also disproportionately large. The ivory is veined, like flesh, and the sculptor has turned it into supplely creased skin.

I looked at El Cristo de Carrizo for five minutes, then turned to Bill. "I've seen enough. I'm leaving."

"Don't you want to look at all these other things?"

"No."

I left the museum and went back to the bar, sat down, and ordered Cinzano *sin alcohol*—bitter Cinzano without the alcohol, and nibbled on toasted, salted almonds, while I thought about the pale perfection of the crucified Christ figure. It was all out of proportion—yet that made it seem more human. It was a caricature, really, but somehow that made it seem more believable, rather than less. After all, it represented a man-God who was killed but then came back to life. How could one portray such a symbolic act realistically? The near-life-size, blood-dripping

Christ of Burgos, with its buffalo-hide skin, I found repulsive; meant to look real, it looked obscene. But this small crucifix of polished ivory, with outsized hands and outsized head, evoked the mystery, expressed the myth.

An hour later, Bill joined me, and for half an hour we sat and drank and nibbled on toasted, salted almonds. Then we went into the restaurant. It was deserted; Spaniards eat dinner around 10 p.m., and it was only 9. They served us anyway.

The restaurant of San Marcos is known for its fine food. I ordered *escalopines madrileños*—breaded veal medallions in tomato sauce. They looked pretty and tasted delicious—a contrast of crisp golden-fried veal, smooth red sauce, and fresh sprigs of parsley. Bill ordered *ancas de rana*—a casserole of tender little frog legs, sauteed in oil and garlic, then baked in a colorful—and spicy—mixture of green and red peppers and chilis. A wonderful odor wafted up from the bubbling contents of the earthenware dish.

Bill saw me watching him eat and offered to share his frog legs with me. Soon we were using pieces of bread to soak up the last bits of sauce. We washed them down with a fine, locally produced red wine. The dinner was the kind that is not only sensorilly stimulating but also intellectually satisfying; I paused with each bite to think about the subtle interplay of taste and texture, of odor and substance.

Although we were satiated, our waiter recommended a well-aged *Manchego* cheese and fruit for dessert, followed by cognac.

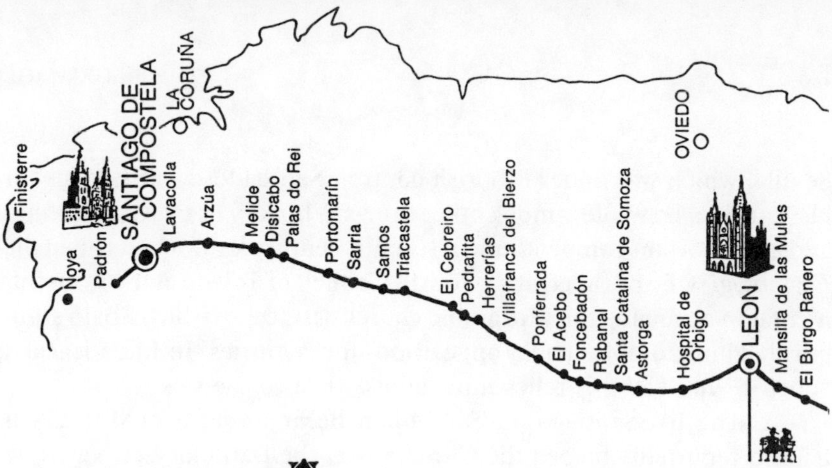

Day 30: August 8

The next morning we were rested, but Bill wanted to stay another day to make sure we had more time to recover from the strain of the last few weeks. I agreed; besides, there was a lot to see in León. After breakfast of *churros* and chocolate in the hotel, we started walking towards the center of town.

> Toledo en riqueza,
> Compostela en fortaleza,
> Y León en sutileza[24]
>
> (Toledo in wealth,
> Compostela in endurance,
> León in 'airy elegance')

According to a sixteenth-century poem, the Kingdom of León had 24 kings before Castilla had laws. And at one time the city of León reportedly had 27 churches, 17 *hospitales* for pilgrims, numerous palaces and impressive homes, and Moorish, Frankish, and Jewish neighborhoods. But by the nineteenth century, León was markedly less impressive—at least according to the English traveler Richard Ford, who described the city as dull, deserted, and decaying.

Today it is a thriving urban capital, full of newly constructed apartment buildings and stores, as well as well preserved medieval walls and monuments. I particularly wanted to visit two of these monuments, the Collegiate Church of San Isidoro and the cathedral, Santa María de la Regla, famous for its *sutileza.* We followed the medieval city walls until we reached the Colegiata de San Isidoro. After waiting for half an hour in the lobby, we took the obligatory guided tour.

In 1063, at the behest of Doña Sancha and her husband Ferdinand I, the relics of Saint Isidore (ca. 560–636), Archbishop of Sevilla and "Doctor Egregius" of the Visigothic church, were transferred to León from

Sevilla, which was under Moorish control. San Isidoro was famous for his learning; he wrote, among other things, a history of the Gothic kings and an important compendium of seventh-century knowledge, called the *Etymologies;* he presided at the fourth Council of Toledo and was instrumental in arranging the Mozarabic church service, to which Spain stubbornly clung, despite papal opposition, for centuries. In life a learned "doctor," in death his relics miraculously healed the sick.

And he, like Santiago and San Millán, became a slayer of Moors. San Isidoro reportedly helped the Christians at the Battle of Las Navas de Tolosa in 1212; an eighteenth-century carving on a gable over the Puerta del Cordero—the Door of the Lamb—the main portal of the Church of San Isidoro, depicts the saint as a warrior, mounted on horseback. According to Georgiana King, Saint Isidore was often substituted in legends for Santiago and was the successor of the native bull-god; in addition, he was connected with bees and was similar, in some ways, to the Cretan Zeus. His feasts were on the solstices—July 25 and December 30—as are Santiago's. Once again, syncretism has obviously been at work. Syncretism and politics, because it appears that a conscious effort was made to dramatize and publicize the importance of Isidore and León, thus drawing off—or drawing back—some of the fame and financial benefits that were going to Santiago de Compostela.

The relics were reburied in what had been a simple, ninth-century church dedicated to John the Baptist, a church destroyed by Almanzor in 988 and rebuilt by Alfonso V and later by his daughter, Doña Sancha, and Ferdinand I. In honor of the new relics, the church was renamed the Church of San Isidoro. Soon, miracles attributed to the relics were reported to have occurred. It became a popular church: el Cid and Jimena were married there, and she frequently attended Mass in San Isidoro. In addition, pilgrims who were unable to reach Santiago could receive their plenary indulgences in León, by passing through a doorway on the south called the Puerta de Perdón—the Door of Pardon.

Little of the eleventh-century church remains, and most of the present basilica is from the twelfth century. But what interested me most was not the church itself but the eleventh-century Royal Pantheon, burial vault of the kings of León, with its twelfth-century paintings. Here, until Marshal Soult's troops desecrated the chapel in 1808, were the tombs of 11 kings and 12 queens, including Alfonso V, Fernando I, and Doña Sancha, 21 Infantes and many other nobles. The Pantheon measures 23 feet by 30 feet; stubby, sand-colored columns support the vault, their capitals elaborately carved with biblical themes, animals, and floral designs.

But it is the wall and ceiling frescoes which are memorable. The Royal Pantheon has been called the "Sistine Chapel of the Romanesque," and it has been said that the Royal Pantheon is to Romanesque painting as Altamira is to cave art—comparisons which take us forward to theology and backwards to nature worship. Painted between 1160 and 1180 in blue, ochre, red, black and now-faded yellow and green tempera on a white background, the frescos depict Christ and the Evangelists, the Annunciation to the shepherds, the apocalyptic vision of St. John, the Last Supper, the signs of the Zodiac. Rustic scenes of pastors, of hunting, and of daily life are dramatically contrasted with the central presentation of Christ, surrounded by Apostles and mystical symbols. On the inside of one arch the daily tasks associated with each month are shown; by looking at them, I could imagine what medieval daily life—admittedly stylized—was really like. So popular—and so evocative—are the frescoes that part of the scene of the Annunciation is used on posters distributed by the Ministry of Tourism to advertise the Año Santo Compostelano.

The guide hurried our group out of the Pantheon and up to the treasury of the church, pointing out medieval fabrics, important enamels, and boxes. There was an eleventh-century casket decorated with ivory plaques, the heads sticking out at an odd angle from their bodies; there was a casket of twelfth-century Limoges enamels, still brightly colored blues and greens and golds; and there was the chalice—or a chalice—of Doña Urraca, made up of two Roman agate cups, mounted in the eleventh century in a gold setting and inlaid with jewels. Most of the library had been burned by Marshal Soult, but an illustrated bible of 960 was still on display.

I wondered if medieval pilgrims had seen the same caskets and chalice, the same bible as we were seeing. In the Middle Ages, churches displayed their wealth—not to tempt thieves but to demonstrate the power of the relics which they housed. Following the decree of the Second Council of Nicaea, in 787, in order to be consecrated all churches had to have relics—bits of bone, wood, fabric, blood, or other materials associated with the saints, the Virgin, Christ. All churches had to have relics, but miracle-producing relics were the focus of major contributions, which in turn drew more worshippers to the shrine, convinced that they were onto a good thing, and that, in turn, meant more contributions to the church. After all, faith reinforced faith; popularity bred more popularity. The drawing power of important relics was so great that in the Middle Ages there were frequently elaborate—and often successful—plots to steal important ones, thus transferring the power—and contributions—to a new locale. The rationale given for such a violation of Christian commandments was that, after all, if the saints—still present in their relics—didn't want to move to a new location, no power on earth could have moved them!

We left the church and strolled down the busy streets of León, looking in elegant store windows displaying expensive Swiss and French watches and gold, emerald, and sapphire jewelry, showing the latest Paris fashions. I looked at my travel-worn clothes, my shabby sandals. Well, we were on a pilgrimage; luxury was walking without a pack on my back, walking without pain.

Stopping at a kiosk displaying magazines and newspapers, I bought an English-language *Herald Tribune* and read about nearly current events. Feeling hungry, we started reading the menus posted outside of different restaurants and decided to stop at one advertising *cocido* as the low-price *menú del día. Cocido:* a boiled dinner of soup, served first, garbanzo beans and cabbage, served next, and beef brisket, served last. A mainstay of Leonese cooking.

Afterwards, we walked over to a row of canopy-covered tables in a narrow plaza next to the tourist office and the post office and across from the west wall of the cathedral. Sitting under the shade of the canopy, I ordered *café con hielo*—iced coffee—and Bill ordered an *horchata*—a creamy drink made out of ground almonds or squash seeds, water, and sugar.

As we ate and drank our refreshing drinks, we looked at Pulchra Leonina, called the loveliest Gothic cathedral in Spain, the most purely French of all—or so the guidebooks say. Built over Roman hot springs and an ancient Romanesque church, the present cathedral was begun in the mid-thirteenth century and finished in the next. Tall and slim, it seemed more glass than stone, and its two, dissimilar, airy towers soared on either side of a central rose window. The three west doorways were partly blocked with scaffolding; attempts were being made to repair the delicate carvings, damaged by the destructive effects of car exhaust fumes.

Santa María la Blanca stands over the central doorway, child in her arms, surrounded by statues of the apostles. Perched on stone pedestals, the large figures—including one of Santiago, adorned with scallop shells—seem to be caught in the midst of idle conversation. On the tympanum, Christ stands in judgment with angels and instruments of torture. In the frieze below, an angel with the scales of justice separates the saved from the damned. The archivolts repeat the theme, graphically depicting the tortures of the damned. Sinners are tossed into caldrons, devoured by grotesque beasts—the punishments of Hell are vividly displayed, but the joys of Heaven look boring. Why, I wondered, are artists always so much more inventive in showing misery? Is it because there are so many ways to suffer, but happiness is all the same?

We entered the cathedral. The interior is narrow and long—298 feet long, 131 feet wide, 128 feet high over the nave—and the aisled nave has no flanking chapels. My eyes were unavoidably drawn to the glowing stained glass windows: light passed through them and emerged, staining the air and the floor the color of sapphires and emeralds, rubies and amethysts. Georgiana King, so sour about Sahagún, exclaimed that "It is the only church in which one feels as if one is in the heart of a jewel," and Walter Starkie said, "In this cathedral are all of the colors of the sunrises and sunsets of Paradise!" In all, there are 125 large windows, 57 small round windows, called oculi, and three huge rose windows. They make up so much of the structure that it has been called "the cathedral of stone, without stone"; in fact, they actually endanger the walls.

Stained glass probably originated in the Far East, and it was first used in Byzantine churches in Constantinople. By the fourth century, its use had spread to France. The art of stained glass reached its height in the twelfth and thirteenth centuries. Originally, stained glass was used for purely decorative windows, set in plaster or stone. But by the tenth century the designs were not only decorative, they were also didactic—storybooks for the illiterate masses, telling the legends of saints and heroes and kings. Making medieval stained glass required five kinds of craftsmen: designer, glassmaker, glazier, painter, and builder. Manganese, copper shavings, red ochre, or blue cobalt were added to molten glass to give it color. Then the glass was blown to the proper thickness, put in an oven, flattened, cooled, and cut to the shape of the design. Next, grooves were scratched into the glass to indicate details. Sometimes, the grooves were filled with enamel, and then the glass was baked in a kiln. Finally, the stained glass pieces were assembled, soldered together, and put into place.

The earliest stained glass in the cathedral in León is from the thirteenth century, but artisans of later centuries also contributed their skills. Some of the windows are filled with twining vines and flowers; others depict famous personages and heraldic crests; still others tell biblical tales and portray saints. The west front rose window and three central choir chapels contain the oldest glass, from the thirteenth to the fifteenth centuries.

We entered the Chapel of Santiago, illuminated with fifteenth-century stained glass, some of which came from Flanders. Jacobean motifs—Jacobean comes from *Jacobus,* the Latin word for Jacob or James—filled the room. We saw a young pilgrim kneeling before the altar.

When we left the cathedral, we saw another pilgrim: blond, about thirty, sitting on the ground next to his backpack. Wilhelm told us he was from Holland and had started walking, alone, from Paris. Why was he going? Looking slightly puzzled, he acknowledged that he wasn't sure. Somehow, it had seemed like the thing to do: he was between productions—he was a prompter in a theatre—and wanted to think about his future. Why was he following the Camino? For the history, the experience, to walk in the footsteps of his ancestors. We wished him well.

For the rest of the afternoon we wandered around town, walking around the still-arcaded old Plaza Mayor, looking at the carved crests on decaying buildings in the Barrio Húmedo, then up a narrow alley lined with stores. On the sidewalks on either side, street vendors sold their wares: Africans displayed ivory and ebony carvings on blankets; Moroccans hawked cheap radios and watches; young Spanish "hippy-craftspeople" sold colorful jewelry and imported Indian scarfs.

We turned off the alley and entered the Plaza de San Marcelo, across from the Casa de Botines, built by Antonio Gaudí in 1892-1894. The five-story building, now a savings bank, looks like a Disneyland idea of a castle: grey stone, black slate roof, circular turrets in the corners, wrought-iron bars on the arched windows. We bought cone-shaped, waffle-like cookies from a vendor in the plaza, and I dropped bits of mine on the paving stones for the pigeons to eat. Next to a store in one corner of the plaza, a blind man tapped his cane and called out, trying to interest passersby in buying the lottery tickets he had clipped to his shirt.

I wanted to be alone, so Bill left me in the plaza. I sat there on the cold stone steps, watching the pigeons, watching the blind man, watching the passersby. I listened to the sounds of traffic, the shrill sound of a traffic cop's whistle, the beeping of the street lights before they changed color, the tapping of the blind man's cane. I listened to the chattering of Spaniards strolling by; every so often, I heard French, and German, and English.

A slightly crippled young man walked by, pack on his back, scallop shell on his hat. One of his legs was very thin, apparently the result of polio.

I called out, "Peregrino?"

He nodded, smiled, and walked over to me.

"Going to Santiago?"

"Yes, but I'm following the Camino de las Estrellas, not the Camino de Santiago."

"The Milky Way?"

"Yes. It is the true and ancient path of spiritual death and rebirth. The Camino de Santiago was just a later Christian attempt—organized by the French—to camouflage the true way."

He pulled a book out of his backpack and showed it to me: it was a guide to *España Mágica*—Magical Spain.

"How do you find the 'real' way?"

"By staying within a certain latitude—the latitude of the Milky Way—and trying to pass through places with the names of mystical birds and animals."

"Like the Montes de Oca?"

"Yes. Oca, Ganso—names like that. The ancients left carvings, too—sometimes, the churches themselves have secret symbols on them, which only the initiates can read."

"How have you learned about this?"

"Well, it is a bit difficult. The problem is that the initiation rites were secret and carried on by word of mouth—so nothing was written down. We are only now beginning to reconstruct them."

I offered him some of my waffle cone.

"You know," he said, "the Camino doesn't stop at Santiago. It goes on to Noya, where Noah's ark landed, and then on to Finisterre."

He told me he carried money only for emergencies but preferred to ask for charity: that was the proper way to make a pilgrimage. So far, he said, he had always been given food when he was hungry and shelter when he needed it.

I asked him if Santiago meant anything to him.

"Not to me. I am making a pilgrimage for myself—and on behalf of some of my friends in Barcelona. We belong to a 'study group' together, to learn about ancient religions. We also study yoga and occult sciences."

"So why are you making the pilgrimage?"

"To experience a spiritual rebirth. The pilgrimage is like life—a road to follow, with dangers and challenges along the way. Like life, there are wrong turns, you get lost, you find your way, you ask for help." He paused, then added, "I want to learn about myself, break free of my limitations." He got up to go. "I have to leave now—I have to go to the church of San Isidoro to ask for shelter for the night."

I wished him good luck, and, waving goodbye, he limped away. I watched him disappear in the crowd, then looked at the pigeons scrambling for crumbs in the plaza. I didn't know his name. I had met a number of pilgrims on the pilgrimage—but how many did I know by name? Only one or two. And all the people I had talked to in bars along the Camino, all the people who had given us food, given us advice: how many of them did I know by name? None. They were strangers. We were strangers and pilgrims, just passing through.

What was I doing there, in León, in Spain, traveling the pilgrimage road? Pilgrims for centuries had traveled this road—whichever road it was, road to Santiago, road to the stars—driven by faith, drawn by faith. They had traveled it—and continue to travel it today. I had entered and admired the churches, the monasteries, the cathedrals that they entered; I had been impressed by the artistic masterpieces, both great and small, that they had created and commissioned. I had seen the traces of the monuments to the power of their belief. I had seen them praying, either to gods or one god, to goddesses or the Virgin. Their religious devotion and dedication were something I no more understood than a color-blind person could see color, or a deaf person could hear a symphony. Like a deaf person, I could hear vibrations—but not the complex, varied harmony.

I sat there on the cold stone steps of the plaza, wondering why I was making this pilgrimage, why I would keep on making it till I—till we—reached Santiago. And then? I wondered what would happen then. After all, what did I think I would find there, in the great cathedral in Compostela?

Of course, I knew that medieval pilgrims traveled not just for faith. They traveled—for curiosity, for adventure. They traveled for—escape, as well as for fulfillment of a vow or the hope of a miracle. But regardless of the complexity of motives, most of them—many of them—traveled with faith as their companion. Even the crippled pilgrim on his magical mystery tour had faith.

I looked at the gaily chatting tourists. I wasn't a tourist—I was a pilgrim. And to me, that meant participation in a particular kind of process: a sacred journey, a "time out," a "time between," a journey where past and present joined together, where the physical and the spiritual were joined together—and pulled apart. I was, literally and figuratively, walking in the footsteps of my ancestors, searching, as they had searched, for meaning.

Slowly, I walked back to our fancy hotel.

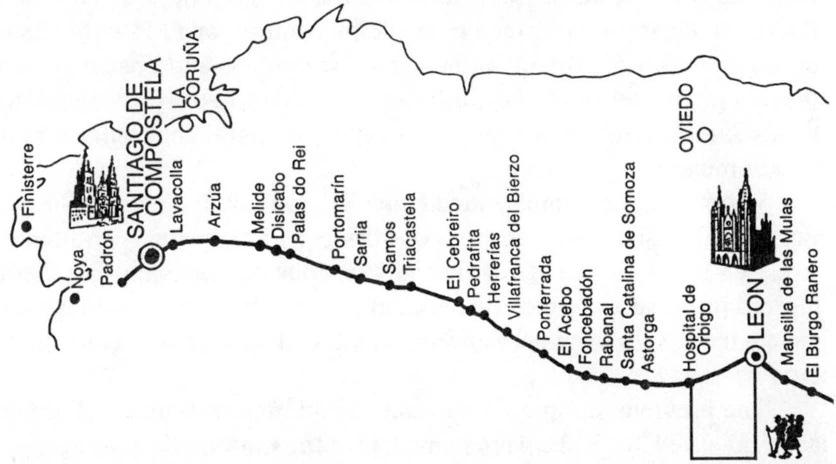

Day 31: August 9 North of León are mountains, the Cordillera Cantábrica, and through the mountains runs a road leading to and from Oviedo, a northern coastal city. There is a popular Spanish saying about the Christ figure in the cathedral in Oviedo:

Quien va a Santiago
y no a Salvador,
Sirve al criado
y deja al senor.

(Whoever goes to Santiago
and not to Salvador
Serves the servant
And ignores the master.)

In other words, whoever goes to Santiago de Compostela and doesn't also visit the famous statue of Christ in the Cámara Santa in the cathedral in Oviedo, visits the servant—Santiago—and ignores the master—Christ. Since the Middle Ages, many pilgrims have traveled along the northern coast to Oviedo and then cut south, hiking over the high mountain pass of Puerto de Pajares to León. From there they have continued to Santiago on the Camino de Santiago.

We could reverse the direction and travel from León to Oviedo, but we decided to ignore history, in this case, and tradition: there was no time and no way we were going to climb over any mountains we could avoid climbing over. Besides, I had seen pictures of the mountain-shrouded Puerto de Pajares—described in an old pilgrimage song as "without sun or moon, maker of orphans and maker of widows"—and I had no desire to cross it. Furthermore, the ninth stage of journey in the *Codex* leads towards Santiago, not Oviedo. It goes from León to Rabanal, a distance of 64 kilometers.

We left the shell-emblazoned Hotel San Marcos and crossed the Río Bernesga on a sixteenth-century stone bridge. Since there was no alternative, we walked on the edge of the highway, dodging trucks and cars. León blurred into a suburb, Trobajo del Camino, and then into the village and Sanctuary of La Virgen del Camino, six kilometers from the center of the city.

The previous summer in Sahagún, I had met a girl named Camino and had asked her if she were named after the Camino de Santiago; no, she told me, she was named after La Virgen del Camino, patroness of León. La Virgen reportedly appeared in 1505 to a shepherd and instructed him to have a hermitage built on that specific spot. After miracles occurred to convince the skeptical church officials, the hermitage was built. Recently, it was rebuilt.

Never had I seen such religious architecture in Spain. Built in 1961 by the Portuguese Dominican architect Francisco Coello, it has a tall, triangular, cement steeple. The front of the angular sanctuary is decorated with an enormous bronze frieze of thirteen Giacometti-style figures, each six meters tall, standing rigidly against a backdrop of abstract glass and lead. They looked like emaciated scarecrows, lined up against a jigsaw-puzzle backdrop. They are, we were informed, the twelve Apostles, posed beside the Virgin, sculpted by the renowned Catalan artist, José María Subirachs.

Inside, the building is equally contemporary—with the exception of a Baroque retable made in 1730 and the sixteenth-century figure of the Virgen del Camino. Somehow, the figures on the church front seemed much more dated than the four-centuries-old Virgin. Was this because we are used to certain ways of presenting religious forms, and so we consider them timeless? Or because of the difference between abstract and stylized, the former drawing upon the artist's idiosyncratic, pared-down vision, the latter drawing upon a culture-wide symbolic code?

Since 1954 the sanctuary has been under the rule of the Dominicans, and we went to look for one of them to stamp our pilgrimage cards. We found the office, but the priest was busy with other pilgrims—the two Dutch women we'd met outside of Calzada and two women from Brittany. Pleased to see each other again, we exchanged stories. They said they had had trouble finding a place to stay in Estella and in Frómista—and they were willing to pay, they added. Although they had wanted to stay in a hostel in Frómista, they had been turned away from all of them. We weren't the only ones to be told there was no room at the inn. They, like us, had ended up in the Casa de Peregrinos. The Dutch women added that they had stayed in a private house—the charitable Señora Diego had a room where she let pilgrims sleep. But, they said, the beds were full of bugs and the room was dirty.

Bill asked, "Do you really think there was no room in the hostels?"

They looked puzzled. "Of course. There were lots of tourists. We just had bad luck."

Since the priest was waiting, we said goodbye. Maybe we would meet them again on the Camino. The priest stamped our cards with a modern, abstract seal, showing the angular church with its triangular steeple. After discussing where we came from and what we had encountered along the way, the priest shook our hands and showed us out. He was quite congenial—the first congenial priest we had encountered, or so it seemed.

Just outside of La Virgen del Camino we saw the yellow arrows again; following them, we climbed down a small embankment onto a cobblestone and gravel path: "real" Camino. Or so the yellow arrows suggested. The countryside had been flat and dry but soon the road began to climb and fall a bit, in gentle waves. Our path continued parallel to the highway, which was broken up by construction work; they were building a superhighway to connect Oviedo and León. That would make the trip easier for tourists in cars—and, I supposed, for pilgrims, since the new road surface would be easier to walk on. But would it be "authentic"?

We climbed up a small mound and looked around; it was a depressing vista. To the east, the cement tower of the Virgen del Camino. To the west, the village of Valverde de la Virgen. To the north, and further west and southwest, mountains. In between, an immense, barren, rolling plain: the Páramo Leonés. After crossing the Páramo we would have to climb the Montes de León to the west.

We walked quickly through Valverde de la Virgen, then two kilometers more to San Miguel del Camino. In the twelfth century there was a *hospital* for pilgrims there. Now it was gone. From the name of the village we knew we were following the "real" Camino—even if, most of the way, it was now coated with asphalt. Scattered along the road were houses, gas stations, bars. Unlike the tightly clumped adobe villages of Tierra del Campos, this part of León is characterized by suburban sprawl.

At frequent, irregular intervals, we stopped at gas stations for Cokes and so that I could use the bathroom. Often the bathroom consisted of a ceramic-lined hole in the floor with ceramic footsteps on either side to stand on, or of a toilet bowl without a toilet seat. The toilet paper, if there was any, was either the consistency of crepe paper or of brown wrapping paper. Ah, the things I had taken for granted before the pilgrimage!

Six kilometers beyond San Miguel del Camino we reached an *urbanización*—a newly constructed residential development, called Camino de Santiago. New development, new camino.

It was hot. I had stomach problems again—from the heat? The exertion? With misgiving, I took some of my recently acquired Spanish pills. Another kilometer, we reached Villadangos del Páramo. Villadongos is an ancient town that existed during Roman times. It was the site of a battle in 1111 between the troops of Alfonso I of Aragón, el Batallador, and those of his wife, Queen Doña Urraca, daughter of Alfonso VI and inheritor of the Kingdoms of León and Castilla. Urraca and Alfonso never got along, and their domestic squabbles soon turned into royal battles.

We entered the town on a road still called the Camino Real Francés and went to see the Church of Santiago. On the door was a carved relief of Santiago on his horse, leading a group of six horsemen, scenes from the legendary—and probably imaginary—battle of Clavijo. On the door of the church next to the Hospital del Rey in Burgos, Santiago had led pilgrims; here he led knights. Moor slayer, apostle, pilgrim's guide, a recurrent presence on the Camino.

After walking a little further, to San Martín del Camino, I quit. My feet, legs, and hands had suddenly swollen up like balloons. Bill pressed his fingers into my left calf. It left a deep dimple. Maybe it was the pills I was taking. At any rate, I couldn't walk. We looked for a bus.

We stopped in a bar and asked the bartender, who told us to walk down the street and wait for the bus by the side of the road. While we waited, a young boy and his black-dressed mother drove cattle across the street with a stick. A group of a dozen young people wearing hiking clothes walked by.

"Peregrinos?" I asked.

Smiling, they shook their heads no and explained they were a parish youth group, walking a stretch of the Camino as part of an "encounter experience." In the evenings, the priest led discussions and they prayed.

"We're just walking 100 kilometers, for four days. We're not trying to reach anywhere—it's just an opportunity to get to know each other better. And at the end of the four days, we will join up with another parish youth group, who've been walking from the other direction."

They said goodbye and walked on.

The bus came and we bought tickets to the next large town, Hospital de Orbigo, seven kilometers down the road. As we rode to Hospital de Orbigo, I remembered the first bus ride we'd taken, a month before, from Bayonne to St. Jean Pied de Port. I'd had stomach problems then, too, and I had been afraid. But now I knew we would make it to Santiago. I wasn't worried.

We crossed the Río Orbigo, celebrated site of battles between Suevis and Visigoths in 456 and between Moors and Christians during the reign of Alfonso III. On the right I could just barely see the Puente de Orbigo, the long Roman bridge over the broad, marshy river bottom, which had been made famous by the foolish—or chivalrous—challenge of the Leonese knight, Don Suero de Quiñones, in the Año Santo Compostelano of 1434.

Don Suero, an example of chivalry carried to an extreme—of decadence or of fantasy—was passionately in love with a coy lady in whose honor on Thursdays he wore an iron fetter around his neck. As a declaration of his love—or of his madness—he vowed to joust with all knightly challengers over a period of one month, beginning July 10, 1434. He gained permission for the tourney from King John II, then sent a letter to be read at all the courts in Christendom.

News of the *Paso Honroso* soon spread across the land, and Suero de

Quiñones and nine companions prepared to fight all comers. Elaborate arrangements were made and suitable lists were constructed for jousting, each 146 paces long and enclosed by a palisade the height of a horse. There were seven galleries built around the lists, and the fields were covered with bright-colored tents and canopies. On July 10 or 11 (the sources differ) fanfare was sounded, the church bells rang, and numerous knights, ladies, and companions emerged from their tents and went to Mass.

Tilting and feasting continued day after day, stopping only on July 25, the Día de Santiago, until, on August 9, 1434, Suero de Quiñones appeared and told everyone that he had broken 300 lances, guarded the Honorable Passage for thirty days, and would now remove the iron fetter. In all, 727 courses were run, one knight killed, eleven wounded. Soon afterwards, Suero de Quiñones and his companions went as humble pilgrims to Santiago, where he donated a gold bracelet to St. James, a substitute for the iron fetter. It can still be seen, draped around the neck of the bust of St. James the Less in the chapel of relics.

At Hospital de Orbigo, we got off the bus and looked for a place to stay. But there was no place to stay. The hostels all were full, or so they said. I, for one, believed them—there were a number of people sitting at outdoor cafes, and when we walked around the town I saw a large camping area, filled with tents. Obviously, this was still a popular place to spend some time. I was frustrated and concerned: where would we stay?

"What are we going to do?"

Bill said, "We can always sleep out. That camp ground looks nice."

I was upset. "You don't have 'the runs,' Bill. I need a bathroom. Besides, I'm worried about my swollen legs."

"Sorry." He went off to ask for advice, and an old man directed him to go to a hostel on the main highway.

So we walked back to the highway to a service station/restaurant/hostel, where we asked for a room. The hostel was new and, apparently, not yet popular; we were given a nice room, down the hall from the bathroom.

Washed and rested, we went down for dinner, expecting standard restaurant/truck stop fare. Instead, we learned the owner/chef had learned to cook in Catalonia and he prided himself on his innovative style. Bill ordered fried trout, I ordered *cangrejos*—crayfish—even though I felt sick to my stomach. When dinner came, I couldn't eat. Bill ate for both of us.

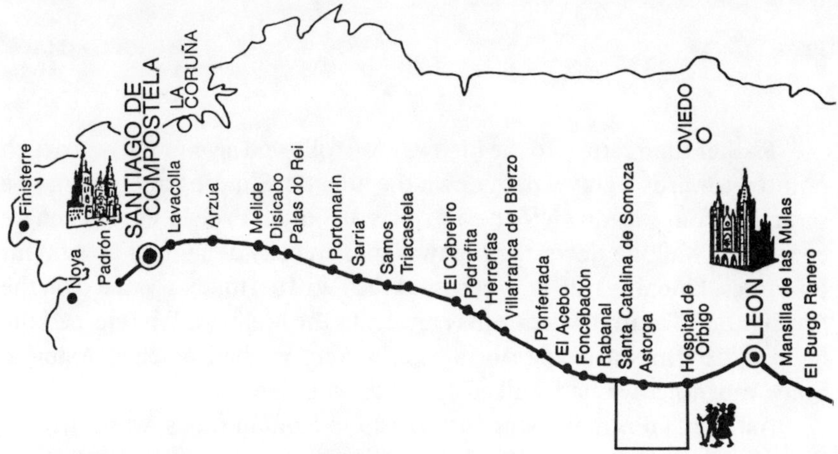

Day 32: August 10 I had stopped taking the pills,and although my legs were still swollen, my stomach was better. Looking at the package insert, I tried to translate the ingredients. How much I took for granted about medication in the U.S.: pills were generally safe, carefully monitored. But both times I had used Spanish pills, I'd had bad reactions.

We went downstairs to breakfast, a Spanish specialty called *torrijas*—bread soaked in sweetened cinammon and lemon-flavored milk, then dipped in egg, fried, and sprinkled with more sugar and cinnamon. It was delicious with the freshly brewed *café con leche.*

Well fed, we said goodbye to the friendly innkeeper and started down the road again. We had two weeks to reach Santiago before the festival. Briskly, we started towards Astorga, fourteen kilometers away. The day was cool, which was a relief, and, since I had not taken any more pills, the swelling started to go down. Walking, though not easy, was not terribly difficult.

Ten kilometers down the road we saw a cross on a small rise and walked over to it. It was the Crucero de Santo Toribio. While we rested at the foot of the cross, a grey-haired gentleman and his grandson drove up in a new Renault. The man told us that Santo Toribio was the bishop of Astorga in the fifth century; fed up with the disbelief and decadence of the inhabitants, he gave up his title and honors and went to live as a hermit.

We walked over to the edge of the hill; in front of us, situated slightly below us in a valley, was the city of Astorga, its cathedral's towers pointing skyward. Imposing Roman walls with regularly spaced, semi-circular towers protected one side of the city. Astorga rose sharply out of the plain, silhouetted against the Montes de León, which we would have to cross.

Rather than return to the highway, we followed a yellow arrow which pointed towards a gravel path down the hillside. Slipping and sliding, we scrambled our way down to the outskirts of San Justo de la Vega. Then we continued walking down the highway, past blocks of cement apartment buildings. Dodging traffic, we crossed the Río Tuerto, then walked on the "authentic" Camino which runs parallel to the highway. We rejoined the highway to cross a Roman bridge, and soon we had reached Astorga. Since morning, we had walked fourteen kilometers.

Astorga, known as Asturica Augusta in Roman times, was called by Pliny "a magnificent city." It was a juridicial center for the Romans and a meeting place of six Roman military routes. As we had seen, some of the twenty-foot-thick Roman walls still surround the city, though now they are quite battered and stripped of their original covering.

An important Episcopal seat since the Christianization of Spain, medieval Astorga was a town which welcomed pilgrims. Two pilgrimage roads—the Camino Francés and the Vía de la Plata, a route going north and south—joined at Astorga. At one time, there were twenty-two *hospitales* for poor people and pilgrims in Astorga, a number second only to those in Burgos. Many were run by confraternities or lay brotherhoods; the most famous, which can still be seen, is the Hospital de las Cinco Llagas—the Hospital of the Five Wounds. St. Francis reportedly stayed in one of these *hospitales* on his pilgrimage to Santiago between 1213 and 1215; perhaps as a result of his visit, the Franciscans became an important religious group in Astorga.

In the Middle Ages a number of foreign pilgrims passed through Astorga, and some of them stayed: the Franks established the Cofradía—lay brotherhood—of Our Lady of Rocamador. We had visited a sanctuary dedicated to her on the hilltop at Estella. The English established the Confraternity of Saint Thomas of Canterbury. Astorga also had a Frankish quarter, two Jewish quarters and a synagogue.

In addition, Astorga was—and is—the capital of a region known as the Maragatería. The Maragatos are an ethnic group of unknown origin, descendants perhaps of Berber highlanders who came to Spain with the Moorish invaders, or perhaps descendants of Goths who sided with the Moorish invaders, or maybe descendants of an ancient Asturian tribe. Perhaps because the Maragatería is a difficult place to earn one's living, the Maragatos developed an unusual life style. Famous all over Spain as taciturn but honest mule cart drivers, the men would be gone from their homes for long stretches of time, transporting goods. The *cigueña*—the stork—became the symbol of the Maragato woman: like the stork, the Maragata's spouse was usually not around, and she had to tend to the children and the fields alone. Theirs was probably a matriarchal society, one in which the women were in charge of their own lives and families. After all, the men were rarely there.

Astorga is still the center of the Maragatería, and two costumed Maragatos, Colasa and Perico, cast in bronze, strike the hour on the Maragato clock on the facade of the town hall. Although the Franks and Jews are gone from Astorga, now a town with a population of 11,000, there are still Maragatos in the surrounding hills, though radically decreased in number: people have found easier ways to make a living than tilling the hostile soil or driving mule carts.

Now they wear their folkloric Maragato costumes only for rare occasions: the men dress in tight-fitting leather vests, embroidered shirts, wide, dark, billowing pants, and round-brimmed felt hats; the women dress in elaborate jewelry and embroidered dresses with long aprons. And then they dance to one of the traditional songs, perhaps "La Peregrina," the story of a young Maragato hopelessly in love with a *peregrinita*—a charming young female pilgrim to Santiago—who has disappeared in the uproar of the *romería.* At last he sees her again, wearing her pilgrim's cape, white shoes, silk skirt, and fine hat, carrying her pilgrim's wallet and staff.

We visited the Palace of Gaudí, another building designed by the architect who built the Casa de Botines in León. And, like the Casa de Botines, the Palace of Gaudí resembles a Disneyland castle, constructed of grey-white stone with a black slate roof, with turrets, rounded towers, pointed steeples, and arched, stained glass windows. Built in 1889 as an Episcopal palace, it is now the Museum of the Caminos de Santiago de Compostela. We walked through the rooms, looking at relics and memorabilia of the Camino: lead scallop shells, memoirs, statues, paintings. So many pilgrims had passed this way before, leaving bits and pieces behind. We had our pilgrimage cards stamped at the information desk.

Then we found a restaurant where we could sit outside, shielded from the sun by the shade of a red and green umbrella. Since we were in Astorga, we ordered a local specialty: *cocido maragato*—a three-course meal made out of a one-dish stew. We began with the meat: cured pork shoulder, bacon, chicken, pig's ears and feet, and *chorizo*; next came the garbanzos, potatoes, and cabbage. And last of all came the broth in which it had all been cooked. In León, our *cocido leonés* had been served in the reverse order, but the Maragatos claim that one should begin with the meat and potatoes, either to "tone" the body or because if some of the cocido is left over, it is better that it should be the soup rather than the substance. Perhaps the economizing Leonese hoped one would fill up on the soup and leave the substance for another meal. For dessert we had *natillas,* a soft custard sprinkled with cinnamon. Then we walked over to a bar and drank espresso, waiting for the day to cool down.

Around 4:00 we took a stroll and stopped at a peculiar little barred window between the chapel of San Esteban and the church of Santa Marta. By peering in the window we could see a tiny room, completed walled up, filled with mud and stone. Above the window was a Latin inscription carved in stone: "Remember my condition: to me yesterday, to you today." This was the cell of the *emparedadas vivas*—the "immured alive" ones. Legend says it was either a jail for women of bad repute or a voluntary prison for women who, for spiritual reasons, had themselves sealed into the cell for the rest of their lives. It reminded me of the self-imposed penance of the mother in *The Hunchback of Notre Dame.* Her only contact with the world: a small slit between iron bars, just space enough for someone to push through a piece of bread, a cup of water.

Rather than do any more sightseeing we decided to start back on the Camino. On the way out of town we stopped and bought several *empanadas de bonito*—pastry turnovers filled with tuna and tomatoes—and a box of the local specialty, *mantecadas de Astorga,* those light and fluffy muffin-cakes we had had elsewhere in Spain. According to a story told in Astorga, the recipe for the local *mantecadas* was invented more than a century ago by a flirtatious nun in the Convent of Sancti Spiritus. She left the convent, married, and set up a manufacturing company. So successful was her recipe—and business sense—that today they even make her *mantecadas* in Osaka, Japan.

There are two Caminos leading from Astorga to Ponferrada, both following the routes of Roman roads. The one to the north is a highway that passes through the Puerto de Manzanal and Bembibre, locale for the famous Spanish novel, *El Señor de Bembibre,* by Enrique Gil y Carrasco. The other route is more southern, a country road that goes through Rabanal del Camino and Foncebadón. Picaud describes the road through Foncebadón as the pilgrimage route of choice in the twelfth century; but in the late fifteenth century Hermann Künig warns against it, saying that it is very difficult. We decided to follow Picaud's advice rather than Künig's warning since the Bembibre route was a newly paved highway and much more heavily trafficked than the back country road, part of which had not been asphalted until 1981 or 1982.

We headed out of town towards Valdeviejas, which once had had a *hospital* for pilgrims; now, instead, there was a Mesón La Peregrina. We went inside to buy a bottle of wine. At Murias de Rechivaldo, the road forked; the main road went towards Castrillo de Polvazares, a National Historic-Artistic Monument, famous for its classical Maragato houses and folkloric weddings. It is also the locale of Concha Espina's novel, *La esfinge maragata*—"The Maragatin Sphinx." But we didn't want to take any detours, so we took the steeply inclined road to the left. On the right side of the road was a sign—"Camino de Santiago—Chemin de St. Jacques." It was the first time I had seen a road sign in French on the Camino.

We headed up the rough-surfaced country road to Santa Catalina de Somoza. Dreary stone houses clustered together, low stone walls divided up the land, subdividing one person's patch of ground from another's, forming a maze of small pieces of nearly useless land, each patchwork piece too small for efficient use. At least the numerous stone fences were a convenient place to put the rocks which occurred as frequently as the soil. Our road led through town, and we looked for the Grand Hospital, a medieval *hospital* for pilgrims, but it had disappeared. We walked past thatch-roofed stone houses and low stone walls covered with matted straw and twigs. Thirsty, we looked for a "club" but saw no sign and no one to ask.

At last a bent old man with a cane came hobbling down the street, and we asked him where we could buy something to drink. He pointed to a doorway in a wall, so we went there and knocked. A woman came to the door and, after we had explained what we wanted, she ushered us into a large courtyard and told us to sit down at a wooden table. Soon three or four children—or maybe grandchildren—joined us, staring at us curiously, silently, and an old man came and sat near us in a wooden chair, propped against a wall. She returned, carrying bottles of warm Coke and a chunk of cheese. We thanked her, ate the cheese, drank the Cokes, and asked if we could buy bread, but she shook her head; there was no bread, except what she had bought three days before for her family. The delivery truck would not return for several more days.

Looking at our packs, she nodded in sympathy and approval. "Qué sacrificio."

We agreed and asked if there were anywhere we could spend the night. She suggested we could sleep outdoors, in the fields.

I asked, "Do we need permission?"

"No. Just find somewhere to sleep."

I had theorized that besides being a gesture of Christian charity, offering shelter was a way of controlling strangers. But this woman didn't seem to care where we went.

We walked past the outskirts of town and climbed over a low stone fence into a field that sloped down the side of a hill. Finding a somewhat level spot, we spread out our plastic rain ponchos and put down our sleeping bags. We ate our *mantecadas* and tuna pies, and drank our cheap wine straight from the bottle. Sound carried over the hills, and we heard the occasional noise of a car, a dog barking, people shouting. Then the night became quiet and still.

A month before, I had been afraid to spend the night in the shelter of an unfinished building; now, I was happy to sleep in the fresh, sweet country air. Away from city lights and city pollution, the night sky was wonderfully clear. We saw the Milky Way spreading its starry trail like a protective blanket over us. It had pointed out the way to Charlemagne, it pointed out the way to us. A star lifted out of the sky and dropped. It seemed to fall into the field below us. A thousand years ago, would I have thought that was a message from God and gone to find the buried tomb, the hidden statue? And what would we find, if we went to look?

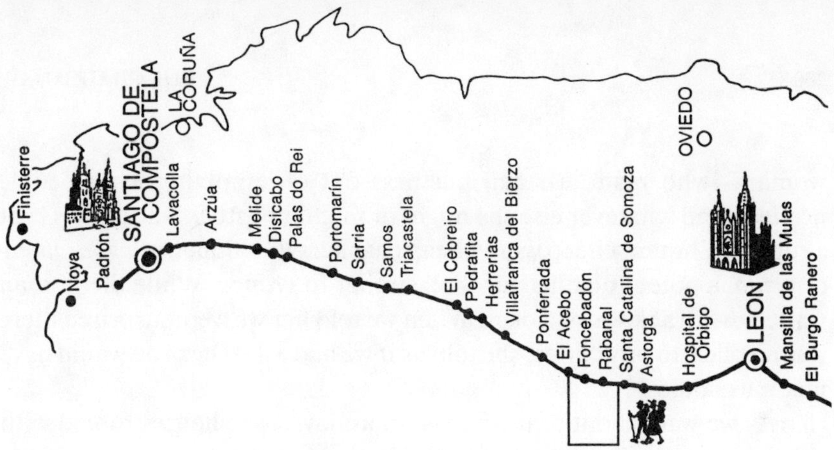

Day 33: August 11 We woke up as the sun rose; the sky was the color of ripe lemons and soft peaches. The dew on the fields glistened, the village looked black and heavy, still unlit by the sun. Shaking the dew off of our sleeping bags and packs, we got dressed and started up the road.

We were in the heart of the Maragatería. To the left of us was el monte Teleno—the mountain of Teleno—believed by the Romans to personify Mars. Over 2,000 years ago, Romans had lived in these hills and walked this same route—not quite the same, though, since the road from Santa Catalina to Rabanal had been asphalted in 1971 in preparation for the Año Santo. We passed a wooden cross with a *concha*—the scallop shell—on the crosspiece. The pilgrims' cobblestones, like the Roman road, lay hidden beneath the modern asphalt surface. We walked silently down the narrow, pebble-surfaced asphalt road, walking past dry, stony fields, walking towards the mountains.

After four kilometers we reached El Ganso—the Gander—a poor village, half abandoned, with clumps of matted straw drying on the tops of low stone walls, with low stone houses thatched with straw. El Ganso: mate of the *oca.* The name reminded me that we were following the pre-Christian, Celtic initiation route, the Camino de las Estrellas, as well as the Camino de Santiago and the ancient Roman road. And the modern highway. In whose footsteps were we traveling?

In 1142 El Ganso had a *hospital* for pilgrims and a monastery, and the church of the village is still dedicated to Santiago. We looked for a bar for our morning coffee but found none; a woman we asked said there was no bar, so we asked her if we could buy supplies somewhere in town. She told us to wait a moment and went to her home, returned with a set of keys, and took us to a storehouse full of canned goods, bottles of wine and brandy, bottled soda, and slightly past-ripe fruit.

It seemed as if all of these villages had someone—usually a

woman—who made a small business out of supplying what people needed. And whatever else she might or might not stock, she always kept a supply of liquor: cheap wine, cheap cognac, sweet liqueurs, *aguardiente* or *orujo,* a potent distilled alcohol, similar to *grappa.* While the woman waited, we drank warm Cokes. When we told her we were surprised there was no place to buy coffee, she told us if we had asked her, she would have made us some.

As we walked out of town, past more low stone houses roofed with straw, we saw a church with a stork's nest on the top: symbol of the Maragatan woman.

Our road curved up and down, through an abandoned, parched, yellow countryside, with occasional clumps of scrubby trees. I took frequent refuge behind them; without the pills, my stomach problems had returned in full force. At the Puente de Pañote we stopped and looked off towards the right. According to the guidebook, on top of a hill 700 meters to the right there had been a Roman gold mine, called La Fucarona. But we didn't have time or energy to follow the forest trail to the mine, even though it was supposedly almost intact.

Our path led down the side of the hill, past several hermitages, an arroyo, and then up towards a town, Rabanal del Camino, end of the ninth stage of journey in the *Codex.*

I had expected a larger town, but Rabanal was a semi-abandoned village, a bit larger, a bit more prosperous than El Ganso—but just a bit. Our road into town was paved with stones, with a drainage ditch running along the sides. We passed by the Casa de las Cuatro Esquinas—the House of the Four Corners—where Philip II stayed in the sixteenth century—and continued into the village, stopping at a fountain and a church, once property of the Templars of Ponferrada. At one time, the Hospital de San Gregorio had sheltered pilgrims; now, it was gone, but I knew the town authorities would let pilgrims sleep in the old school house. We walked down towards the main plaza and a bar, Camino de Santiago. Combining bar, cafe, grocery store and liquor store—the bar was full of young people. We asked if we could buy bread, but we were told no. However, we could buy sandwiches, which we did, then started off again. As we walked past a clearing, we saw men playing *bolos,* a local sport. They took turns tossing a flat-bottomed stone at rows of cone-shaped stone bowling pins.

We left town on a one-lane-wide strip of asphalt, laid down over the dirt and gravel in 1981 or 1982; earlier road maps show no road past

Rabanal. In front of us, filling the horizon, was a mountain range. We started walking towards it. Soon we crossed a dry channel, which had been used by the Romans to carry water for—or from?—the mines of La Fucarona. Several kilometers later we passed a sign, "fuente." In this nearly abandoned countryside, someone had taken care to show pilgrims where they could find spring water. It was reassuring and made me feel less isolated as we climbed up the narrow, paved road, up the mountainside towards the summit of Monte Irago.

At last we approached Foncebadón, located on the eastern side of Monte Irago, eight kilometers from Rabanal. In our guidebook, the name "Foncebadón" was printed in the same size print as Astorga, so we had thought it was a large town; we hoped to spend the night there. Just before Foncebadón, the road splits: the narrow, paved road skirts the pueblo, the Camino goes through it. We took the Camino, an unpaved gravel path, through town. Or, more accurately, through what had been a town, for it was desolate, almost entirely abandoned, black slate roofs slumping over the brown stone walls of deserted houses.

The Camino, now called the "Royal Road," was the only street through town. Lined up on either side of it were abandoned buildings, collapsing where they stood, falling in on themselves and forming neat piles on the ground. As we passed by, we saw that one or two of the buildings showed signs of recent reconstruction—renovation would be too grand a word—and in front of them were cars with Madrid or León license plates. Apparently, some people had returned to their ancestral homes for a holiday. Or maybe they were squatters for the summer season.

There was a crude wood cross on a pile of slate in the middle of the road. It seemed a warning, rather than an acknowlegement or a benediction. I remembered Dante: "Abandon hope, all ye who enter here."

Once, Foncebadón had been a larger, more important town, full of hospitality to pilgrims. In the tenth century, an important religious council had taken place there, convoked by Ramiro II. In the eleventh century the hermit Guacelmo founded a *hospital* and church to aid pilgrims; and in the twelfth century there was probably at least one hospice, church, and monastery in the town. According to one traveler, in 1554 the town had fifteen inhabitants and was very well supplied.

Tradition says that villagers were excused from taxes in exchange for establishing a pilgrimage hospice and maintaining 800 stakes in the ground, indicators of the road to travelers. Like Roncesvalles, Somport, and Cebreiro, this was a difficult pass to cross in winter. During heavy snow storms, the stakes helped keep pilgrims on the proper path. Now the village was all but abandoned; only two people lived in Foncebadón year around: an old widow, named María, and her son, Angel. They were pastors of sheep, not of pilgrims.

We walked down a slope across a field to the ruins of what was probably the *hospital* of pilgrims. Most of the stones had been carted away, used to form the walls of the nearby cemetery. All that remained was a fragment of wall and the archway of a window, standing as a desolate monument.

Rather than return to the road, we clambered up the side of the next hill. In the distance I saw the Cruz de Ferro. I suggested we just cut across the top of the hill. Bill was surprised: I had always been so afraid of getting lost. I had been afraid of getting lost—walking through the forest trail to Roncesvalles, where there was no conceivable way of missing the path; walking through the fields of Navarra, where we did get lost. But I could see where we were heading, and the thought of walking a little extra if I were wrong and we couldn't get there the way I thought, no longer filled me with anxiety. So we headed across the top of the hill.

Every so often we saw stakes driven into the ground. In the Middle Ages, villagers used stakes to mark the route. In winter, snow could be quite deep in the mountains, but the six-foot-tall stakes would have poked up above the surface of the snow. We followed the stakes across the hill to the Cruz de Ferro, crossing from the Maragatería into the Bierzo.

On top of the 1,490-meter-high Monte Irago is a huge, conical pile of stones, and on top of that is a five-meter-high oak staff, and on top of that is the one-and-one-half-meter-high Iron Cross—the Cruz de Ferro. Over the centuries, as the pile of stones has grown higher, the pole has had to be lengthened and, on occasion, replaced: sixty years ago, it fell over. The pole stands out in high relief against the dark green hills. According to pagan tradition, to placate the gods, travelers were supposed to throw a rock on the pile of stones, a boundary marker known as a "mountain of Mercury." Pilgrims traveling to Galicia and Galician harvesters passing into Castilla for the first time continued the pagan custom. We walked down to the road, picked up some pebbles, and threw them on the mound, adding our stones to those of all who had traveled this way before. I climbed up the mound of stones to look more closely at the cross, as had many before me.

Throughout the centuries, travelers have come and gone; pilgrims have passed through; *pueblos*—the Spanish word means both village and a people—have been born and died, have grown and decayed. The pile of stones remains. Symbol of man's quest, of religious rituals lasting through the centuries, symbol of the travelers who had passed this way for millenia. Originally pagan, a gesture to appease the gods, tossing a pebble on the mound had been continued by Christian travelers; the ritual remained, the meaning changed—or is it now devoid of meaning? Or is the meaning still the same—a gesture of hope, a request for help—but the gods appealed to different?

An insignificant gesture, tossing a pebble on a mound. Asking for, hoping for, some response from the silent hills, the silent sky. Through the millenia the mountains have remained, the bits of crumbled mountains have been piled on a mound; the insubstantial wooden pole with its iron cross has toppled over and faithfully been erected again and again, defying, with man's help, the wind, the snow. Fragile symbol of potent faith, poking upwards toward the Milky Way.

In the distance I could see the mountains of the Bierzo and Cebreiro, mountains which we would soon have to climb. I climbed carefully down the slippery heap of pebbles. Someone called out to us, and we saw a man standing on the road below, near a small cement building, the Hermitage of Santiago, built in 1982. Dark haired, about 30 years old, he carried a patchwork leather bag, slung onto two carved wooden sticks, held on his back by two leather straps. A small lyre stuck out of the bag, and a suede leather *bota* swung from one side. He wore a leather hat, adorned with scallop shells.

He asked us, "Pilgrims?"

We nodded yes, and together we walked away from the Cruz de Ferro and down the mountainside. His name was Peter, he said, and he was from Belgium, where his father owned a large Belgian endive farm. He had spent a lot of time in Central America and then had returned to Belgium to work as a manager on his father's farm. But he had decided to go on pilgrimage, and he had walked to Lourdes. And then he had decided to continue on to Santiago.

I asked him, "Where did you get that unusual backpack?"

He smiled. "I didn't plan to carry anything, but I went to a fair near Lourdes and bought a lyre. I couldn't leave it behind, so I bought a bag and made this pack."

Bill envied his lack of baggage and told him he would like to travel with as light a load. The thought of traveling without a pack made me anxious, not envious: I was ready to get rid of excess baggage—but to travel with none at all? Besides, it looked uncomfortable.

We saw a sign, "Fuente de Peregrinos," on the left and Peter stopped. "I stop at every fountain and fill my *bota* with water."

So we headed down the green hillside, past a ruined building, toward the spring. A dark haired woman in a multi-patterned skirt and blouse was filling an earthenware jug with water; near her were half a dozen cattle. We greeted her and, as we filled our respective water vessels, she told us she was from the south, but every summer they transported the cattle north by truck to escape the heat and fatten on the grass.

The road zigzagged down the hill. According to the map, the next village was Manjarín, where we planned to spend the night. But when we reached Manjarín we found it in ruins. The inhabitants of the pueblo had either died or emigrated. Broken houses lined the street, houses falling in on themselves, abandoned, once filled with life, now filled with debris and silence. Instead of solid roofs we saw the skeletal framework of branches that had supported the slate or straw.

We followed the narrow highway through the ruined village and down the hillside. It was getting late and we were tired, but there was nowhere to stop; the hillside was covered with a thick mat of low, prickly bushes and weeds. To the right, in the fading light, we saw a huge antenna: a military base and helicopter port were built on top of a hill in the midst of the deserted countryside. We took a brief break, sitting at the edge of the road, sharing cheese and fruit. Then we started walking again, watching the sun set behind the mountains.

At first, I had thought we would spend the night in a village, sleeping in a bed, eating restaurant food. When that looked unlikely, I had hoped we would spend the night in some kind of shelter and purchase supplies from someone's storehouse—some bread, some cheese. Later, I had hoped we would find a place to camp out in the fields, without food, without a toilet. Now, I just wanted to find a place to stop—but in the dark it was impossible. In the distance occasionally we saw lights, appearing and disappearing, blocked out by the road as it curved its way up and down, up and around the hills. Suddenly a car came around an unseen curve and headed towards us; nearly blinded by its lights, we jumped into the scrub at the side of the road.

Eight kilometers from abandoned Manjarín was the village of El Acebo; it, too, might be abandoned. We just kept on walking, walking and talking. It was after 11 p.m.

In the distance we heard dogs barking—but whether they were close or far we could not tell. At last we rounded a curve in the road and the darkness lightened a little; looming in front of us were buildings. The paved road ended and we started walking on cobblestones. Suddenly, two dogs came running towards us, barking loudly, and a man appeared, carrying a lantern. He walked up to us and lifted the lantern towards our faces. We saw his face, dark, heavy with shadows.

"Peregrinos?"

We nodded. He lowered the lantern and gestured for us to follow him. He led us down the street to a small bar, where people were sitting on the porch, smoking, drinking, talking in the cool night air. When they saw us, they stopped talking. He gestured towards us: "Peregrinos." They looked at us and moved aside, and we climbed the stairs to the porch and went into the bar. Suddenly it became noisy, as people started talking again and everyone crowded in behind us.

The bar owner came forward and gestured to us to take off our packs and sit down. Exhausted, we did. After all, we had walked 29 kilometers through the hills. Then he asked us what we wanted to drink—wine? Bill and Peter nodded yes; I asked for a Coke. Wiping her hands on her apron, the man's wife appeared, listened, and then returned to the kitchen. Soon she returned, carrying plates full of *chorizo* and cheese sandwiches. The bar owner came over, carrying a large earthenware pitcher full of wine and three earthenware cups, which he filled. We drank, we ate, we drank and ate some more. And then we paused and answered questions. Where were we from? How far had we walked? How many kilometers did we travel a day?

It was tourism, in reverse. Instead of us coming to see the sights, we were the sights and we had come to them.

The owner brought out a large guest book and asked us to sign it. Looking through the pages, I saw poems and sketches, lengthy accounts and brief statements, detailed street addresses and single-line national designations, crudely printed names and elaborately embellished autographs. German, Italian, French, Dutch, French, Britons, Brittans, a Japanese—and now, two Americans, one Belgian.

An hour after we had arrived we were well fed, relaxed, and tired of talking. The wine had added sleepiness to exhaustion. The man with the lantern stood up, picked up his lantern, and gestured for us to follow him out the door. Everyone stood up and followed us. What a midnight parade we made: a man and lantern, three weary pilgrims, two dogs, and a dozen villagers, walking down the cobblestone street. They took us to the empty schoolhouse and unlocked a door. We could sleep there. Before the man with the lantern left, he told us that there were other pilgrims sleeping in another part of the building. They had arrived three hours before.

We took off our packs, spread our sleeping bags on the cold cement floor, and climbed into them; Peter spread a thin blanket on the floor. Usually, he said, he slept in a knotted string hammock he carried in his pack.

Trying to sleep, I thought about our reception in this tiny village, far from the highway and the cities. Was this typical of how medieval pilgrims were received? With open arms and warm greetings? Or was this no more typical than the hostile reception in Navarra, or the uninterested reception in Hornillos del Camino, or the lack of reception in Frómista? In the Middle Ages, monasteries and lay brotherhoods had taken care of pilgrims, and villagers had not had much responsibility. Today, few monasteries or lay brotherhoods existed, and in small towns, the mayor appeared to have taken over responsibility for pilgrims. But in El Acebo, our reception by the villagers themselves had been impressive. Because of Christian charity? Because of the strength of pilgrimage traditions? Because of boredom?

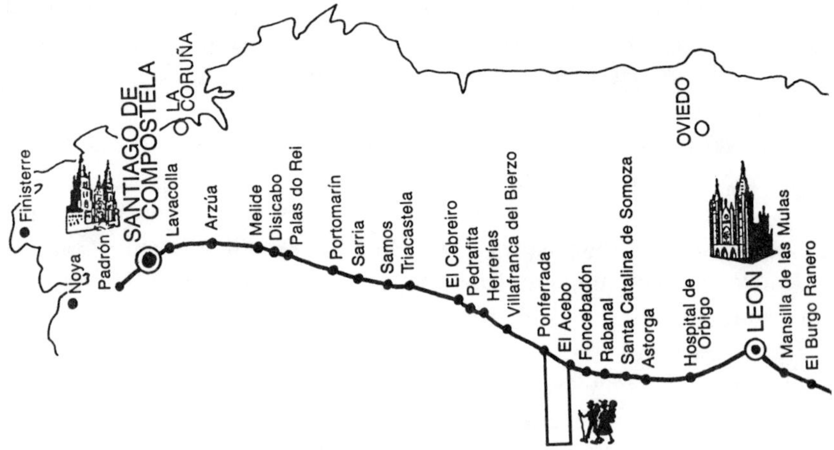

Day 34: August 12 In the morning, I could hardly walk. My feet felt like mush. Peter looked at my hobbling gait and laughed.

"It's called 'the pilgrim's dance,'" he said.

I winced. "My arches feel as if they will collapse without my shoes to support them. Besides, I'm stiff."

He offered me some Belgian after-ski muscle balm, similar to Ben-Gay. "Be careful—don't use too much, or you'll feel like your skin is on fire."

We went outside to wash in the fountain. The pilgrims who had arrived before us were already there: two Dutch women we'd met before. They knew all three of us, but they didn't seem very pleased to see Peter. After saying hello to us, they nodded briskly at him and left.

In the daylight we could see El Acebo: two rows of narrow two-story stone houses with slate roofs, leaning against each other, leaning towards each other across the narrow, cobblestone street. The second story of the houses had wooden balconies, protruding a meter or so over the lower level. We walked quietly through the still sleeping village.

Somewhere to the left of El Acebo is what remains of Compludo, where San Fructuoso founded his first monastery in the seventh century, and where a medieval ironworks run by water still functions. And somewhere else nearby are the Roman mines of las Médulas; all that remains today of the rich excavations is red, dismembered hills, hollowed out by the incessant labors of 60,000 slaves digging away the gold that lay buried within them, washing it and the hillsides away with channels of water. We would have liked to see the Médulas, but we needed to reach Santiago as quickly as possible. Briskly, the three of us walked down the hills to Molinaseca, talking while we walked.

"Peter, why are you going to Santiago?" I asked.

He paused a moment, searching for words. "For me, Santiago represents the ancient Christian church, from before the schism between Catholics and Protestants. So it is a very powerful place, closer to the old beliefs."

Bill asked, "When you say 'old' beliefs, do you mean pre-Christian ones?"

Peter looked at us. "Maybe. At any rate, I don't think the pilgrimage ends at Santiago."

"No?"

"No. I think it just begins at Santiago."

"Then where does it end? At Noya?"

"Maybe never. But I think that Santiago is just the beginning of the pilgrimage, not the end."

I wondered if he were right. For after all, something was—and is—

set in process by the pilgrimage—a change of state, a change of place, a change of self. And how could that just end? After all, life is a pilgrimage. But then, what would we find at Santiago?

We had walked nearly three kilometers on the highway before we came to a gravel road, the "real" Camino, which we followed to Riego de Ambros, a small village with several fountains. Before going further we wanted to get something to eat and drink, so we asked a woman we saw for directions. She pointed to a doorway and we knocked. Soon, a woman appeared and opened up the cafe/bar. She made us coffee and sandwiches of the famous local *chorizo* and cheese. Friendly, expansive, hospitable people seemed to live in these isolated mountain villages. We thanked her and left.

The countryside had changed from the brush-covered hills of the day before. Now we walked through hillsides sprinkled with groves of aged chestnut trees, their years visible in their knotted trunks and scarred, wrinkled branches. Cutting across the hillside, we rejoined the paved road just outside of Molinaseca.

On the right was the semi-ruined sanctuary, la Hermita de las Angustias. Medieval pilgrims had chipped splinters of wood from the sacred doorways, carrying them away as relics; to protect the doors, they had been covered with iron. Crossing over the Río Meruelo on a medieval bridge, we entered Molinaseca. In the Middle Ages, Queen Doña Urraca reportedly lived there, and there is a large house with towers where the important Balboa family lived. We walked down the central cobblestone street, looking at the large doorways on the houses and the large carved shields.

Peter wanted to see the local priest, so we went with him to find him. A woman directed us to the house near the church where the priest lived.

Peter explained, "I make a habit of two things: filling my *bota* with water from every spring and getting stamps from every priest. It gives me a connection with people, an opportunity to talk. Otherwise, this pilgrimage would be very lonely."

Bill asked, "Have you walked alone most of the time?"

"I've had companions, but since I walk so fast and so much—50 kilometers a day, often—my companions quickly fall behind."

How transitory were fellow pilgrims on the road. Stability lay in the mountains, in the stones. And even those crumbled. But Peter seemed to find some stability through priests and springs.

The priest said we would have to go with him to the church to get the stamp, and while there he gave us a tour and pointed out the more important works of art. I was impatient to go on, but Peter seemed to enjoy the tour, and Bill seemed to enjoy Peter's company. At last we were finished with the tour and, thanking the priest, we left.

We passed the abandoned hermitage of San Roque, a reminder that here, too, the plague had come, brought out of the mountains by travelers and pilgrims. From there, our route became one with the highway, which we followed out of the hills. On a hill in the distance was Ponferrada. Our route bifurcated: on the left was a road which led to Campo, a small town, and then to Ponferrada; on the right was a highway, leading directly to Ponferrada. That route looked less authentic, but shorter, so we followed it, crossing the Río Boeza on the bridge known as the Paso de la Barca, the "Crossing of the Boat." Originally there had been a Roman bridge there, but it collapsed in the eighteenth century and a replacement wasn't built until the nineteenth century. In the meantime, a *cofradía* made a boat available for pilgrims to cross the river.

Soon we crossed a series of railroad tracks and walked up labyrinthian cement streets, past urban industrial sprawl, up into the center of town. At a small, tree-lined plaza, we stopped to rest. Bill and I were tired, but Peter said he wanted to continue walking, so we said goodbye and watched him disappear down the street.

Bill and I decided to spend the day—and the next—in Ponferrada, resting. Even after a month of walking, we could still only manage to walk two or three days before we had to rest for a day or two. We found a cheap hostel—$14 for the two of us, per night—and washed up, then went out for lunch.

Ponferrada, which may have been the Roman Iteramnium Flavium, takes its name from the Pons-Ferrata—the Iron Bridge—a stone bridge with iron railings, built over the Río Sil by Osmundo, the bishop of Astorga, at the end of the eleventh century. The town is situated on the high ground between the Ríos Boeza and Sil, and that bridge was one of several built to aid pilgrims trying to reach Santiago. On the highest ground, the Templars, who also helped pilgrims on the road, had built a castle, begun in the twelfth century. Ponferrada is full of sanctuaries and *hospitales,* including the Hospital de la Reina, founded by Queen Isabella in 1498.

Today the town is a mining and industrial center of 50,000. It is the capital of the Bierzo region, a saucer-shaped basin between the León Mountains and the Galician Massif, drained by the gorge of the Río Sil.

Ponferrada is full of monuments from the past, including churches, monasteries, and the 1692 town hall, and numerous hotels, restaurants, shops, and high-rise buildings commemorating the present. As we walked around town, we saw the iron mines across the river from the city, the iron mines which have brought new prosperity to the town: not only the Romans found mineral wealth in the region. Spread out before us was the fertile valley of the Bierzo, encircled with high mountains and, tallest of all, the peaks of Cebreiro, which we would soon climb.

We were determined to have a good meal after several days of bread, cheese, and *chorizo*, so we stopped for *la comida* at a popular restaurant next to a church. When we asked what the specialties were, we were told there were several: *botillo berciano, chanfaina, calamares en su tinta,* and *pulpo al ajillo.* The last two we knew: squid in its ink and octopus in garlic; the first two were new to us, so we asked the waiter to list the ingredients. The *botillo berciano* was a kind of pork stew, made up of ribs, backbone, and tail of the pork, seasoned with pimiento, white wine, garlic, and oregano, then cooked with *vejiga,* whatever that was, and fat, stuffed tripe—the *botillo.* The *chanfaina* was a stew of such things as head, lungs, feet, and spleen.

We decided to skip the *chanfaina* but to order the other three. The *calamares en su tinta* came: tiny cuttlefish floating in a thick, dark sauce, fragrant with garlic and wine. The *pulpo al ajillo* came: tender bits of octopus, spiced with garlic and hot chili pepper. Then we ate the *botillo*—an enormously filling dish, and washed everything down with a fine, local Bierzo wine. For dessert, a slice of *tarta helada*—ice cream pie, this time flavored with chocolate and brandy.

After lunch we strolled around town, walking past the Basílica de Nuestra Señora de la Encina—"Our Lady of the Evergreen Oak"—named after an ancient carving reportedly found concealed in an evergreen oak tree. In 1958 she was made Patrona of the Bierzo, and the sixteenth-century church was raised to the status of basilica. Then we walked over to the medieval Castle of the Templars. It is imposing, with tall stone walls, rounded towers with crenelated tops, toothed battlements, colorful flags waving from the portico. Made of unevenly shaped stones fitted tightly together, discolored with mold, age, and pollution, the castle looked like a well-worn, large-scale cardboard cutout. When compared with the "real thing," the Gaudí castles we had seen were playful parodies.

To enter the castle, we climbed up the imposing stairway, passed through a massive doorway, and saw—a packed-earth courtyard with a stage at one end. Workers were setting up scenery for a medieval pageant show.

For the next few hours, we walked up and down the streets of Ponferrada, past large buildings with elaborate facades, past blocks of plaster-covered houses. From the sidewalk to one meter up, the houses were painted brown; above that to the roof, they were painted light beige. Substantial apartment buildings rose directly from the sidewalks; there were no lawns, except in front of churches and monuments and in the plazas. This was a big, expanding industrial city. At the bottom of the town, we found the Tourist Office, where we had our pilgrimage cards stamped and picked up brochures describing the pilgrimage road.

I was tired. Although walking with the backpack was tiring, that was a different kind of tiring than sightseeing in the city. Walking was physically wearying, but I could recover from it by resting for a while—especially under the shade of a tree, or in a flower-strewn field, or by the side of a stream. Walking in the city, on the other hand, was emotionally wearying: the noises, the jumble of sights, the people, the traffic, the exhaust fumes, the variety of quick impressions. I wasn't used to the speed. I needed not just rest but withdrawal. I wanted to be alone.

Bill went off on his own, and I sat on a stone bench in a tree-lined plaza near the Basílica. I read through the guidebooks, I breathed in the scent of the trees that filled the quiet corner I had found. People walked quickly by, cars honked, children cried. I sat quietly and let it wash over me like waves, trying to sink below the surface upheaval to the tranquility that was in the mountains, in the trees, in the stone. Trying to see beyond the incessant variation to some structure, some pattern. All these pilgrims, walking in the footsteps of their ancestors, placing their feet one by one on the same path. I fell asleep.

Day 35: August 13 Still in Ponferrada, recovering from our different kinds of weariness. We had originally planned to visit several outlying churches: San Tomás de las Ollas, a tenth-century Mozarabic church; Santa María de Vizbayo, an eleventh-century Romanesque church; and Santiago de Peñalba, a tenth-century Mozarabic church, declared a National Monument. But when it came time to go, I was too tired for the lengthy excursion; besides, I wanted to be alone. Again. I told Bill to go by himself, but he didn't feel like going, either. While I stayed in the hostel, Bill went off for a short walk around town.

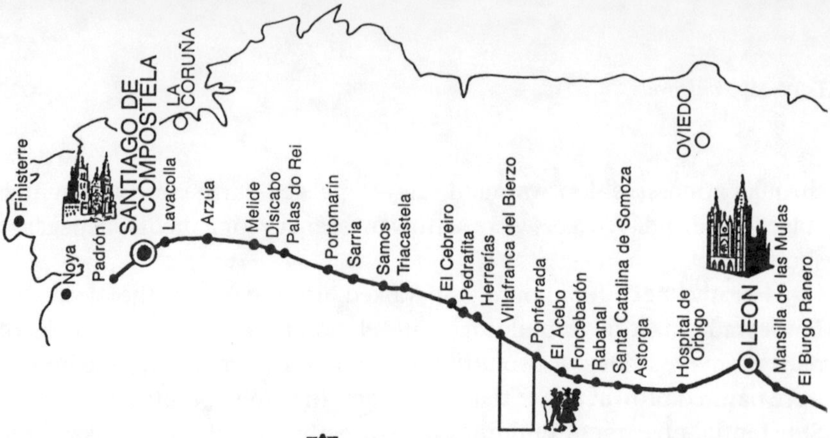

Day 36: August 14 We were in the middle of the tenth stage of journey in the *Codex,* from Rabanal to Villafranca del Bierzo, a distance of 50 kilometers. With luck, we could make the remaining 21 kilometers in one day. After all, just two days before we had walked 29 kilometers in the mountains in one day, twice as far as we had managed when we began our pilgrimage in the Pyrenees. And, although I still had stomach problems, they, like the pain in my feet, were a discomfort I had gotten used to.

When we came downstairs from our room, three heavy-set, middle-aged Spanish women were sitting in the lobby of the hostel. They looked at our backpacks with great interest.

The first one asked, "Peregrinos?"

We nodded yes.

The middle one said with disbelief, "Walking to Santiago? Actually walking? Surely you are taking the train."

The third said in puzzlement, "Why would you want to walk to Santiago?"

The first spoke again, "Vale la pena!"

We walked past the Castle of the Templars and down the hill, through the Barrio de Santiago to the tourist office, where we turned left and crossed the Puente Ferrada. Then we followed the highway out of town, past the slag heaps of Compostilla. At Columbrianos, after carefully picking our way past various highways, we reached a small stretch of "authentic" Camino—still called the Camino Real—and walked on that to Fuentes Nuevas. There we stopped for Cokes and had a long conversation with a man in the bar. He said he'd seen a Japanese pilgrim and several others on horseback that summer, and lots of French and Germans walking the Camino. I asked him whether he thought Santiago was important.

"Of course he's important! He's patron of Spain!" He looked at our backpacks. "Vale la pena!"

We started off again. We were in a large basin between mountain ranges; to the east was the pass at Foncebadón; to the west was the pass at El Cebreiro. The Camino passed through rolling hills covered with groves of fruit trees and green fields of low-lying grape vines. At Camponaraya, which once had had two pilgrim *hospitales,* our "real" Camino de Santiago rejoined the heavily trafficked highway to La Coruña, but on the other side of town it separated off again.

Still striving for authenticity, we followed the gravel Camino across the fields of grapes, growing bush-like in the furrowed soil. At one place, the Camino crossed the highway, but then it continued on through the countryside, and soon we were walking on a stretch of authentic *calzada romana*—Roman paving stones. The authenticity was short lived: at the Hermitage of San Roque the highway obliterated our ancient road. We crossed the Río Cúa and entered Cacabelos.

Until the end of the nineteenth century, Cacabelos was under the bishopric of Santiago de Compostela. In 1108 the powerful Archbishop of Santiago, Diego Gelmírez, found the town destroyed and ordered it rebuilt in greater glory. At one time, Cacabelos had at least three churches and three pilgrim *hospitales;* it still has several monuments, including the Church of Santa María and the Sanctuary of the Quinta Angustia, mentioned in 1199. The Archeological Museum displays some of the artifacts that have been discovered nearby.

When we reached the center of town, we stopped at a restaurant for lunch: hamburgers and french fries. The restaurant was a sort of Spanish quick-food shop, with formica-topped tables. Displayed on shelves behind the counter were bottles of local wine and jars of the famous Cacabelos preserved cherries, brown-red globes floating in amber liquid. At a nearby table were two young French pilgrims; he was wearing shorts, she was wearing a bathing suit. We nodded at each other but didn't talk. Looking at my skirt and blouse, I wondered if my modesty was really necessary.

South of Cacabelos, at Carracedo, are Roman ruins and a Cistercian monastery, founded in 990 and rebuilt in 1138. Nearby are a ninth- and thirteenth-century palace and sixteenth-century domestic buildings. Carracedo is a favorite stopping place for tourists, but we didn't take the detour. Our road climbed slowly towards Pieros, located to the right of the highway. An ancient Asturian city, conquered in A.D. 26 by the Romans, it is noted for its ancient Suevic fortifications, some of which are still standing, twenty-five feet high, and for the Church of San Martín de

Tours, consecrated on November 19, 1086. On a knoll to the left of the highway is an archeological site, the Roman Castrum Bergidum, which gave the region its name.

It was late afternoon, but the walking had been easy. In the distance we saw a few buildings nestled between green hills: we were approaching Villafranca del Bierzo, end of the tenth stage of journey in the *Codex*. Our road curved around a hill, and the buildings disappeared. To the right we heard sharp cracking sounds and saw a large number of cars: there was a clay pigeon shooting club there, and they were having a meet.

Leaving the highway at Prados de Valdonege, we turned right onto a narrow road. Our guidebook indicated that the "authentic" Camino was no longer passable, so this narrow road had been designated as an "authentic" substitute for it. Obediently, we followed it up a small hill and turned left on the Camino de la Virgen. Two kilometers and several undulating hills later, we were on the outskirts of Villafranca del Bierzo. Manier described it as "a little city in frightful mountains where it is shut in as by a precipice."[25]

Soon we were resting beneath a Romanesque doorway of the twelfth-century church of Santiago de Villafranca. Except for its two carved doorways, it looked like a fortification, not a church: it is plain, box-shaped, with just a few tiny windows placed high up on the brown stone walls. In the Middle Ages, pilgrims who could go no further were able to earn their Compostelan plenary indulgence by entering this church through the Doorway of Pardon—just as at San Isidoro in León. This privilege still exists; in Año Santo 1965, a sick and weary Frenchman, unable to proceed, asked for the door to be opened. Passing through it, he earned his indulgence.

We walked down the steep cobblestone path towards town. On our left was the sturdy castle of the Marqueses of Villafranca. Begun in 1490, it is square and squat, built of stone, with a black slate roof. Each of its four corners has a large round tower, towers which were destroyed in the War of Independence but since rebuilt. We heard dogs barking and saw what looked like curtains on some of the deep-set windows.

The road curved around and soon we were walking down the famous Calle del Agua, so-called because an irrigation canal used to cut through the street. The Calle del Agua—often in the past filled with dirty water—is lined with impressive *palacios* on either side, their white stucco and beige stone walls emblazoned with carved coats of arms. Here are the fifteenth- and sixteenth-century palaces of Torquemada and Alvarez de

Toledo, and the chapel of Omañas. It was on this street that Fray Martín Sarmiento, the writer, was born, as was the romantic novelist and poet Gil y Carrasco. Most of the houses are three stories tall, with ornate wrought iron balconies on the second story. Their round-arched entries are defended by thick wood doors studded with metal; their first floor windows are carefully barred with iron grids.

Turning right, we headed towards the Plaza Mayor, looking for a place to spend the night. There was a parador in Villafranca, but I didn't know where it was. It didn't matter: there were a number of hostels in this town of 6,000 people. On our way to the plaza we saw a sign for a *fonda* outside a bar; we went in and asked about a room. The bar owner looked us over and said there was a room, and we should ring the doorbell next door, which we did. After a few minutes, a shabby, slouched man appeared and looked at us suspiciously. We explained what we wanted; he looked at us and shut the door.

Soon a tired woman dressed in a faded skirt and blouse and faded apron, with scuffed slippers on her feet, appeared at the door and we repeated our request; she also looked at us suspiciously but let us in. We followed her retreating back up the stairs and down a corridor. Silently, she pointed to an empty room, then went back to washing the hall floor. Although this was supposedly a *fonda*, they hadn't asked for our passports, and there was no rate card posted.

Bill looked around, checking the connecting glass door to the next room, making sure it was locked. He lay down on his bed, sat up, and put his hand under the mattress, and pulled out a savings book.

"What do you think this is doing here?"

I looked at it. "Maybe someone left it under the mattress for safe keeping and forgot it."

Bill looked skeptical. "Maybe."

"What do you think—they killed last night's guests? I suppose it's possible. After all, we're all just strangers passing through. Who would ever know?"

We looked at each other and rechecked the doors. Cautiously, we took turns washing up—there was no hot water—and then went back to the bar next door.

While we drank our Cokes we talked with the owner. Did he know a good restaurant? Of course he did—his own. Behind the bar was a large dining room where we could eat as much as we wanted for a set price. He told us to return around 9:30, when dinner would be served. Did he know anything about the castle? Of course. It now belonged to the Counts of Peñarramiro, who live there. According to the bar owner, the Countess's husband is a concert pianist. Reassured by the owner's friendliness, we decided to keep the room and go for a walk before dinner.

Villafranca del Bierzo, like so many other towns on the Camino, was established because of—and for—the pilgrimage to Santiago. Franks were settled there during the reign of Alfonso VI. The Frankish influence was great, not only from settlers but also from French religious groups: Alfonso VI erected a church dedicated to Nuestra Señora, maintained by Benedictine monks from Cluny, hence its popular name, de Cluniaco—of the Clunies—and later de Crunego.

At one time, the town belonged to Doña Urraca Alfonso, daughter of the first Portuguese king and wife of Fernando II; afterwards, it was given to a series of other noble families until, in 1486, the Marquesado de Villafranca was created. The still inhabited castle we had seen was built soon afterwards. Villafranca's more recent claim to fame was as the independent capital of the province of the Bierzo from its creation in 1822 until its demise in 1833.

Villafranca was not only a popular town for Franks and Spanish nobility; it was also a popular town for religious orders. According to the guidebook, Nuestra Señora de los Angeles, the church of San Francisco, was founded in Villafranca by San Francisco himself in the thirteenth century. And there is the seventeenth-century Colegiata de Santa María—the successor to the earlier de Crunego building. In addition, there is the Jesuit convent of San Nicolás—now of the Paulists—founded in the seventeenth century, and a convent of San José and another of the Divina Pastora, originally called the Hospital de Santiago. There is also the Convent of La Anunciado, originally founded as a Franciscan convent in 1606 by the fifth Marqués de Villafranca for his headstrong daughter, María. She wanted to be a nun, he wanted her to marry; he imprisoned her, she escaped. Defeated, he reportedly said, "If you must be a nun, be a founder!" and built her a convent.

After drinking espresso at a sidewalk cafe in the plaza, we walked back to our bar/restaurant/*fonda* and ate dinner. At a nearby table was the group of four French bicycle pilgrims we had seen earlier on the road. We nodded to each other in greeting.

The owner had told the truth about his restaurant; the food was good, cheap, and plentiful. Everything was "family style": the waiters served the food from large platters and tureens that they brought to the table. There was a salad made of lettuce and onions but no tomatoes, and a *caldo gallego*—a vegetable-meat soup of rich stock, potatoes, turnip greens, salt pork, and white beans. This was followed by thin, pan-fried beef steaks and fried potatoes. And there was wine. In the late fifteenth century, Künig had reported that the wine was excellent; it still was.

Afterwards, we went for a leisurely walk around town. It was full of large, well maintained monasteries and impressive houses. There were colorful, well kept yards and flowerbeds; people nodded at us pleasantly. The rest of the town seemed normal enough, but our *fonda* was definitely peculiar. Unwillingly, at last we returned to our room, locked both doors carefully, and got ready to go to bed. As a precaution, I propped a chair against the glass connecting door; Bill did the same to the door that opened onto the hallway.

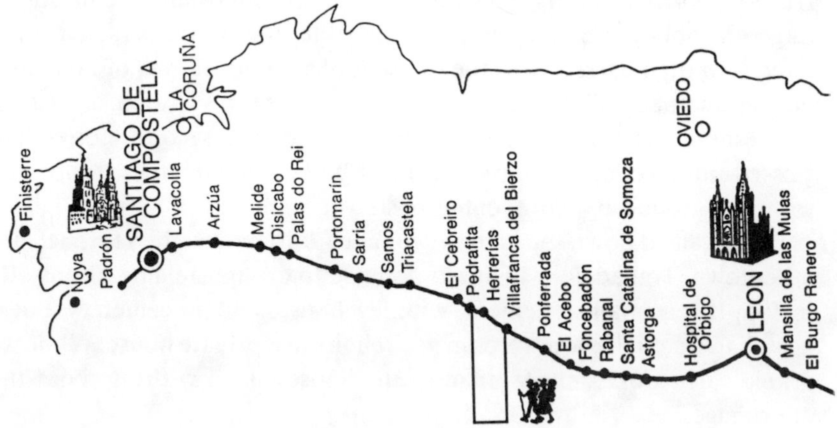

Day 37: August 15

The eleventh stage of journey in the *Codex* is from Villafranca to Triacastela, 47 kilometers in the mountains. We hoped to make it in two days. When we got up, there was neither hot water nor electricity. We left quickly.

We walked out of town and across the Río Burbia on the heavily trafficked two-lane highway through the Valcarce Valley to La Coruña. For centuries, the Valcarce has been a strategic passageway to and from Galicia. Soon we came to a tunnel, which we ran through, trying not to breathe the gasoline-drenched air. On the other side of the tunnel, the highway covered up both the pilgrim's road and the earlier Roman road.

Because the Valcarce Valley is quite narrow—its name means narrow valley imprisoned by mountains—there was nowhere else to build a road, and nowhere else to walk. The road was narrow, without shoulders; we walked on the edge, trying to avoid traffic.

To our left was a sign advertising a fish farm. Also to our left, rising up to and falling below the level of the road, was the bubbling and gurgling Río Valcarce. A yellow arrow outside of Pereje, a small settlement just off the road, indicated that the "real" Camino went through the village, so we left the highway and followed the Camino through the town. In 1118, Queen Doña Urraca gave Pereje to the Aurillac monks at El Cebreiro, and their monks built a *hospital* in town, which sheltered pilgrims during the winter months when snow blocked the pass of Cebreiro. This donation of Urraca's caused a great dispute with the Clunies of Villafranca. Over a period of time, Doña Urraca, Alfonso IX, Urbano III, the bishop of Astorga, the archbishop of Compostela, the bishop of Lugo, the abbot of Samos, and assorted other important personages entered into the quarrel. Now the quarrel, like the town, was of no consequence and nearly forgotten. We passed a cemetery, a church, a few two-story stone houses with dark roofs. Some of the second stories had glassed-in banks of windows, but most had open balconies, supported from the ground by worm-eaten posts.

We walked down the highway for a few kilometers, then through another town, Trabadelo, which was donated to Compostela by Alfonso III in 895. It is a small settlement, with few houses and no cemetery. But it has a bar—actually, a storeroom with chairs in a private house. While we drank warm Cokes, the woman of the house talked with us about the pilgrimage.

"Es bonito, no? Y qué sacrificio!"

Outside of Trabadelo we saw two Frenchmen on horseback. They saw us and stopped.

"Peregrinos?" we asked.

In a mixture of French and Spanish they explained that they came from Paris and were making the pilgrimage on horseback to Santiago—a *peregrinación a caballo*—for the experience and to experience the history. I told them riding horses looked much easier—and much more fun—than walking, but they assured me it was much more difficult. They had to spend one hour every morning and two hours every night caring for the horses. In addition, they couldn't go sightseeing in the cities but had to stay outside with the horses because it was dangerous for and hard on the horses to be in the city. They also had to avoid traffic as much as possible, which was extremely difficult on this stretch of the road, where there was no other trail. The pavement was hard on the horses' hooves, and the swiftly passing trucks and honking cars were very hard on their nerves.

Finding a place to stay and finding food were additional problems. In Castilla and León it had been easy, but in this part of Spain it was quite difficult. They had a horse van, which their two girlfriends drove, and in it they carried feed for the horses. If necessary, they could transport the horses for a distance, but usually they bought food from villagers and camped in the fields outside of town. Now I knew why I had heard about but not seen horseback-riding pilgrims: they avoided the highways, they skirted the towns.

There is a Frenchman who organizes horseback pilgrimages to Santiago, and I had thought it would be romantic and authentic to take a horseback pilgrimage someday. After all, medieval pilgrims often traveled by horse. But conditions were different, then. There were no cars, no asphalt roads, no cities to avoid. Of course, in the Middle Ages there were bad water, bad fodder, and horse thieves to avoid, instead.

They said goodbye and rode on down the highway. I wondered: were they pilgrims? Did it matter?

We walked slowly down the highway, past the ruins of the Castle of Auctares, a fortification of great fame. It is the Uttaris of the Roman itinerary of Antonino. Centuries later, it provided shelter for bands of bandits who assaulted travelers and pilgrims and charged outragous fees for letting pilgrims pass. In 1072, Alfonso VI mandated that the pilgrims not be charged; he explained his intervention by saying, "pilgrims have no other protectors than God and the King."

When we reached Portela, we stopped again, this time at a roadside inn. We had walked twelve kilometers from Villafranca and were very hungry. The inn was extremely crowded, so we had to wait for almost an hour for a table; but at last we ordered *chorizo* sandwiches, *tortilla bocadillos,* and Cokes. While we waited, an old woman commented on our backpacks, the hot weather, the difficulties of walking such a distance.

"Es bonito, no? Y, qué sacrificio! More for the woman than the man."

After we left, a young boy came running after us with a melon and a knife. He asked, timidly, "Peregrinos?" We nodded yes and he grinned, then cut two slices of melon for us. He said he was traveling with his parents, and they'd visited some town near Santiago and now were returning home to Burgos. After we thanked him, he ran back to his parents, watching from the inn. They waved; so did we.

Although the day was hot, there was a pleasant breeze and there was shade. A good day to walk. In addition, the green hills made it seem cooler than it actually was. Walking through the lush green hills of the Bierzo was much pleasanter than walking through the flat brown Tierra del Campos, even if we did have to avoid traffic on the busy, narrow, two-lane road. The Río Valcarce kept gurgling along, slightly lower than the road.

"Bill, people in cars are missing so much."

"Mmh? Sure—pain, weariness, boredom—"

"Oh, come on. They're missing all this beauty! They drive by in their cars, windows closed, radios on. They don't see the river, they don't hear the birds. They don't see the flowers or pick wild berries by the side of the road. They're not going somewhere—they're just getting somewhere!"

Bill looked at me. "You're in good spirits. I take it your feet don't hurt."

"Right. And yours?"

"Mine don't either."

"That moleskin really helps, doesn't it?"

"It sure does. Let's stop and I'll put on some more."

We climbed over a fence and part-way down to the river. We sat down on the grass-covered bank and replaced the moleskin pads on our feet. We were learning how to take care of ourselves and of each other.

The road kept winding up into the hills, ascending the Valcarce Valley, following the Roman road, following the route of Almanzor in the tenth century, following the line of Sir John Moore's retreat in January, 1809, when hundreds of his men perished from the cold, the fault of the wine of Ponferrada—or rather, of their overindulgence in the same. So many footsteps, so many ancestors.

Soon we would reach the summit of the Sierra de Ancares, the Pass of Pedrafita, where Sir John Moore's men had tossed the heavy treasure chests into a ravine in order to lighten their loads and speed their retreat.

We passed more little settlements—several houses long, nothing more—stretching out along the side of the road. Ambasmestas: the name stands for "waters coming together"—where the Ríos Valboa and

Valcarce join. A small village of forty-five inhabitants. Ambascasas. Vega de Valcarce. To the left, on a hill, the ruins of the Castle of Sarracín, dating from the fourteenth or fifteenth century. Ruitelán, another tiny village. According to local tradition, in the ninth century San Froilán left Lugo and retired to Ruitelán, hoping to lead a hermit's life; later he had to abandon his hermitage and take up the episcopal seat of León.

The next village was Herrerías, a mixture of freshly painted white houses and decrepit, grey stone buildings. While we rested, wearily, by the side of the road, we consulted the guidebook. Either we followed the old Camino on the left side of the valley, through Hospital—where there had been a *hospital* for pilgrims—La Faba, Laguna de Castilla, and up to Cebreiro, or we followed the highway on the right to Pedrafita—and later on to Cebreiro. The route on the right was taken by Künig, who cautioned that one could get lost on the difficult route of La Faba. We had already walked twenty kilometers and I was ready to quit at any time. But our road continued to go uphill to the Pass of Pedrafita.

According to our guidebook, the road on the right would be longer—but it also was a paved highway, not a gravel path, so there seemed to be more likelihood of finding somewhere to stop for the night. So we took the route to the right, the same that Kuñig had taken in the fifteenth century. Our road was paved with asphalt; his, if paved, had been paved with cobblestones. The road wound up and around the side of one hill, then another. It went slowly, steadily uphill. We had hoped to find an inn on the road, but there was none. And the hills were steep—too steep to sleep on—and heavily cultivated with wheat and rye. I wondered how anyone could work such steep fields; obviously, all the farming had to be done by hand. It would be difficult not to fall down the hillside. The Bierzo is a rich, fertile region, full of grain, fruits, chestnut and poplar trees, but it was difficult land to farm, and the villages all looked extremely poor. The village of Lamas, precariously perched on a hillside, consists of a few rough stone houses, nothing more.

High above us, spanning the hills, supported on huge cement pylons, was the new Madrid-Coruña superhighway under construction. Someday soon the old road we were walking on would be like U.S. Highway 30, abandoned bits of broken, weed-tufted pavement running alongside the gleaming white super-road—just as now, our asphalt road covered the medieval trail and offered an alternative to yet another, more ancient path.

Bill suggested we climb up to the flat surface of the superhighway to sleep. I refused. We didn't have food or water, and I wanted to keep going. Pedrafita couldn't be much further, I thought.

Bill hoped that Pedrafita would be around the next curve. It wasn't. We kept on walking. We took a short break, then we walked some more. We rounded the curve, then another curve. We walked under the shadow of the elevated superhighway. One kilometer, another kilometer, another. All uphill.

Bill wanted to quit but he wouldn't admit it. I didn't want to quit. For the first time in over a month of walking, I was feeling nothing except exhilaration. No pain. No blisters. No exhaustion. All I felt was the determination to get to Pedrafita. I had no intention of quitting just because Bill was tired. Why should I always be the considerate, acquiescent one?

Bill looked at me. "Let's take a break."

We took a fifteen-minute break and then I got up.

Bill looked at me. "What's your rush?"

"Bill, it is easier for me to keep going than it is for me to stop and get started again."

"I'm just the opposite."

"I know. I've noticed it before: you want to stop within half a kilometer of a town to rest. I hate that!"

"And you! Once you see the goal, you keep on going with a compulsive determination. I hate that!"

We looked at each other and started to laugh. A few weeks earlier, we would have gotten angry.

According to the map, Pedrafita was ten kilometers from Herrerías, but we didn't know how far we had come. When we had stopped at Herrerías, I had been tired; since then, I had felt unstoppable—I was loaded with adrenalin. I'd never experienced that before.

Two or three curves later, we were still walking uphill. At last we saw a town in the distance, on top of a hill. Bill got a sudden burst of energy and he managed to keep up with me as we rounded the last curve into town. We passed a sign, "Province of Lugo," and soon we entered Pedrafita. We'd walked 30 kilometers uphill! We felt like celebrating! But first, we had to find a place to sleep.

There were two hostels in town. The first was closed. The second was full.

"Full?" Bill asked, his voice expressing disbelief.

The man behind the desk repeated. "Full. My son is getting married, and the hostel is filled with wedding guests."

I looked at him. "Could you suggest somewhere else for us to go?"

"Well, the other hostel is closed." He thought a bit. "My wife will take you to a *casa particular*—a private home where you can spend the night."

We thanked him and waited till his wife came, and then we followed her around and behind the hostel, down a narrow alley, and up to the second floor of a stark, ugly, modern, two-story apartment building. She knocked on the door, and a woman dressed in black opened it. Gesturing towards us, our guide explained the situation. We listened, too tired to talk; suddenly, we could hardly stand up. After looking at us, the woman nodded and ushered us in to her home. It was clean, bare, and narrow, like a railroad car: a corridor stretching the length of the building, and the rooms were all entered from the right side of the hallway.

She told us we could sleep in an unused bedroom at the end of the corridor, and she gave us fresh towels and told us how to turn on the gas hot water heater for the bath. We returned to the room and collapsed. Lying on the sagging mattress, my head resting on the lumpy bolster, I thought about how odd it felt to sleep in a stranger's home. But they didn't seem worried. Nor had our friends in St. Jean Pied de Port. I wondered if Americans were less trusting. Bill pointed out the Spaniards had bars on their windows and the hotels had a light switch near the bed. More trusting? He doubted it. Besides, what could we do to harm these people? We were pilgrims.

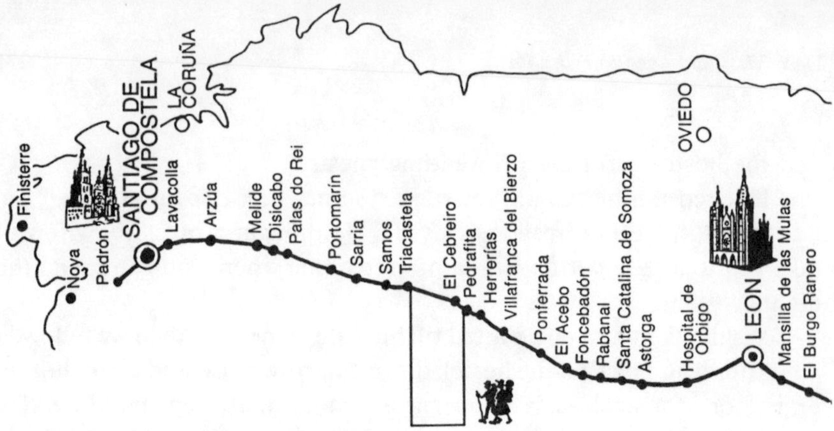

Day 38: August 16 We got up early, felt rested, and started towards Cebreiro. The air was thick with fog. We could barely see the road signs and the road. Walking along the side of the broken-surfaced road, we tried to avoid being hit by the cars that appeared and disappeared silently, abruptly in the fog. Looking over the side of the road, we could see nothing except the guard rail.

The road kept going up. I had thought that the Pass of Pedrafita was a high pass, at 1,109 meters, but apparently it was not the only or the highest pass we had to reach. We kept on climbing up the Monte de Cebreiro, described in the old pilgrims' guides as the most difficult ascent of the entire route; it stretches upward for seventeen continuous kilometers at an altitude of over 1,000 meters, from Laguna de Castilla—on the La Faba route, near Pedrafita—to Filloval. Although instead of taking the road through La Faba we had taken the road through Pedrafita to Cebreiro, we still had to make the same lengthy, steep climb.

Five kilometers from Pedrafita the road forked; we saw a road sign and walked up next to it to read it: Cebreiro to the left. In the fog, we passed a ghostly cross and then dark shapes loomed up in front of us to the right: a damp, grey stone church, low, elliptical thatched huts, another damp stone building. We'd reached Cebreiro, at an altitude of 1,300 meters.

Cebreiro is spelled Cebrero in our guidebook but spelled Cebreiro on the new roadsigns, in acknowledgement that the Gallegan spelling is more valid than the Castilian—a political judgment, not a grammatical one—an indication that Galicia, like other Spanish regions, is reclaiming itself. Galicia with its sonorous bagpipes, Galicia with its Celtic past, Galicia with its own language, Gallego, a mixture of old Castilian and old Portuguese. Galicia, most western of the Spanish provinces, famous for its fishermen, its forests, its legends of sorcerers and witchcraft, its mid-

Fog obscures the deep valleys surrounding El Cebreiro. This building is a prehistoric, Celtic-style palloza, part of an ethnographic museum run by the parish priest, Elías Valiña Sampedro, a scholar and supporter of the Camino. Pilgrims can spend the night in the palloza, which smells of animals and damp straw.

night magic and apple-laden, blue-flamed *queimada* punch. Galicia, famous for its shrine of Santiago de Compostela.

Cebreiro was supposedly inhabited sometime before 300 B.C.—people fleeing one set of invaders after another ended up huddled together on this lonely mountain top which no one else wanted. Later, Cebreiro was the site of one of the first mountain refuges built for pilgrims to Santiago. And pilgrims needed shelter, up there on the high, isolated, windblown mountain ridge. The mountain is covered with snow in winter, and blizzards are frequent; fog persists throughout the year. The pass is comparable to those of Roncesvalles, Somport, and Foncebadón; crossing it would perhaps have been easier, because pilgrims were in better shape, but it would have been harder for pilgrims weakened by weeks of illness and exertion on the road.

The stone church is pre-Romanesque in style and dates from the ninth and tenth centuries. In 1072 Alfonso VI placed Cebreiro under the control of the monks of the abbey of San Geraud d'Aurillac; in 1487 Cebreiro was given to the Benedictine monks of Valladolid. They controlled it until 1854 and the *desamortización,* after which it was placed under the jurisdiction of the diocese of Lugo.

Today, the church, *hospital,* and huts form an important historical-artistic monument; Elías Valiña Sampedro, the parish priest of Pedrafita and an authority on the Camino de Santiago, has actively promoted their preservation and development. In 1965 the remains of the primitive *hospital* and residence of the monks was refurbished and converted into a *meson* for tourists and pilgrims passing through to Santiago. The *pallozas*—those strange, elliptical stone huts—are now used as an ethnographic museum—a sort of "Living History Farm"—and one of them serves as a refuge for modern-day pilgrims who need a place to sleep.

Cebreiro gained fame not only as a shelter for pilgrims in the mountains but also for a miracle which purportedly occurred around 1300. According to the legend, one day a villager from the nearby pueblo of Barjamayor climbed up to Cebreiro to hear Mass, despite a fiercely blowing gale. The Mass was celebrated by a monk of little faith, who ridiculed the sacrifice the villager had made to reach the church in such foul weather. "Fool," thought the priest, "to travel here for just a bit of bread and wine!" But then, to his amazement, a miracle occurred; in the moment of the consecration, the communion wafer was converted into flesh and the wine into blood.

The word spread quickly, carried across Europe by the feet and tongues of pilgrims, and the fame of Cebreiro and its miracle grew. In 1486 the Catholic monarchs visited Cebreiro on their pilgrimage to Santiago; they admired the twelfth-century chalice in which the miracle occurred and later donated a rock crystal reliquary to the church to house the relics of the miracle. Later, Wagner may have drawn on the legend for his musical creation, *Parsifal*.

Cebreiro: home of the Holy Grail—not the Arthurian one, of course, for that holy grail dates some seven or eight hundred years earlier. But perhaps the Galician legend owes something to that other holy grail—after all, there were Celts in northern Spain, and pilgrims traveling through would carry tales in both directions. Besides, who is to say that there was only one grail, or that they were not the same? Holy grails, miracles, apparitions of Virgins: occurring repeatedly, replicating themselves on mountain tops, in caves.

The day we arrived, Cebreiro was cloaked not only in mystery but also in fog. We walked through the thick, clotted air to the *meson*. Inside the air was full of the smell from a cracklng fire and freshly baked bread, the sound of conversation: we saw a crowded room, wooden tables and chairs, pilgrims, priests, tourists. A group of middle-aged visitors invited us to sit with them. One was from Germany, two were Swiss, three were French, one was a relative of the priest, Don Elías, whom, unfortunately, we could not meet—he had just driven down to Pedrafita. I wondered if we had seen his car, its yellow headlights appearing and disappearing in the fog.

Warmed and rested, we went out to see the church and the *pallozas*. A guide took us first to the *pallozas*—low, circular and oval buildings made of flat stones layered together haphazardly. The *pallozas* crouch on the mountaintop, huddle into the ground for shelter from the winds and snow. The conical-shaped thatched roofs, made of straw laid down in rows, reach almost to the ground. The *pallozas* have one or two doors, several small, deep-set windows. There is no chimney; smoke just seeps out through cracks in the walls, the doors, the windows. Inside, animals and people shared a common living space and warmth.

We entered one of the *pallozas*: it was dark, cramped, damp, the air still thick with the stench of wet fur and decay, of rotting grain and unwashed animal skins. According to our guide, these ancient Celtic huts undoubtedly resembled the prehistoric Iron Age homes of Europe. Although ancient, one of the *pallozas* of Cebreiro was lived in until twelve years ago. And just the night before, a group of pilgrims had slept in the one we were standing in.

Walking past two large, circular gateposts, their flat, rough-edged stones softened by the fog, we crossed a small courtyard. In front of us was the church, a well preserved example of ninth- and tenth-century Asturian-style architecture, even though this is Galicia, not Asturias. In the fog, the church was barely visible, but I could see that it was all stone walls and roof, a simple church, with a low, squat bell tower and a sheltered entryway. We went inside.

The silver-crowned, twelfth-century figure of Santa María la Real greeted us, solemn and serene, a moon-faced Virgin holding a wise—and large—child Jesus on her lap. We saw the miraculous chalice, and the relics of the bread and wine, the flesh and blood. A holy chalice, evocative of the Holy Grail of Arthur's knights, of true believers and doubting priests: the search for purity, the quest for miracles, led on by faith. I wondered what would have happened to those knights if they had found their grail. Would they have dropped dead on the spot, utterly fulfilled? Or would they have been doomed thereafter to a life of anticlimax?

What happens when you find what you are searching for? Maybe it is the quest that really matters, not the goal. I was neither the villager nor the priest, neither Gawain nor Parsifal. I was the pilgrim, on a different quest. Unlike them, I knew where I was going—but not what I was looking for. What would I find at Santiago? And after?

The fog had cleared. All around us were deep valleys, high hills—a patchwork of dark emerald and light lime; it looked like Norway or Switzerland. I walked over to the edge of the mountain top, next to one of the *pallozas.* What a lovely view. And what awful winters the inhabitants must have had, with nothing between them and the bitter wind but stone and straw, the heat of a smoky fire, the warmth of each other and their animals.

We started up the highway. And up and down. A road to the left led to Rubiales, an important lead and zinc mine, but we kept on the highway leading to Triacastela, 21 kilometers away. Already we were tired. Usually, after two or three days of walking, we rested for a day. But today we would have mountains to climb before we could stop in Triacastela. Bill had the chills, and my stomach was very bad again.

According to the guidebook, Lagua de Tablas, called the "cradle of the Knights of Santiago," was to the right of the highway. We passed through Liñares, the Linar de Rege of Aymeric Picaud, a place mentioned as early as 714. Liñares has several churches, similar in appearance to the one in Cebreiro, and several houses. We kept on walking. There was supposed to be a beautiful view several hundred meters off the highway, a view of the picturesque valley formed by the Río Lor and of the village of Veiga de Forcas, home of the Armestos, famous knights of the Order of Santiago; in the background, we would be able to see the distant mountain ridge topped by the peaks of Capeloso, Faro, and Piopaxaro—the spelling of the latter reflecting the replacement of the Castilian "j" with the Gallegan "x"; the pronunciation remains the same—a silent "h"—but the politics are different. Although the scenic overlook was only 200 meters off the highway, we didn't go to see it. We'd see the mountains soon enough, and the valley. Unlike car travelers, we would not only see them—we'd walk through them.

In some of the hills we saw old limestone quarries, the quarries whose rocks pilgrims had transported to Castañeda to help make mortar for the cathedral in Santiago. We saw a building with empty soft drink crates stacked outside and a sign, "Casa Jaime"—the usual Spanish word for James. The name Santiago, however, is derived from the Latin Jacobo and the Greek Iacobus. In German, he's referred to as Jakob—and the Camino is called "Jakob's Way." That's also how we get the term, "Jacobean pilgrim." Gradually, the name changed from Jacobo to Iago, the same name as Shakespeare's character in *Othello*, but with the addition of "San" for saint; eventually, the name changed from San Iago to Santiago.

We stopped in Casa Jaime for a Coke. The place was a large room, full of supplies piled on the floor and hanging from the ceiling: hot water bottles, agricultural equipment, huge rubber overshoes, wooden shoes called *zuecos,* canned goods, bottles of liquor and warm soda pop.

Refreshed, we started out eagerly, but soon our energy flagged again. We were climbing the Alto de San Roque, 1,264 meters high. Scattered along the side of the road and the hills were isolated houses and occasional bars. We passed by Hospital da Condesa—the Gallegan "da" replacing the Castilian "de la"—named for a pilgrim's *hospital* which was founded there perhaps by the end of the ninth century.

Hospital da Condesa's church is typical of the region: built in a low-lying area, of flat local stone laid unevenly in random layers, with unadorned, round-arched doorway and windows. The stone bell tower is low and square, covered with a vaulted stone roof, topped with a cross. In Hospital da Condesa the cross was the cross of Santiago. What a change from the light-hearted, elaborately decorated churches of Castilla and

León, standing on a prominence, pointing sculpture-covered towers towards the sky. Those churches aimed at heaven; these burrowed in the earth.

We passed several stucco-and-stone houses. Behind them were vegetable gardens, planted with grape arbors and strange, tall stalks with a green head on the top—a kind of cabbage allowed to grow tall, plucked leaf by leaf. After passing through the town, we climbed over a low stone fence and rested in a field full of purple heather.

The road kept going up, past groves of ash trees, their branches lopped off to feed village oxen. Soon we left the highway and followed the "authentic" Camino through Padornelo, an important village in the twelfth century; the Brothers Hospitaliers of San Juan de Malta built a hospice there for pilgrims. Today, only three people live in the village, and all that remains are several buildings, a church, another church in ruins, and a cemetery.

The road kept going up, and at last we reached the top of the pass and a newly painted sign, "Alto do Poio, 1,337 meters high." Our guidebook used the Castilian spelling—Alto de Poyo; the sign post, however, used the Gallegan spelling. In the Middle Ages there was a hermitage at the top of the pass, called Santa María del Poyo and dedicated to Mary Magdalene. The vista was impressive. To our right, the valley of the Río Navia. Behind us, and now distant, El Cebreiro. All around us, light green, dark green, and yellow patchwork hills.

We rested, then we started walking again. Soon we reached a small village called Fonfría del Camino—the name comes from Fons Frigida, meaning "cold spring." From 1535 until the nineteenth century, there was a hospice in Fonfría for pilgrims, the Hospital de Santa Catalina. The monks provided firewood, salt, and water and a bed with two blankets to pilgrims, without charge; to the sick, they gave bread, eggs, and lard.

The villages we had seen that day looked the same: uneven grey stones wedged together to form the houses, jagged rocks filled the yards and the street, grey-brown stones piled on grey-brown stones formed low barriers around the buildings. The houses seemed scattered at random in the lowest lying land. In Navarra, the stone houses had looked well cared for and substantial, made of carefully fitted, evenly cut stones, brightened with colored edging on the windows and doors and with decorative stone trim on the corners. In Castilla and León, most of the houses had been brown, mud brown, adobe smooth and rounded, their windows blocked off by metal blinds or green bamboo shades. They clustered together, presenting high blind walls to the curious passerby. Often, they lined up along the Camino.

In comparison, these villages in Galicia looked destitute, the houses made of haphazardly shaped stones, haphazardly layered together, haphazardly arranged. Maybe the building style was unavoidable, but I couldn't shake the feeling that this was a much more primitive region, that as we walked forward into Galicia, we were walking backwards into the Middle Ages.

According to our guidebook, at Fonfría the Camino separated from the highway. We saw an old man walking down the road and asked him where the Camino was; he advised us to stay on the main highway to Biduedo. Unlike elsewhere on our pilgrimage, where people had blithely urged us to take the Camino, assuring us that it was easier and shorter when it wasn't, people here seemed to know what they were talking about. Perhaps they had less room for fantasy.

At Biduedo, the highway and the Camino came together and separated again. An old man sitting outside a stone hut watched us pass by. Dressed in faded black, he sat upon a chair, smoking a hand-rolled cigarette. We walked over to him, and Bill offered him a Gitano from his pack, which he took and put in his shirt pocket. He offered Bill a cigarette in exchange. After a while, he told us that two pilgrims had taken a shortcut through the hills that morning but had gotten lost. He repeated the instructions for us, but his dialect was hard to understand. It sounded like: go past some springs, follow the yellow arrows. Off we went, up the steep side of the hill behind the village.

We passed water dripping out of a moss-covered limestone hillside: was this the spring? We tasted the water; it was cold, mineral-filled. Bill squeezed a bit of lemon into it, making it more refreshing. While we wiped our sweaty faces with the water, a tractor passed us on the narrow dirt road. Following the old man's directions, we walked up the trail, looking for yellow arrows and a pillar. Soon we were hiking on a barely visible rocky path up and over the heather-covered hills. Far below us was the highway, twisting its slow, cautious way around the hills; we watched one model-sized car, then another, winding their way along the road. Our route was obviously shorter, and even, possibly, authentic.

We stopped and rested awhile, staring out at the lush, green hills, trying to locate the little villages of Lamas and Vilar, somewhere on the highway. My feet hurt terribly from walking across the rough, uneven, rocky trail; Bill's tendonitis was acting up again. He continued to rest while I went off behind a hillock: I still had severe stomach problems.

At the village of Filloval, end of the difficult 17-kilometer stretch which had begun before Pedrafita, the Camino came down from the hills and crossed the highway. Then it took off again over the hilltops while the highway wound around the hills. We were following the Camino, but somehow we lost the way and came up against a stone fence. Far below we saw the highway, so we climbed over the fence and slid and limped down the hillside, cutting across a stubble-filled field. When we reached the highway at the valley floor, we rested beneath a large chestnut tree. Then we walked down the highway for a short distance until we saw a yellow arrow which pointed to a path to the left and below the level of the road.

The packed dirt path was two meters below the surface of the soil, worn down through centuries of use and erosion. Oak and chestnut tree roots dangled out of the banks on either side. We walked in shadow; the sun couldn't reach that far below the surface of the ground. On either side, above the level of our heads, trees, moss, weeds, and bushes grew. The air smelled of earth. Suddenly, the bank on the left diminished in height, and we saw a clearing and a village, As Pasantes.

On the other side of As Pasantes, the bank grew higher again and then diminished again. We reached another clearing and another village: Ramil, the Ranimirus of the ninth century. The villages were as medieval as the trail: stone houses, rutted dirt paths, animal dung, the sound of cattle, the smell of pigs. It seemed as if we had walked back into the Middle Ages—but then I saw an electricity line and a TV antenna.

Our ancient trail rejoined the highway and around the next curve was the town of Santiago de Triacastela—now called Triacastela—end of the eleventh stage of journey in the *Codex.* We had walked 29 kilometers.

To our left was a church dedicated to Santiago. The town already existed in the ninth century—or at least a monastery did, dedicated to Saints Peter and Paul, donated by Count Gatón and his wife Doña Elvira and fitted out with books, ornaments, curtains, and other necessary paraphernalia. In 1112 Archbishop Gelmírez of Santiago accompanied Queen Doña Urraca to Triacastela during a military campaign against her husband, Alfonso I el Batallador. But it was Alfonso IX who really developed the town; he wanted to raise a large city at the foot of the mountains of El Cebreiro. His project was only moderately successful, although at one time there was a *hospital* for pilgrims and various hospices.

Innkeepers in Santiago de Compostela used to send agents to

Triacastela, where they would improvise encounters with innocent pilgrims; striking up an acquaintance, the agents would recommend particular hospices in Santiago. When the pilgrims stayed in them, they would be cheated in numerous ingenious ways. For example, the innkeepers would charge them too much to purchase things and give them too little in exchange for their foreign coins.

Exhausted and hungry, we wanted to find somewhere to spend the night. As we walked through the village, we saw a modern-looking bar/hostel, so we went in and asked for a room. The man behind the counter said there was no room. There was no room at this hostel, but he owned another one and there was room there. We walked over to it and got a room, paying $12 for one night with breakfast included. The wallpaper peeled off the walls; there was no lock on the door. But there was a bathroom and cold running water.

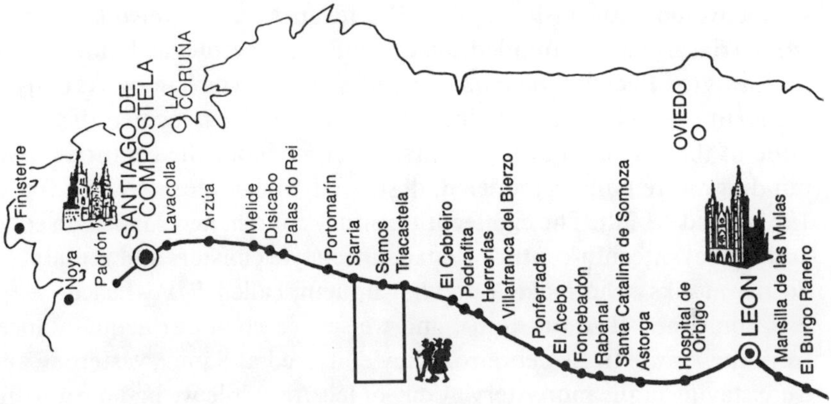

Day 39: August 17 We were both exhausted, and Bill was sick, but we didn't want to stay in Triacastela. We agreed to try to walk some more. But first we had to choose which route: we could follow the Camino Real, Camino Francés, Camino de Santiago—the road had many names, all the same—to Sarria, passing through San Xil; or we could follow the highway to Sarria, passing through Samos. Which was authentic? What did it matter. Given our condition, we decided to follow the highway: we might have to hitchhike.

As we walked out of town, we passed a large, triangular-shaped stone monument to the pilgrim to Santiago. At the top was a statue of a pilgrim wearing a long cape and a wide-brimmed hat, holding a staff. They honored pilgrims in this town—if only the memory.

The air was cool and fresh, and the highway was paved—a welcome change from the rocky authentic Camino of the day before. Although the road went up and down, mostly it went gradually down, winding gently through the valley of the Río Ouribio. There were fields and small villages, the houses grouped close together but not walled together as in León. In the distance, I saw a young boy riding his bicycle up and down the road, making long, lazy loops.

Soon we stopped for a Coke at a bar/store. The woman behind the counter asked if we were going to Santiago to fulfill a promise; when we said no, for the experience, she was puzzled. She told us that it seemed like a long way to come, just to walk the Camino. Shaking her head, she said it wouldn't have surprised her if we'd gone to Lourdes, or Fátima—but to come to Spain to walk the Camino?

With an effort of will, we left the bar and walked some more. My feet were covered with blisters; Bill had a fever. At last, twelve kilometers from Triacastela, we rounded a curve and there before us, hidden in the hills, was the Benedictine monastery of San Julián de Samos. As early as the sixth century, a Benedictine monastery had been located there, but none of the original building remains. Throughout the centuries more buildings were built, remodeled, destroyed—most recently, by a fire in 1951—and rebuilt. The eighteenth-century church, neoclassical in style, and the seventeenth-century Renaissance-style cloisters still remain. So do the monks, who make a popular liqueur, called *Pax*—Peace.

Someone called out to us, and we saw some of our acquaintances from the *meson* in El Cebreiro. They'd arrived at Samos yesterday and were staying at the monastery. A day of leisure, while we had been struggling up and down mountaintops. With their help, we got our pilgrimage cards stamped, admired the cloisters, the paintings, and the chapel.

On one monastery wall was a list of names, chiseled into the stone: the patriots who had died for their country during the Civil War. The memorial only listed those who had died on the winning side. It seemed inappropriate, carved into the monastery wall: a blatant reminder of the strong connection between the Church, the military, and Franco.

Since it was time for lunch, we left our companions, who were eating in the monastery, and went to a small restaurant next to the gas station across from the monastery. A sign in front advertised *parrilla.* When we went in, we saw that the restaurant served only one thing: *parrillada,* a selection of grilled beef steaks, pork and lamb chops, and kidneys. It was run by a husband and wife, who talked to us while he grilled the meat on an open fire in one corner and she took care of a little baby. We told them where we had come from and that we didn't think we could walk much further—our feet were terribly sore. The man said he had heard that hot salt water was the best treatment for tender feet. While we talked, we ate the juiciest, best-seasoned *parrilla* I ever ate in Spain.

Then we went outside and sat down by the side of the building, across from the monastery, wondering what to do next. I couldn't walk any further—my feet were swollen and covered with blisters; Bill's feet were also covered with blisters, and he had a fever.

As we rested wearily against the side of the building, a bus pulled up in front of us. On the back of the bus was a banner: "Pilgrimage from Costa Brava to Santiago." The bus doors opened, and gaily dressed people spewed out. When they saw us, they came rushing over. One man offered us an open bottle of wine, a woman gave us a handful of nuts, several people took photographs of us. After all, we were real, authentic pilgrims! And what, I wondered, were they? Their pilgrimage was a few days of vacation on a bus going to Santiago, with sightseeing excursions along the way. Theirs was a a communal experience, crushed together in the bus, speeding over the pilgrimage road. They were not footsore and weary. They were not pilgrims like us.

Soon their guide led them across the street for an organized tour of the monastery. We stumbled to our feet and went to find a taxi to Sarria. Ten kilometers, $5, with a scenic tour thrown in for free.

In exquisite comfort, we drove out of the narrow valley of Samos and arrived twenty minutes later at Sarria, 10 kilometers away. I had no idea what those ten kilometers of the Camino looked like, but I didn't care. I'd seen enough. The driver dropped us off at the Hotel Roma and we went in. The place smelled of fresh paint.

Bill asked, "Do you have a room?"

"Yes."

I asked, "With private bath?"

"Yes."

"With bathtub?"

"No, with shower."

"No bathtub?"

"Sorry, no."

Bill looked at me. Why was I quibbling? I said, "It sounds fine—we'll take it."

We climbed up the stairs to our room. The room, like the hotel, had just been redecorated. And we had our own, private bath, and I just knew there would be hot water. I really wished there were a tub, not a shower, so that I could soak my sore muscles, but I wasn't going to complain—too much. After all, sometimes I needed to remind myself that part of the pilgrimage was learning to appreciate what I had. Hot water, a shower—they would do just fine.

I went into the bathroom and turned on the faucet—nothing. Zero. *Nada.* Not a drop. I went downstairs and complained. Shrugging his shoulders, the hotel clerk said he was sorry, but at the moment apparently there was no water. There must be something wrong with the water supply. Perhaps later. . . .

What a joke—what a lesson! I had been complaining because there was no bath—I had felt deprived because all I had was a shower—and it turned out there was no water.

Just two days before, I had blithely said how pleasant walking was—I could even understand why people went on a nice little 30-kilometer stroll—without backpack—in the Pyrenees. I had felt rested, fit; I had actually enjoyed walking through the hills. But, then, we had had to climb 10 or more kilometers uphill without a break, and although at the time I had been charged with adrenalin, afterwards, I was exhausted. And the next day we had had to walk 28 kilometers more, up and down mountains, on rocky paths which ruined my feet. On top of that, instead of resting after three days of exertion, we had walked twelve more kilometers to Samos. Lest I forget: this was not a pleasure trip. It was a pilgrimage. When it started getting easy, something would start to get difficult.

Bill had a fever, my feet were badly swollen and my blisters bloody; we decided to spend the next day resting in Sarria. We went to bed early. During the night, Bill was burning with fever, heat radiating from his body. I gave him aspirin and plenty of water, and worried about how I would find him a doctor if he needed one. And what going to a Spanish doctor would be like.

Day 40: August 18 I woke up first, got dressed, and went to a cafe across the street to buy coffee and croissants for Bill. He woke up at the smell, ate them, drank the coffee, and went back to sleep. While he slept, I went downstairs and bought postcards at the registration desk. I sat down at a sidewalk cafe next to the hotel. A young, solitary pilgrim walked silently by, weighed down by his pack.

Later, Bill was feeling well enough to eat *la comida,* so we went downstairs to the hotel restaurant, located in the basement and decorated like a *bodega.* There was an elaborate stone and iron fireplace in the middle of one wall, on which they were grilling *parrilla*—not as good as the *parrilla* at the tiny, plain restaurant at Samos. Then we went back to the room and slept.

We woke about around 5 p.m, and felt better, so we decided to see the town. Called Flavia Lambrio by the Romans, Sarria was an important stopping place for pilgrims in the Middle Ages; now it is a thriving industrial town of 16,000 people. As we walked downtown, we passed brightly colored graffiti painted on cement fences and vacant walls: "25 de Xulio, Día de la Patria Galega"—Day of the Galician Fatherland. Although July 25 is the Día de Santiago, the feast day of St. James, patron of Spain, in Galicia the Galicians were now claiming it as their own day, not Spain's, claiming it as a symbol of their struggle for separation or autonomy from the rest of Spain.

On the outskirts of town, on top of a hill, reached by climbing a set of steep granite stairs, are the remains of a medieval castle and a convent. We looked up at them from down below, then turned around and went back to the hotel and back to bed.

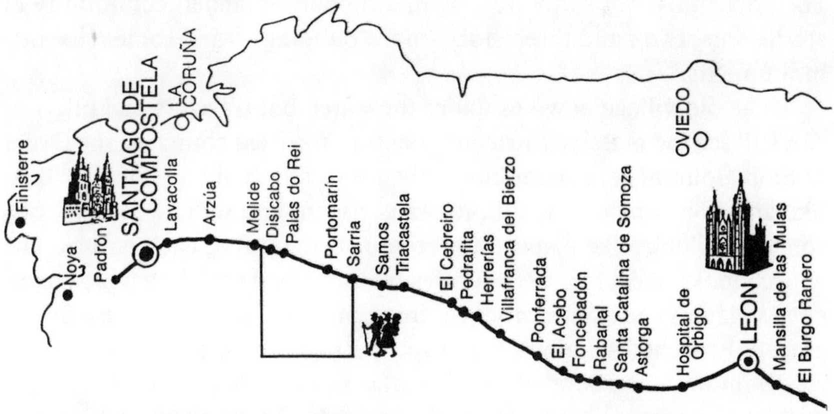

Day 41: August 19 Since Bill felt better, we decided not to rest another day in Sarria. We wanted to be in Santiago by August 22 or 23; and, although we couldn't make it all the way to Santiago on foot by then, we still hoped to walk most of the way. We debated whether to plan

ahead which sections of road to walk and which to skip, or whether to continue walking as far as we could and then skip a "chunk" at the end. Which was truer to the "spirit" of the pilgrimage? After much discussion, we agreed to take a taxi 20 kilometers to the next large town, Portomarín, skipping ahead one day's walk.

Portomarín is a new old city. Originally, the village of Portomarín—or Puertomarín—stood beside a strategically located bridge over the Río Miño. The original Roman bridge was destroyed during a battle between Alfonso I el Batallador and his wife Doña Urraca and rebuilt in 1120 by Pedro Peregrino—Peter the Pilgrim. Another bridge was built in 1929, and the present bridge replaces that one. For centuries, Portomarín was an important stopping place for medieval pilgrims, with several churches and hospices.

The town and its monuments withstood fierce medieval battles and the nineteenth-century *desamortización,* but then the government decided to build a reservoir, the Embalse de Belesar, and the village was submerged under its waters in 1963. But not everything was lost. The more noteworthy buildings were taken apart block by block, numbered, moved to a nearby, higher site, and then put back together. Although this wasn't Abu Simbel and the Aswan Dam, it was the same idea. New off-white stucco apartment buildings were built for the villagers, since their homes had not been considered worth preserving. Today, a new old Portomarín overlooks the reservoir, a modern, planned community of sterile one-, two-, and three-story stucco buildings—and some relocated monuments.

The old village now lies under the water, but travelers and pilgrims can still see the massive thirteenth-century fortified church of the Order of Saint John of Jerusalem, now called the church of San Nicolás. Box-like and imposing on the hill, its walls rise up and up to a saw-toothed roof; what looks like a guard tower adorns the top of each corner. The church looks like a fortress and presumably was; I could imagine frightened villagers and noble princes hiding behind its sheltering walls. Small, gracefully arched windows interrupt the high walls, and an enormous rose window—surrounded by a circular stone halo, half the size of the wall itself, permits light to enter the obscurity. On the elaborately carved archivolt of the main doorway, twenty-four old musicians sing and pluck their way through the Apocalypse.

Visitors can also see the little twelfth-century church of San Pedro, the sixteenth-century Casa del Conte, and the seventeenth-century Palace de Berbeteros, for they, too, were saved. And they can enjoy the restful view of the green hills from the new *parador,* built in a style to match the creamy colored stucco and beige stone architecture of the new old town. Once, there were several *hospitales* for pilgrims and a leprosarium in Portomarín; now they, like the villagers' homes, lie under shifting waters.

We followed the new cobblestone road through town, looking at store windows on the arcaded central street. A group of tourists were drinking espresso and eating local sweets at a sidewalk cafe. Several pilgrims on bicycles passed through without stopping. There wasn't much to see: an artificial town, an artificial lake. Bill thought he heard the tourists laughing at the sweaty bicycle pilgrims. As usual, I argued with him: after all, what could possibly be funny about it? But he was sure they had laughed. After all, he said, such strenuous effort must look unnecessary—and humorous—to the tourists, who are traveling to Santiago in comfort.

Still tired, we decided to take another taxi to Palas de Rey, 23 kilometers away, and stay there for the day. Going by taxi was the most convenient way, and we no longer quibbled about "authenticity" or walking every foot of the Camino—after all,the Camino was very long, and some parts of it were more authentic than others. Besides, we had run short of time.

As we drove along, our driver pointed out villages and local sites and occasionally told us where the "real" Camino de Santiago could be seen from the highway. We missed that part of the pilgrimage. Not just that part of the Camino, but that part of the pilgrimage: we missed the experience of walking past those tiny villages off the highway, seeing the churches, drinking Cokes in the bars, cooling ourselves with water from the public fountain, exchanging pleasantries with the villagers. We missed the weariness, the pain, the pleasure, the accomplishment.

We missed walking through Toxibó, Gonzar, Castromaior and Hospital. We missed Ventas de Narón, Prebisa, Lameiros, Ligonde, Eirexe, Portos. Names on the map, villages of one or two houses on the road. We missed Vilar—or Villar—de Donas, a National Monument, named after a group of *dueñas—doñas* or ladies—who founded a convent in the town or, perhaps, for a family named Donas. In 1184 the Order of the Knights of Santiago was installed there in the Church of El Salvador; today, numerous sarcophagi still line the walls, tombs of the Galician Knights who fought to keep the Camino safe from bandits, who fought against the

Moors. The apse is covered with frescoes painted in 1386 or slightly later—frescoes of delicately painted young women—the *doñas*?—with penetrating glances. "Giocondas of Galicia," according to Cunqueiro, "of mysterious and thoughtful smiles." We missed them.

Soon we reached Palas de Rey: Palas do Rei, according to the newer spelling on the road sign; Pallatium Regis, according to Picaud's guide. The end of the twelfth stage of journey in the *Codex* and the beginning of the thirteenth and final stage.

Palas do Rei is the center of a large municipality, and we had arrived on a day when most of the municipality, and many of its animals, were walking up and down the narrow streets of Palas do Rei. A *feria*—a cattle market—as well as a produce market were in progress. Open-backed trucks displayed imported fruits and vegetables, open carts displayed home-grown produce. Tables were heaped with fabric, trims, towels, and clothes. There were food vendors, offering cheeses and dried country ham and *pulpo a la feria*—boiled octopus, sliced in tiny pieces, marinated in oil, garlic, and spicy paprika. The smells reminded us that it was 2:00 and we were hungry.

Some children stopped us and asked where we were from and how far we had walked. Then a *guardia civil* stopped us and asked if we were coming back from or going to Santiago. Since he seemed quite amiable, we asked him for directions to a restaurant. Courteously, he walked with us down the street, around a corner, and pointed towards an open door. We entered.

The restaurant was very popular—every seat was taken. Along with a number of other hungry people, we stood by the door. We wondered what the proper procedure was: to wait for someone to take our names? To stand behind a table and play musical chairs? We didn't know, but we were very hungry and hoped the wait would be brief. We stood and waited for more than half an hour, talking with other, equally hungry people. But they seemed to come and go; we stayed. At last, we saw a table being cleared, and our companions urged us to go sit down at it. We did.

The waiter placed a brown ceramic carafe of cheap red wine on the table and asked us if we wanted pork or beef stew. Our efforts to get Cokes were unsuccessful. The food—a salad, a stew of short-ribs, potatoes, and vegetables—was nourishing and filling, the bread was excellent. We ate quickly—other people were waiting behind our chairs—and paid and left.

Although originally we had planned to spend the day in Palas do Rei, we changed our minds because of the *feria.* Refreshed by lunch, eager to leave the uproar, we decided to begin walking the 63 kilometers to Santiago, the final stage of journey in the *Codex.* An old man pointed us towards the Camino de Santiago—called, there, the Campo dos Romeiros.

We crossed the Río Roxán and left the road, climbing to the houses of Aldea de Riba, and then Gaiola de Riba, the name of the last house in the settlement. The houses had names, just like families. According to the map, there was a Gaiola de Baixo, too. The equivalent in Castilian was Gaiola de Arriba—up above—and de Abajo—down below. I wondered why two different names when they were so close together.

After climbing up to de Riba we climbed down an arroyo and then up to a hilltop, shaded with oak trees. Then we descended again, to the village of San Xulián do Camiño—in Castilian, San Julián del Camino—a small settlement of twenty-five people. There we saw a sign pointing towards the left: "Castillo de Pambre," described by the Gallegan writer Emilia Pardo Bazán in her novel, *Los Pazos de Ulloa.* For the first time on the pilgrimage, we decided to take a sightseeing detour off the Camino.

We started down the gravel path which led to Castle Pambre. An old man saw us turn off the Camino and called out to us, telling us we were on the wrong road to reach Santiago and offering us directions. We thanked him but said we wanted to see Castle Pambre. He shook his head: pilgrims sightseeing?

We strolled down the gravel path. On either side were fields and meadows separated by thick, solid hedgerows or barbed wire. Cattle grazed in some of the fields—Galicia is renowned for its veal and for its cheese. The houses were arranged in scattered settlements, standing alone, surrounded with low stone walls, each separate and fenced off from the rest, guarding its property from neighbors' eyes. Beside the houses were elevated grain-drying sheds, rectangular in shape, with slotted cement sides and a cross at the top at one end. In the yards, there were two-meter high, rounded cones of straw draped around a central pole; the top was covered with a cloth, perhaps for protection from the rain. There were gardens, as well, filled with the elongated cabbage stalks and grape vines, elevated off the soil on wooden trellises. Outside of one house, we saw two men working. Neither wore the berets we had seen on most Spanish men; they wore, instead, a sort of Irish golfer's cap. More Celtic influence? When they saw us, they turned away.

Our gravel path turned into a gravel road that wound beside the Río Pambre. The sounds of chattering birds and of the gurgling river were broken into by the sputtering sound of a car coming up behind us. We stepped aside, but the car stopped; a young Spanish couple offered us a ride. He was from Santiago, she was from Madrid; he was a medical student, she was his fiancée. They were surprised that we were walking to Santiago.

We rode the last two kilometers to Castle Pambre, only to find that it was closed. The caretakers were at the *feria* in Palas do Rei, according to the handyman. Our Spanish companions tried to convince the handyman to let us enter, but he refused. I would have liked to have seen the inside of the castle; according to our guidebook, it is one of the most complete medieval fortresses in Galicia.

Disgusted, the medical student said, "These Gallegos! They are so suspicious of strangers!"

His girlfriend agreed. "Not like people in Madrid."

I suggested, "Maybe it is because this is such an isolated place."

He snorted. "No, it's just the Gallegan mentality. Unfriendly and suspicious. Except for me, of course. But then, I am more educated. It is the rural people who are ignorant."

In Spain each region has its stereotype—and has its stereotypes of all the others. "They" say that the Leonese are serious and hardworking—hardened by the harsh environment. "They" say the Andalusians are fun loving and gay—and unreliable. "They" say the Gallegans are taciturn, suspicious, untrustworthy, and withdrawn. And "they" say all rural people are ignorant.

Since we couldn't get in, we walked around part of the fortress, built in the fourteenth century by the Ulloas, counts of Monterrey. Its beige stone walls are well preserved, although greenery hangs in clumps from the battlements and the square towers. Near one of the towers was a storage bin: a two-meter-high woven wicker basket, topped with a conical straw lid.

The Spanish couple offered us a ride back to the road, which we refused. We felt like walking. Soon we reached Sambreixo and stopped to look at an unusual display: under a canopy supported on stone columns, enclosed by a sturdy fence and locked gate, was an elaborate pictoral presentation of the Passion—a carved stone crucifix, covered with all the relevant symbols—the cock, the sponge, the carafe of vinegar. According to the guidebook, it was a typical *crucero* of Galicia. We walked past the crucifix into the village, a green and shady place, and drank some Cokes in the local bar.

Looking at our backpacks, the woman behind the bar said, "Vale la pena!"

Another woman added, "Es bonito, no?"

We nodded in agreement.

When we traveled by taxi we missed those spoken affirmations—those statements of approval, of support—the acknowledgement, the recognition that walking this pilgrimage was *un sacrificio,* that it was worthwhile, that it was a lovely thing to do. Was it because we were told those things so often that we came to believe them and see our pilgrimage in those terms—and experience it in those ways? How many times had Bill said, "It's a sacrifice. You have to suffer." How many times had I thought, "We are pilgrims—and they are not—because we are undergoing such hardship." Justification? Rationalization? Tradition? Truth? We could have quit. We could have responded to the sneers, the disbelief, the exhaustion, the excruciating pain by deciding that this really was a stupid undertaking. Instead of that, we had continued—and continued to affirm it.

The woman behind the bar gave us directions back to the road to Santiago. Taking shortcuts through forests of rustling oaks and sharp-scented pines and shimmering, spicy smelling eucalyptus, we walked up into the hills. At Couto—or Coto—we left the Province of Lugo and entered the Province of La Coruña. At a clearing in the forest, we came to a bar. Sitting outside were four pilgrims, collapsed on a bench. They said they had walked 40 kilometers already and had to walk seven more before they stopped for the day, since they planned to sleep in the town hall in Melide. The two women were Spanish, in their midtwenties, and had begun walking at Puente la Reina. The men were in their midtwenties, one Spanish, the other Belgian. The Spaniard had started walking at Burgos, the Belgian at St. Jean Pied de Port.

Why had all of us started our pilgrimage at a specific spot on the Camino de Santiago? After all, a pilgrimage could start anywhere, and medieval pilgrims had started their pilgrimages when they left their homes. Was it because we had no rite of separation, no clear beginning point—except for a place on the map? Because we wanted to follow the "authentic" road as much as possible—walking in the footsteps of our ancestors—and so we couldn't start until we reached the Camino? Were we turning a metaphor into a ritual act?

Bill told the Belgian we had met another Belgian, earlier.

"Named Peter? With a leather backpack?"

"Yes."

Hesitantly, the Belgian asked, "Where is he now?"

"Somewhere up ahead."

He looked relieved. The women kept silent. Why was there this guarded response whenever Peter was mentioned? It had happened before, at El Acebo, in the morning. The two Dutch girls had obviously not wanted to renew their acquaintance with him. Although I was curious, I didn't ask, perhaps because of an excessive respect for the privacy of strangers I would never see again.

Struggling to their feet, the quartet started down the road to Melide. We waved goodbye, finished our Cokes, and followed far behind. For part of the next kilometer, we walked on fragments of ancient paving stone; descending a small incline, we crossed Picaud's Campus Leporarius—Campos de Liebres—the Fields of Hares—into the village of Leboreiro. We passed the lichen-covered stone church of Santa María, with a beautifully—but simply—carved medieval Virgin above the doorway. In front of the church was an ancient house that had been used as a *hospital* for pilgrims as late as the nineteenth century. Next to it was a large wicker storage basket. The medieval pavement continued, down an arroyo and across a medieval, single-arched stone bridge over the Río Seco, nearly hidden in the trees. We crossed the bridge and walked past the few houses in Disicabo. Then we crossed the nearby highway and entered a small roadside bar.

It was a tiny bar, with a few small tables and four unstable chairs. We put down our backpacks and found an empty table—several other people were already there. Behind the bar was an old, nearly toothless woman. Soon one man insisted on buying us drinks—bottles of warm orange Kas—and wanted to know where we were from, how long we'd been walking, how much we walked each day—the standard questions we had been asked all along the Camino. Was it just a way of making conversation, like talking about the weather? Or a way of participating vicariously?

His wife asked, "Do you go to fulfill a promise?"

I replied, "No."

"For tourism, then?"

Indignantly, I said, "No, it is too hard for that!"

She replied, "Of course, it is a sacrifice! And to come from the U.S. to go on a pilgrimage earns you exceptional merit."

Another man drinking in the bar joined in the conversation, asking us about our blisters, our shoes. He also bought us bottles of warm orange Kas. According to him, there were a number of pilgrims that year—mostly French.

We asked where we could spend the night, and they agreed no one would object if we camped out in the fields.

Since our supplies were low, we asked the old woman if she would sell us some food. We bought smoky Gallegan cheese, called *queso tetilla* because of its breast-like shape, a loaf of bread, and a bottle of wine, poured from a large cannister and corked. The wine was fresh, so fresh that it was still cloudy with yeast. After saying goodbye, we left the bar and walked down the road, looking for a place to camp out for the night.

We climbed a fence and walked through a field towards a large oak tree, under which we spread our sleeping bags. As we ate our dinner of chewy country bread, fresh creamy cheese, and green wine, the sky clouded up and it looked like rain.

"Ellen, what should we do if it rains?"

"Well, we're sheltered by the tree, and we've got rain ponchos—we can just cover ourselves up!"

"That's not quite what I had in mind—I meant, did you see any shelter nearby?"

"No. But what are you worried about? The worst that happens is that we get wet!" How much I'd changed.

Bill grumbled something and went off down the road; soon he returned. He'd found a building a bit down the road. If it got really bad, he said, we could run for shelter. By then, I thought, we would be soaking wet anyway, so why bother?

After dinner we crawled into our sleeping bags. I looked up at the dark night sky, looking for the Milky Way, but all I could see was steel grey clouds floating over the moon.

During the night it sprinkled just a bit, but we covered ourselves with the plastic ponchos and kept sleeping.

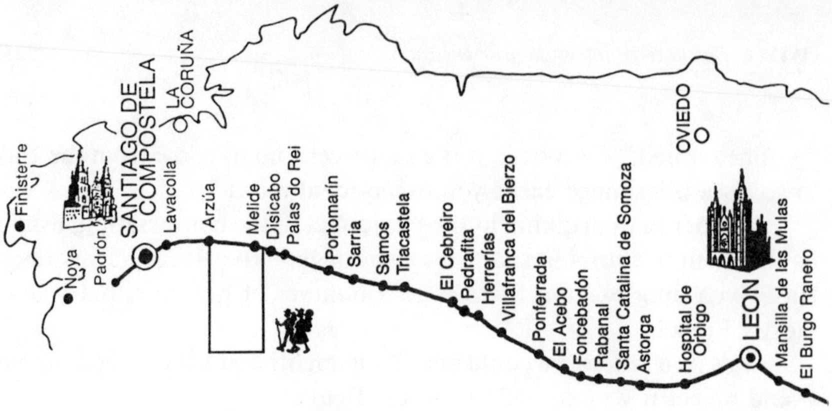

Day 42: August 20 The air smelled fresh after the light shower; there was just a hint of damp earth, cut grass, and manure. After we shook the moisture off our ponchos and packed up our sleeping bags, we started down the trail to Melide—also spelled Mellid. This stone Camino was authentic, worn by the footsteps of all the pilgrims who had passed that way before. At the Río Furelos we crossed a large medieval bridge and entered Furelos, which once had had a *hospital* for pilgrims. Then we continued out of town and up the medieval road to Melide. We were literally following in the footsteps of millions of other pilgrims.

Melide, center of a rich agricultural zone, is a large city, with several interesting churches and convents and with a number of modern stores. As in Sarria, some of the cement walls of the town were decorated with graffiti: "25 de Xulio, Día de Independencia." In recent years—since Franco's death—there have been riots in Santiago on July 25, riots between the leftist-separatist group called BNPG and the police. Some of the notices we saw urged supporters to attend the demonstrations, and they had.

We passed several large bars with striped canopies over the front, advertising the green wines of Ribiero. We chose one and went in for coffee and sweet rolls. While Bill had a second cup of coffee, I used the bathroom at the back. No toilet paper, as usual.

Melide has been inhabited since prehistoric times, and there have been a number of archeological finds in the area. In the Middle Ages, it was an important city; here, the Camino de Santiago united with the route of pilgrims coming down from Oviedo via Ribadeo and Villalba. There were several *hospitales* for pilgrims, including ones next to the churches of Santa María and San Pedro, and one founded in 1375 and placed under the direction of the Frailes Menores de Sancti Spiritus—the Franciscan Brothers. Today, pilgrims like the four we had met in the clearing would be given shelter in the town hall.

Just outside of Melide, to the left and below the highway, is the twelfth-century church Santa María de Melide, which still has well-preserved fifteenth-century frescoes. We looked at it briefly, then followed the old, "authentic" Camino past Carballal into the middle of a forest of pine and eucalyptus trees. We forded the quickly flowing Río Raído by stepping across on some large, flat stones. Our path climbed up to Raído, met the highway, then went off again into the deep, green forest. We followed a gravel cart trail up and down, up and down, through the rustling trees.

At Boente de Riba/Boente de Baixo, we stopped for lunch. A woman in a bar made us *chorizo* and cheese sandwiches, and we ate two apiece and drank Cokes as we ate and rested. While we ate, I noticed a rack of cassette tapes on the counter. Curious, I spun it around, looking at the slightly faded labels. I found several tapes by an Argentine singer, Jorge Cafrune—tapes no longer available in the U.S.

Once again, we started down the road. An old man and his son called out to us, telling us the proper way to go—on the Camino, not the modern highway. Although his son was concerned we might lose the way, the old man assured him it was well marked with yellow arrows. We walked through thick green forests, tree branches forming a canopy overhead. Pale green, speckled light filtered through the leaves. It resembled the trail in the Pyrenees: it seemed as if the Camino had come full circle, by going straight.

We passed scattered homesteads, small villages of two or three houses. Then we reached Pomariño, a settlement formed by four houses; from its elevation, we could see an extensive, fertile valley below us. To our right was the settlement of Castañeda. According to Picaud, pilgrims carried limestone rocks from the mountains of Cebreiro to be turned into lime mortar in the furnaces of Castañeda. The mortar was then used to build the cathedral in Santiago. We walked across the field to Castañeda, sat down in a bar, rested again, and drank more Cokes. Walking was hard, even though the countryside was beautiful and serene. There was no traffic to dodge, no burning sun, but still it was hard. Maybe it was because the journey was almost over.

At the bar, villagers told us about shortcuts we could take to Arzúa. When we left, a woman came running after us, pointing out the way to the Camino de Santiago.

We walked some more, then took another break, this time sitting on the steep side of a hill. Our Camino went nearly straight down to the bottom of the valley, where there were several houses—a community called Río—and a medieval-looking bridge. Then, our Camino went up the other side of the hill. The highway curved lazily around the side of the valley.

We watched a bus on the highway go around the curve below. On the back window was a sign: "Pilgrimage to Santiago."

We took the Camino down, and up, and down and up again, past Ribadiso de Baixo and Ribadiso de Riba. At Ribadiso da Carretera our Camino joined the highway, which we followed through the forests to Arzúa.

That day, walking was very hard. I don't know why. After all, we hadn't walked much the day before, and the route was scenic—trails through eucalyptus and pine forests, gravel paths through the countryside. When we reached the outskirts of Arzúa, we had only walked eighteen kilometers, but we had had it. We walked past a large restaurant with flags waving gaily from the roof; it looked like a popular spot, since there were many cars parked in front. I wanted to go in, but Bill wanted to continue into town. Pushing limits, still pushing limits. Some days I pushed, some days Bill did.

We walked into town. The road split in two: the highway went to the right, the Camino to the left. We went left and the road went down a hill and soon we were almost out of town. I stopped. I couldn't go any further. That seemed to be my pattern, I realized: one minute I'd be weary, but walking; the next, I would be incapable of taking another step. I could go no further. While I waited in a nearby bar, Bill walked back into town to a hostel we had seen. I waited in a smoke-filled room, watching groups of dark-clad, grey-haired men playing cards. The place reeked of Spanish cigars, stale cigarette smoke. There were no other women. There rarely were in bars, I realized, at least not in the late afternoon. And not alone.

Bill had found us a room. Slowly, we walked back up the hill to the hostel and I took a nap. Later, we went out for a walk. Somehow, after a short rest, without my backpack on my back, I was eager to walk around town. Exhaustion was so relative—and so transitory.

We saw more posters announcing the July 25th demonstrations in Santiago and passed by the Church of La Magdalena, once a convent of the Augustines and a pilgrimage *hospital.* Now, the parish priest frequently offers shelter to pilgrims in need. In the plaza we saw two French women with enormous backpacks on the pavement beside them. One was slicing a large loaf of bread.

We asked, "Peregrinos?"

They nodded yes and invited us to join them. Close friends, they had wanted to make the pilgrimage together. The older one, in her midforties, was a school teacher in Paris; the younger one, in her early thirties, was a student.

The older one said, "I wanted to get away from urban life—to have time to think about things, to listen to the birds—to contemplate nature. To make a pilgrimage."

Bill asked, "How is it going?"

"Just awful! We are exhausted! Never again!"

I asked her, "Have you walked all the way?"

Ruefully, the younger one replied, "There wasn't time. Two weeks ago we left our car in Burgos. Some of the time we walk, some of the time we take the bus or the train."

The older one added, "We walk a bit, and then we are so tired, and our feet hurt so much, we take a bus."

I said, "When we started, we were always exhausted. But now we've gotten used to it and it's easier. We've got more endurance."

Bill added, "It's actually pleasant, much of the time."

Skeptically, the older woman looked at him. "It's hard to believe this could ever be pleasant!"

I tried to explain. "You get a real sense of accomplishment—of achievement."

She shook her head. "All I feel is total exhaustion. I'm too weary and in too much pain to think about anything."

They told us they had walked from Pedrafita to Cebreiro, where they had slept in a *palloza,* after spending most of the night singing and dancing with other pilgrims in the *meson.*

The younger woman said, "Fellow pilgrims? I thought they lived in Cebreiro."

The older woman repeated, "Fellow pilgrims—I think. And they had a van to carry their baggage for them."

We left the women slicing their bread for sandwiches and walked back to the hostel.

After an early dinner—a casserole of spicy octopus, a plateful of mussels marinated in onion, garlic, hot peppers and oil—we went out. I wanted to be alone to write in my journal, so Bill left me at a sidewalk cafe while he continued his stroll around town. I wrote:

"As we near the end, I think about the people we've met; some were helpful, some were not. Some nodded and smiled, shouting encouragements, wishing us well—yesterday, some old women we met called out, 'Vaya con Dios'—Go with God. Go with God. Others ignore us or look at us with some hostility. Most often, we encounter curiosity and helpfulness. Distrust seems to occur more in the cities than in the small villages, and more when we were far away from Santiago—in Navarra, in Santo Domingo de la Calzada, in Frómista.

"I still think that Bill is unnecessarily suspicious. He blames the lack of hotel rooms on the fact that we are pilgrims. Much of the time, there really is no room at the inn. Of course, sometimes people are hostile. Not to us as individuals—they don't even know us—but to pilgrims to Santiago as a class, as a category. Or maybe just to strangers of whatever sort. But not everyone is like that, and not all the time. And some people's initial wariness can be breached. I've been too naive, refusing to acknowledge the negative—but Bill has been too distrustful.

"We are nearing the end of the road. Santiago is so close—just 35 kilometers away. Should we rush to get there—or postpone the end? Yesterday, it felt right to lengthen the journey a bit, take an excursion to Castle Pambre, and not walk much further. We could have hurried to Santiago, pushing ourselves to the limit; instead, we are lengthening the time, drawing out the journey. I, for one, want to experience the final days fully, taking time, holding time, walking the old roads step by step. I am afraid of reaching the end—I am afraid of a letdown when I get there. We will have reached our goal. And then what?

"How did medieval pilgrims feel? I suppose they were eager to arrive, eager to reach the goal, filled with ecstatic longing, with overwhelming enthusiasm. But then what? How did the knights searching for the Holy Grail feel when they completed their quest? Of course, they never could. . . .

"Not that reaching the end was all that sure a thing. William X, Duke of Aquitane, wrote a poem describing the longing and uncertainty felt by many pilgrims:

> Where will yon lonely pilgrim wander,
> Where will my ancient pilgrim roam?
> Away on the road to Compostella,
> Who knows when he'll reach his goal?
> His weary feet are stained with gore
> And he can tramp no more.[26]

"He, at least, reached his goal. He died in Santiago on Good Friday in 1137.

"I am afraid to reach the end, afraid that after all this effort, stopping will be very difficult, that instead of feeling complete, I will feel empty, that instead of being filled, I will be a vacuum.

"And what about Bill and me and our relationship? What a struggle it's been to get past knee-jerk, stereotyped responses, to stop trying to please him, to stop trying to meet his expectations. To learn to set my own limits and determine my own limitations. And for him—to learn to compromise, to be supportive, to learn to cooperate, not compete, to acknowledge weariness and need. It hasn't been fun. Or easy. But what we have shared!

"Yesterday Bill said that, unlike me, he was looking forward to reaching the goal—he was savoring the sense of accomplishment. But this morning his feelings had changed, and he admitted that he was trying to deal with a sense of anticlimax. There was nothing for him to look forward to between Melide and Santiago. I want to savor the remaining footsteps, but he just wants to be there, not get there. Suddenly, for him, the journey is over.

"Peter the Belgian said that Santiago was just the beginning. Maybe he's right—but the beginning of what?

"I have had several similar dreams during the pilgrimage, dreams of packing, of leaving in a hurry, of leaving things behind. Anxious, wrenching dreams of hurriedly sorting through things in preparation for leaving, ending up leaving things behind, leaving parts of myself behind. But the night before last, in Sarria, I had a different dream: it began as usual, a dream about rushing to the airport without being prepared, without being completely packed; but this time I looked at the stuff in the back of the car and said, 'I don't need this old baggage anymore'—and I went off without a second glance. I joked in Estella about getting rid of unnecessary baggage. Maybe I finally have. But what have I gotten rid of?

"I am filled with a sense of accomplishment—and with fear and dread. We've almost reached Santiago. But reaching Santiago was never really the goal—it just looked that way.

"In my guidebook there is a poem by León Felipe:

> Ser en la vida
> romero,
> romero sólo que cruza
> siempre por caminos nuevos;

ser en la vida
romero,
sin más oficio, sin otro nombre
y sin pueblo. . .
ser en la vida
romero . . . romero . . . sólo romero.
Que no hagan callo las cosas
ni en el alma ni en el cuerpo. . .
pasar por todo una vez,
una vez sólo y ligero, ligero, siempre ligero.[27]

(To be in life
a pilgrim,
only a pilgrim who travels
always on new caminos;
To be in life
a pilgrim,
without other occupation, without other name,
and without home . . .

To be in life
a pilgrim . . . a pilgrim . . . only a pilgrim.
Who doesn't take things hard,
neither in the soul nor in the body . . .

To pass through everything once, once only
and lightly, lightly, always lightly.)

"The first time I read the poem, I found it depressing—the pilgrim was always moving, always passing through: no name, no people, no connections. Alone, lonely, only a pilgrim. The second time I read it, I knew the poet was absolutely wrong; obviously, he was not a pilgrim, he was an escapist! A real pilgrim would know that one feels everything—pain, pleasure, loneliness—with great intensity. Now, reading the poem again, I am deeply moved; what, after all, is wrong with always traveling through? Isn't that better, somehow, than reaching the end? Or than not going anywhere?"

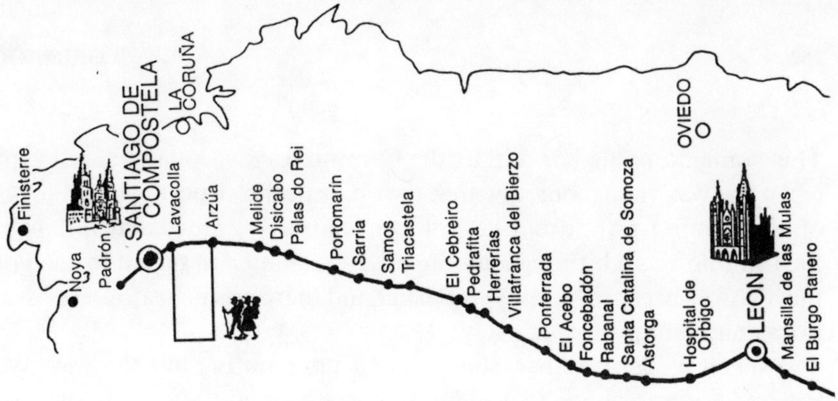

Day 43: August 21 Since we planned to reach Santiago the next day, we decided to spend the last full day walking on the old, authentic Caminos.

Leaving Arzúa, we passed by the ancient *hospital* next to the church, Santa María Magdalena, then passed the "Fountain of the French," now abandoned. We descended into an arroyo and scrambled up and down over brambles, finally reaching Raído. We followed yellow arrows. We followed the pointing fingers of friendly villagers. We followed our guidebook. Our journey was quite scenic—through eucalyptus and pine forests, through green and gold pastures and fields covered with yellow-purple brambles.

Our route consisted of every possible kind of road: medieval—possibly Roman—stone *camino,* with ruts carved into the stones by the passage of cart wheels over the centuries; green mossy *camino,* velvet stepping stones cut in the forest glen; a rocky footpath littered with trash; a broken trail, blocked by construction of a new highway, so that we had to clamber over cement blocks and muddy gashes in the hillside; a cobblestone path blocked by fallen, fungus-covered trees; a slippery, worn earthen *camino,* deeply eroded below the level of the ground, with water trickling down the middle of the trail (was it a road or a stream bed?); and asphalt pavement and cement highway *camino* when there was no alternative.

We passed lichen-covered stone houses, scattered along the road. Some of them had names: Tabernavella, Calzada, Calle, Boavista, Alto, Salceda, Xen, Ras, Brea; Empalme, where we stopped in a bar for sandwiches of *chorizo* and cheese; Santa Irene, Rúa, Burgo, Arca, San Antón. We passed cattle grazing in the pastures. We passed villagers. Some were friendly, pointing out the way; others turned away.

Late in the afternoon, we stopped for a Coke at Amenal, where the ancient, rutted stone Camino crosses the asphalt highway to Santiago.

The woman tending bar told us the Camino to Lavacolla was well kept when she was young, but now that they'd built the airport, which blocks off the Camino, no one took care of it any more. She added that, although the Camino was a bit rough, all the pilgrims wanted to take it instead of the highway because the air was fresher and there was no traffic. Besides, it was authentic.

When we left the bar, she followed us, pointing out the way. We hesitated—the highway looked inviting—so she came after us to show us exactly where the proper Camino began—behind some buildings, up past the village trash heap. Authenticity—and her obvious desire that we follow the "real" Camino—won out. Why did she care? Were we making the pilgrimage for her, with her? We followed her directions while she watched.

Slippery and wet, the dirt path was littered with garbage. It wound behind another settlement, Cimadevila, and then joined a wide logging road through the pine and eucalyptus forest. We passed farmers and ox carts loaded with hay they were bringing back from the fields. Going the opposite direction, we headed up the hill—and ran up against a tall cyclone fence: the airport of Lavacolla. Once, the Camino had gone straight across that expanse; now, we had to walk around the blocked-off airfield.

It was a day of contrasts: medieval villages, a modern airport; ancient stone trails, a modern highway; pristine forests, a village garbage heap; ox carts, automobiles and planes. Past and present, we were walking in the footsteps of our ancestors—footsteps which were being obliterated by modern technology. But the pilgrimage and the Camino remained.

At last we reached Lavacolla, the Lavamentula of the *Codex.* The name means "to wash one's body," and for centuries, before entering the holy shrine in Compostela, pilgrims have washed themselves in the Río Lavacolla—cleansing their flesh in preparation for cleansing their souls.

Instead of looking for the stream, we looked for a hostel. People were not helpful—in fact, they turned away. At last, a man responded to our query and told us to go ask at a bar down the road. We walked over to the large, new building. Behind the bar was a teenager.

Bill asked him, "Do you have any rooms?"

He looked at Bill and wiped the counter with a rag. "I don't know."

"What do you mean, you don't know?"

"Maybe we do, maybe we don't."

"How do you plan to find out?"

"I suppose I could ask my father."

Bill lost patience. "Ask him!"

The kid left, presumably to find his father. Soon he returned and nodded. "There's a room, but you have to wait a while."

We waited. While we waited, we struck up a conversation with an older man who was working in the bar. He told us he approved of what we were doing—it was good for the body to walk. He, I noticed, was badly overweight.

Fifteen minutes later, the owner came into the bar, and he led us out of the bar and up an outside set of stairs to the second floor. He and his family lived in part of the building and rented out rooms in the other part. It was quite an efficient arrangement: below, the bar and restaurant; above, sleeping quarters and paying guests. He didn't ask for our passports.

We heard familiar voices, and, coming out of the communal bathroom was the younger of the two French women we had met in Arzúa. She looked very tired. We greeted her, agreed to meet later, and went to our room.

I heard church bells and—for the first time on the trip—wanted to go to Mass. So we walked over to the nearby parish church, climbed up the grey granite steps, and entered the church. Once inside, I wasn't sure what to do. But Bill had been raised a Catholic, so I copied his gestures. Afterwards, we took a short walk, then Bill went back to the hostel; I returned to the empty church and sat outside on the cold stone steps, looking at the night sky.

It was getting dark, and I could see the Camino de las Estrellas in the sky, that glittering Milky Way that we had followed—that had been guiding us—from the mountains in the Pyrenees, across the hills of Navarra and the flat, dry *mesetas* of Castilla and León, into and out of the rich green valleys of the Bierzo, and up and up into the mountains of Cebreiro and the pine and eucalyptus forests of Galicia. Tonight, the milky trail seemed to dip down towards the west. Was it touching the cathedral spires in Santiago? Was it showering more stars on our Camino? Would we find them scattered before us in the morning, showing us the way?

Slowly, silently, I walked back to the hostel for dinner. The French women sat at a table next to us, and we toasted each other and chatted while we ate garlicky grilled lamb chops and french fries. The older one told us again how disillusioned she was—all she could think of, all she could talk about, was how tired they were, how disappointed they were.

Wearily, the older woman shook her head. "Never again!"

Presumably, they would never attempt this again. They had thought this would be a fine experience—combining outdoors tranquility, philosophical reflection, and friendship. Not really exercise—a pilgrimage. But their packs were heavy, loaded with the paraphernalia of civilization, and they hadn't walked enough to ever get past the pain and exhaustion.

I knew just how they felt. In the beginning I had thought it strange that pilgrimage, which was supposed to focus on the spirit, made me so very conscious of the weakness of my flesh! Once that had seemed like a contradiction. Now I realized that the physical suffering was a way to experience the spirit: the two were complementary.

If we had been physically fit and healthy when we started, the pilgrimage would have been a very different experience. The soccer player outside of Nájera learned about endurance. The French pilgrim I had met the previous summer, traveling alone, fresh out of the military, learned about solitude. Perhaps in every pilgrimage, what people learned—what they had to learn, what they needed to learn—was different.

We had walked through the pain, the exhaustion. We still ached, we still got tired, but we had endured. And more than endured: we had overcome our limits and changed them in the process. The Frenchwomen hadn't had enough time to let the pilgrimage develop, to let the journey unfold.

They, however, looked towards tomorrow and the arrival in Santiago with relief and enthusiasm. I looked towards tomorrow with dread. What could I possibly find in Santiago except the end of the road?

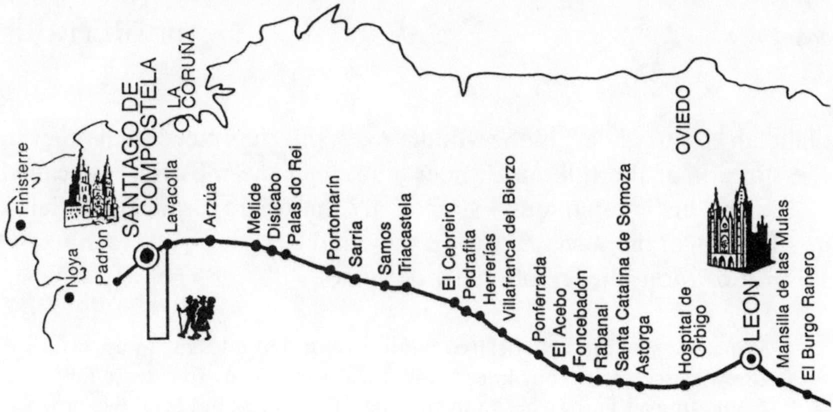

Day 44: August 22 Ten kilometers to Santiago. We crossed the Río Lavacolla but did not stop to wash in its waters. We were in a hurry. My misgivings of the day before had disappeared; now I was eager to reach Santiago.

We walked alongside the busy highway: here, close to the end of our "traditional" pilgrimage, there was no "authentic" Camino left. The road curved up the hillsides and I climbed steadily upward, energized by the magnetism of the holy shrine. Bill plodded along behind, trying to keep up. At the village of San Marcos, we left the highway and headed up a path towards the Hill of Joy—Monte del Gozo, Montjoie, Monte Gaudi, Monxoi—the hill from whose summit pilgrims could first see the towers of the cathedral of Santiago. In 1425, it was described in these words:

> Upon a hill stondez on hee
> Where Sent Jamez ferst schalt thou see,
> A Mount Joie, mony stonez ther ate.[28]

On the first night of our pilgrimage, we had collapsed in the Pyrenees near the site of one of Santiago's reputed miracles. It was there that the faithful Lombard knight stood guard over his dead comrade and called out to St. James for aid. And Santiago came, mounted on his milk-white steed, summoned by the knight's true faith. In just one night Santiago transported the knight and his dead companion to the Hill of Joy. It had taken us over a month to reach Mount Joy, but who could be sure that St. James hadn't helped us, too?

Montjoie: battle cry of Roland and his troops; Mount Joy, from the top of which we would see the spires of the cathedral of Santiago, appearing, according to Eugenio Montes, "like a shell in the pilgrim's cape of the

Galician countryside." In the Middle Ages, pilgrims raced each other to the summit of the hill, and whoever reached the top first was called "King" by his companions—supposedly the origin, among Spaniards and French, of the surnames Roy, Leroy, and Rey. Laffi, on reaching the summit of Montjoie, emotionally declared:

> When we saw the long-desired Santiago but half a league away, we threw ourselves on our knees, and such was our joy that tears fell from our eyes and we began to sing the "Te Deum": but after two or three verses we could continue no more, such were the floods of tears we shed and the sobs that choked our song.[29]

Bill and I raced up the hill hand in hand. It was not a competition any more; it was a shared endeavor. We reached the top and, walking past wooden crosses placed there by other pilgrims, we looked out towards Santiago. Unfortunately, our view was partly blocked by a new house someone was building on the side of the hill.

We walked over a little ways and looked again. The view was still a partial one, but better. Soon we would be at the cathedral, soon we would pass through the Puerta Santa, the Holy Doorway through which pilgrims entered during Años Santos; soon we would fulfill our promises to give "un abrazo al Apóstal" and light the candles we had been asked to light.

We walked slowly down the hill and back to the highway. Dodging traffic, we rushed across the Atlantic Superhighway. In front of us was a road sign, "Camino de Santiago: Santiago, 0 kilometers."

This was the end of the thirteenth and final stage in the *Codex.* Somewhat hesitantly, almost unwillingly, we walked up the Calle de los Concheiros—*concheiros* was another name for pilgrims to Santiago, derived from the *concha*—the scallop shell emblem of the shrine. Eager to arrive, yet eager to postpone the moment of arrival, we stopped at a bar, dropping our backpacks inside the doorway.

On top of the countertop was a selection of filled pastry pies, the famous *empanadas* of Galicia. We ordered two wedges, one of tuna and one of pork and veal. It has been said that *empanadas* are popular in Galicia because they suit the character of the people—the contents are hidden from view, just as the Gallegans are aloof and secretive.[30] True or not, Gallegans make marvelous meat pies—flaky pastries filled with green peppers, onions, herbs, and spices.

When I turned around to carry our Cokes and slices of *empanadas*

The author on top of the Monte del Gozo—Monxoi or Monte Gaudi—the spot where for a thousand years pilgrims have had their first, long-awaited glimpse of Santiago de Compostela. Unfortunately, someone was building a house on the side of Mount Joy and the view would soon be blocked.

over to a nearby table, the woman behind the bar started to giggle.

"Why did she do that, Bill?"

"Look at the back of your skirt."

I looked. The back of my India print cotton skirt had been worn almost transparent by the rubbing of my backpack.

Leaving the bar, we started walking again, faithfully following the traditional pilgrim's way through town: up the narrow, winding Rúa de San Pedro, through the Puerta del Camino, which used to be called the Porta Francigena—according to Picaud, this is where the Vía Francigena begins which leads to Paraíso—Paradise—the cathedral's north door. It is also, according to Starkie, where the Camino Francés, which begins in the Rue St. Jacques in Paris, ends. Beginning and ending: it all depends on your point of view.

We continued up the street called Casas Reales, past the Plaza de Animas, past the Plaza de Cervantes, onto the street called Azabachería, which leads to the Plaza Inmaculada and the north door, the "Paraíso" of Picaud. We stopped there, in front of the damp, lichen-flecked, grey-brown granite cathedral. Santiago is the rainiest city in all of Spain.

Medieval pilgrims arrived at the cathedral singing the Flemish Pilgrims' Song:

Herru Sanctiagu
Grot Sanctiagu,
E ultreja e sus eja!
Deus adjuva nos.

(Lord Santiago
Great Santiago,
Onwards and upwards,
God help us!)

We arrived silently.

The grey, lichen-encrusted baroque façade of the cathedral of Santiago de Compostela. Pilgrims cross the Obradoiro Plaza, climb up the double staircase, and enter the cathedral. There, they eagerly receive forgiveness, complete their vows, renew their faith, or simply finish their pilgrimages.

It was noon, time for the Pilgrim's Mass. Plaza Inmaculada, in front of the Paradise Door of the cathedral, was filled with people: sales people standing behind stalls and selling souvenirs; shabbily dressed people walking through the plaza begging; weary women, black shawls over their heads, sitting on blankets, motionless babies in their laps, hands outstretched; well-dressed parents bringing their well-dressed children out of the crowded church so that they could throw up in a corner of the plaza or urinate against a wall.

We tried to enter the cathedral but it was impossible: people were packed tight inside. Hoping to have better luck at another entrance, we walked around the cathedral to the Plaza del Obradoiro—also called the Plaza de España—and the main entryway—but that, too, was overflowing with people. So we went back to the Plaza Inmaculada and sat down against a low stone wall, watching beggers with extended hands come up to tourists and pilgrims, pleading for *limosna,* watching gaily dressed tourists buying yellow plastic pilgrim's staffs and green and red plastic Gallegan bagpipes.

While we waited, the two Frenchmen on horseback we had met near Villafranca del Bierzo came over and said hello. They had arrived the day before and had ridden their horses up to the Plaza del Obradoiro; the local newspaper had taken pictures of them posing before the cathedral and had interviewed them for a story. We watched the people in the plaza and we talked, exchanging stories of the pilgrimage road. According to them, Santiago and the cathedral hadn't been crowded the day before.

We waited for the service to end.

More children were brought out, threw up, urinated in the corner. Finally the Mass ended, and people started to leave the church. Fighting against the flow, we managed to enter the still packed cathedral. It was hot, stuffy, filled with the smell of incense, of burning candles, of sweat. The noise was astounding: instead of a silent house of worship, instead of the resonant, melodious sounds of communal prayer—a discordant blast of shouts, cries, frantically repeated prayers, screams, shoes scraping on stone floors, exclamations of pain.

We jostled our way to the Puerta Santa. How I had looked forward to passing through the sacred doorway, a right specially reserved for pilgrims during the Año Santo. But crowds of people were pushing and shoving to pass through the Holy Door, crying out in joy, reciting prayers and promises, feverishly tracing the crosses on the doorway with their fingers, frantically raising crucifixes to the carved crosses, lifting each other off their feet in their urgency, elbowing each other in the ribs, nearly trampling each other in their rush.

I had thought that only pilgrims could pass through the Holy Doorway—and we and our companions from the road were the only pilgrims I knew of. We were "real" pilgrims; we had walked the Camino for over a month to reach Santiago, the cathedral, the Holy Door. Who were all these other people and what were they doing there, filling the huge cathedral, crushing against us?

They had come by car or bus—maybe, even, in one of the buses that had passed us on the Camino. They hadn't walked. They had ridden in comfort. But according to the Church, they were pilgrims too. Pilgrims, just like us. We were all strangers and pilgrims. The realization shocked me. They were pilgrims, just like us. They were pilgrims just like us.

Turning away, I gave up trying to pass through the Puerta Santa and went over to "dar un abrazo al Apóstal"—to embrace the larger-than-lifesized figure of the Apostle—something I had promised people I would do, something I had looked forward to doing. But there, too, a huge crowd of shouting people, of jostling, pushing and shoving people, created chaos instead of an orderly line: a squirming mass of frenzied people all tried at once to climb up the staircase that led to a platform behind the Apostle. I turned away, repulsed by the agitated mob. I told myself that medieval pilgrims probably acted just the same—in fact, there had been riots and even murders in the cathedral in the Middle Ages, and special arrangements had to be made for the frequent re-sanctification of the church. But I didn't care if this was "authentic"—it was awful.

I wasn't prepared for the frantic press of people trying desperately to rapidly perform ritual acts. I tried to tell myself that if they had come on a tour bus, they only had a limited amount of time allotted to perform these acts, so of course they were in a rush. But visions of Catholic fanaticism, of Inquisition, of slaughtered martyrs, of mass movements of whatever sort—of mindless belief—rose before my eyes.

I couldn't participate in that kind of rite. It was ironic: they had come by bus and threw themselves into this ecstatic state at the pilgrimage shrine; I had walked the Camino for one and a half months, for 800 kilometers, and couldn't bring myself to join in their frenzy. But after all, who was the fanatic? I was the one who had suffered on the Camino, who had forced myself to keep going, despite excruciating pain, despite exhaustion, so that I could make a pilgrimage.

For some reason, I had thought we would have a separate reception, a special line at the Holy Door—we were the "real" pilgrims, after all, not they—but there was no different treatment for us than for the hordes of others who had effortlessly arrived by busloads or by car—despite our sacrifice. I thought we would be treated—differently. I thought we were—"special." We were not.

I tried to explain to Bill, who thought my attitude was a bit elitist, though he understood. He pointed out that the pilgrimage was between us and—God. The Church had nothing to do with it, so why should the Church acknowledge its special importance? Besides, he added, perhaps the Church preferred the more controllable, organized frenzy of "bus" pilgrims. They were more easy to understand and to control. They were more traditionally religious, trying to get their plenary indulgences as quickly as they could. We were the strange ones: not religious, yet struggling 800 kilometers on foot to make a pilgrimage.

I tried not to cry with disappointment at—at everything. Obviously, the Church had nothing to do with my pilgrimage. I wasn't even a believer! And what I had sacrificed was between me—and the Camino.

My reaction was in part response to the shock of being in the middle of a huge, noisy crowd after having walked in the peaceful wilderness for weeks. The contrast between private quest and shared frenzy, between personal experience and organized religion, between nature and civilization—was just too much.

We left and went to find a place to stay for the night.

"Let's splurge, Ellen."

I answered glumly. "Sure, why not."

"Let's stay at the Hotel de los Reyes Católicos."

"Okay. Why not."

The Hotel de los Reyes Católicos is a five-star hotel, run by Entursa—as stunning as the Hotel San Marcos in León and even more luxurious. Across the Plaza del Obradoiro from the cathedral, it was originally a pilgrimage *hospital,* built in the early 1500s by the Catholic Monarchs Ferdinand and Isabella. During subsequent centuries it was used for many things, including a medical hospital. In the mid 1950s, it was converted into an elegant hotel. We walked over to the elaborately carved entryway and were stopped by the uniformed doorman.

"Pilgrims or tourists?" he asked us.

Bill quickly replied, "Tourists."

He let us by. We entered and asked for a room for the night.

"No room."

We left and went down the streets of the town, looking for another hotel. We tried several medieval looking hostels, without luck.

"No room."

Bill looked at me.

"Now, Bill, it can't be because we are pilgrims! The town is full of pilgrims!"

"But we are 'real' pilgrims, Ellen. Maybe that makes a difference."

We walked down to the new part of town and tried another hotel. No room. I asked the desk clerk why there was no room, and he explained that this was the busiest season of the year—and most people made reservations three or four months in advance. Trying to be helpful, he suggested a rooming house down the street which might have a vacancy. It did: a small bedroom, at the end of a dark corridor.

Walking back towards the cathedral on the Rúa Nueva, we passed a number of bars and cafes. In front of one of them we saw the two French women we'd met at Arzúa and Lavacolla; they invited us to join them for a drink.

The older woman pointed at her legs, covered with welts. "We took the 'authentic' Camino to Monxoi—and got lost in a bramble patch!"

Her companion added, "It took us hours to get here. But at last we're here!"

I asked, "Did you go into the catheral?"

The younger woman replied, "Not a chance. We tried to—but it's a circus! The Camino was better than this. There are just too many people!"

The older woman continued, "It was better on the Camino—this is a madhouse. We're leaving as soon as we can."

Bill was surprised. "You're not staying a few days to see the town?"

They shook their heads.

We walked a little further down the arcaded street and saw the two French horseback riders again, this time with their girlfriends. They waved at us and we joined them. Introductions were made: Jean, David, Suzanne, and Marie.

"How is it going?" Jean asked us.

I shook my head, sadly. "Too many people. We couldn't even get into the cathedral when we arrived."

David agreed: "It is a circus."

Bill asked, "Are you going to leave soon?"

Suzanne said, "Maybe tomorrow. Or the next day. After all, there should be something worth seeing in Santiago."

We drank espresso and talked about the Camino and pilgrimage.

Jean said, "Now that we've done it by horse—next time we'll do it the 'real' way—on foot!"

I was surprised. "But don't you think riding horses is the same?"

Shaking his head no, Jean continued, "Walking—that's the real way to do it. You really experience the Camino, then. You really walk in the footsteps of your ancestors."

Bill said, "By the way, we saw the two Frenchwomen with the heavy packs—"

"The ones at the table down the way?"

"Yes. Do you know them?"

Quickly, they exchanged a look; then Jean volunteered, "They say they are pilgrims, but they took the train most of the way. So how can they be 'real' pilgrims? You have to make more of a sacrifice than that!"

I asked, "And what about these masses of 'pilgrims' in Santiago—the ones who come by bus?"

They looked at me. "They're obviously tourists visiting a pilgrimage shrine."

"But they're so—fervent!"

Laughing, Jean explained, "Of course they are! They're on vacation! They're not exhausted from making the pilgrimage!"

After they left, we sat silently for a while, drinking more espresso. Then we went to a nearby restaurant for dinner. Dinner began with *coquilles St. Jacques,* of course, and we got to keep the shells. Then *cabrito*—roast baby goat—for me and *angulas* for Bill. We thought *angulas* were sliced conger eel, but when the plate came, it was heaped with what looked like spaghetti—spaghetti with tiny black dots. The dots were eyes. *Anguila* was conger eel; *angulas* were baby eels, the size of bean sprouts. Lightly stir-fried in olive oil, seasoned with garlic and hot peppers, they were delicious.

After dinner was over, we went for a walk. But the contrast between my let-down and the gay tourist-pilgrims we encountered was too much. I resented their enthusiasm, their cheerfulness. Tired, worn out, not in the mood to celebrate, we returned to our room.

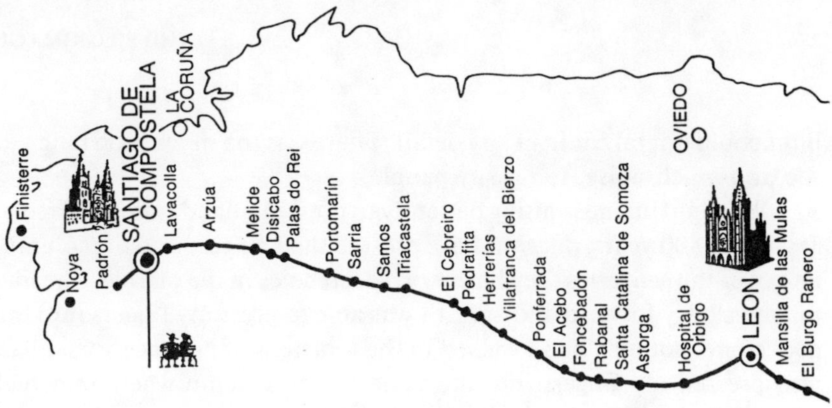

Days 45–46: August 23–24 We slept most of the morning, then went sightseeing. Santiago de Compostela has 71,000 inhabitants and numerous monuments: old medieval quarters, churches and convents, university buildings, museums. We walked up and down the Rúa del Villar and the Rúa Nueva, the narrow, arcaded streets in the old part of town, preserved, as are all the buildings in the old part of town, as they were in the Middle Ages. The streets are lined with shops, small cafe bars and restaurants, and when it is not raining the sidewalks are lined with tables and chairs. I could almost imagine that, in the shadows, medieval pilgrims sat and watched us walking by.

We walked back to the cathedral, determined to complete the promises we had made to people on the Camino. We had chosen a good time: the lines were not as long, the crowd was not as thick. As we climbed the double staircase outside the main entry, I looked at the impressive granite cathedral. It was originally built between 1060 and 1211 on the site of a basilica built in 899 on the site of the original ninth-century mud and daub church. In the sixteenth through eighteenth centuries the cathedral was remodelled, its simple Romanesque lines covered with elaborate baroque adornments and towers. We entered the cathedral through the ornate baroque doorway. There before us was the famous Pórtico de la Gloria, the Doorway of Glory, carved between 1166-1188.

The Pórtico is actually three doorways side by side, each with an elaborate tympaneum and archivolt, each with beautifully detailed figures carved on the columns supporting the arches. The vault above is painted white, providing a stark contrast to the greyish stone carvings, slightly tinted with color. The center support of the middle doorway is a column; forming the lower section is the marble Tree of Jesse, genealogical tree of Christ; Santiago sits on top of the twining tree; sitting above him is Christ. I knew this was a masterpiece of Romanesque carving—

but I could not take it in in any detail. There was too much. Too much to see, too much noise, too many people.

We stood in line, waiting patiently to press our hands into the Tree of Jesse. For 800 years, pilgrims have pressed their fingers into the column, and over the centuries they have worn deep holes in the marble. The line moved slowly forward and at last I was able to press my fingers into the cool stone: not only had I walked in the footsteps of my ancestors, I had also pressed my fingers into the same carved column where they had pressed theirs. They were pilgrims, just like me.

Behind the Tree of Jesse is a small statue of Master Mateo, architect of the cathedral. The statue faces towards the Capilla Mayor, the high main altar which displays the richly decorated statue of the Apostle. It is customary for people to bump their heads on the head of Master Mateo's statue—with the hope that a little of his creative genius will rub off on them. While I watched, several people bumped their heads on the wrong statue.

We walked through the noisy cathedral towards the main altar. The high walls of the cathedral are unadorned grey stone, focusing attention on the statue of the Apostle, sitting like a jewel-encrusted oriental potentate under an enormous, incredibly elaborate canopy covered with gold and silver angels and twining vines and leaves, thrusting their way up to the distant ceiling. The glittering, larger-than-life-sized statue of the Apostle sits, impassive, on a large chair, decked out in silver, gold, precious stones, carved scallop shells, and—according to my guidebook—bullet casings. On his chest is the red cross of Santiago. In his left hand he holds the pilgrim's staff and gourd. This is a far different Santiago from the wise and gentle pilgrim who guided us along the pilgrimage road; this

One-third of the Pórtico de la Gloria, the twelfth-century entryway sheltered behind the Obradoiro facade. The center support (not shown) is the Tree of Jesse; behind that, the figure of Maestro Mateo; behind that, at the end of a long soaring corridor, the gold-encrusted figure of Santiago, waiting to be embraced.

is Santiago as pontificate, waiting to receive devotion, waiting to grant requests, waiting to accept penance, waiting for the offerings which were his due.

I could see movement around the neck of the statue—the hands of pilgrims, embracing the Apostle. We walked up to the staircase beside the ornate altar and, since the lines were shorter this time and there was not such a frenzied crowd, I stood in line and slowly began to climb up the stairs on one side of the statue. Patiently, I waited for my turn to "dar un abrazo al Apóstal." How pagan it seemed, to embrace a statue. But after all, I had promised people along the Camino. On the platform at the top of the stairs, a young man handed out cards with a prayer printed on them:

> Lord, you have led our steps to the Sepulchre of St. James, the first of your Apostles who sealed with his blood the faith in Jesus Christ. Receive now the joyous proclamation of this same faith which he preached to us. . . .

Reading it, I realized this had nothing to do with me. This had nothing to do with the pilgrimage. What was I doing there, anyway, getting ready to embrace a gold-encrusted statue?

A middle-aged Spanish woman in front of me looked at the statue from behind and started to walk on. The young man stopped her.

"You have to embrace the Apostle."

She looked startled. "Embrace the Apostle? Why should I do that?"

"It is a sign of respect."

She hesitated but embraced the statue.

My turn came and I did the same, feeling nothing except that I had, at last, completed the requests which had been made to me; I had discharged the obligations I had had. I had been a sort of spiritually charged vehicle for some people's hopes. Give "un abrazo al Apóstal." I had. Maybe it made a difference to someone, somewhere.

After I climbed down the staircase, I walked down another set of stairs, stairs that led beneath the main altar to the crypt, where the bones of the Apostle and his two disciples are buried in a bright silver casket. Kneeling, I prayed briefly at the shrine, as millions had done before me.

There is reason to doubt whether the bones I prayed before were Santiago's, whether his bones were ever in Spain and whether he ever preached in Spain. One authority goes so far as to say that "The honest beginning to any enquiry about the origin of the cult of Santiago is to admit that we know nothing about it at all."[31]

Some theorists suggest that the bones which were discovered in the eighth century were actually those of Priscillian, a heretic who was executed at Trier in 385 and whose body was then returned to Spain for burial. He was the first schismatic heretic executed by secular authorities at the request of the orthodox Church authorities, and his relics became the center of a cult in Galicia. Perhaps these silver-encased relics, focus of a thriving pilgrimage shrine directly tied to the conservative Catholic church and Franco's State, are actually those of a heretic. Luis Buñuel uses this theme in his film *La Voie Lactée—The Milky Way*—a story of modern pilgrims going to Santiago who encounter Priscillian and other heretics.

Although St. Jerome and several other writers of the fourth and fifth centuries believed an unnamed apostle—possibly Paul—had preached in Spain, no one suggested it was St. James the Greater, until perhaps the seventh century. In the *Breviarium Apostolorum,* an abbreviated Latin list of the apostles' mission fields based on Greco-Byzantine sources, someone copied—or rather miscopied—that St. James evangelized Hispaniam (Spain) in place of the usual Hierusalem or Hierosolyman (Jerusalem). The *Brevarium* also states that St. James went to Spain and was buried there. Writing in 776, the Asturian monk Beatus of Liebana credits "Iajocobus" with bringing Christianity to Spain in his *Commentary on the Apocalypse,* a commentary on the "Book of Revelations." And sometime around 783 to 788, a hymn in honor of St. James, "O Dei verbum patris," was composed in the Asturian Kingdom. But all that this proves is that there was a story going around and gaining in popularity. There is little evidence that it was a story based on fact.

Nonetheless, by the ninth century there was a firm belief that St. James was buried in Spain. The *Martyrology* of Usuard of St. Germain des Pres, dated A.D. 865, gives St. James's feast day as July 25 and says his body was transported to Spain and worshipped there. Most convincingly of all, the remains, or so-called remains, of St. James were discovered at some time between 813 and 842 by the shepherd Pelayo or the hermit Pelayo. The relics were authenticated by Bishop Teodomiro of Iria Flavia, and he himself was buried at Compostela, evidence that Santiago was a revered place by the time he died.

In 1946 archeological excavations were begun in Compostela and showed that the cathedral was built alongside a major north-south

Roman trade route. Under the cathedral, archeologists discovered a number of Roman tombs, what appear to be early Christian burials, and a Suevi necropolis, dating from A.D. 100 to A.D. 650 or so; they also discovered the ninth-century tomb of Teodomiro. These finds would indicate that the name Compostela comes not from *Campus Stellae*—Field of Stars—but from *compostela*—cemetery. They would also indicate that the tomb was not abandoned from Santiago's burial in ca. A.D. 44—if he were buried there—until its miraculous rediscovery early in the ninth century.

Regardless of the early history of the site, in the 800s bones were found and identified as those of Santiago and his two disciples, the relics were worshipped, and the church grew in size and importance. Early skeptics about Santiago's presence—and apostolate—in Spain existed, but by the 900s they fought a losing battle. Nonetheless, the Creed of Santiago, which required belief in his presence in Spain both before and after death, has been the subject of criticism and attack throughout the centuries. Regardless of the skeptics, pilgrims flocked to the shrine to worship—and regardless of the presence or absence of Santiago in Spain, the pilgrimage became a reality, the Camino de Santiago became a reality, and the power of faith was itself a miracle.

At some time—probably in the 1700s—the bones were moved and hidden to save them from possible desecration by invading forces. Somehow, their hiding place was forgotten. In 1879 excavations were conducted, bones were discovered under the floor of the altar, and they were validated as the proper bones by Pope Leo XIII in the Apostolic Letter "Deus Omnipotens," November 2, 1884. Soon pilgrims again began to flock to Santiago.

The crypt was getting crowded, and my knees hurt from kneeling. I stood up and walked back upstairs.

At the bottom of our pilgrimage cards, it said to take the completed cards to the Palacio de Rajoy, across from the cathedral, to get a pilgrimage certificate. But the young clerk behind the information counter didn't know what we were talking about. He sent us back to the cathedral. We went back to the cathedral and asked a man selling tickets for a tour of the cathedral archeological museum, treasury, room of tapestries, and the Palace of the Archbishop Gelmírez. He said we had come at the wrong time—the Chapter office was closed. Pointing at a nearby door, he said we would have to return at 4:00 when the office was open. It was only 1:30, so we went out to eat at a nearby restaurant.

At 4:00 we returned and waited by the door. No one came in or out. At 4:45 a priest came out of a different office, and we went up to him and showed him our pilgrimage cards. In irritation, he waved them and us away, telling us that we would have to wait until after Mass. Apparently, we had been waiting at the wrong office door, and now we would have to wait some more. As if we had nothing better to do than sit around and wait—or go to Mass!

Bill was fed up. "To hell with it!"

"Come on, Bill, we've waited this long—we can wait a while longer."

"I have no patience for this kind of rigmarole—they just want to let us know who's in charge!"

We had waited a month and a half for this—but the idea of waiting an hour more was frustrating and annoying. We had no tolerance for petty bureaucracy any more. We walked around the noisy cathedral, trying to decide what to do next. One of the Spanish women we had met outside of Melide came up to us.

"How is it going?"

Sadly, she shook her head. "The only places to stay are the Franciscan night shelter—and it is full of bums and derelicts—and a seminary, far out of town. It's a long walk back. And the cathedral is so noisy it is impossible to hear the Mass. I wanted to hear the Mass, but it was impossible." She shook her head again. "It's a circus here. I'm leaving as soon as I can."

Bill asked, "Do you know where we can get our pilgrimage certificates?"

She brightened up. "Yes—I got mine already, and it is really beautiful—all in Latin! There is an office around the corner. . ."

We talked a bit more, then said goodbye. As she left, she said, "Santiago no está aquí—está por el Camino!" (Santiago isn't here: he's on the road.)

We went in search of the other office and ran into the same man who had told us to wait at the wrong door. We told him there was another office, but he said there was not. He said we had to wait. He was very rude. I got angry, and he said something under his breath and stomped off. Furious, we left the cathedral without our pilgrimage certificates and went for a long walk around town.

We walked around some more, looking at the souvenir stands, the numerous gift shops. Since the Middle Ages, Santiago has been famous for its jet and silver work; shops line the street, their window displays full of finely made silver spoons, jewelry, book marks, bells, serving pieces, plates, and scallop shells and jet carvings of the Apostle or of the shell of Santiago. Other stores specialize in less expensive goods: plastic gourds, plastic replicas of the Gallegan bagpipes, plastic copies of the cathedral that light up from inside. Moveable stands set up around the plazas sell a profusion of the usual tourist souvenirs: postcards, guidebooks, keychains, ornaments.

I didn't feel like buying anything—not even a postcard. What would I write? "Wish you were here!" "Having a wonderful time—it's all I ever dreamed it would be!" I was a pilgrim, not a hypocrite.

During the rest of the day, we tried to recognize pilgrims—our kind of pilgrim—by their appearance. Hiking boots were a giveaway, as were sunburned faces, faded clothes, and a certain look about the eyes. We would ask, "Peregrinos?" And almost always that query led to an acknowledgment and a lengthy conversation.

At one time I saw a tall, bearded, attractive blond man walk by, dressed like a hiker. I went up to him and asked, "Peregrino?" Definitely. He was a thirty-year-old artist from Munich who had traveled alone. He told us many stories, including about staying in the Franciscan convent in Astorga, and about hiding in an abandoned car during a thunderstorm. After we had talked for a while, I asked him why he had come to Santiago.

"I always wanted to make a pilgrimage. I had promised myself someday I would. When a friend of mine died, he willed me a book about the Camino de Santiago, so I went."

We saw the young Dutchman connected with the theatre whom we had met earlier. Curious as to whether his motives had changed, I asked him why he had come. He paused a while before answering.

"Well, I'm not sure I know. I guess because I wanted to walk in the footsteps of my ancestors."

Later we talked to other pilgrims, and I tried to ask them all the same question. Now, I knew they might not be honest, or they might not know, or there might be many motives—some more conscious than others. But I wanted to understand—if not my own motives, perhaps theirs. Few of them thought Santiago the saint was important, and few of them admitted to being very religious. So why were they making the pilgrimage? Something about the importance of the Camino, of the process itself, of the experience.

A middle-aged Spanish professor of music told me, "I wanted a 'time out.' I could have spent a month walking in the Pyrenees, but then I would have had to decide where I was going—and when I was done. This way, it was done for me. Besides, this way I was walking where millions of pilgrims have walked before, for centuries."

Some of these pilgrims had arrived a week before, before the city got crowded, and they had formed a network of fellow pilgrims who ate together and went dancing together in the evenings. They talked about how they would make the pilgrimage the next time—more "authentically"—without money, perhaps, or without companions; always asking for charity, perhaps, or always walking. Now, they said, they knew where the "real" road was. They knew how to find it, how to follow it. They knew how to make a pilgrimage.

Some of them had cried in the cathedral, overcome with joy. But, some of them said, now that Santiago had gotten so full of tourists, it was too crowded—it wasn't "their" town or "their" cathedral any more, and they felt like leaving.

We also felt like leaving. We had planned to leave on August 25, since Bill was flying home from Madrid on the 27th, the day my parents were flying in with my son. Now we considered leaving immediately, instead.

Although I didn't want to stay, I also didn't want to leave. I felt caught in the middle, incomplete. How, and where, and when would my pilgrimage end? I had been participating in an extended rite of passage, during which I had become a pilgrim. But how did I end the rite? I had had no ecstatic sense of completion at the shrine itself. Traditionally, pilgrims reached their goal at Santiago and were filled with elation—they were cured, healed, forgiven, saved. When they returned home, they were greeted with community recognition and celebration. Sometimes, when word arrived that they were close to town, community members would go out to meet them and welcome them back.

But my arrival was a disappointment and I wasn't returning home—my son and I were going to spend the year living in Sahagún. Of course, my friends and family would ask how it had gone—but there would be no ceremonial "taking-off" of the pilgrim's cloak, just as there had been no ceremonial "putting on" of the pilgrim's garb.

I had reached the end of the quest—and nothing was there. Santiago wasn't there—he was "on the road." It was the process that mattered, and now that was over. I told myself: Peter the Belgian had said the pilgrimage just began at Santiago.

It was time for lunch. At least my appetite was not impaired. We found a small restaurant and selected our meal from an huge platter of raw shellfish. Soon the waiter brought the freshly broiled seafood and a carafe of green Gallegan wine, which we drank out of small pottery cups. For dessert, we ate slices of a *tarta de Santiago*—an almond-paste cake, decorated with powdered sugar in the shape of the pointed cross of Santiago.

We walked around a bit, drank espresso, and waited until 4 p.m. Then once again we returned to the cathedral to get our pilgrimage certificates. I hoped that the certificate would give me some sense of completion. This time the priest was in his office, and he was quite friendly. He examined our pilgrim's cards, asked us to sign a register, and then gave each of us a personalized copy of the pilgrimage certificate—a twentieth-century version of a fourteenth-century document. Once, this certificate would have been important proof of the completion of the pilgrimage, and presenting it would have given special privileges. Now, the certificate was just a memento of the journey—with one exception. According to the priest, we could present it at the Hotel de los Reyes Católicos and, if we were one of the first ten to do so that day, we would be entitled to three free meals in the kitchen. Once, the Hotel de los Reyes Católicos had served pilgrims; now it served tourists.

We had a light dinner, then walked around town again. We saw more of our fellow pilgrims from the Camino, including the young Belgian. Had he seen Peter, we wondered? He had—but Peter was gone. He had stayed only one night in Santiago and then had left to walk to Finisterre—the end of the known earth in Roman times, the end of the Camino de las Estrellas. The Road of the Stars, after all, was not just in the sky; it was also on earth, buried beneath the Camino de Santiago. According to the young Belgian, Peter had said that the Camino didn't end at Santiago—it couldn't. And he had left town.

I remembered a poem I had read:

> My field a universe,
> The Milky Way the pathway where I walk
> With stars for flowers.[32]

We returned to the cathedral, drawn by its spires, its promise, its reservoir of hopes and miracles. Tourists, pilgrims, and tourist-pilgrims strolled across the huge plaza, and the sounds of Celtic pipes and drums drifted down the streets from the bars.

Under the arcaded front of the Palacio de Rajoy, we saw a group of about a dozen young men dressed like courtiers from the seventeenth century, wearing beribboned black velvet capes, and black tights. They carried guitars, several lute-like instruments, and several tambourines. College students, they were members of the *tunas*—traditional music groups—of the University of Santiago. Soon they began to play romantic Spanish music. Gradually, the arcade filled with strollers drifting across the plaza to hear the music. Leaning against a wall, we listened to the *tunas*.

By 1 a.m. the plaza was nearly empty. A group of six slightly drunk, middle-aged Spaniards—three couples, presumably tourist-pilgrims—came strolling across the plaza, singing songs. Supporting each other, arms on each other's shoulders, they looked so happy. We were not.

I tried to see the Milky Way: did it really lead to Santiago? Did it end there, showering its stars over the cathedral towers? The lights of the arcade were too bright. I could see nothing but darkness.

Day 47: August 25 We rented a car and drove out of town, eager to get as far away as possible as quickly as possible. But we didn't drive back to Madrid; instead, we drove to the sea.

"Santiago no está aquí. Está por el Camino."

We drove to Padrón, the Iria Flavia of Roman times, where the boat bearing Santiago's body supposedly landed in A.D. 44. According to the guidebook, there was a commemorative monument, but we couldn't find it. Then we continued up the highway to Noya, where supposedly Noah's ark once landed, an important stop on the Camino de las Estrellas. Noya was also *en fiestas,* so we waited while a parade marched across the street.

We drove out to the sea and kept on driving along the rocky coast, driving as far as we could—driving on and on to the ocean, driving until we reached the end of the road, at Finisterre. Finisterre, the End of the Earth. We walked out to the sea, and then we sat there on a rocky prominence watching the sun set into the ocean. We sat without speaking, smelling the salt breeze, watching the waves break against the shore, listening to the eternal rhythm of the sea.

At last the stars came out, first one, then another, then all in a rush the sky was filled with white, glittering stars: the Milky Way. The Milky Way stretched across the sky. It didn't end at Santiago—it kept going, across the ocean, around the world.

Afterword

One year later, back in Princeton, I went to an anthropology department party. I told Jim, a new instructor, about my pilgrimage. He asked if I knew the poem "Ithaka," written in 1911 by the Greek poet C. V. Cavafy. No, I didn't know it—or the poet. Jim recited the poem:

As you set out for Ithaka
hope your road is a long one,
full of adventure, full of discovery.
Laistrygonians, Cyclops,
angry Poseidon—don't be afraid of them:
you'll never find things like that on your way
as long as you keep your thoughts raised high,
as long as a rare excitement
stirs your spirit and your body.
Laistrygonians, Cyclops,
wild Poseidon—you won't encounter them
unless you bring them along inside your soul,
unless your soul sets them up in front of you.

Hope your road is a long one.
May there be many summer mornings when,
with what pleasure, what joy,
you enter harbors you're seeing for the first time;
you may stop at Phoenician trading stations
to buy fine things,
mother of pearl and coral, amber and ebony,
sensual perfume of every kind—
as many sensual perfumes as you can;
and may you visit many Egyptian cities
to learn and go on learning from their scholars.

Keep Ithaka always in your mind.
Arriving there is what you're destined for.
But don't hurry the journey at all.
Better if it lasts for years,
so you're old by the time you reach the island,
wealthy with all you've gained on the way,
not expecting Ithaka to make you rich.

Ithaka gave you the marvelous journey.
Without her you wouldn't have set out.
She has nothing left to give you now.

And if you find her poor, Ithaka won't have fooled you.
Wise as you will have become, so full of experience,
you'll have understood by then what these Ithakas mean.[33]

Notes

1. Eusebio Goicoechéa Arrondo, *Rutas Jacobeas* (Estella [Navarra]: Los Amigos del Camino de Santiago, 1971), p. 59. (Translation by Ellen O. Feinberg.)

2. Luis Vásquez de Parga, José María Lacarra, and Juan Uría Ríu, *Las Peregrinaciones a Santiago de Compostela* (Madrid: Consejo Superior de Investigaciones Científicas, 1949), Vol. III, p. 67. (Translation by Ellen O. Feinberg.)

3. Derek W. Lomax, *The Reconquest of Spain* (London and New York: Longman, 1978), pp. 31–35.

4. Walter Starkie, *The Road to Santiago* (New York: E. P. Dutton and Co., Inc., 1957), p. 165; de Parga et al., *Las Peregrinaciones,* Vol. II, pp. 101–103.

5. de Parga et al., p. 103.

6. Ibid., pp. 113–14.

7. Ibid., pp. 115–16.

8. Arrondo, *El Camino de Santiago,* p. 60.

9. Penelope Casas, *The Foods & Wines of Spain* (New York: Alfred A. Knopf, 1983), pp. 399–401.

10. Antonio Machado, *Poesías Completas* (Madrid: Espasa-Calpe, 1981), p. 246. (Translation by Ellen O. Feinberg.)

11. Starkie, p. 189.

12. de Parga et al., pp. 157–58. (Translation by Ellen O. Feinberg.)

13. Starkie, pp. 204–5.

14. *The Travels of Leo of Rozmital through Germany, Flanders, England, France, Spain, Portugal and Italy, 1465-1467,* Second Series, No. 108, trans. and ed. Malcolm Letts (Cambridge: Hakluyt Society, at the University Press, 1957), pp. 79–80.

15. Richard Ford, *A Handbook for Travellers in Spain* [1845], ed. Ian Robertson (Carbondale: Southern Illinois University Press, 1966), Vol. III, p. 1338.

16. Ramón Menéndez Pidal, *The Cid and His Spain* (London: Frank Cass and Co., Ltd., 1934).

17. Angus MacKay, *Spain in the Middle Ages: From Frontier to Empire, 1000-1500* (London and Basingstoke: The MacMillan Press, Ltd., 1977), pp. 36–57.

18. Miguel de Cervantes Saavedra, *Don Quixote of La Mancha,* abridged ed. trans. and ed. Walter Starkie (New York: Mentor Books/New American Library, 1957), pp. 360–61.

19. *Travels of Rozmital,* p. 86.

20. John Esten Keller, *Alfonso X, El Sabio* (New York: Twayne Publishers, 1967), pp. 64–95.

21. Walter Muir Whitehill, *Spanish Romanesque Architecture of the Eleventh Century* (Oxford: Oxford University Press, 1941), p. 209.

22. Georgiana Goddard King, *The Way of Saint James* (New York and London: G. P. Putnam's Sons, 1920), Vol. II, pp. 120–21.

23. Alfonso el Sabio, *Las siete partidas del Rey Don Alfonso el Sabio* (Madrid: la Imprenta Real, 1807), Vol. I, p. 497. (Translation by Ellen O. Feinberg.)

24. Starkie, p. 244. (Translation by Ellen O. Feinberg.)

25. King, p. 368.

26. Starkie, p. 320.

27. León Felipe, *Obra Poética Escogida* (Madrid: Espasa-Calpe, 1977), pp. 49–50. (Translation by Ellen O. Feinberg.)

28. *Purchas His Pilgrim,* 1425, quoted by Starkie, p. 305; also see King, *The Way of Saint James,* Vol. III, p. 573.

29. Starkie, pp. 305–6.

30. Casas, p. 52.

31. T. D. Kendrick, *St. James in Spain* (London: Methuen & Co. Ltd, 1960), p. 187; see also Jan van Herwaarden, "The origins of the cult of St. James of Compostela," *Journal of Medieval History* 6 (1980):1–35; R. A. Fletcher, *Saint James's Catapult: The Life and Times of Diego Gelmírez of Santiago de Compostela* (Oxford: Clarendon Press, 1984), pp. 53–77.

32. Quoted with no attribution in Starkie, p. 308.

33. *C. P. Cavafy: Collected Poems,* ed. George Savidis, trans. Edmund Keeley and Philip Sherrard (Princeton, N.J.: Princeton University Press, 1975), pp. 67, 69.

Additional Reading

Now that we have traveled the Camino de Santiago together, perhaps you would like to continue the pilgrimage on your own—on foot, by car, or from your armchair. Hundreds of informative books and articles exist to show you the way, but I only have space to mention a few.

Guides for walking the Camino: *El Camino de Santiago, Guía del Peregrino,* by E. Valiña Sampedro et al. (León: Editorial Everest, 1985), contains carefully drawn maps as well as brief descriptions of sites, cities, and shelters. *Rutas Jacobeas: Historia, Arte, Caminos,* by E. Goicoechea Arrondo (Los Amigos del Camino de Santiago de Estella, Aptdo. 20, Estella, Navarra, 1971), provides 708 pages of artistic, historical, and musical information, as well as details of the Camino and a hiker's map of the route; the map section and a slide series can be purchased separately. *Le Chemin de St. Jacques en Espagne (Guide du Pèlerin),* by Abbé Georges Bernès and René Brynaert, is a favorite of French-speaking pilgrims; it contains detailed sketches and sketchy historical information on the Camino. To purchase a copy, contact Abbé Georges Bernès at Tillac, F-32170, Miélan, France. Even if you don't read Spanish or French, you will still be able to follow the maps in these books—and the yellow arrows painted on trees, walls, and roads.

Guides for driving the Camino: ask the Spanish Tourist Office (665 Fifth Ave., New York, NY 10022) to send you an English-language brochure on the Camino de Santiago. The brochure shows the highways to follow and gives the distances between cities and gas stations; it also describes major historical sites. In addition, the Spanish government has labeled the Camino with highway signposts and historical markers. Travel books such as the *Blue Guide* and the *Michelin Green Guide* describe parts of the route. *En Vacances: Sur le Chemin de Compostelle,* by René Brynaert (Paris-Gemblous: Editions Duculot, 1981), includes a bit of history, information on local festivals, and interesting asides. Intended for car tourists who may also want to walk, it provides detailed descriptions of hiking excursions on (and off) the Camino.

Guides for seeing the Camino from your armchair: *Rutas Jacobeas* (mentioned earlier) can be purchased with an extensive set of slides. *The Pilgrim Route to Santiago,* by Brian and Marcus Tate (Oxford: Phaidon, 1987), is a coffee-table book of glorious photographs of the Camino. *Spain: a Phaidon Cultural Guide* (Englewood Cliffs, NJ: Prentice-Hall, 1985) includes lovely photos of architecture and art in cities along the way to Santiago. Some university art history departments and libraries have slide series on the Camino, and many books mentioned in this bibliographic essay include photographs.

First-hand accounts of the pilgrimage: *The Way of Saint James,* by Georgiana Goddard King (Hispanic Society of America, 1920), is a charming, erudite, art historian's interpretation of the Camino, which she traveled by foot, mule, and other assorted means. Walter Starkie's *The Road to Santiago* (New York: E. P. Dutton, 1957), is a raconteur's account of his rambles on the Caminos in France and Spain; it is full of literary allusions, historical references, and intriguing encounters. *The Pilgrimage to Santiago,* by Edwin Mullins (New York: Taplinger Publishing Co., 1974), is a slightly cynical but interesting description of a quick trip on the Caminos de Santiago; it includes historical and artistic commentaries. Other travelers' accounts—and there have been many—are mentioned by these authors; additional references can be found in my footnotes.

Second-hand accounts of the pilgrimage: The *Codex Calixtinus,* the twelfth-century guide to Santiago, has been transcribed in three volumes by Walter Muir Whitehill as *Liber Sancti Jacobi, Codex Calixtinus, texto transcripción* (Compostela, 1944). Book V, "The Pilgrim's Guide," has been translated into French by Jeanne Vielliard as *Le guide du pèlerin de Saint Jacques de Compostelle,* (Mâcon 1950, 1963). Bits and pieces of the *Codex* and "The Pilgrim's Guide" are translated in various English-language books on the Camino. For example, *Santiago de Compostela: In the Age of the Great Pilgrimages,* by Marilyn Stockstad (Norman: University of Oklahoma Press, 1978), includes translations of "The Pilgrim's Guide," although Stockstad's focus is on the city of Santiago in the eleventh and twelfth centuries. Horton and Marie-Hélène Davies's *Holy Days and Holidays* (East Brunswick, NJ: Associated University Presses, 1982) provides an interesting description of the art and architecture along the route and of the medieval pilgrimage; it has extensive footnotes. The classic three-volume *Las Peregrinaciones a Santiago de Compostela,* by Luis Vázquez de Parga, José María Lacarra, and Juan Uría Ríu (Madrid, 1949; reprinted in Oviedo by the Diputación de Asturias, 1981), includes important essays on the pilgrimage through the ages, individual pilgrimages, hospitality, medicine, and art; a step-by-step description of the history of locales along the road; photographs; and an extensive appendix. *Rutas Jacobeas* (previously mentioned) focuses on the art, music, and history of the Camino. My unpublished dissertation, "Strangers and Pilgrims on the Camino de Santiago in Spain" (Princeton University, 1985), is an anthropological analysis of the modern-day pilgrimage; it also has a lengthy bibliography on the pilgrimage to Santiago and on other pilgrimages.

Books on other pilgrimages: Alan Kendall's *Medieval Pilgrims* (New York: G. P. Putnam's Sons, 1970) is a brief, straightforward introduction to the topic. *Pilgrimage: An Image of Medieval Religion,* by Jonathan Sumption (Totoway, NJ: Rowman and Littlefield, 1975), is a historical examination of this exciting period. *Image and Pilgrimage in Christian Culture: Anthropological Perspectives,* by Victor and Edith Turner (Oxford: Basil Blackwell, 1978), provides a good introduction to the anthropology of pilgrimage. Oliver Statler's *Japanese Pilgrimage* (New York: Morrow, 1983) is a delightful description of a foot pilgrimage around the island of Shikoku.

Pilgrimage organizations: several exist—both for those who have gone to Santiago and for those who think about going. In France, contact Les Amis de Saint-Jacques de Compostelle (87, rue Vieille-au-Temple, F-75003 Paris; or contact Mlle Warcollier, Secretary General, 4, square du Pont de Sèvres, F-92100

Boulogne-sur-Seine, France). In Spain, a number of new affiliates of Amigos del Camino de Santiago have been established. A bi-monthly magazine, *Peregrino,* is being published to help coordinate this effort. In 1988, an annual foreign subscription cost 1,500 pesetas. For information, write to *Revista Peregrino,* Aptdo. 60, 26250-Sto. Domingo de la Calzada (La Rioja), Spain. In the United States, efforts are underway to establish a national Association of Amigos del Camino.

Index

ELLEN OKNER FEINBERG was born in Champaign, Illinois, grew up in Ames, Iowa (with a year off in Sri Lanka), attended Stanford University, graduated from Iowa State University with honors and distinction in English, and received an M.A. in Anthropology and a Master of Public Administration from the University of Kansas. She then worked as an administrative assistant for the Kickapoo tribe of Kansas and as a health planner for the Kansas State Office of Health Planning. She earned her Ph.D. in Anthropology at Princeton University in 1985, during the course of which she spent 1½ years doing fieldwork in Spain. She has traveled the Camino de Santiago several times, including once on foot in 1982.

Ellen Feinberg now lives in Ames, Iowa, where she directs the national High-T_c Superconductivity Information Exchange and edits an international newsletter, *High-T_c Update*. She lives with her teenage son, Jesse L. Reynolds, and looks forward to the day when they can walk the Camino together.